Family Matters

In 1960, consensual sodomy was a crime in every state in America. Fifty-five years later, the Supreme Court ruled that same-sex couples had the fundamental right to marry. In the span of two generations, American law underwent a dramatic transformation. Although the fight for marriage equality has received a considerable amount of attention from scholars and the media, it was only a small part of the more than half-century struggle for queer family rights. *Family Matters* uncovers these decades of advocacy, which reshaped the place of same-sex sexuality in American law and society – and ultimately made marriage equality possible. This book, however, is more than a history of queer rights. Marie-Amélie George reveals that national legal change resulted from shifts at the state and local levels, where the central figures were everyday people without legal training. Consequently, she offers a new way of understanding how minority groups were able to secure meaningful legal change.

Marie-Amélie George is a legal scholar and historian whose work focuses on the LGBTQ+ rights movement. She is Associate Professor of Law at Wake Forest University.

See the Studies in Legal History series website at
http://studiesinlegalhistory.org/

Studies in Legal History

EDITORS

Lisa Ford, University of New South Wales
Thomas McSweeney, William & Mary Law School
Reuel Schiller, University of California College of the Law,
    San Francisco
Taisu Zhang, Yale Law School

Other books in the series:

Simon Devereaux, *Execution, State and Society in England,
1660–1900*

Giuliana Perrone, *Nothing More than Freedom: The Failure of
Abolition in American Law*

Christian G. Fritz, *Monitoring American Federalism: The History of
State Legislative Resistance*

Ada Maria Kuskowski, *Vernacular Law: Writing and the Reinvention
of Customary Law in Medieval France*

E. Claire Cage, *The Science of Proof: Forensic Medicine in Modern
France*

Kristin A. Olbertson, *The Dreadful Word: Speech Crime and Polite
Gentlemen in Massachusetts, 1690–1776*

Edgardo Pérez Morales, *Unraveling Abolition: Legal Culture and
Slave Emancipation in Colombia*

Lyndsay Campbell, *Truth and Privilege: Libel Law in Massachusetts
and Nova Scotia, 1820–1840*

(*Continued after the Index*)

Family Matters

Queer Households and the Half-Century Struggle for Legal Recognition

MARIE-AMÉLIE GEORGE

Wake Forest University School of Law

CAMBRIDGE
UNIVERSITY PRESS

CAMBRIDGE
UNIVERSITY PRESS

Shaftesbury Road, Cambridge CB2 8EA, United Kingdom

One Liberty Plaza, 20th Floor, New York, NY 10006, USA

477 Williamstown Road, Port Melbourne, VIC 3207, Australia

314–321, 3rd Floor, Plot 3, Splendor Forum, Jasola District Centre, New Delhi – 110025, India

103 Penang Road, #05-06/07, Visioncrest Commercial, Singapore 238467

Cambridge University Press is part of Cambridge University Press & Assessment, a department of the University of Cambridge.

We share the University's mission to contribute to society through the pursuit of education, learning and research at the highest international levels of excellence.

www.cambridge.org
Information on this title: www.cambridge.org/9781009284400

DOI: 10.1017/9781009284417

First published 2024

Printed in the United Kingdom by TJ Books Limited, Padstow Cornwall

A catalogue record for this publication is available from the British Library.

Library of Congress Cataloging-in-Publication Data
NAMES: George, Marie-Amélie, author.
TITLE: Family matters : queer households and the half-century struggle for legal recognition / Marie-Amélie George, Wake Forest University School of Law.
DESCRIPTION: Cambridge, United Kingdom ; New York, NY : Cambridge University Press, 2024. | Includes bibliographical references and index.
IDENTIFIERS: LCCN 2023056081 (print) | LCCN 2023056082 (ebook) |
  ISBN 9781009284400 (hardback) | ISBN 9781009284431 (paperback) |
  ISBN 9781009284417 (ebook)
SUBJECTS: LCSH: Homosexuality–Law and legislation–United States–History. | Gay rights–United States–History. | Sexual minorities' families–United States. | Parent and child (Law)–United States. | Gay parents–Legal status, laws, etc.–United States. | Children of gay parents–Legal status, laws, etc.–United States. | Custody of children–United States. | Gay adoption–Law and legislation–United States.
CLASSIFICATION: LCC KF4754.5 .G46 2024 (print) | LCC KF4754.5 (ebook) |
  DDC 346.7301/308664–dc23/eng/20231214
LC record available at https://lccn.loc.gov/2023056081
LC ebook record available at https://lccn.loc.gov/2023056082

ISBN 978-1-009-28440-0 Hardback

For my family.

Contents

Figures

Acknowledgments

Writing a book is never a solitary endeavor. Countless colleagues, mentors, friends, and others influenced my research, enriched my thinking, and inspired me to keep writing. I am grateful to have the opportunity to recognize their insights, kindness, and support.

No one shaped this project more than Reuel Schiller. Reuel is an infinitely patient and generous editor. He read numerous drafts, pressing me to hone my arguments and refine my writing style. He offered unfailing advice on everything from chapter structure to word choice, balancing his apt criticisms with unwavering faith and boundless enthusiasm. Reuel provided a level of engagement and support that is rare in academic publishing, but that enriched this book in every possible way. I cannot express how fortunate I have been to have had him in my corner.

Like many first books, this one began in graduate school, where I was lucky to be surrounded by remarkable professors and mentors. Joanne Meyerowitz, my dissertation committee chair, was the best advisor a fledgling historian could hope to have. She willingly read and reread drafts, responding with incisive questions and detailed line edits that made me a better scholar. John Witt's guidance was equally invaluable. He shaped my understanding of legal history, inspired me to think more broadly about my research, and provided helpful insights on both the dissertation and the book manuscript. John's keen intellect has improved my work at every turn. I am likewise grateful to George Chauncey, who shared both his passion for gay and lesbian history and his deep expertise on the subject. He and his work continue to be an inspiration.

In drafting the book, I benefited immeasurably from the feedback and guidance of colleagues in my field. My deepest thanks go to Scott

Cummings, Felicia Kornbluh, Anna Lvovsky, Douglas NeJaime, and Ron Wright, who generously read the full manuscript. Their comments improved the book dramatically. I am also grateful to Margot Canaday, Sally Gordon, and Serena Mayeri, whose thoughts and counsel at an early stage prompted me to reconsider the book's narrative. Fellow participants in the Wallace Johnson First Book Program, Pedro Cantisano, Amanda Kleintop, Kalyani Ramnath, Evan Taparata, and Adnan Zulfiqar, shared their ideas, enthusiasm, and support at the book's inception. I am additionally indebted to my colleagues at Wake Forest University School of Law, who generously read chapters and offered their feedback on the book's contents. Thanks in particular to Meghan Boone, Alyse Bertenthal, Chris Coughlin, Brenda Gibson, Allyson Gold, Heather Gram, Mark Hall, Raina Haque, Esther Hong, John Knox, Ellie Morales, Sarah Morath, Stratos Pahis, Eileen Prescott, Zaneta Robinson, Sid Shapiro, Kenneth Townsend, and Jesse Williams for discussing ideas over coffees, lunches, workshops, drinks, and panicked phone calls.

Beyond these scholars and colleagues, I am indebted to the many academics who have helped me grow as a researcher and writer. I am particularly thankful to Deborah Dinner, Katherine Franke, Russell Gold, Suzanne Goldberg, Clare Huntington, Michael Klarman, Gillian Metzger, Carol Sanger, Karen Tani, and Andrew Verstein, who have offered generative conversations, astute comments, and detailed line edits over the course of many years. I am additionally grateful to the participants of the American Society for Legal History Annual Meeting, Family Law Scholars and Teachers Conference, Harvard Law School Legal History Workshop, Michigan Law School Public Law Workshop, Mid-Atlantic Family Law Scholars Roundtable, William & Mary Law Faculty Workshop, UNC Law Faculty Workshop, and Washington University School of Law Faculty Workshop. These scholars' astute comments and probing questions helped me develop and refine the book's arguments.

Many people made this book possible in very practical ways. I relied on sources from a number of archives and libraries, and I am grateful for the generosity of the staff at all of the institutions. At Wake Forest, Sally Irvin went above and beyond in tracking down files from clerks and state archives. Kate Irwin-Smiler procured numerous articles from obscure journals and newspapers, often despite my having only provided limited bibliographic information. Many archivists also helped me identify and gather sources, including Brenda Marston at Cornell University, Isaac Fellman at the GLBT Historical Society, Michael Oliveira and Loni Shibuyama at ONE Gay and Lesbian

Archives, Benoit Shoja at the New Hampshire State Archives, Shawn Wilson at the Kinsey Institute, and Tim Wilson at the San Francisco Public Library. In addition to professional librarians and archivists, I am grateful to the individuals who helped me track down historical photographs, which have helped bring the book's stories to life. Thank you to Tricia Gesner and Donna Binder, who scoured microfilms and negatives to find images from decades ago. I am additionally indebted to everyone who spoke with me about their lives and experiences. I am especially grateful to Tom Brougham, who shared both his time and private photographs, and Jeff Weinstein, who gathered documents to supplement my records. I am also thankful for the students who devoted their time to helping me research and polish the manuscript. The book benefited immensely from the work of Summer Allen, Sophie Barry-Hinton, Berfin Bediz, Sam Brady, Caleb Coffelt, Lily Drake, Emily Franklin, Lucas Helton, Edowaye Idahor, Julia Johnson, Creighton Knight, Kit Kniss, John Payne, Jacob Padillo, Emily Washburn, Brianna White, Emily Wilmink, Andrew Wilson, and Katie Wooten. The book is also clearer and better written as a result of Liz Scheier, who lent her sharp editorial eye to the project. I am extremely grateful for her assistance.

I could not have completed this project without generous financial support. I was able to conduct the archival research the book required thanks to the Phil Zwickler Memorial Research Grant, Wake Forest Pilot Research Grant, Yale University Fund for Lesbian and Gay Studies Research Award, Yale University History Department Pre-Dissertation Research Fellowship, and Yale University John Morton Blum Fellowship. The Wallace Johnson First Book Program helped me transform the dissertation into a book. The Wake Forest University Humanities Institute supported the project in its final stages through a Book Development Grant. Wake Forest Law also made this project possible by giving me a crucial year away from the classroom to write. I cannot express how grateful I am for Jane Aiken and Wendy Parker, who reconfigured my teaching schedule so I could focus on this project. I could not have produced this book without the time that they gave me.

Parts of Family Matters draw on material that has appeared in the *Alabama Law Review*, *Harvard Civil Rights-Civil Liberties Law Review*, *Journal of the History of Sexuality*, *Law and History Review*, *Northwestern Law Review*, *Wisconsin Law Review*, and *Yale Law* and *Policy Review*. I thank those publishers for helping me improve my work and granting me permission to reprint the material here. I am just as indebted to the team at Cambridge University Press for their helpful suggestions and careful editing. I was fortunate to be able to work with Cecelia Cancellaro, Lisa Carter, Jem Langworthy, Victoria Phillips, and Jasintha Srinivasan. I also benefited enormously from the work of indexer Derek Gottlieb. I am thankful to all of these individuals for sharing their talents with me.

Finally, I am deeply grateful to the friends and family who have reassured, entertained, and distracted me during the many years it took to complete this book. Thank you to Betsy Barre, Claudia Calhoun, Justin Esarey, Emily Johnson, Carrie Johnson, Yumi Kim, Devin McGeehan Muchmore, Molly Pachence, Arie Rubenstein, Lauren Tilton, Jess Rogers, Ruthie Vishlitzky, Charles Wuest, and Alexa Zimmerman. Archival research and scholarly writing can be extremely lonely endeavors, and all of you made the process significantly easier. My partner, Stephen Tiley, has improved my life in every way imaginable. I have been fortunate to have his unwavering confidence in both me and this book. Finally, my parents, Claude and Martine George, have supported me in countless ways, as have my sisters, Emma and Caroline. I cannot thank them enough.

Abbreviations

ACLU	American Civil Liberties Union
AJC	*Atlanta Journal-Constitution*
ALI	American Law Institute
APA	American Psychiatric Association
BAR	*Bay Area Reporter*
BG	*Boston Globe*
CDSS	California Department of Social Services
CEE	Citizens for Excellence in Education
CM	*Concord Monitor*
CT	*Chicago Tribune*
CUAV	Community United Against Violence
DCYF	Division of Children, Youth, and Families
DOMA	Defense of Marriage Act
DSM	Diagnostic and Statistical Manual
ERG	Employee Resource Group
GAA	Gay Activist Alliance
GCN	*Gay Community News*
GLAAD	Gay and Lesbian Alliance Against Defamation
GLAD	Gay and Lesbian Advocates and Defenders
GLDC	Gay and Lesbian Defense Committee
HRC	Human Rights Campaign
LAPD	Los Angeles Police Department
LAT	*Los Angeles Times*
LGTANY	Lesbian and Gay Teachers Association of New York
LMNDF	Lesbian Mothers' National Defense Fund
MDSS	Massachusetts Department of Social Services
MPC	Model Penal Code

MUM	Mainers United for Marriage
NASW	National Association of Social Workers
NCLR	National Center for Lesbian Rights
NGTF	National Gay Task Force
NGLTF	National Gay and Lesbian Task Force
NIMH	National Institute of Mental Health
NOW	National Organization for Women
NYN	*New York Native*
NYT	*New York Times*
PFLAG	Parents and Friends of Lesbians and Gays
SFC	*San Francisco Chronicle*
SFE	*San Francisco Examiner*
SFS	*San Francisco Sentinel*
SV	*Southern Voice*
UL	*Union Leader*
WSJ	*Wall Street Journal*
WB	*Washington Blade*
WP	*Washington Post*

Introduction

Del Martin was terrified. Her husband, Jim, had found a cache of love letters that she had written – but never sent – to the woman who lived next door. Jim told Del that, if she persisted in filing for a divorce, he would use the letters against her in court, making it unlikely that she would ever see their young daughter again.[1] In 1945, same-sex attraction was widely understood as a psychological disorder. Del knew that a court would never grant a lesbian visitation rights, let alone custody of a toddler.[2] Sick with fear and shame, she could not even bring herself to warn her attorney about the letters. To her immense relief, the judge determined the documents contained nothing more than an expression of chaste female friendship.[3] He may have been compassionate, or simply naïve. Regardless of the reason for the judge's ruling, Del got her divorce, as well as custody of Kendra.[4]

Del was not yet the out and proud lesbian who would lead a queer rights revolution. Born in San Francisco in 1921, she realized from an early age that she was attracted to women. However, Del also knew that those feelings were forbidden. As a teenager, she repressed her desires by burying herself in schoolwork and extra-curricular activities.[5] She adopted the same approach at San Francisco State University, where she majored in journalism and joined the staff of the school newspaper. It was at the journal's offices that she met Jim, the paper's business manager. The two quickly discovered they had a great deal in common and, before long, they were engaged. Nineteen-year-old Del accepted Jim's proposal in part because she had convinced herself that she was in love with him. But just as importantly, she wanted to prove that she could be like every other American woman.[6] By her third year of college, she was pregnant. The family moved to a house in the suburbs, where Del became increasingly unhappy in the relationship. She cared for and respected her husband, but she was also attracted to her female neighbor. When she finally asked Jim for a divorce, he shocked her by asking whether her misery had anything to do with the woman next door. She had never suspected that he knew her secret.[7]

Del may have ended her marriage because of her sexual orientation, but she did not yet identify as a lesbian. That was unsurprising, given that she had never even heard the term. When she finally came across it, in her mid-twenties, she raced to the library to learn everything she could. What she discovered turned her euphoric feelings of self-discovery into a well of suicidal despair.[8] Everything she read framed homosexuality as a pathological condition, a crime, or both. She wondered how she could identify with something so terrible.[9] Over time, she built up the courage to voice her sexual confusion to two close friends. Neither believed that Del was a lesbian, but they commented that she could settle her doubts by going to the bars in San Francisco's North Beach, one of the city's first queer neighborhoods.[10] After Prohibition's repeal, a series of gay and lesbian-owned and operated nightclubs had opened in the area, leading members of the queer community to rent rooms near the cluster of establishments that catered to them.[11]

Del gave little thought to visiting those bars until a year later, when her life had changed enough for her to venture into queer life. Her first lesbian relationship, with a close friend, had come to an end. She had also agreed to relinquish custody of Kendra. Jim had remarried, and he had convinced her that his two-parent home would be better for their child.[12] Bereft and looking for companionship, Del began frequenting gay and lesbian bars and clubs. She quickly learned that doing so was perilous, as vice officers regularly harassed and arrested the patrons.[13] As Del left the Chi-Chi Club one night, a policeman stopped her, demanding to know her name and where she worked.[14] When she refused to answer, the officer let her go, but the incident rattled her enough that she decided to look for employment opportunities elsewhere. She hoped it would be easier to transition out of the closet somewhere new, away from the vestiges of her old life. When a specialty magazine in Seattle offered her a position, she jumped at the opportunity.[15] On her first day at the office, she met Phyllis Lyon, the woman who would become her life partner.

Like Del, Phyllis had also grown up in California, and she too had followed her journalism career to Seattle.[16] Phyllis had also known early on that she was different, but she thought it was only because she was uninterested in marriage or homemaking.[17] Although Phyllis recognized that she felt more comfortable in the company of women, it never occurred to her that these relationships could extend beyond mere friendships.[18] In fact, until Del disclosed her attraction to women at after-work drinks one night, Phyllis had never met a lesbian.[19] What Del did not reveal during that conversation was that she had fallen in love with Phyllis. Del had experienced so many unrequited loves that she had resigned herself to Phyllis being nothing more than her "good straight friend."[20] It was not until two years later, when Phyllis was about to relocate to San Francisco, that Del worked up the courage to reveal her feelings.[21] As it turned out, Phyllis had been waiting for Del to make the first move. When Phyllis left town soon after that fateful night, Del followed her.[22]

The women struggled to blend their lives and personalities. They had been close friends for three years, but a relationship was something else entirely. When Del would leave her shoes in the middle of the room, Phyllis became so frustrated that she threw them out of the window. Del, on the other hand, became infuriated when Phyllis would disengage from their arguments. Del would later joke that they only stayed together for the sake of their kitten.[23] After a tumultuous first year, the women were able to resolve their differences. They began looking for friends as a couple, but found themselves reluctant to visit the city's queer establishments due to Del's earlier encounter with the police in North Beach. At the time, there were few alternatives to the bar scene. Consequently, in 1955, they founded the Daughters of Bilitis, a lesbian social group, where women who loved women could socialize in the safety of one another's homes. Soon, they changed the group's mission, turning it into the first lesbian rights organization in the country – and launching their life's work in the process.[24]

Over the next five decades, Del and Phyllis would fight tirelessly for LGBTQ+ rights. They lobbied to declassify homosexuality as a mental illness, decriminalize consensual sodomy, and secure sexual orientation antidiscrimination protections.[25] The women took on projects at the local, state, and national levels, often combining queer rights advocacy with feminist activism. In 1966, they joined the National Organization for Women (NOW), where they made waves by insisting on the membership rate offered to spouses. The duo quickly convinced the group to make lesbian rights part of its political platform.[26] In 1977, both attended the International Women's Year Conference in Houston to ensure that the agenda would include lesbian rights. The following year, Phyllis chaired the San Francisco campaign against a California ballot measure to ban gay and lesbian teachers from public schools. By that point, Del was already serving on the city's Human Rights Commission.[27] The couple continued their work through the 1990s, when both served as delegates to the White House Conference on Aging. Thanks to their efforts, the conference – for the first time in its thirty-eight-year history – addressed discrimination based on sexual orientation.[28] The women's final contribution to the LGBTQ+ rights movement was filing a lawsuit challenging California's discriminatory marriage law.[29] In 2008, just a few minutes after the state's highest court ruled in their favor, the women legally wed.[30] By that point, they had spent fifty-five years as a devoted couple. Two months after the ceremony, Del passed away.[31] Phyllis was devastated, but took some comfort in knowing that they were able to undertake a formal vow of love and commitment before their time together came to an end.[32]

FIGURE I Del Martin and Phyllis Lyon marrying at a ceremony officiated by Mayor Gavin Newsom at San Francisco's City Hall, 2008. The public celebration of their union illustrated just how much views of same-sex sexuality had changed over the course of their fifty-five-year relationship. Photo by Marcio Jose Sanchez/AFP. Courtesy of Getty Images.

Del and Phyllis lived through a remarkable transformation in American law. At the time that the women began advocating for queer rights, the state went to great lengths to suppress homosexuality, insisting that it was deviant, immoral, and socially harmful.[33] State-sanctioned discrimination infused statutory codes and legal policies, impeding the ability of many gays and lesbians to work, form communities, and create households. One of the main tools that the state wielded to repress queer life was its family law doctrines. Gay and lesbian parents, like Del, risked losing the children they loved because of their sexual orientation. Another weapon in the state's regulatory arsenal was its criminal codes. As Del had experienced firsthand, penal laws rendered every sexual liaison dangerous. Queer individuals risked arrest, prosecution, and punishment for seeking affection, companionship, and comfort. Officials did not always agree with the law's harsh punishments. Some turned a blind eye, like the judge who heard Del's case may have done. Others used their discretion to dismiss charges against homosexuals.[34] These small mercies mattered a great deal to individual gay men and lesbians, but they did little to dissipate the fear that pervaded queer life. Additionally, the existence of punitive criminal laws did more than make same-sex sexual activity illegal. By defining gays and lesbians as outlaws, the state reinforced social disapproval and stigma. Gays and lesbians consequently faced an oppressive legal regime, one that made the prospect of law reform seem daunting, if not impossible.

Yet the law changed – dramatically – in a surprisingly short period of time. In 1960, consensual sodomy was a crime in every state in America. Homosexuality was considered a mental illness, a designation that prevented gays and lesbians from serving in the military, obtaining federal employment, and securing custody of their children. Just fifty-five years later, in 2015, the Supreme Court ruled in *Obergefell v. Hodges* that same-sex couples had a fundamental right to marry. Over the span of two generations, advocates like Del and Phyllis had transformed American law from a regime that criminalized gay and lesbian relationships to one that recognized and affirmed the dignity of queer families. By the time the Supreme Court ruled in favor of same-sex marriage rights, gay men no longer feared being arrested, imprisoned, or institutionalized because of who they were. Lesbians did not live with the constant anxiety of losing their livelihoods if their sexuality became known.[35] Instead, they could overwhelmingly celebrate their relationships with pride. Del and Phyllis had begun their relationship in secret, unable to go out as a couple without risking police harassment and arrest. Five and a half decades later, they wed at City Hall, in a ceremony officiated by San Francisco's former mayor and attended by hundreds of well-wishers.[36] The celebration of their commitment could not have been more public.

The fight for gay and lesbian rights has become one of the most conspicuous social justice movements in American history, with *Obergefell* marking advocates' remarkable progress. Because the *Obergefell* decision was so consequential, numerous scholars and popular writers have detailed the history of the campaign for marriage equality, tracing the evolution of same-sex marriage rights in courts, legislatures, and administrative offices.[37] But the struggle for marriage equality was only one small part of a more than half century-long movement for queer family rights. Decades before the United States became embroiled in debates over same-sex marriage, advocates were working to support and promote the rights of queer couples and their children. The queer community faced an oppressive legal regime, one centered on the assumption that same-sex sexuality was inherently dangerous to children. Through painstaking efforts, advocates secured changes to criminal codes and family law doctrines that allowed gay- and lesbian-headed households to become more prevalent and visible. These families, in turn, reshaped the place of same-sex sexuality in American society and law. By the time the Supreme Court held that the Constitution required states to recognize same-sex marriage, the law was no longer protecting children *from* gays and lesbians, but rather protecting the children *of* gays and lesbians.

These decades of queer family advocacy are largely unknown. Yet without this history, it is impossible to understand how the marriage equality movement secured so much, so quickly. *Family Matters* provides this crucial missing piece of the puzzle. As it explains, changes to criminal codes and family law doctrines allowed same-sex couples to become increasingly open about their sexual orientation. The country consequently came to see gays and lesbians as both partners and parents. Battles to protect the community from hate violence also encouraged the straight mothers and fathers of gays and lesbians to become advocates for queer rights. By making public their love and support for their gay sons and lesbian daughters, these parents high-lighted that gays and lesbians were embedded within traditional households not just as parents, but also as children. The visibility of both types of queer families – the families that gays and lesbians created, as well as their straight families of origin – had a significant effect on the law. These households were consequential because they provided evidence of same-sex sexuality's ubiquity and projected a new vision of what it meant to be queer, one that was centered on "conventional" domestic life. What this book therefore demonstrates is that "family matters" – issues relating to the family – were essential to the evolution of American law and the rise of queer rights. At the same time, family rights were crucial to members of the gay and lesbian community, for whom family *mattered*.

This book consequently highlights the legal reforms that predated the movement's focus on marriage, rather than focusing on the fight for marriage equality. These changes transformed society, such that advocates could conceive of and pursue marriage rights. By presenting this history, *Family Matters* reveals a deep irony at the heart of the gay and lesbian rights movement: although marriage traditionally marks the start of a family, gays and lesbians had to form legally and socially recognized families before the law would allow them to marry. Marriage equality may be the queer rights movement's best-known success, but it was a postscript to decades of family-centered strategies.

Advocating for Queer Families

In a 2015 speech from the White House Rose Garden, President Barack Obama lauded the Supreme Court's marriage equality decision. The president explained that the ruling, which the Court had handed down earlier that day, "affirmed what millions of Americans already believe in their hearts" about the worth of queer households.[38] Love, the nation had come to see, was love. The president concluded that the decision was a triumph not only for gays, lesbians, and their families, but America as a whole. Marriage equality brought the country closer to fulfilling its founding premise that everyone was created equal.[39] The speech thus connected gay and lesbian rights to American values, a link that would have been unimaginable when Del and Phyllis first began their work in the mid-twentieth century. That it came from President Obama, who just seven years earlier had voiced his opposition to same-sex marriage, made the declaration all the more remarkable.[40]

The president's views on marriage equality, like those of most Americans, shifted as the queer rights movement made its case for eliminating discriminatory bans on same-sex unions. By the time the Court issued its decision, marriage equality had spent more than two decades on Americans' minds. After advocates won their first judicial victory in 1993, the country debated the issue of same-sex marriage with an unprecedented intensity. During those years, many Americans had learned, through their everyday interactions, that gays and lesbians created families just like their own. As a result, the United States Supreme Court's declaration in *Obergefell*, that the Constitution protected same-sex couples' right to marry, cemented what they already believed about the value of queer relationships. The gay and lesbian rights movement's signature achievement thus depended on the existence and visibility of queer families, which more than fifty years of advocacy had made possible. Over the course of half a century, advocates had secured legal reforms that produced new social understandings of homosexuality. Where same-sex relationships had once meant psychopathy, predation, and deviation, they now had become another means of expressing love, care, and commitment. Those changes meant that, for many Americans, marriage rights no longer seemed incongruous with queer life.

As *Family Matters* explains, this transformation in attitudes about same-sex sexuality had three equally important causes. The first was a dramatic change in law at the state and local levels, where revisions to criminal code provisions and family law doctrines helped to reshape Americans' perceptions of gays and lesbians. Penal laws during much of the twentieth century defined queer life as a public menace. Police raids on bars, arrests at cruising spots, and prosecutions for same-sex assignations all reinforced the public's perception of homosexuality as deviant. Criminal law reforms in the last three decades of the twentieth century allowed gay and lesbian couples to interact in public without fear of prosecution. Changes to family law were equally significant. Developments in custody and adoption laws made queer-headed households possible, such that gays and lesbians became visible as parents. Domestic partnership registries, which emerged in the 1980s, revealed that same-sex couples were devoted and committed partners, much like their straight counterparts. Together, these legal changes allowed gays and lesbians to create "conventional" families – nuclear households composed of caring parents and beloved children.

Family law and criminal law reform efforts also made visible another dimension of the queer family. Gays and lesbians were not just partners who raised children. They were also the sons and daughters of straight parents. In the 1980s, these parents of queer children "came out" in droves, becoming central players in the effort to protect sexual minorities from hate. That project became particularly urgent during the AIDS epidemic, when rates of violence against gays and lesbians soared. Enraged assailants would descend upon queer individuals, perpetrating attacks that terrified the entire community. Advocates tried to stem the tide of hatred through police reform and hate crimes legislation, but the progress they made was slow and uneven. They likewise tried to change school curricula to inculcate tolerance for same-sex sexuality, but religious conservatives opposed these efforts with such furor that the queer community made little headway. It was not until Americans heard from the parents of gay and lesbian children, who spoke about the heartache that prejudice inflicted on their families, that the country started reckoning with the dangerous consequences of antiqueer sentiment. These parents of queer children emphasized that support for gay and lesbian rights and support for family values were one and the same. When combined with the increased visibility of queer parents, these changes promoted a particular image of gays and lesbians, one that highlighted their roles as partners, parents, and family members.

If state and local law provides an unexpected geographic locus for the origins of change in national constitutional law, the second source for the law's transformation may seem equally surprising. Advocates were able to secure radical legal change by appealing to tradition. They self-consciously put forward a limited vision of gay and lesbian life that centered around conventional domesticity and an immutable identity. Over the course of five decades, as advocates fought for couples and their children, the most conspicuous markers of gay and lesbian life shifted from bathhouses and bars to playgrounds and PTA meetings. Legal victories in the criminal and family law context allowed gays and lesbians to be open about their sexual orientation, with individuals then projecting a vision of same-sex sexuality that highlighted how gay and lesbian couples were committed partners.

As increasing numbers of queer individuals raised children, they fought for legal recognition as parents to protect their families. When these legal remedies became available, other lesbian mothers and gay fathers seized upon them, making clear just how many queer families existed. The parents of gay sons and lesbian daughters, who emphasized their love for their queer children, reinforced the message that same-sex sexuality was consistent with domestic life. The increased visibility of these many types of queer families provided fuel for further reform, which in turn gave rise to a legal system in which queer families increasingly belonged.

The movement's emphasis on conventional households was an accurate representation of the lives of many community members whose legal battles shaped the movement's trajectory. It was also strategically necessary given the strident opposition that queer rights engendered. However, these arguments also minimized that many gays and lesbians did not fit this norm. Advocates' focus on families also did not address the most pressing needs of less privileged members of the gay and lesbian community, as well as those who deviated from social convention. Many of these individuals would have preferred that the movement address other issues, such as eliminating discrimination in employment and housing, expanding access to health care, and ensuring the physical safety of low-income, racial minority, and gender nonconforming queer individuals.[41] Yet by emphasizing how gay and lesbian households conformed to convention, queer rights advocates promoted the rights of all members of the LGBTQ+ community. Their appeal to tradition ultimately proved to be quite subversive, changing how Americans understood both same-sex sexuality and the family. The legal victories they secured for same-sex couples and their children reformulated ideas about marriage, parenthood, and the traditional household.[42] The movement thus did not just grant the queer community access to established legal institutions – it also challenged and reshaped legal and social norms.

The third cause for the law's transformation may be just as unexpected as national change coming from advocacy at the state and local levels, or a legal revolution deriving from arguments about conformity. As *Family Matters* shows, the crucial actors behind the transformation of criminal codes and family law doctrine were not just lawyers, legislators, and judges. As often, the central figures were social scientists, business leaders, social workers, police officers, teachers, school board members, and media consultants. These individuals did not necessarily see themselves as agents of legal change. Their efforts nevertheless instigated essential shifts in social perceptions of gays and lesbians, as well as the legal doctrines that shaped their lives. By helping to inspire changes in Americans' attitudes and law, these nonlegal actors helped to make queer family rights possible.

By the time the Supreme Court issued its *Obergefell* decision in 2015, American law and society had changed decidedly. Both had become more pluralistic in their definition of families, which increasingly encompassed queer households. The movement's extensive advocacy for same-sex couples thus produced legal and social changes that opened the door to marriage equality. Putting the *Obergefell* ruling in its historical context demonstrates that the legal victory depended on decades of prior rights gains on behalf of same-sex parents and their children. That fact does not reduce the importance of the marriage equality ruling, which conferred crucial rights and privileges on queer households. The Supreme Court's decision made hundreds of thousands of same-sex couples eligible for countless federal and state benefits. It also conferred significant dignitary rights on queer families.[43] At the same time, unearthing the evolution of queer family rights demonstrates that demands for marriage equality were the natural outgrowth of a movement that had long focused on the needs of queer couples and their children. The turn to marriage, in other words, was simply the next stepping-stone on the path to gay and lesbian rights.

The Turn to Marriage

In the fall of 1989, the queer community became embroiled in a fierce debate over whether to press for marriage rights.[44] Two attorneys from Lambda Legal Defense and Education Fund, a prominent queer legal rights organization, set out the competing considerations in the pages of a widely circulated gay and lesbian magazine.[45] The group's executive director, Tom Stoddard, argued that the movement should prioritize same-sex marriage because that strategy provided the surest path to equality.[46] Marriage, he argued, was much more than a legal relationship. It served as the centerpiece of America's social structure. As a result, until gays and lesbians were legally allowed to wed, they would always be second-class citizens.[47] Paula Ettelbrick, the organization's legal director, disagreed. She conceded that marriage provided "the ultimate form of acceptance" and "an insider status of the most powerful kind."[48] That fact, however, was the problem. Gays and lesbians, she argued, should not have to assimilate to the norm to secure legal equality. The queer community's distinct perspectives and experiences were something to be valued, not erased.[49] Moreover, the state should support all families, rather than create a "two-tier" system in which only married couples were entitled to respect, protection, and public support.[50] She therefore urged the movement to focus its resources on securing meaningful alternatives to marriage.[51]

Ettelbrick lost the debate. In the decades that followed, gay and lesbian rights groups would litigate and lobby for marriage equality, ultimately securing their victory at the Supreme Court. The *Obergefell* decision reflected a profound change in how legal decisionmakers conceptualized same-sex sexuality. But for those familiar with gay and lesbian rights advocacy, the movement's victory raised an important and troubling set of questions. When gay liberationists first began pressing for their rights, they vocally demanded sexual freedom. These self-proclaimed radicals flaunted their difference, making no apologies for pursuing a new social order. They sought the right to define, explore, and experience their sexuality without fear of legal prosecution.[52] Given the movement's revolutionary origins, many commentators have denounced advocates' decision to prioritize marriage equality. Some have gone so far as to charge national organizations with squandering gay liberation's potential. In their view, marriage equality was a poor substitute for the freedom that the movement promised.[53] Many of these critics were also troubled by the sanitized image of queer life that advocates put forward to secure marriage rights. These commentators argued that the movement's strategies did little to address the visceral disgust for same-sex intimacy that undergirded social and legal discrimination.[54] Other critics of the marriage equality movement expressed discomfort because the victory primarily benefited the most privileged members of the LGBTQ+ community, given that white, educated, and wealthier individuals are the ones who are most likely to marry.[55]

As *Family Matters* demonstrates, these criticisms overlook the history that both shaped the movement's evolution and limited the arguments that advocates could make. Community members' goals shifted over time, coming to center on marriage equality, in part to secure benefits that people urgently needed. Because so many rights depend on marital status, the law's refusal to recognize queer households as families inflicted significant financial, psychological, and dignitary harms. At the state level, child custody, inheritance, and medical decision-making rights all turn on whether a couple is married. Marital status matters just as much at the federal level. More than 1,000 federal statutes make marriage a factor in accessing benefits, including tax credits, social security payouts, and insurance coverage.[56] Obtaining these forms of state financial assistance became particularly pressing after the economic downturn of the 1970s. As inflation spiked and unemployment soared, governments cut social support programs to balance their budgets.[57] Yet even as the state shrunk the size of its overall safety net, it continued to confer benefits on married couples.[58] The law's refusal to recognize queer households as families consequently deprived gays and lesbians of one of the main remaining forms of government support. Indeed, these pragmatic considerations were what led three same-sex couples in Hawaii to file the lawsuit that sparked the marriage equality movement.[59]

Advocates were able to establish some alternative forms of family recognition that made certain benefits available to same-sex couples, but none were as robust as marriage. These rights also did not confer the important symbolic and dignitary benefits that came with marriage equality. The state's discriminatory marriage laws communicated that same-sex couples were somehow lesser than their different-sex counterparts. By denigrating the dignity and worth of same-sex relationships, the laws expressed that gays and lesbians did not belong in American society. They consequently harmed all members of the queer community, even those who did not live in nuclear family structures. Today, organizations' pursuit of marriage equality may seem like a narrow goal, one at odds with the movement's desire to radically transform society and promote justice for those who deviated from accepted norms.[60] Such a characterization, however, ignores how direly members of the queer community needed the rights that came with marriage. It also overlooks the expressive benefits of marriage equality, which helped to counter the enormous resistance that the gay and lesbian rights movement faced.

Indeed, critics of the movement for marriage rights often ignore the power of Christian conservatives, who constrained the strategic choices of queer rights advocates. By the late 1970s, objections to queer rights had crystallized around the claim that gays and lesbians were harmful to children. The religious right insisted that homosexuality was a behavioral choice, rather than an immutable identity. Christian conservatives also maintained that same-sex sexuality was a lifestyle that children learned from adult role models. To prevent homosexuality's transmission, they argued, the state should deny civil rights protections to gays and lesbians. In their view, doing so would reduce the likelihood that minors would interact with gay or lesbian adults and thus become homosexual themselves. Promoting the rights of gay parents, partners, and families thus meant launching a direct assault on the fundamental beliefs of those who most vocally denounced same-sex sexuality. Emphasizing queer households may have rankled religious conservatives, who were especially invested in the traditional family, but it also made gays and lesbians appear more familiar, and less threatening, to large swaths of mainstream society.

To counter the power of the religious right, advocates also had to demonstrate that homosexuality was an innate and unchangeable trait. Doing so ran counter to the goals and aspirations of gay liberationists and lesbian feminists, most of whom rejected efforts to base legal arguments on homosexuality's status as an immutable identity. For gay liberationists, arguments based on homosexuality's biological basis missed the point. Individuals should have the freedom to express their sexual desires, regardless of where they originated.[61] Lesbian feminists echoed these arguments, with some claiming that lesbianism was both a sexual identity and a political choice, one that all women should adopt to challenge the patriarchal social order.[62] However, Christian conservatives' child protection rhetoric required queer rights advocates to underscore homosexuality's status as an immutable trait, as only by doing so could they reduce the concerns of a public anxious that same-sex sexuality was a learned behavior. To some modern readers, emphasizing family visibility and homosexuality's immutability suggests a conservative approach.[63] From a historical perspective, however, the movement's goals and strategies appear more radical.

As this explanation suggests, analyzing how gay and lesbian rights advocates succeeded in transforming American law necessarily requires examining how conservative opposition framed and influenced the movement's priorities and arguments. The rise of conservativism and religious fundamentalism in postwar America had a significant influence on gay and lesbian rights advocacy, making strategic concessions necessary to attain legal gains. This history is not unique. Scholars of other rights movements have demonstrated how conservative political pressures channeled, narrowed, and consequently defined the parameters of postwar liberalism, influencing the arguments that legal organizations could successfully pursue.[64] Although the religious right ultimately lost the fight over marriage equality, it indelibly shaped the evolution of queer rights by constraining the arguments that advocates could make. Because of the power of Christian conservatives, the movement could not pursue the more politically challenging goals that advocates like Ettelbrick championed. They also could not root these arguments in sexual freedom, but rather had to base their claims on homosexuality's status as an innate trait.

The movement's history consequently demonstrates that contemporary criticisms of the marriage equality movement are deeply flawed. Advocates did not sacrifice the movement's revolutionary potential on the altar of conformity, while gaining little of substance in return. These commentators ignore that advocates often found themselves stymied by political headwinds they could not control. They also overlook the pressing needs of many queer community members, which only marriage rights could meet. Of course, critics are correct that the gains the movement attained were uneven, leaving the most marginalized members of the LGBTQ+ community – racial minorities, the economically disadvantaged, and gender nonconformists – with the fewest legal protections. Indeed, although the *Obergefell* decision was an important marker of larger progress on behalf of queer families, marriage equality did not address the rampant discrimination, harassment, or violence that members of the LGBTQ+ community continue to endure. Marriage equality's limitations are such that, although *Family Matters* is an account of a successful campaign to promote the rights of queer families, it is not a triumphalist narrative of gay and lesbian legal victories. The right to marry was simply one step in the fight for full legal equality, which gays, lesbians, and other members of the LGBTQ+ community are still working to attain. Queer rights continue to be contested, with advocates experiencing defeats as well as victories.

The book thus uses marriage equality as a marker of change, rather than casting it as an end point for the legal movement. At the same time, by placing marriage rights within the broader context of queer family mobilization, *Family Matters* demonstrates that advocates' focus on marriage equality was not a symbolic white whale that narrowed or diverted the movement's ambitions, as some have claimed. To the contrary, what this book demonstrates is that the fight for marriage rights was the natural next step for advocates, given their long-standing focus on creating legally recognized queer families. Moreover, the intense resistance that advocates encountered makes it clear just how significant the movement's achievements were. Indeed, that detractors can characterize advocates' focus on marriage rights as conservative and unimaginative is a testament to how dramatically gay and lesbian rights advocates transformed both American society and law.

The queer rights movement, in other words, did not simply secure the right of same-sex couples to marry. It attained profound social and legal changes. The *Obergefell* ruling symbolized how much advocates had accomplished since the middle of the twentieth century, when the state actively repressed and punished same-sex sexuality. In addition to conferring practical and dignitary rights, the decision was consequential because it served as a reminder that the law could have a transformational effect. *Family Matters* thus offers more than a history of gay and lesbian rights. By tracing the movement's evolution, the book suggests how advocates for minority rights may be able to unlock the potential of law reform.

Securing Meaningful Change

John Stevens brushed the tears from his eyes as he and David Daily exchanged vows. Just a few hours after the Supreme Court ruled that the federal Constitution protected their right to marry, the couple of thirty-nine years wed in Detroit, Michigan. Stevens, a retired computer programmer, had spent weeks checking a website that live-blogged the Supreme Court's actions, awaiting the decision with equal parts hope and trepidation. He later confessed that he never truly expected to see the day when he could marry the love of his life.[65] Around the country, gay men and lesbians who had lived through decades of state repression echoed Stevens's sentiments. Their moments of joy came as a surprise. None had thought marriage equality would happen in their lifetimes.[66]

These members of the queer community were not the only people who marveled at the legal change. The gay and lesbian rights movement's rapid, extraordinary success has mystified academics, advocates, and the public alike. The legal system is known for moving at a glacial pace, rather than lightning speed. Judicial decisions all too often deliver hollow victories, rather than meaningful social change. Many have thus been left wondering how the gay and lesbian rights movement was able to defy those conventions. At stake in these debates is whether the struggle for queer rights serves a model for the many other groups clamoring for their rights. What *Family Matters* shows is that the gay and lesbian rights movement is distinctive, because historical forces beyond advocates' control often shaped the law's evolution. At the same time, the movement's past offers new ways of understanding how reform movements are able to attain consequential legal change. This book is thus as important to understanding the systemic manner in which rights become embedded in law and society as it is to understanding the state of the law around same-sex sexuality.

Gay and lesbian rights advocates necessarily had to chart a new path to achieve their goals, given the singular nature of their cause. The reasons for antiqueer animosity shifted over time, with each new justification fueling another wave of state regulation and repression. What also made the fight for gay and lesbian rights unique was the host of external political, legal, economic, and cultural changes that shaped the movement's evolution. During the second half of the twentieth century, conceptions of sex, gender, and the family were in a state of flux.[67] In the 1960s, feminist activists launched an assault on gender norms, questioning the need for sex differentiation in society.[68] The rise of feminist liberation coincided with the wider availability of contraception, which helped to spark a sexual revolution.[69] Around this time, states made it easier to divorce by instituting no-fault regimes. Consequently, the rates of couples ending their unions soared.[70] American households had always been multifaceted, but in the 1970s, they became more visibly diverse. Most households continued to comprise two married adults and their children, but an ever-greater number consisted of single parents, unmarried couples, and blended families.[71] These changes produced pitched political battles over the state of the family, helping to launch a new conservative movement.[72] To the religious right's consternation, same-sex couples were increasingly able to present themselves as just another deviation from the norm. The queer rights movement was consequently pushing against a door that was poised to open.

The particular historical moment in which gay and lesbian rights advocates operated thus explains some of the movement's successes. At the same time, the movement's victories were more than a matter of fortunate timing. They were also the product of deliberate choices, one of which was sustained attention to reform at the state and municipal levels, where small groups of motivated citizens were able to secure legal changes that would have been unthinkable in other parts of the country. Many of the debates over gay and lesbian rights took place in liberal cities like Los Angeles, New York City, and San Francisco. However, municipalities across America responded to these developments, which queer rights advocates – and their opponents – brought to local officials' attention. Sometimes they did so with sympathetic laws that mirrored the actions on the coasts. Just as frequently, however, elected officials enacted legislation or policies that demonstrated their hostility to gay and lesbian rights. Yet even in the face of this resistance, successes at the state and local levels undermined conservatives' strident opposition. These developments allowed for small-scale experiments that made unthreatening queer families more visible. The conspicuous existence of these households, in turn, generated legal, political, and constitutional change at the national level. In other words, it was not that decisions in progressive enclaves represented national trends, but rather that they provided the foundation for widespread change.

Family Matters consequently provides a history of law reform across the United States, but does so by examining law from the ground up. Only by studying the day-to-day struggles for equality in cities and towns around the country can the successes and limitations of the gay and lesbian rights movement as a whole be understood. It thus analyzes episodes throughout the country, then weaves them together, to explain the transformation of American law writ large. This focus on the state and local is a methodological innovation that is essential to understanding legal change more generally. Many accounts of the fight for gay and lesbian rights have focused on federal constitutional law and national politics – understandably so, given that federal policies had an important effect on gay and lesbian life, from prohibitions on serving in the military to funding research on AIDS.[73] Legal histories of other rights movements have likewise concentrated on federal actors, congressional enactments, and Supreme Court decisions, which shaped rights across the country.[74] At the same time, legal historians have produced exceptional local studies of efforts to combat discrimination, both in the context of gay and lesbian rights advocacy and other rights movements. However, their works have tended to be case studies rooted in specific cities, rather than the country as a whole.[75] They have likewise typically focused on a singular legal issue or limited their analysis of local developments to court cases.[76]

By examining seemingly disparate locales and areas of the law, *Family Matters* demonstrates how they are integrally related, with each forming a piece of a larger puzzle. What *Family Matters* reveals is that the causes of change in constitutional law and national policy often came from outside of the capital. Moreover, the impetus for change frequently originated outside of the courts, where state legislative enactments and municipal administrative decisions often had little to do with the Constitution's protections. Focusing on state and local advocacy efforts, as well as the links between them, demonstrates how many small shifts in discourse can make national change possible. As a result, the book showcases a broader array of legal experiments and experiences than analyzing federal developments alone. This attention to the state and local is not meant to minimize the role of federal law, but rather to extend the possibilities for consequential reform beyond the halls of Congress, the White House, and the Supreme Court. Likewise, identifying how advocates connected the changes in various parts of the country does not diminish any one effort. Instead, it helps to illuminate important, but previously overlooked, mechanisms for national law reform.

This state and local lens also focuses attention on the important role of nonlegal actors in securing meaningful legal change. *Family Matters* consequently provides a different narrative than typical accounts of law reform, which until recently have focused on lawyers, judges, and legislators.[77] The traditional loci of law reform scholarship are important, given that litigators and elected officials had a substantial influence on the development of the law. Indeed, they also appear in this book's pages, playing a crucial role in battles over gay and lesbian rights. However, they are only part of the story. Administrative agencies and ballot measures were also integral to law reform, as were the nonlegal actors whose work shaped decisionmakers' actions. This book thus expands the study of legal change beyond both the traditional players and the typical branches of government, identifying how reform occurs in unexpected places. Social scientists, local civil servants, social workers, teachers, business leaders, and the media were important actors that made it possible for advocates to succeed. Identifying their contributions to the gay and lesbian rights movement provides an account of legal change that is neither top-down, nor entirely bottom-up. Instead, it emphasizes the distinct and indispensable role of those who operate in between.[78] By presenting this history, *Family Matters* demonstrates that civil rights law is based on more than cases, statutes, and administrative regulations. It also includes a diversity of other sources, including employment contracts, scholastic policies, and public education campaigns. Expanding the focus of law reform in this way reveals a wider range of opportunities for change, by a greater variety of people.

Family Matters takes as expansive an approach to legal argumentation as it does to legal actors. Gay and lesbian rights advocates often rooted their claims in traditional forms of legal reasoning, focusing their briefs and oral arguments on doctrine and established precedent. However, many queer rights battles were fought in the court of public opinion, where advocates discovered the power of appealing to emotion.[79] Their opponents had already learned this lesson, securing antiqueer laws by stoking fears that gays and lesbians would harm children. The queer rights movement adapted conservatives' strategy. Rather than calling upon dread, however, they emphasized love and

affection. Advocates underscored the bonds between straight parents
and their children, as well as the devotion of same-sex couples to their
sons and daughters. This affective reasoning convinced many members
of the public to support queer rights, but the framing strategies did
more than reshape popular opinion – they ultimately informed legal
arguments. By the time the marriage equality movement took its cases
to the Supreme Court, its attorneys were emphasizing the lasting
bonds between same-sex couples, as well as the decency, dignity, and
humanity of gays and lesbians. Social movement scholars have noted
that the divide between political and legal mobilization is often
porous.[80] Activists routinely draw upon legal principles to achieve
their political goals. They likewise demand that the state intervene
on their behalf, giving rise to enforceable rights. Nowhere was the line
between law and politics thinner than in the gay and lesbian rights
context. The arguments that featured in public education campaigns
quickly peppered court filings, with both reshaping the place of same-
sex sexuality in America.

Family Matters' methodological innovations reinforce one another.
Its state and local lens brings together a varied and unexplored set of
public policy issues, which in turn illuminate the role of diverse actors
and arguments in bringing about legal change. Together, they allow
the book's insights to apply beyond the LGBTQ+ community, to the
legal system more generally. The speed of the gay and lesbian legal
revolution – especially as compared to efforts to secure civil rights for
Americans of color and women – has challenged conventional wisdom
about the law's resistance to change and its ability to produce meaningful results.[81] The book's emphasis on the state and local, as well as
the role of nonlegal actors and emotional rhetoric, offers keys to
understanding the processes of law reform and how social movements
can secure consequential legal victories. Those lessons are particularly
important, given that the story it tells also serves as a reminder that, for
people suffering at the hands of state oppression, legal change cannot
come fast enough.

The Path Forward

Clive Boutilier had a quiet life in Brooklyn, New York. He lived in the
same building as his mother and stepfather, although in a separate

apartment.[82] During the day, he worked a custodial job in Manhattan.[83] On nights and weekends, he bowled and attended Mass.[84] Then, in 1959, the 26-year-old departed from his routine. He met a stranger and they engaged in a quick tryst – one that led to his arrest for consensual sodomy. For Boutilier, the problem was not the criminal charge, which the district attorney's office soon dismissed.[85] Instead, it was that he was a Canadian citizen at a time when America's immigration law barred gays and lesbians from entering the country. He and his family had emigrated from their Nova Scotia farm in 1955, after his mother married a United States citizen.[86] When Boutilier applied for citizenship in 1963, the Immigration and Naturalization Service learned of his arrest, and thus of his homosexuality. The agency ordered him deported.[87] He spent six years fighting their decision, only to have the United States Supreme Court rule against him. The distraught Boutilier attempted suicide, which left him in a month-long coma. When he finally awoke, it was with brain damage and physical disabilities that would last for the rest of his life.[88]

Like Boutilier's encounters with the law, *Family Matters* begins in the 1950s, a time when the state went to great lengths to punish queer identity. The book traces legal changes through 2015, when *Obergefell* was decided, detailing reforms to penal codes, child custody standards, domestic partner benefits, adoption regulations, hate crimes laws, and educational policies. It recounts this history in seven chapters, arranged in three sections that proceed in loosely chronological order. The first section addresses the rise of visible same-sex couples, as well as how gays and lesbians came to be seen as parents. Chapter 1 begins with the laws and legal practices that created an imposing barrier to reform, detailing the web of criminal provisions that punished, stigmatized, and isolated homosexual men and women in mid-twentieth-century America. The chapter then turns to initial efforts to dismantle the discriminatory regime. It explains how and why lawmakers began decriminalizing gay and lesbian life in the 1960s and 1970s, which made it possible for same-sex relationships to flourish. Chapter 2 turns to early efforts to secure the rights of queer parents, analyzing custody disputes in the late 1970s and early 1980s. These lawsuits gave rise to visible gay- and lesbian-headed families, setting the stage for broader changes, including demands for affirmative protections during and after the HIV/AIDS crisis of the 1980s. Chapter 3 takes up the rise of domestic partnership registries in the mid-1980s and early 1990s, which granted concrete benefits to gays and lesbians and made a symbolic statement concerning the ubiquity and acceptability of same-sex couples. Chapter 4 details foster care and adoption policy reforms during this time period, demonstrating how the changes allowed an increasing number of gays and lesbians to become parents. Chapters 1 and 3 thus address queer partners, while Chapters 2 and 4 discuss queer parents.

The second section presents a different dimension to the queer family, which was more than simply gay- and lesbian-headed households. Gay and lesbian adults began their lives as queer children, and the overwhelming majority had straight parents. Chapters 5 and 6 explain how antiviolence advocacy in the 1980s and 1990s helped to make this aspect of the queer family visible. The AIDS crisis unleashed a torrent of animosity against the queer community. As hatred rose, so did levels of violence. However, attacks did not just come from outside the community. Queer youth also responded to society's hatred by inflicting harm on themselves at alarming rates. By the end of the 1980s, suicide had become the leading cause of death for gay and lesbian youth. Both chapters detail how parents of queer children became involved in antiviolence efforts, pressing the American public to take seriously the plight of their sons and daughters. These families of origin helped to bridge the gap between the queer and straight worlds by showing that gays and lesbians were members of close-knit, "traditional" households.

Family Matters' final section examines marriage equality and its aftermath. Chapter 7 discusses the movement for marriage equality, demonstrating how battles over domestic partnerships, custody, foster care, adoption, and hate violence shaped arguments for marriage rights. Over the course of the 1980s and 1990s, same-sex couples had become visible as partners and parents. They were also increasingly recognized as integral members of straight families. Advocates drew upon these themes in both their legal briefs and their public opinion messaging, creating a framework that helped many Americans to become more accepting of same-sex sexuality. The chapter consequently demonstrates how previous victories on behalf of queer families made marriage equality possible. The epilogue then extends these arguments by addressing debates over queer rights since the Supreme Court's same-sex marriage ruling.

Crafting this narrative required piecing together archival fragments and combining them with a range of other sources. Much of the information in this book comes from the records of gay and lesbian rights organizations, whose newsletters, memos, press releases, and other materials memorialized their work. Movement leaders, advocates, and community members also preserved pamphlets, fliers, speeches, and other documents that contained crucial details and revealed connections between events in various parts of the country. Dozens of oral history interviews with individuals involved in battles over gay and lesbian rights – including attorneys, activists, elected officials, government administrators, social scientists, and educators – helped to fill in the missing pieces. So too did government reports, legislative histories, newspaper accounts, magazine articles, documentaries, scientific studies, and published sources.

Some of the materials for the book were particularly difficult to obtain. Family court decisions are typically unreported and sealed for the protection of the children involved, while the records of criminal courts are often spotty when they are first created, and are not always maintained for posterity. Because of these limited institutional records, putting together the narrative meant finding the unpublished judicial opinions and case files that lawyers, litigants, and advocates had entrusted to libraries, as well as collecting reports of decisions scattered in the newsletters of local queer rights organizations. Uncovering the more ephemeral materials that were crucial to the fight for gay and lesbian rights, such as television commercials, meant scouring internet databases, contacting producers, and visiting far-flung repositories.

These sources contained numerous stories of courageous individuals, whose efforts to secure justice contributed to the transformation of America's legal system. When discussing specific people, the book uses last names, except when two or more people share a moniker. Under those circumstances, the book employs first names to avoid confusion. Where individuals – like Del and Phyllis – are widely known to the queer community by their given names, the chapters reflect that common usage. In the historical records in which queer community members appeared, people with same-sex attractions described themselves in varying ways. The terminology that this book deploys consequently depends on the time period in question. Discussions of the 1950s and 1960s use the term *homosexual,* while chapters on later periods primarily deploy *gay* and *lesbian.* The chapters also rely on the generic *queer* to refer to those who engaged in same-sex practices, even though that word sometimes departs from those individuals' self-conceptions and risks eliding bisexuals, who have long been marginalized within the queer community.[89] It additionally uses *queer family* as a descriptor for households with gay or lesbian family members, who might be partners, parents, or children. Using "queer" risks introducing a modern term into a historical narrative, but it is also a necessary descriptor for complex, shifting, and diverse identity categories.

The term queer is also a useful means of recognizing that many of the individuals who suffered at the hands of state discrimination – and fought to overturn unjust laws – included transgender, nonbinary, and other gender nonconformists. The pages of this book focus on people who self-identified as men and women, offering a history of gay and lesbian rights. However, state repression extended to all parts of the queer community, whose members often banded together to combat discrimination. Much like the language that individuals used to describe themselves, the labels for the movement that represented their interests have changed over time. Since the book focuses on the work of people and groups in the 1980s and 1990s, it primarily describes the legal movement as "gay and lesbian." Many national rights groups became *LGBT* in the late 1990s and early 2000s, and today would identify themselves as *LGBTQ* or *LGBTQ+.*[90] This work uses these acronyms when appropriate, which depends on both the historical time period and the rights at issue.

As the varied and changing terminology indicates, the place of same-sex sexuality in twentieth-century American society and law shifted significantly. Over the course of five decades, both queer and straight society developed new understandings and conceptions of same-sex sexuality. These changes would prompt legal reform, giving rise to a significant transformation in American law. The events that would change the country include inspiring accounts of resistance, heartwarming tales of affection, and humorous moments of wit. Some were headline-grabbing theatrical protests, such as when a queer rights activist literally shut the mouth of evangelical leader Anita Bryant by hurling a banana cream pie at her face. The gay and lesbian press reveled in the fact that he self-identified as a "Groucho Marxist."[91] Others were personal moments of activism, like the elderly lesbian couple who contributed to the cause by coming out in the newsletter of their assisted living community.[92] Still others were painful stories of hardship, agony, and injustice, experiences that all too often dominated the lives of those who fought against America's discriminatory legal regime.

Perhaps no account illustrates the dangers that gays and lesbians faced in the middle of the twentieth century more vividly than the tale of Bert Chapman, who spent thirty-one years confined to psychiatric hospitals because he was gay. In September 1940, Michigan police arrested Chapman for having been sexually intimate in his own home with another man.[93] What led law enforcement to Chapman's home that night has been lost to history, as the clerk's office overlooked his files when converting its paper documents to microfilm.[94] The few remaining records, however, paint a grim picture of Chapman's life after the arrest. Instead of sending him to jail, the court confined the 35-year-old to a psychiatric institution until he "fully and permanently recovered" from his homosexuality. In the decades that followed, Chapman repeatedly appealed his confinement. He was finally able to secure his release in 1971, after convincing a jury that he was no longer a danger to society. At that point, he was 68 years old. His mother had died a year before the verdict, at the age of 90, having spent the last three decades of her life trying to secure her son's freedom.[95]

Chapman's experience provides a sobering reminder that, in the mid-twentieth century, the legal landscape for homosexuals was bleak. The extreme nature of Chapman's ordeal was the exception, not the rule, but he was also far from the only gay man who suffered prolonged periods of confinement because of his sexual orientation. At the same time, Chapman's release also demonstrates that the law could and did in fact change. Given that the state relied so heavily on its penal codes to humiliate, denigrate, and abuse homosexuals, initial reforms perhaps unsurprisingly focused on the criminal law. The story of the gay and lesbian rights revolution thus begins with the fight against surveillance, arrest, and imprisonment, all of which dominated the lives of homosexual men and women in mid-twentieth-century America.

Part I

Queer Partners and Parents

In the 1940s, being a gay man in America required hiding in plain sight. Dale Jennings understood this rule all too well. He may have been a talented dancer who traveled in bohemian circles, but Jennings was so anxious to conceal his homosexuality that he wed three times. Each of those marriages was brief and quickly annulled.[1] In 1952, however, the decorated World War II veteran defied convention in the most public way possible. He came out to the world after he was arrested for soliciting an undercover officer in Westlake Park, a popular Los Angeles cruising site. At the urging of his friends in the Mattachine Society, a homophile rights group he had cofounded two years earlier, Jennings decided to fight the charge. At the trial, he admitted to being homosexual, but steadfastly denied having made any sexual overtures. The jury deliberated for thirty-six hours, only to report that they were deadlocked. Eleven members wanted to acquit, but one juror was holding out for a conviction. Upon hearing their report, the district attorney's office dismissed the charges.[2]

Jennings left the courthouse that day stunned at his victory. He had expected to go to jail, not to walk free.[3] His goal in defending the case was to draw attention to police entrapment practices, which he hoped would prompt homosexuals to join the Mattachine Society. The group formed to secure acceptance for same-sex sexuality, but being associated with homosexuality was so dangerous that its members did not dare to meet in public. They gathered in one another's homes, holding their meetings in windowless basements to preserve anonymity. If the

host did not have a cellar, they drew the shades tight to avoid being
seen.⁴ Jennings's case changed the organization's fortunes.
Membership multiplied after the trial, leading chapters to form in cities
on both coasts.⁵

Jennings's legal battle marked the start of a new legal movement,
one that would transform American society. In the years that followed,
gays and lesbians increasingly dared to come out and demand their
rights. They first secured changes to criminal laws, which allowed
same-sex couples to interact in public without fear of prosecution.
Over the course of the 1960s and 1970s, as leftist social movements
proliferated, gay and lesbian rights groups adopted a more radical
posture. They made greater demands, which they pursued through
increasingly confrontational tactics. Around that time, the movement's
focus also shifted, expanding to include family law reforms. That was
a change that neither Jennings nor the Mattachine Society had anticipated, yet their work set these efforts into motion. Over time, gay and
lesbian rights advocates convinced the state to recognize same-sex
couples as partners and parents. As queer households proliferated,
they changed the dominant image of gay and lesbian life, from furtive
assignations in dark cruising grounds to family meals in suburban
homes. Neither view of the gay and lesbian community had ever been
entirely accurate, as queer life had always been as diverse as queer
individuals themselves. However, making families the dominant image
of same-sex sexuality helped advocates secure the legal rights that
community members needed.

After his trial, Jennings became known as the Rosa Parks of the
queer rights movement.⁶ His courage in publicly admitting his homosexuality inspired others to fight for justice. They initially devoted
themselves to securing reforms to criminal laws, which required gays
and lesbians to hide their sexual orientation. It took decades, but states
eventually began eliminating their prohibitions on consensual sodomy.
Soon thereafter, other criminal code provisions that police wielded to
repress queer life would also fall away. Those changes would help
bring an end to the days of fear, silence, and secrecy that plagued the
lives of gays and lesbians.

I

Legalizing Queer Life

Alfred Kinsey and Criminal Law Reform

Thomas Earl and Eldridge Rhodes did not know that police were following them on the evening of July 1, 1962, as they walked through San Diego's Gaslamp Quarter. The vice squad had stationed two officers in the area after receiving a series of complaints about two Black men soliciting clients for female prostitutes waiting at area hotels. Rhodes, who was Black, fit one of the suspects' descriptions; the police assumed that Earl, who was white, was a potential client. Upon spotting the men, police followed them to their destination – a room at the Service Hotel. There, the officers positioned themselves outside the door, where they heard kissing and the bed squeaking. Hoping to catch the men violating the state's antipandering law, the officers looked through a half-inch wide opening between the room's door and its frame. However, instead of seeing an encounter with a female prostitute, they witnessed two undressed men embracing on the bed. To get a better view, one officer gave the other a leg up to reach the door's glass transom, then fetched a stool from the hotel manager so the officers would not need to take turns looking through the pane. Upon witnessing the men engaging in oral sex, the officers broke down the door and arrested Earl and Rhodes for violating California's anti-sodomy statute.[1] Both men were convicted of the felony.

Laws prohibiting consensual sodomy were only one of the many criminal provisions that the state wielded to suppress queer life in the mid-twentieth century. Police also arrested gays and lesbians for vagrancy, disorderly conduct, lewdness, and solicitation. These statutes did not target same-sex sexuality directly, but officials interpreted them broadly and readily deployed the laws to repress the queer world. Police often relied upon the provisions to harass homosexuals simply for standing on the street, as well as to shut down places where the queer community socialized. The statutes and their heavy-handed enforcement rendered gays and lesbians invisible, as venturing into queer life meant risking arrest and public disgrace.[2] Contact with the police could force gays and lesbians out of the closet, which jeopardized their family relationships, friendships, and careers. Criminal laws reflected American society's abhorrence of same-sex sexuality, but by defining gays and lesbians as outlaws, penal codes also reinforced their outsider status. These laws encouraged employers, landlords, and other decision-makers to act on their prejudices against gays and lesbians.[3] This was particularly the case when homosexual parents petitioned for custody of children after divorcing their different-sex spouses. One judge colorfully explained that he would not permit "children to be placed in a home where the felony of sodomy is committed at least twice a week."[4] Criminal laws thus had far-reaching consequences, anchoring a legal regime that condemned same-sex sexuality.

In the 1960s, gays and lesbians were thus living in a world that defined their very existence as an aberration that deserved punishment. That oppressive legal regime, however, was beginning to change. Had Earl and Rhodes lived in Illinois at the time of their arrest, their actions would not have been illegal. In 1961, a year before officers witnessed the men's assignation, Illinois had become the first state to decriminalize consensual sodomy. Other states soon followed suit. By 1978, almost half of states had repealed their consensual sodomy laws.[5]

What helped to make these reforms possible was that, as dire as the American legal system was for gays and lesbians, the web of laws that punished the queer community was also a relatively recent development. For most of the nation's history, federal and state officials had not condoned same-sex sexuality, but they had not explicitly targeted gays and lesbians. Homosexual activity was not yet seen as a marker of identity. Instead, it was a deviant behavior in which some members of the population engaged.[6] Only in the 1930s did governments begin suppressing queer life, after experts popularized a new conception of same-sex sexuality, one that framed homosexuality as a psychological disorder. Homosexuality became an affliction that would both mar the lives of individuals and corrode American society. That notion spurred antiqueer laws and discriminatory policing, but it would also prove to be the key to legal change.

Creating Criminals

Sergeant Sonnenshein served in the military during World War I. He was known in his unit as "Tessie" and "fairy Sonnenshein." His fellow soldiers mocked him for being "perhaps a little queer" and would degrade him by demanding sexual favors. Sonnenshein would ignore their taunts, sometimes simply smiling in response. In 1918, the military court-martialed Sonnenshein, alleging that he had tried to fellate another man in the latrine. Although the judge advocate general agreed that Sonnenshein was "an effeminate type," that was not enough to sustain a conviction. Sonnenshein returned to duty.[7] Twenty years later, Sonnenshein's sexual orientation would have been sufficient for the military to expel him. Until the 1930s, however, the state was concerned with same-sex conduct, not homosexuality per se. As the political and medical context changed, so did social perceptions of same-sex sexuality. What had once been seen as a personal moral failing was now understood as a danger to society. Consequently, the state undertook wide-ranging efforts to repress homosexuality.

American states had criminalized same-sex intimacy since the nation's founding, but until the Second World War, the state's regulation of homosexuality was only incidental to its larger efforts to address crime, poverty, and social disorder.[8] In the colonial period, sodomy was punishable by death, a penalty that reflected biblical injunctions against the "crime against nature."[9] Yet state authorities typically ignored consensual same-sex activities, focusing instead on prosecuting forcible rape.[10] In the nineteenth and early twentieth centuries, the federal government took a similar approach in their law enforcement efforts. Immigration officers searched out homosexual immigrants not because of their sexual orientation, but because inspectors linked perversion and dependency. According to the theories of German sexologist Richard von Krafft-Ebing, who popularized the argument that homosexuality was an inborn constitutional defect, same-sex attraction was a nervous and hereditary disorder that produced weaker physical bodies.[11] His conception led immigration officials to conclude that homosexuals would become economically dependent on the state, in violation of a provision that barred any immigrants who were "likely to become a public charge."[12] When they excluded or deported homosexuals, it was because same-sex sexuality was a proxy for dependency.

In the 1920s, a new framework for understanding homosexuality emerged – one that would lead officials to start targeting gays and lesbians because of their sexual desires. During this period, psychiatric theories reconceptualized homosexuality not as an innate trait, but rather as a flaw in psychological development. Homosexuals were individuals who were frozen at a pre-adolescent developmental stage. As a result, they were emotionally immature and impulsive. These same ideas also linked same-sex attraction to pedophilia. Since homosexuals related to children on a developmental level, psychiatrists reasoned, they were more likely to search them out as sexual partners.[13] Under this new theory, the "effeminate homosexual" constituted one extreme of sexual deviance. At the other end of the spectrum was the violent sexual predator.[14] In the 1930s, psychiatrists combined both poles into one diagnostic category: the sexual psychopath.[15] Psychiatrists explained that homosexuals were like violent sex offenders because both were immature and lacked self-control. Popular books, magazines, and newspapers echoed this theory, repeatedly linking uncontrolled sexuality and childishness.[16] For example, readers of *Parents' Magazine* learned that sex offenders "are immature, frequently with no more control over their impulses than the child who wants what he wants when he wants it."[17]

This new psychiatric category became a legal classification in the 1930s, when a sex crime panic swept the nation. A series of highly publicized, violent sex crimes against children prompted public outrage. Citizens consequently pressed elected officials to protect innocent victims from assault, leading thirty states and the District of Columbia to enact sexual psychopath statutes.[18] Under these laws, individuals convicted of sex-related offenses, including consensual sodomy, could be institutionalized in psychiatric hospitals, rather than imprisoned. These statutes cast offenders as patients rather than criminals, ostensibly portraying them in a more sympathetic light. However, the laws did not replace the penal code provisions that punished gays and lesbians for their homosexuality. Moreover, because many of the statutes allowed sexual psychopaths to be institutionalized indefinitely, the civil commitment laws could be just as punitive as criminal codes. The sexual psychopath laws varied not just in the length of time a person could be committed to a psychiatric hospital, but also in how they defined sexual psychopathy, which – depending on the jurisdiction – could include everything from rapists and pedophiles to sadomasochists, exhibitionists, voyeurs, and homosexuals.[19] As broad as the statutes were, the psychiatric definition of sexual psychopathy was even more expansive. Some psychiatrists included in the category anyone who engaged in extramarital or premarital sex.[20] The diagnostic label was so imprecise that it generated significant controversy within the scientific community, with one prominent psychiatrist deriding it as a "wastebasket" classification.[21]

Because sexual psychopath laws were blunt instruments, judges and prosecutors did not level them against all defendants who fell within the statutes' wide scope. Instead, they often reserved the weapons for the most dangerous offenders.[22] Yet the laws' very existence was a terrifying specter for gay men, who could be institutionalized until "cured." Prosecutors often wielded the threat of commitment under sexual psychopath laws to convince defendants to plead guilty to nonviolent offenses.[23] They sometimes also proceeded with adjudications under the laws. Although commitments for sexual psychopathy typically involved cases of forcible rape, gay men arrested for consensual sodomy were likewise adjudicated under the statutes.[24] Because of California's sexual psychopath law, Thomas Earl's conviction for sodomy was only the start to his legal troubles. Soon after issuing the verdict, the court adjudicated him a sexual psychopath and transferred him to Atascadero State Hospital.[25] In most states, sexual psychopaths received therapy, but medical professionals in California took a more aggressive approach. Doctors at Atascadero were known for treating their patients with shock therapy, as well as punishing those who tried to decline the sessions with solitary confinement in cold cells.[26]

Psychological theories that cast homosexuality as inherently dangerous to children gave rise to more than just this sexual psychopath regime. They also produced a host of discriminatory provisions at the federal level. These were not criminal laws, but they nevertheless reinforced to the American public that same-sex sexuality was a threat to the social order that needed to be contained. During World War II, the military instituted a ban on homosexuals, fearing that gays and lesbians could not control their desires, and therefore would not be able to adjust to the rigors of military life.[27] The policy cast same-sex sexuality as antithetical to patriotic duty. Similar concerns about national security led the federal government to target homosexual employees in investigations into disloyalty. Authorities feared that gays and lesbians were emotionally unstable and susceptible to blackmail, a particularly dangerous proposition during the Cold War. Under the theory that "one homosexual can pollute a Government office," the federal civil service tried to purge itself of queer employees.[28] As the Cold War raged, more gays and lesbians lost their federal jobs than suspected communists. Federal officials, for their part, emphasized the similarities between homosexuals and communists, arguing that individuals in both groups could pass undetected and tended to participate in underground subcultures.[29]

The federal government's depiction of homosexual men and women as state security risks consequently framed same-sex sexuality as a grave danger, one that could corrode American society. Writers in the 1950s reinforced that notion by routinely using the metaphor of disease to describe homosexuality.[30] That language resonated with Americans, who feared that sexual and political threats to the nation were contagious and spreading as queer communities expanded in the late 1940s.[31] The country's mobilization during World War II had led gay men and lesbians to leave their homes and neighborhoods for war-related work in urban centers. There, they discovered more permissive environments – and one another.[32] After the war, many remained in these cities, giving rise to new queer communities. Bars and restaurants that catered exclusively to gays and lesbians proliferated not just on the coasts, but all around the country, opening in cities as diverse as Denver, Colorado; Kansas City, Missouri; and Richmond, Virginia.[33]

The public's concern about homosexuality only grew as gays and lesbians began organizing for their rights. In 1950, Dale Jennings and four others formed the Mattachine Society, the first homophile rights organization.[34] Several of its founders were members of the Communist Party, and all traveled in leftist circles.[35] In 1953, Paul Coates, a Los Angeles newspaper writer, revealed to his readers that the group's legal adviser had been an "unfriendly" witness before the House Un-American Activities Committee, invoking his Fifth Amendment right to avoid providing answers to its questions about his communist activities. Coates noted that, with approximately 200,000 homosexuals in the Los Angeles area, "[a] well-trained subversive could move in and forge that power into a dangerous political weapon."[36] The Mattachine's ties to communism reinforced the image of homosexuality as sinister, corrupt, and a danger to American society.[37]

Thus, by the 1950s, all levels of government were on alert against the menace of homosexuality. The federal government's discriminatory policies resulted in thousands of suspected homosexuals losing their jobs.[38] Yet that number paled in comparison to how many queer individuals would suffer detention, arrest, conviction, and imprisonment at the hands of local law enforcement officials – vice patrol squads that, in the 1950s and 1960s, launched extended campaigns to suppress homosexuality. Vice officers would raid the taverns and clubs where gay men, lesbians, and gender nonconformists gathered, using every option they had available to penalize queer life. Their sustained efforts made it dangerous for gays and lesbians to venture into the few bars and restaurants that welcomed the queer community.

Penalizing Queer Life

Hazel's was a lively and popular queer bar located in San Mateo, California, a city just south of San Francisco. Founded in 1939 by Hazel Nickola, the bar survived World War II's economic downturns and, by 1956, was once again thriving. Hazel's welcomed Black, white, and Asian patrons alike to its convivial space, where a bawdy humor reigned supreme. Most of Hazel's patrons were homosexual men, who would dance, kiss, and caress their partners within the haven of the bar's accepting ambiance, but women likewise found themselves drawn to the bar's unrestrained atmosphere.[39] The freedom the queer community enjoyed at Hazel's came to a terrifying end shortly after midnight on February 19, 1956, when San Mateo County Sheriff Earl Whitmore led a raid on the bar. His uniformed officers rounded up the almost 300 patrons, arresting 90 of the regulars who undercover agents recognized from their prior investigations. They charged those individuals with vagrancy for their illicit behavior. At the time, police often relied upon vagrancy statutes – which gave law enforcement virtually unlimited discretion to arrest individuals who seemed to threaten the social order – to suppress queer life.[40]

The officers also arrested Hazel's owner for permitting lewd dancing. Soon thereafter, Hazel's lost its liquor license for becoming "a resort for sexual perverts."[41]

Hazel's was just one of the many queer bars and clubs that police raided in the 1950s and 1960s.[42] In these sweeps, mass arrests for dancing, flirting, or kissing members of the same sex were common, with police typically charging the patrons with vagrancy, lewdness, disorderly conduct, or solicitation.[43] At a time when the country was already on alert because of the Cold War, these large-scale raids reminded Americans that one of the significant dangers they needed to guard against was same-sex attraction. Each arrest underscored homosexuality's status as a crime, which reinforced social stigma against gays and lesbians. The sweeps also served as warnings to members of the queer community. Gays and lesbians were constantly aware that they risked detention and prosecution if they dared to seek out the companionship of other homosexuals. That fact made it even more difficult for individuals to obtain the support and encouragement they needed to challenge society's discrimination.

Police departments were able to make mass arrests, like the one at Hazel's, because they had a wide array of criminal statutes at their disposal to ensnare the queer community. But the panoply of charges that officers levied against those rounded up in bar raids was only the tip of the proverbial iceberg. Vice patrols could be remarkably creative in their efforts to target gays, lesbians, and those who served them. They eagerly arrested queer bar-goers who made the mistake of jaywalking to their car parked on the opposite side of the street, or who failed to stop their vehicles when exiting the parking lot.[44] In Miami in 1954, police arrested a bartender at a queer club for his "noisy jukebox" and another for "serving a drunk."[45] Notably, police did not have to make arrests to discourage gays and lesbians from congregating in the few social spaces that welcomed them. Common police tactics – entering a bar every half hour to check patrons' IDs or parking a marked patrol car outside – could ruin a night out.[46] Patrons quickly learned to stay away, leaving the bars no choice but to shutter their doors.[47] To avoid this type of harassment, bar owners often resorted to bribing corrupt vice officers or paying organized crime for protection from the police.[48] Constant police surveillance meant that danger and fear infused queer nightlife.

FIGURE 2 Drag performer José Sarria entertaining patrons at San Francisco's Black Cat, a queer club, 1950s. Singers, dancers, and cabaret hosts who transgressed gender norms were a mainstay of queer nightlife in the mid-twentieth century. José Sarria Records, 1996-01. Courtesy of Gay, Lesbian, Bisexual, Transgender Historical Society.

Vice departments' efforts also extended beyond closing queer social spaces. Officers actively rooted out homosexuals by patrolling parks, beaches, and other known locations of same-sex activity. To ferret out gay men looking for sexual partners, vice squads sent undercover agents to movie theaters, bathhouses, gyms, and hotel lobbies.[49] They also sent officers to flirt with men in bars and parks, hoping to entice propositions, often successfully.[50] These police practices generated large numbers of arrests, in the process heightening gay men's anxieties about approaching potential sexual partners.[51] Longing looks and suggestive language could indicate someone's interest, but they could just as easily be a trap for the unwary. Women, who typically did not engage in sexual encounters at cruising sites, shouldered less of the brunt of police activity, although they nevertheless suffered from vice patrols' constant surveillance.[52] Police routinely arrested female bar patrons because of their "mannish" dress, taking their sartorial choices as evidence of their lesbianism and, therefore, their vagrancy.[53] Conventional wisdom in lesbian circles quickly became that women needed to wear at least three items of female clothing to avoid arrest.[54] Vice squads thus focused on suppressing every manifestation of sexual deviance, which meant that queer individuals chanced harassment, arrest, and imprisonment simply for being who they were.

Police most often arrested members of the queer community for solicitation, vagrancy, lewdness and disorderly conduct, crimes that were easy to prove given that the offenses took place in public. It was much more difficult for vice squads to charge gay men with consensual sodomy, given that the crime typically occurred in private and between willing participants. That challenge did not deter law enforcement officials, who went to great lengths to catch same-sex couples *in flagrante delicto*. Officers would typically hide themselves behind peepholes in public restrooms where gay men were known to meet for sex, hoping to spot queer sexual encounters. Open windows, adjacent closets, and air vents all provided officers an opportunity to stake out would-be sodomites.[55] Surveillance campaigns could last months, requiring officers to spend long hours at their dark and dank stations.[56] Vice squads also overcame off-putting logistical challenges to enforce anti-sodomy laws against gay men.[57] Where restrooms lacked natural observation posts, police created them. Some departments cut holes in ceilings, camouflaging the gaps with false air vents, while others drilled openings in the back walls of toilet stalls.[58] Gay men were so familiar with these tactics that an observant lavatory cruiser marked one such hole with the warning: "Cop's Peephole. Beware."[59] The vice squad found this caution more of a help than a hinderance. By plugging the opening with toilet paper, the officers were able to lull lavatory patrons into a false sense of security. They then used another aperture to view the sexual encounters, allowing the squad to make felony arrests.[60]

These extensive clandestine observations were extremely successful, allowing vice squads to dramatically increase their arrests of homosexual men for consensual same-sex sodomy in the 1950s and 1960s.[61] Officers focused on securing these charges because the law reserved some of its harshest punishments for consensual sodomy. Several states had five-year mandatory minimum sentences, which some judges were all too happy to impose.[62] In other jurisdictions, offenders could be subject to life imprisonment.[63] For some Americans, including judges, these consequences appeared far too punitive. Judges who considered the punishments inappropriate responded either by imposing the lowest penalty they could or using their discretion to reduce the charges to misdemeanors.[64] As a result, defendants charged with consensual sodomy could leave the courthouse with probation and a fine, much like those arrested for other misdemeanor offenses, such as vagrancy and lewdness.[65] But regardless of the ultimate sentence, the arrests for consensual sodomy mattered: each one reinforced homosexuality's status as a crime. Unlike vagrancy, lewdness, and solicitation, which applied to large swaths of the population, consensual sodomy laws were uniquely associated with homosexuality. Arrests under consensual sodomy provisions therefore made clear that the state considered homosexuality a threat to society.

Members of the public often agreed with the state's assessment, expressing their disapproval by meting out their own punishments. They sometimes learned of the offenses through local newspapers, which often printed the names of defendants arrested in gay bars or in public toilets on their broadsheets, sometimes adding their home addresses and places of employment.[66] Even if the charges were later dismissed, these individuals had to face the stony judgment of their family, friends, and coworkers.[67] Americans were sometimes willing to dismiss same-sex assignations as unfortunate aberrations, so long as the individuals were married. The solution in those cases was for the people involved to recommit to their different-sex spouses and dedicate themselves to overcoming their deviant desires.[68] Despite some community members' willingness to overlook what they identified as mistakes, the social punishments for same-sex sexuality were often harsh. In the wake of an arrest, many people lost their jobs, if not their careers.[69] In Florida, 29-year-old Harris Kimball lost his license to practice law in 1957 after being arrested for lewd and lascivious conduct.[70] Doctors, dentists, teachers, and even hairdressers had their licenses suspended, putting their livelihoods in jeopardy for years.[71] Of course, members of the queer community did not need to be arrested to be found out and punished. In 1963, a male Columbia University student, who was using binoculars to peer through nearby dormitory windows, spied two Barnard College women having sex. Barnard administrators promptly expelled the female students, but the Peeping Tom remained enrolled at his Ivy League institution.[72]

Typically, however, discovery came from being caught in a police dragnet. Because arrests could be so personally devastating, many gays and lesbians approached social interactions with insecurity, anxiety, and dread.[73] One man in San Francisco described the "constant fear" of meeting police decoys in streets, parks, and other public places.[74] In deciding whether to spend an evening at a bar, gay men and lesbians calculated the likelihood of being swept up in a raid, weighing this against the comfort of a night spent amidst queer compatriots.[75] Criminals also took advantage of the community's precarious situation, with potential partners all too often transforming into extortionists who demanded large sums of money in exchange for their silence.[76] When willing sex partners became thieves, their victims could not turn to the police for help.[77] A homosexual man in Tampa learned this the hard way in 1957. After he reported the robbery to police, officers charged him with sodomy.[78]

Since gays and lesbians who made even the most tentative forays into queer life could suffer extreme repercussions, it was difficult for these individuals to be out, let alone fight for their rights. The personal costs were far too great. In the 1950s, those few who banded together to argue that homosexuality was neither dangerous nor perverse kept their activities as secret as possible.[79] As it turned out, these individuals did not need to disclose their sexual orientation to press their case, as a powerful advocate had emerged from outside of the queer community: a zoologist with a penchant for bow ties named Alfred Kinsey.

Questioning Criminality

Those who knew Kinsey growing up would never have expected him to become an expert on homosexuality or sex crimes. The Eagle Scout from Hoboken, New Jersey, was raised as an evangelical Protestant.[80] Every Sunday, he walked to church, where he attended both morning services and evening prayer meetings.[81] Kinsey earned his PhD from Harvard in 1919 with a prize-winning dissertation that classified thousands of gall wasps.[82] Kinsey soon found himself teaching biology, entomology, and insect taxonomy at Indiana University in Bloomington. Then, in 1938, Kinsey made a decision that changed the course of his life. That year, he volunteered to teach a class on marriage and the family. At the time, few people in the United States had access to candid information on sex and reproduction. Many stores, even in cosmopolitan cities like New York, kept their books on the subject under the counter, limiting access to the few patrons who dared to request a copy.[83] Students were captivated by Kinsey's class, which addressed masturbation, pre-marital sex, and birth control.[84] They often met with Kinsey in private, trusting him with their questions and anxieties. In those sessions, Kinsey learned that his students engaged in a surprising variety of sexual behaviors. He consequently began interviewing student volunteers about their sexual histories, starting the research that would stun the country.[85]

In 1948, Alfred Kinsey and his colleagues published *Sexual Behavior in the Human Male*, which quickly became a blockbuster for its shocking findings about Americans' sexual habits. Readers flocked to purchase the 804-page book, which spent months on the national bestseller lists, ultimately selling almost a quarter million copies.[86] The tome was so popular that, as late as mid-1949, the New York Public Library had stopped adding names to its lengthy waiting list.[87] Derivations of the work were almost as successful as the original: a 25-cent summary of Kinsey's findings sold three-quarters of a million copies.[88] Media outlets, from national magazines to small-town news-papers, reported extensively on Kinsey's controversial work, such that his findings were even more widely known than they were read.[89]

What captured the public's attention was the study's revelation that there was a wide chasm between what society prescribed as appropriate sexual behavior and what Americans actually did behind closed doors. One of Kinsey's most shocking findings was that same-sex sexuality was much more common than anyone had previously thought. His research showed that at least 37 percent of men in America had engaged in some kind of same-sex sexual conduct and that 13 percent of the American population was "predominantly homosexual." As Kinsey and his col-leagues explained, "persons with homosexual histories are to be found in every age group, in every social level, in every conceivable occupa-tion, in cities and on farms, and in the most remote areas in the country."[90] Kinsey's data was decidedly skewed. His study dispropor-tionately relied on unrepresentative populations – college students, prison inmates, and gay men.[91] The report's accuracy, however, was less important than its effect on the popular imagination.

What the public took from Kinsey's work was that homosexuals were not a separate population, but rather existed in every part of society. These findings astounded Americans, who understood same-sex attrac-tion as a pathological deviation. Kinsey's research also shook the foun-dation on which the country's antiqueer laws were based. The

conception of same-sex sexuality as a mental illness had undergirded the
military's ban, the civil service's purge of homosexual employees, and the
nation's sexual psychopath statutes. However, the scientist's findings
that a large percentage of adult men had participated in same-sex activity
called into question whether homosexuality was necessarily pathological. Kinsey's work thus directly undermined the theories on which
these laws were based. Moreover, his research demonstrated that states'
criminal codes were ineffective, as applying the sexual psychopath laws
as written would have required states to institutionalize approximately
6.3 million men.[92] Kinsey's study raised similar concerns as to consensual sodomy laws. Given that 13 percent of the male population was
"predominantly homosexual," police necessarily were only apprehend-
ing a small percentage of those who engaged in consensual sodomy.

FIGURE 3 Sexuality researcher Alfred Kinsey working with staff to prepare
the final manuscript of "Sexual Behavior in the Human Female," 1953.
Kinsey's findings, which indicated that a significant percentage of the
American public engaged in same-sex activity, prompted states to reevaluate
many of their criminal laws. Photo by Hulton Archive. Courtesy of Getty
Images.

Kinsey's findings led him to criticize America's sex offender codes, which he characterized as archaic, moralistic, and unnecessarily punitive.[93] After publishing his study, he readily corresponded with attorneys defending men charged with sex crimes, providing them with statistical information so they could better represent their clients.[94] To a lawyer who asked for advice in a case involving a man who had been "charged with carnally knowing a pig by the anus," Kinsey noted that "a fair proportion of the population" engaged in this type of behavior.[95] His research had shown that 17 percent of men completed sex acts with animals and nearly 30 percent of men attempted to do so. Using this information, the attorney secured a reduction in his client's charge – from a felony that carried a fifteen-to-twenty-year sentence to a misdemeanor.[96] Even in an instance of bestiality, Kinsey's research had a significant effect on how officials applied the law.

Although Kinsey routinely denounced both consensual sodomy and sexual psychopath statutes, he was adamant that he was not a reformer.[97] In 1953, when the Mattachine Society asked Kinsey to serve on its advisory board, he not only declined the invitation, but threatened to sue the group. Kinsey's objection was that the Mattachine Society had been using his name when contacting other potential advisors, thereby making it seem as though the scientist was involved with the organization.[98] Kinsey was furious. The power of his work, he believed, came from its scientific objectivity. In such a controversial and fraught field, he knew it was particularly important to cast himself as a scientific expert, even as he ignored critiques of his methodology. Yet the same year that he feuded with the Mattachine Society, Kinsey forcefully condemned American penal codes in his follow-up study, *Sexual Behavior in the Human Female*.[99] He described consensual sodomy and sexual psychopath laws as "completely out of accord with the realities of human behavior."[100] Moreover, by criminalizing commonplace acts, the statutes made it possible for police to blackmail otherwise harmless members of society.[101]

Kinsey may not have wanted to be associated with the shadowy Mattachine Society, but he meant his work to lead to tangible legal reform. It would soon have the opportunity to do just that.

Rethinking Sexual Psychopathy

Morris Ploscowe, a New York magistrate judge, did not need Kinsey to tell him that penal codes were out of date. From the bench, the Harvard Law graduate had seen for himself that many people went to jail for engaging in commonplace sexual activities. Ploscowe described the criminal law as "an instrument of repression" that gave rise to extortion and police corruption.[102] As a result, when the Prison Association of New York asked him to draft a sexual psychopath statute to submit to the state legislature, Ploscowe excluded both consensual sodomy and disorderly conduct as provisions that would trigger the statute. He explained that police only ever used disorderly conduct laws to arrest men who engaged in sexual activities in subway and theater toilets. In his view, neither activity was "sufficiently dangerous or anti-social" to warrant classification as a sexual psychopath.[103]

New York's legislature was initially skeptical. They revised Ploscowe's draft and passed a version that included both sodomy and disorderly conduct. But Governor Thomas E. Dewey vetoed the bill. The politician, who served as the Republican Party's presidential nominee in 1944 and 1948, was concerned that the statute did not sufficiently distinguish between various types of sex offenses.[104] He insisted that those "who commit their acts privately ... are their own greatest victims." As a result, incarcerating these individuals was "unnecessarily inhuman."[105] Dewey did not mention gay men or lesbians explicitly, but he did not need to. At the time, New York courts rarely prosecuted private heterosexual consensual sodomy.[106] The legislature could read between the lines. Dewey's objection ultimately carried the day. When the Empire State finally enacted a sexual psychopath law in 1950, the text no longer included references to consensual sodomy or disorderly conduct.

The decriminalization of queer life in other parts of the country began similarly, starting with legislative projects that questioned the sexual psychopath framework. In these other states though, elected officials had hurriedly enacted sexual psychopath statutes in response to public outrage at sensationalized media accounts of violent crimes. Once the furor had died down, legislators then created commissions to analyze the laws' effectiveness. Appointing experts to evaluate criminal laws had become a common practice in the 1920s, with commission members adopting a self-consciously scientific approach to their task. They gathered facts, analyzed the data, and made recommendations based on their findings.[107] Given that commissions were meant to avoid moralism, it was no surprise that members of the sexual psychopath commissions set about their task with Kinsey's admonishments in mind. More unexpectedly, given the widespread social condemnation of same-sex sexuality, the reports they produced ultimately led some lawmakers to reconsider their statutes. As in New York, these reforms did not begin as a queer rights project, but rather as broader investigations into how the criminal justice system applied sexual psychopath provisions. The sexual psychopath commissions would nevertheless have a significant effect on gay and lesbian rights, becoming the first of many instances in which experts became key to securing the queer community's civil liberties.

The commissions devoted themselves to their charge, leaving few stones unturned in their study of the sexual psychopath statutes. They typically held multiple public hearings where they heard from concerned citizens, educators, and law enforcement officers. They also interviewed leading experts and surveyed existing research.[108] No group was more committed than the Michigan commission, where the twenty-three members met more than eighteen times as a full group, at sessions that each lasted an average of six hours. They also interviewed experts – including psychiatrists, criminologists, and lawyers – consulted over 600 books and articles, and convened public hearings to hear from citizens and civic organizations.[109] The seven-member New Jersey commission likewise conducted an exhaustive review of expert material. They invited over 700 experts to testify at hearings. They also sent questionnaires to an additional 300 psychiatrists, school principals, and parent–teacher groups.[110] The commission members engaged in these extensive efforts without pay, making their herculean efforts all the more impressive.[111]

One of the experts who commissioners clamored to meet was Alfred Kinsey.[112] California's commission convened in Sacramento specifically to hear from the sociologist.[113] New York's Committee on the Sex Offender likewise consulted Kinsey before crafting its proposal in 1950. At Kinsey's urging, it recommended reducing consensual sodomy to a misdemeanor.[114] Reformers recognized the role that

Kinsey's findings could play and consequently strategized ways to ensure that commissioners considered his studies. For example, the Illinois Academy of Criminology, which opposed its state's sexual psychopath law, arranged for Kinsey to meet with the commission members before their work officially began.[115] The Illinois commission ultimately sat down with Kinsey on three separate occasions, with the researcher becoming so influential to the group's work that the commission identified him as an advisor in their report.[116] Of course, commissions did not need to meet with Kinsey to incorporate his research. The Pennsylvania commission noted in its findings that, based on Kinsey's study, "there were at least 2,275,760 male sexual deviants in Pennsylvania in 1940."[117] The New Jersey commission likewise argued that, based on Kinsey's studies, a substantial number of men could be committed to a state mental hospital under the sexual psychopath statute.[118] In California, the commission dryly noted that, based on Kinsey's research, "at some time or another, 95 percent of the male population commits a sex offense for which he might be prosecuted."[119]

As the commissions noted, the ways in which authorities applied the laws seemed to prove Kinsey's point that the statutes were unnecessarily punitive. In New Jersey, the commission emphasized that defendants who had been adjudicated as sexual psychopaths had rarely committed violent sex crimes. Instead, the state's cases of sexual psychopathy included an African American man who had followed – but never approached – a white woman, an exhibitionist who exposed himself when drunk, a straight man who met with a female prostitute in a movie theater, and a homosexual man who had written a bad check.[120] None of these people were the danger to society that the public feared. They were also not the types of crimes that had led the legislature to enact the sexual psychopath statute. Moreover, none of them deserved the sexual psychopath law's draconian sanctions. New Jersey's statute was exceptional in how broadly it applied.[121] Yet minor sex offenses gave rise to adjudications for sexual psychopathy around the country, which made reformers question the entire statutory scheme.

The evidence that the commissions marshalled produced a clear consensus: nonviolent crimes should not trigger a state's sexual psychopath statute. The commissions overwhelmingly concluded that the state needed to distinguish between crimes that offended the community's "good taste and morals" from those that constituted physical dangers to society.[122] The crimes with which most gay men were charged – consensual sodomy, disorderly conduct, and vagrancy – clearly fell in the former category. In making this argument, the commissions implicitly challenged psychiatric orthodoxy, which linked homosexuality to pedophilia and violence. The reports suggested that, although gay men might be sexual deviants, they were not dangerous. That reframing undermined not just the criminal laws, but also social perspectives on homosexuality, both of which had made it impossible for gays and lesbians to be out and demand their rights. That the commissions agreed so resoundingly was perhaps no surprise, given that groups often relied on one another's work. Some interviewed commission members from other states, while others simply reviewed the other groups' published final reports.[123] Indeed, the document that the Pennsylvania commission ultimately produced consisted of little more than a summary of the New York and New Jersey commissions' findings.[124] The Keystone State group even reprinted their recommendations in full.

Most of the groups insisted that legislators had erred in crafting their sexual psychopath legislation and urged them to reform their statutes, but some commissions took their conclusions a step further. In California, Michigan, and New York, commissions recommended that the legislatures do more than simply scale back their sexual psychopath laws. They pressed elected officials to amend their criminal codes to differentiate between consensual and forcible sodomy.[125] Under this formulation, gay men would be charged with a lesser crime in recognition that same-sex sexuality was not the same, nor as harmful, as forcible conduct. The Illinois commission recommended an even more radical change to its state's penal laws. It proposed reducing public, consensual sodomy from a felony to a misdemeanor and decriminalizing private, consensual sodomy altogether. That way, the law would "discriminate between socially distasteful and socially dangerous conduct."[126]

Given that these recommendations departed so drastically from convention, legislatures were understandably reluctant to adopt them. As a result, most did not. Although elected officials had entrusted a review of the laws to experts, who produced meticulously detailed studies of the sexual psychopath regime, the public had also demanded that their representatives take aggressive action against sex crimes.[127] Making the changes that the commissions suggested thus meant defying the public will. A handful of legislatures were willing to risk provoking their constituents' outrage, with some moving quickly. It only took New Jersey four months to incorporate all of the commission's suggestions.[128] The few other states that adopted the changes were more sluggish, but the fact that they made any reforms at all was notable. The vast majority of states balked at instituting the changes that their commissions recommended.

By 1955, only four states had removed consensual sodomy from the list of crimes that triggered the sexual psychopath provision. Given that thirty states and the District of Columbia had sexual psychopath laws at the time, these changes did not constitute a wide-ranging shift in the law. Additionally, the reforms did not necessarily limit the state's use of the laws. In California, the legislature circumscribed the scope of its statute in 1950.[129] At the time, the state committed an average of fifty offenders per year as sexual psychopaths.[130] Between 1953 and 1958, however, California applied the law to almost 350 men per year.[131] By the mid-1960s, it was institutionalizing an average of 800 offenders each year.[132] The states willing to amend their sexual psychopath laws were few and far between, and yet there was even less movement on the consensual sodomy front. Although New York reduced consensual sodomy from a felony to a misdemeanor in 1950, no state was willing to decriminalize consensual sodomy altogether.[133]

In the end, the commissions' work only produced minor changes in their states' statutes. Yet these limited reforms were important, because they were the first legal stones to tumble. They started what would eventually become a cascade of reform in favor of gay and lesbian rights, one that would eventually make queer family recognition possible. The next criminal laws to follow were prohibitions on consensual sodomy. At the time the commissions issued their reports, no state was willing to seriously consider decriminalizing consensual sodomy altogether. Even if the commissions convinced individual legislators that they should amend the penal codes, doing so was politically impossible. Within a decade, however, that was no longer true. Once again, Kinsey – along with a cadre of lawyers, law professors, and judges – would be at the center of those reform projects.

Decriminalizing Consensual Sodomy

In 1951, Manfred Guttmacher, a well-known forensic psychiatrist and criminologist, received an unusual request. A Post Office inspector from New York wanted Guttmacher's opinion on whether to prosecute a man who published sadomasochistic pornography. At the time, Guttmacher served as the chief medical officer for the Supreme Bench of Baltimore, overseeing a medical services division that provided psychiatric, psychological, and social work evaluations to the city's court system. His office advised on approximately 400 cases every year, with lawyers, judges, and juries accepting its recommendations in 98 percent of cases.[134] In the pornography case, Guttmacher was conflicted. He reasoned that the materials could help sadomasochists better suppress their desires. But he could also imagine that the photographs could lead people to act out violent sex crimes.[135] Guttmacher turned to the leading expert in the field: Alfred Kinsey. Kinsey assured Guttmacher that pornography was nothing to fear. It provided an outlet for sexual desire, rather than giving rise to imitation. He also cautioned that the Post Office's action was illegal.[136]

Guttmacher often asked the researcher for advice. For example, when Guttmacher became involved in a case challenging the military's ban on gays and lesbians, he turned to Kinsey for support.[137] Guttmacher revered the scientist, describing his work as "a bold, vast project, brilliantly conceived, patiently and sensitively executed, and carried out with the greatest honesty."[138] Guttmacher and his identical twin, a gynecologist named Alan who would later become the president of Planned Parenthood Federation of America, were both taken with Kinsey. The pair even offered to provide their sexual histories to add to Kinsey's data set.[139]

Perhaps because of his familiarity with Kinsey's research, Guttmacher became a strident opponent of sexual psychopath and consensual sodomy statutes. Echoing Kinsey's arguments, Guttmacher described the former as laws that were more likely to "lead to abuse rather than cure."[140] As for the latter, he maintained that they "all too often degenerate[d] into a source of blackmail and police corruption."[141] In 1951, Guttmacher had the chance to help abolish the statutes he abhorred. That was the year that the American Law Institute (ALI), a highly respected organization dedicated to simplifying and clarifying American law, asked Guttmacher to serve on the Advisory Committee for the Model Penal Code (MPC). The MPC, in turn, would help transform American criminal laws.

The MPC was a model criminal code meant to assist legislators in reforming their penal statutes.[142] Since its founding in 1923, the ALI had recommended the reform of state laws in nine areas, including contracts, property, torts, and trusts.[143] When the group turned to criminal law and its administration, American penal codes were little more than ad hoc collections of statutes, and even those were painfully out of date. Only one state – Louisiana – had tried to systematically reform its criminal code since the nineteenth century.[144] Given the dire need, as well as the ALI's distinguished reputation, the MPC was well-poised to have a significant practical effect on states' penal codes. To begin its work, the ALI set up an Advisory Committee to research and draft each section of the MPC. Once the Advisory Committee gave its approval, the Council of the ALI, an elected volunteer board of directors, would vote on the provisions before sending them to the entire ALI membership for a final decision.

The ALI tapped many experts for the Advisory Committee on Sex Offenses who, like Guttmacher, identified Kinsey's research as foundational to their views. The Advisory Committee included Morris Ploscowe, who had proposed that New York exclude consensual sodomy from its sexual psychopath statute's purview. In 1951, he published *Sex and the Law*, which he described as applying Kinsey's sociological research to legal principles.[145] In that text, he set out the two main arguments that the Advisory Committee would make for decriminalizing consensual sodomy. The first was pragmatic and rooted in Kinsey's findings: given homosexuality's prevalence, states simply could not enforce the statutes effectively.[146] The second was more theoretical. Since homosexuality was a psychological condition, rather than a behavioral choice, states had no basis criminalizing consensual sodomy.[147] Homosexuality was not a matter for the state to punish, but rather a condition for the afflicted to address with medical professionals and religious advisors. This framework constituted a notable shift. In the 1930s, psychiatric theories of homosexuality had led states to identify homosexuality as a dangerous pathology requiring the state's intervention. For that reason, lawmakers included consensual sodomy within their sexual psychopath laws. But by the time the ALI drafted the MPC, medical conceptions of same-sex sexuality would form the basis for excluding consensual sodomy from criminal codes altogether.

Ploscowe's dual arguments – one concerning homosexuality's prevalence, the other its status as a mental illness – convinced the Advisory Committee to draft a code that excluded consensual sodomy from its list of sex offenses. But the Advisory Committee took his points a step further. In addition to stating that the laws were unenforceable and that homosexuality was a medical issue, they also declared that same-sex sexuality was innocuous.[148] The Advisory Committee boldly announced that "no harm to the secular interests of the community is involved in atypical sex practice in private between consenting adult partners. This area of private morals is the distinctive concern of spiritual authorities."[149] In other words, the state should not be regulating homosexuality at all. Thus, the Advisory Committee's claim was not just a denunciation of existing criminal laws. It also suggested that governments should eliminate all of their antiqueer policies. The Advisory Committee's statement came at a time when gays and lesbians risked their jobs, homes, and families when their sexual orientation became known. It was a radical change from existing conceptions of homosexuality, both in the criminal law and society at large.

Given the draft's tenor, as well as its departure from existing penal codes, the ALI Council unsurprisingly rejected the Advisory Committee's proposal. Even Council members who agreed with eliminating consensual sodomy in theory feared that its exclusion would torpedo the entire project. The goal was to create a model code that legislators would adopt wholesale, so that states' penal codes would become uniform. Without a consensual sodomy prohibition, legislatures might reject the entire MPC.[150] Others voted against the Advisory Committee's recommendation as a matter of principle. For these Council members, sodomy was a marker of moral decay that the law should at least try to suppress, even if the state was bound to fail at eliminating same-sex sexuality. The Council consequently added a prohibition on consensual sodomy to the draft it sent to the ALI members for ratification. As a compromise, the provision made consensual sodomy a misdemeanor rather than a felony.[151]

The members of the ALI, who had to vote on the final draft, were conflicted on which version to endorse. They knew and understood the competing arguments that had produced the Advisory Committee recommendation and the Council drafts.[152] What ultimately resolved the debate was the argument of Learned Hand, one of the most well-respected judges of the twentieth century.[153] Hand explained to the group that he had changed his mind on the issue. At the Council meeting, he had voted to retain the prohibition against consensual sodomy because he feared that omitting it would risk the MPC's adoption throughout the country. However, he confessed that he had "always been in great doubt" about his decision, because he believed that consensual sodomy "is a matter of morals, a matter very largely of taste, and it is not a matter that people should be put in prison about." He was now urging the members to exclude consensual sodomy because criminal laws should not serve as mere expressions of moral condemnation. If police were not going to be able to enforce the laws, then they should not be on the books.[154]

Hand's argument won the day. After hearing from the esteemed jurist, the members of the ALI voted to eliminate the consensual sodomy provision from the MPC.[155] Notably, Kinsey's name did not appear in the debate, and neither did his studies. His research, however, undergirded the entire discussion. Kinsey's work had established that these laws were futile, given that millions of Americans violated them. The ALI had applied the scientist's research when crafting the MPC, turning his conclusions into law. Indeed, after the members approved the final draft, the ALI sent Kinsey a copy, noting that he would immediately see the extent to which they were indebted to his work.[156]

The MPC inspired criminal law reform throughout the United States. In 1961, Illinois became the first state to decriminalize consensual sodomy when it adopted a draft version of the MPC.[157] By 1978, twenty-two states had decriminalized consensual sodomy, almost all as a result of legislators rewriting their penal codes based on the MPC.[158] Because of these results, the MPC has been described as one of the most successful academic law reform projects in American history.[159] Contrary to the Council's dire predictions, legislative debates over whether to enact the MPC did not focus on the absence of a consensual sodomy provision. Some Republican-dominated states, as well as states in which public opinion favored criminalization, retained their sodomy laws when revising their codes.[160] Other legislators adopted the MPC wholesale because they did not realize the provision was missing.[161] In two states, Arkansas and Idaho, legislators went back to add consensual sodomy laws after they belatedly learned that their new codes did not include prohibitions on the conduct.[162] The nascent gay liberation movement kept quiet during these legislative debates, realizing that legislators were more likely to decriminalize consensual sodomy if the issue remained under the radar.[163]

These penal code reforms eliminated one of the state's harshest punishments against same-sex sexuality. Although few men were subject to these draconian sanctions, the changes did away with a major risk that came with being queer. The changes also began to sever the connection between same-sex sexuality and criminality, given that states limited prosecutions of consensual sodomy to homosexuals. Of course, the effect on the day-to-day lives of gays and lesbians was more limited, as the decriminalization of consensual sodomy did not end police harassment of gays and lesbians. Law enforcement officials continued to suppress queer life by wielding the many other criminal statutes at their disposal. As one gay liberation group noted in 1970, "any homosexual from Chicago, where homosexuality is legal, will tell you that changing the law makes no difference."[164] That was because the MPC had decriminalized activities that took place in private, but gay men and lesbians typically risked arrest when they flirted, danced, and embraced in public spaces like bars, restaurants, and cruising grounds.

The MPC thus inaugurated an important change in penal codes, but it did not make it safe for homosexuals to be out. For that, the queer community needed legislators and judges to revise the other laws that police used to suppress gay and lesbian life. The next challenge was thus to decriminalize vagrancy and lewdness. Only then could it be legal to be openly queer.

Legalizing Queer Life

On December 31, 1966, gay and lesbian revelers – many in drag thanks to a contest at a nearby bar – gathered to celebrate the end of the year at Los Angeles's Black Cat tavern. At the stroke of midnight, as patrons sang "Auld Lang Syne" and kissed, undercover officers announced themselves and began making arrests. The typical bar raid soon turned bloody, with officers throwing punches and dragging men to the curb. Police beat two of the victims so badly that they were left unconscious in the gutter, one with broken ribs and the other with a cracked skull. Onlookers were shocked by the police's brutality. Activists quickly organized a picket along Sunset Boulevard, as well as a rally that more than 200 people attended.[165] The crowd called for an end to police abuse and entrapment, bearing signs that read "Peace Officers – Not Storm Trooper[s]" and "Blue Fascism Must Go."

The outrage the raid provoked demonstrated how much American society had changed in the decade since vice officers shuttered Hazel's bar. One reason for the shift was that, as a result of Kinsey's work, many people realized that homosexuality was much more common than they had ever expected. That, in turn, raised questions as to whether the state should be criminalizing queer life. But the change also stemmed from broader concerns about police techniques and their effect on Americans' civil rights. The MPC had focused on the substantive problems with state criminal laws, but the country was also reckoning with the procedural issues associated with their enforcement.[166] Much of the focus at the time was on the racial disparities in policing, but judges increasingly questioned the police surveillance tactics that produced arrests of gays and lesbians for vagrancy, lewdness, and solicitation.[167] Some bristled at enforcing victimless crimes and considered the prosecutions a waste of police resources.[168] For others, the problem was that police decoys might be tempting vulnerable suspects to yield to latent impulses. Without the vice officers' enticements, these judges reasoned, the defendants might never have succumbed to their desires. Because of these concerns, some judges used their discretion to dismiss the charges or acquit the defendants at trial.[169]

Judges were not the only ones to express discomfort with how police officers enforced the laws. In the 1960s, citizens began voicing similar concerns after they became more aware of vice patrols' work, following the publication of detailed exposés on queer life in national newspapers and magazines.[170] One of the first of these appeared in the June 26, 1964 issue of *Life* magazine, which printed a fourteen-page "report on homosexuality" that featured photographs from inside a queer bar.[171] In the years that followed, the popular press became filled with journalists' forays into gay and lesbian communities.[172]

To uncover the queer world, reporters sought guidance from vice squad officers, who had painstakingly become experts in gay men's clothing preferences, physical cues, and specialized lexicon.[173] Vice patrols took these journalists along on their evening rounds, leading to articles that highlighted how easily officers blended into queer life.[174] Some readers responded with alarm at the queer world's existence. But for others, the stories' revelations of gay and lesbian subcultures were not as concerning as the police tactics the authors depicted. As one woman explained, the government should not have the right to surveil citizens' private lives.[175] Another dismissed the patrols' work as harassment, entrapment, and a simple waste of public funds.[176] Liberal magazines were more likely to run repudiations of vice squads than mainstream publications, often printing them alongside reports of other police abuses. However, as criticisms mounted, outlets across the political spectrum began publishing these denunciations. A year after *Life*'s multipage profile on gay life, it featured an editorial that decried plainclothes decoys as "unjust and repugnant."[177]

Vice patrols' clandestine operations struck a particular nerve because they seemed to be yet another example of how police harassed vulnerable groups. Following the Cold War, when the fight against totalitarian states highlighted their Orwellian encroachments on privacy, such actions seemed distinctly un-American. As a result, an undemocratic air lingered over undercover surveillance.[178] In the 1960s, confrontations between law enforcement officials and civil rights protestors reignited concerns about police abuse. The public recoiled from their television screens, which displayed horrifying images of sheriffs unleashing fire hoses, bull whips, truncheons, and dogs upon peaceful Black demonstrators.[179] Although these events took place in Southern towns, mistrust of police spread around the country. In 1966, one former New York City police commissioner lamented that "[n]ever before in the 150-year history of law enforcement has the police 'stock' been at a lower point."[180] As Vietnam War protests spread around the country, often leading to violent clashes, newspaper headlines increasingly focused on the police's cruelty.

In response to public outcry, many urban police departments began retreating from their controversial methods in the late 1960s. They reduced the number of raids they conducted and diminished their use of decoy patrols. As a result, it became *safer* – even if not entirely *safe* –

for gays and lesbians to socialize in public. That meant that the queer
community could start to be visible in American life. The détente
between police on the one hand, and gays and lesbians on the other,
went even further in certain cities. Some departments began establishing
liaisons between officers and the queer community, as well as instituting
civilian review boards where gays and lesbians could lodge complaints
against officers.[181] In San Francisco, the queer community and law
enforcement began socializing at an annual softball game, where the
ceremonial first ball was painted lavender and covered in glitter.[182]

Changes to police practices were important, but they did not resolve
the queer community's problem. Law enforcement officers around the
country continued to suppress gay and lesbian life, applying vagrancy
and lewdness ordinances to limit queer sociability. In the 1960s, most
gay men and lesbians were unwilling to endure the embarrassment and
expense of challenging the laws publicly.[183] However, the laws' wide
applications led other minority groups to fight against them,
prompting reforms that would alter the lives of queer individuals
around the country. Vice patrols had never wielded vagrancy laws
solely against gays and lesbians, but rather had always used them to
police all social misfits. The statutes allowed police to arrest anyone
who violated social mores, from labor organizers and communists, to
gamblers, hobos, and hippies.[184]

What tipped the scales in favor of law reform was that, in the 1950s
and 1960s, southern officials often deployed vagrancy to arrest civil
rights activists and their allies, tainting the provisions as fundamental
bulwarks of Jim Crow.[185] In 1958, Birmingham police accused three
ministers of lacking proper identification, then arrested them for
vagrancy. The group had traveled from Montgomery to visit
Revered Fred Shuttlesworth, who had cofounded the Southern
Christian Leadership Conference with Martin Luther King, Jr.[186]
The arrests became front-page news, sparking national protests.[187]
Although civil rights organizations used the incident to challenge
vagrancy laws as unconstitutional, the Supreme Court upheld the
provisions.[188] In the years that followed, it was so common for civil
rights workers to be arrested for vagrancy that organizations educated
staff and volunteers on the topic before they traveled south.[189]
An army of lawyers formed to defend civil rights activists when they
inevitably faced vagrancy charges.[190]

Civil rights groups thus continued to fight against vagrancy laws. They spent more than a decade lobbying legislatures, convincing elected officials to revise their penal codes. They also challenged the laws in the courts, leading state high courts to invalidate the provisions.[191] As a result of their efforts, by the late 1960s, vagrancy statutes were on their way out.[192] The death knell for these laws finally came in the early 1970s, when the Supreme Court held them to be unconstitutionally void for vagueness.[193] The petitioners in these cases included four Jacksonville, Florida, residents – two Black men and two white women – who were arrested for "prowling" when they rode in a car along the city's main thoroughfare. Another was a Black civil rights leader who was walking along a city block, looking for a friend. A third was an African American man who had dropped off a woman at her home. The circumstances of each reinforced the laws' excessive breadth, as well as their potential for abuse. The Court struck down the laws after decrying them for encouraging arbitrary arrests, criminalizing innocent activities, and placing far too much power in the hands of the police.[194]

None of the cases involved gays and lesbians, but the Court's decisions had a significant effect on queer life. As a result of the Court's rulings, vice patrols lost one of their main tools for repressing same-sex sexuality. Without these laws, officers could no longer arrest people like the Black Cat bar's patrons for spending an evening out together. For the six revelers who were charged that night – and whose convictions meant they had to register as sex offenders – the decisions came too late.[195] But for other gays and lesbians, who no longer had to weigh the risk of a police raid with the need for community and companionship, the change transformed their lives. The end to vagrancy made it easier for gays and lesbians to gather publicly, thereby giving rise to increasingly visible queer communities.

* * *

With the Supreme Court's decisions striking down vagrancy laws, an era of rampant antiqueer policing ended. By 1971, gays and lesbians did not invariably risk arrest when they socialized. In an increasing number of states, their private sexual activity was no longer a crime. Moreover, lawyers, judges, and psychiatrists denounced the notion that homosexuals should be institutionalized as sexual psychopaths. Kinsey's research had shown that same-sex attraction was widespread, making it less likely that gay men and lesbians were inherently dangerous. His findings gave rise to penal code reforms, such that the queer community was no longer by definition criminals. That is not to say, of course, that the police stopped harassing, intimidating, and arresting gays and lesbians. Antiqueer policing continued in new forms, shifting its focus to cross-dressers and individuals who participated in survival economies, a change that disproportionately burdened gender nonconforming, racial minority, and economically marginalized individuals.[196] But as a general matter, the system of legal oppression – which had made it impossible for gays and lesbians to be open about who they were – had begun to crack.

These changes occurred at the state and local levels, where criminal laws are most typically administered. Because penal codes differ from state to state, and law enforcement practices vary by municipality, many of the legal changes were geographically uneven. Yet the fact that any state decriminalized consensual sodomy was extremely consequential. In addition to eliminating a legal basis for discriminating against gays and lesbians, each legislative enactment helped to chip away at social conceptions of same-sex sexuality as a dangerous menace. Legal changes in one part of the nation thus communicated an important message to Americans all around the country. What made it possible for elected officials to reconsider their sexual psychopath and consensual sodomy laws was growing evidence that gays and lesbians were not deviant. Kinsey's findings had convinced legal experts that penal codes were out of date, punishing ordinary behavior rather than aberrant acts. Sociological research thus opened the door to legal change by identifying same-sex sexuality as a variation on the norm, rather than a difference that warranted punishment. Such a framework was a far cry from acceptance for gays and lesbians, but it was nevertheless a notable change.

For queer rights advocates, reforms to the criminal justice system were important, but only a start. Despite the sea change in penal codes, gays and lesbians continued to experience widespread discrimination, which showed no sign of abating. Advocates demanded the right to live their lives free of judgment and injustice. Being out should not mean losing family relationships, homes, or jobs. Otherwise, the cost would simply be too high. Without these changes, people could not live openly as gays and lesbians. That was particularly true for lesbian mothers and gay fathers, who faced an additional obstacle to leaving the closet: the prospect of losing custody of their children when their sexual orientation became known. As far as family courts were concerned, queer parents were categorically unfit. Same-sex sexuality was incompatible with family life given its long-standing connection to pedophilia and crimes against children.

Criminal laws had assumed that homosexuals were a small group of dangerous predators, while sexual psychopath statutes insisted that gay men were harmful to children. Although the prevalence of same-sex activity had led elected officials to revise their penal codes, these legislative debates did not directly address whether homosexuals were dangerous to youth. In the 1970s, that would become the central issue in a new set of queer rights battles, fought over child custody. As lesbian mothers and gay fathers increasingly went to court to secure rights over their children from different-sex unions, debates over child welfare would become the central issue for decisionmakers. The result of those disputes would determine not just the outcome of any given custody case, but the future of the queer rights movement.

Contesting Custody

Social Science and Queer Parental Rights

Mary Jo Risher sobbed when the Texas jury announced that it had awarded custody of her 10-year-old son Richard to his father, Douglas.[1] The jurors handed down their decision shortly before Christmas, 1975. Four years earlier, when the Rishers separated, Mary Jo had obtained custody of Richard and his older brother, James. Then Mary Jo, a nurse, Southern Baptist schoolteacher, and PTA member, began dating Ann Foreman, a bank auditor with a daughter of her own.[2] Seventeen-year-old James was ashamed of his mother's lesbianism. He moved in with Douglas, who then petitioned for custody of Richard as well.[3] At the trial, Douglas's lawyer implored the jury to not make Richard "a guinea pig in someone else's social experiment."[4] He also repeatedly cited the Bible as a "good source" for learning about homosexuality. The jury foreman later explained that, although the jurors thought Mary Jo provided a good home, they disapproved of the "homosexual lifestyle."[5] Their moral condemnation did not extend to Douglas, who had once broken Mary Jo's nose, had a history of drunk driving, and admitted to impregnating an 18-year-old – before paying for her illegal abortion – soon after the couple separated.[6]

A photographer snapped a picture of Mary Jo's agonized expression as she heard the jury's verdict. The image, which appeared in newspapers around the country, introduced many Americans to what seemed like a contradiction in terms: lesbian mothers. In the mid-1970s, these women became increasingly visible as they came out of the closet and fought for custody of their children in court. Until the early 1970s, most courts considered same-sex sexuality to be an absolute bar to custody. The few lesbian mothers who tried to obtain custody in the 1950s and 1960s invariably lost their battles. By the time Mary Jo filed her suit, however, many courts no longer automatically disqualified queer parents from custody. Some, like Mary Jo, suffered the pain of losing their children. But many others emerged from the courthouse victorious, giving rise to legally recognized gay- and lesbian-headed families. Most of these were lesbian mothers, who filed cases by the hundreds. Their custody battles helped inaugurate new perspectives on same-sex sexuality. They also began reshaping America's vision of the family to include queer parents.

A shift in scientific orthodoxy made this legal transformation possible. Alfred Kinsey's sociological research had inspired the ALI to remove consensual sodomy from the Model Penal Code, leading to criminal law reform all around the country. Then, in 1973, a different scientific field – psychiatry – would become embroiled in the fight for gay and lesbian rights. That year, the American Psychiatric Association (APA) declassified homosexuality as a mental illness. The APA's decision would open the doors to custody claims from queer parents by removing an almost impenetrable barrier to their suits. But once in court, these mothers and fathers would have to confront a growing concern that homosexual parents were dangerous to children. That fear originated in the arguments of the religious right, which came to a renewed national prominence during this period. Christian conservatives claimed that the state needed to protect children from the influence of gay and lesbian adults, who, they argued, served as role models for homosexuality. That political debate over homosexuality's origins would become central to custody cases, shaping courts' decisions. It would also lead scientists to mobilize in support of gay and lesbian parents.

The APA's decision may have sparked a transformation in family law, but the key figure in the battle over homosexuality's diagnostic status was neither a parent nor a psychiatrist. Instead, it was an activist named Franklin Kameny, who led the effort to change homosexuality's diagnostic status. He had not set out to reshape custody decisions, but his efforts would have an indelible effect on the American family.

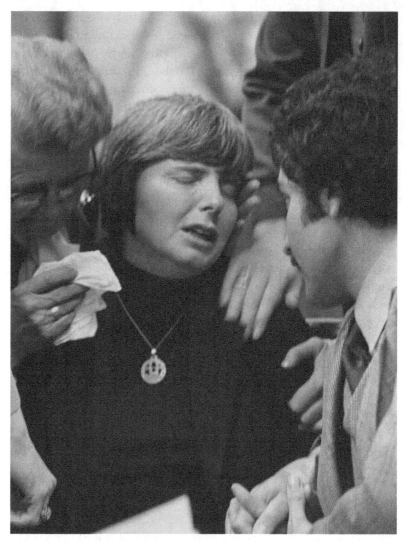

FIGURE 4 Mary Jo Risher after losing custody of her son, 1975. Risher's case introduced many Americans to the existence of lesbian mothers. Photo by Fred Kaufman. Courtesy of AP Images.

Confronting Psychiatrists

Kameny was an unlikely instigator of radical change. In 1957, the astronomer with a PhD from Harvard University was working for the Army Map Service. As the Cold War heated up, the military needed to ensure that intercontinental ballistic missiles would land on their exact targets. The armed services consequently hired specialists like Kameny to draw the precise maps they required.[7] However, Kameny lost his security clearance – and consequently his job – when federal investigators discovered a past arrest for lewd conduct.[8] In 1956, an undercover police officer had arrested Kameny after the scientist engaged in a brief assignation in a public restroom with another man.[9] With his security clearance gone, Kameny could not obtain another job as an astronomer, despite his elite qualifications in a sought-after field. He refused to consider any employment prospects that did not use his specialized training and skills, announcing he would rather starve – which he did.[10] Within two years of his termination, he was penniless and suffering from malnutrition, subsisting on the few frankfurters and potatoes he could buy with his 20-cents-a-day food budget.[11]

Kameny's experience led him to become a leader in the fledgling homophile movement, the first organized campaign for gay and lesbian rights. In that role, Kameny insisted that gays and lesbians had to appear respectable to generate public support. At the demonstrations he organized, Kameny approved every message that appeared on signs and demanded that marchers proceed in silent, single-file lines.[12] He also required the men to wear suits and the women to don dresses.[13] In 1965, two would-be picketers wore informal summer attire to a demonstration at Philadelphia's Independence Hall, where the temperature had reached almost 90 degrees. Kameny sent them away, even though they had traveled nearly 100 miles to participate.[14]

Kameny, like other queer rights advocates, became increasingly militant in the early 1970s. After the Stonewall riots of 1969, where a police raid on a queer club in New York City's Greenwich Village sparked six days of protests and violent clashes, the gay liberation and lesbian feminist movements eclipsed their predecessors, the homophiles.[15] Homophiles had focused their arguments on America's need to tolerate people of every sexual orientation. The gay liberation movement, alongside its lesbian feminist counterpart, made the more radical claim that mere tolerance was not enough. Gays and lesbians deserved social approval, as well as moral, legal, and political equality with heterosexuals.[16] The gay liberation movement also adopted new tactics that promoted visibility, calling on everyone who engaged in same-sex relationships to "come out" publicly.[17] The most conspicuous marker of the gay liberation movement became annual Pride parades, which began a year after the events at the Stonewall Inn. In 1970, several thousand gays and lesbians in four cities marched to commemorate the rebellion. By the mid-1970s, half a million people were flocking to the public celebrations of queer life across dozens of municipalities.[18] These events were lively and loud, in stark opposition to the protests that Kameny had organized a decade earlier.[19] Media outlets brought word of the parades around the country, introducing Americans in far-flung places to gays and lesbians, which further encouraged those in the closet to come out.

Gay liberation and lesbian feminist groups were part and parcel of the radical movements that swept America in the late 1960s and early 1970s. They appealed to younger firebrands who adopted the aggressive language and tactics that came to characterize many on the left at this time.[20] Gays and lesbians occupied the offices of newspapers and magazines that printed antiqueer articles, events that sometimes turned into violent fights with the police.[21] Gay liberationists also drew inspiration from the African American civil rights movement, which had become more militant in the 1960s. Liberationists' slogan, "Gay is Good," mirrored "Black is Beautiful," reinforcing the parallels between the movements.[22] Gay and lesbian rights advocacy took a similar institutional form as well, with gay liberation leaders establishing impact litigation and lobbying groups modeled on civil rights organizations. These included the National Gay Task Force (NGTF)[23] and Lambda Legal Defense and Education Fund. Lambda Legal's founder even borrowed the bylaws of the Puerto Rican Defense and Education Fund when filing the nonprofit's paperwork, illustrating how closely queer rights groups followed in the footsteps of racial equality organizations.[24]

Kameny may have begun as a staid homophile leader, but he quickly learned to use gay liberation's confrontational tactics. His target: homosexuality's status as a mental illness. The APA classified homosexuality as a pathology in its Diagnostic and Statistical Manual (DSM), the guidebook that health care professionals in the United States use to diagnose psychiatric disorders. That diagnostic status had such a pernicious impact on gays and lesbians that Kameny once described it as "the albatross around the neck of the Gay and Lesbian movement."[25] Homosexuality's classification as a mental illness served as the basis for the federal government's purge of gays and lesbians from civil service positions throughout the 1950s.[26] It also justified the military's exclusion of homosexuals.[27] The discrimination even extended to much less sensitive work, demonstrating the diagnostic status's significant role in circumscribing queer rights. The New York City Taxi Commission, for example, refused to license a homosexual driver until he had obtained a psychiatrist's certification of fitness.[28] To maintain his right to operate a taxi, the man had to visit a psychiatrist twice a year to renew the certification.[29]

Homosexuality's diagnostic status also all but barred gay and lesbian parents' custody claims. When Ellen Nadler filed her custody petition in 1967, the court not only granted custody to her ex-husband, but also required that her visits with her child be supervised by another adult.[30] The judge's disgust for Nadler's same-sex sexuality was palpable as he told her: "Frankly, Ma'am, you should take therapy … if you are going to overcome your, beat your psychological problems."[31] The judge added that, if Nadler followed a course of treatment and a psychiatrist could assure him that the child would be protected, then he would permit Nadler unsupervised visitation.[32]

Nadler was one of the few lesbian mothers who filed for custody in the 1960s. Many queer parents refrained from filing suit because they had internalized society's negative views of homosexuality, including the claims of the religious right that homosexual adults were dangerous to children. Indeed, when Del Martin and Phyllis Lyon founded the Daughters of Bilitis, they heard from many lesbian mothers anxious for their children's future. These women feared that their sons and daughters would grow up to be queer simply because they had lesbian mothers as role models.[33] To address these concerns, the group held a meeting in 1956 with a child psychiatrist, who assured the attendees that their children would be fine so long as they were raised in a loving environment.[34] Despite the expert's confidence, many women remained anxious that their sexual orientation would negatively affect their children. They consequently kept their lesbianism hidden from their sons, daughters, and communities.[35] Other queer parents were confident that they provided nurturing homes for their children but did not pursue custody rights because they knew that courts would be hostile to their claims. These mothers and fathers recognized that homosexuality's status as a mental illness meant that gays and lesbians were by definition pathological. Judges would therefore conclude that they were necessarily dangers to their children.[36]

Homophile groups urged gay fathers and lesbian mothers to stay out of court, identifying parental rights as too controversial for the queer community to pursue.[37] Yet even as they discouraged custody cases, homophile leaders were lobbying the APA to eliminate the diagnostic category that prevented these mothers and fathers from pressing their parental rights in courts.[38] They published critiques of the scientific

orthodoxy and circulated petitions to the APA, asking the organization
to reconsider its position.[39] When these restrained tactics did little to
convince the scientific community, Kameny decided to turn up the
pressure. He led pickets and interrupted the group's annual meeting
plenary in 1971, announcing: "Psychiatry is the enemy incarnate.
Psychiatry has waged a relentless war of extermination against us. You
may take this as a declaration of war against you."[40] To avoid disruption at the next year's conference, psychiatrists invited gay activists to
appear on a panel to present their views. At the 1972 convention in
Dallas, Texas, crowds of attendees gathered to hear a cloaked, wigged,
and masked psychiatrist known only as "Dr. Henry Anonymous." Dr.
Anonymous dramatically disclosed his homosexuality to the audience
while speaking through a voice-distorting microphone.[41] Audience
members were shocked to learn that he was only one of several hundred
gay psychiatrists who had been meeting clandestinely during the
Association's annual conventions under the campy name "Gay-PA."[42]
Dr. Anonymous was John Fryer, a psychiatrist on the medical faculty of
Temple University. Sitting in the front row of the audience at the con-
vention was an administrator who would later fire Fryer from the staff of
Friends Hospital for being gay.[43]

FIGURE 5 Dr. H. Anonymous and Dr. Judd Marmor speaking on an APA
panel, 1972. The panel turned heads at the APA, prompting the group's
members to debate whether homosexuality should be classified as a mental
illness. Photo by Kay Tobin. © Manuscripts and Archives Division, New York
Public Library.

The event turned heads within the APA, convincing some of the group's members that they were mistaken in their views of homosexuality as a pathology. Others were persuaded by the growing scientific research that questioned homosexuality's status as a mental illness. Alfred Kinsey's work had indicated that same-sex sexuality was significantly more widespread than anyone previously thought. That fact, however, did not resolve whether homosexuality was a disease that needed to be contained. Eight years after Kinsey published his work, psychologist Evelyn Hooker tackled this issue. Her first study, which she described as "a validation of Kinsey's position," revealed both that homosexuals were well-adjusted and that there was no psychological difference between homosexuals and heterosexuals.[44] Hooker presented her results before a packed audience at the American Psychological Association's annual meeting in 1956, unsettling her listeners and opening a debate over whether homosexuality constituted a mental illness.[45] In the thirteen years that followed, Hooker published twelve papers on homosexuality, all of which challenged scientific norms and conventional beliefs about the pathological nature of same-sex desire.[46]

These studies, combined with gay liberationists' protests, produced a heated debate within the APA about homosexuality's diagnostic status. It ended on December 15, 1973, when the APA's Board of Trustees deleted homosexuality from the DSM.[47] The APA simultaneously issued a press release supporting the civil rights of homosexuals, a resolution that Kameny had drafted with the help of another gay activist. With characteristic flair, Kameny provided the resolution to a member of the DSM drafting committee at a queer bar in Waikiki during the APA's annual conference.[48] The position paper garnered support from psychiatrists who were concerned that the diagnostic category had contributed to discrimination against gays and lesbians.[49] After the Board of Trustees approved the resolution, the NGTF immediately used it to argue for the repeal of sodomy laws and the introduction of antidiscrimination laws in cities and states around the country.[50]

The declassification of homosexuality eliminated one of the main arguments against gay and lesbian rights – that same-sex sexuality was a manifestation of mental illness. It also removed the primary justification for denying custody to lesbian mothers and gay fathers, who, spurred by the gay liberation and lesbian feminist movements, were increasingly pressing their rights in family court during the 1970s. The APA's decision did not, however, ensure that these parents would obtain custody of their children. After the APA declassified homosexuality as a mental illness, lesbian mothers and gay fathers would have to contend with another, equally potent barrier to custody: the notion that the state should repress same-sex sexuality because it was dangerous to children. In the wake of the APA's announcement, this argument – which an increasingly powerful political movement of Christian conservatives forcefully and repeatedly articulated – would take center stage, framing how judges approached the custody disputes. Political battle lines would consequently prove crucial for courts adjudicating what was in the children's best interests.

The Political Battle Lines

Don Mager was in the midst of a divorce when he became involved in the gay liberation movement. It was 1972, and the father of two young children had recently come out. He consequently joined the Detroit chapter of the Gay Liberation Front, as well as an activist group that published the *Gay Liberator*, a community newspaper.[51] In 1973, he printed an article in its pages, entitled "Faggot Fathers," which identified the radical potential of queer parents.[52] In Mager's view, gay fathers destabilized repressive gender roles and, as a result, helped break down harmful, oppressive patriarchal family structures.[53]

Mager, like other gay liberationists and lesbian feminists, had a particular vision for America: a society that embraced gender equality.[54] However, these same ideals were anathema to the religious right, which came to a renewed national power in the 1970s. In the view of Christian conservatives, America was on a wayward path, and only a return to "traditional family values" could correct its trajectory. As part of that, American society needed to reject and repress same-sex sexuality. Lesbian mothers and gay fathers thus increasingly fought for custody of their children at a time when two ascendant political movements – queer rights and the religious right – were fighting one another over how Americans should view same-sex sexuality. At issue was whether homosexuality was a matter of mere difference, as gay liberationists maintained, or harmful and immoral, as Christian conservatives claimed. These debates framed custody battles, such that gay and lesbian parents had to tread into fraught political waters to assert their rights.

The religious right may have become more visible and influential in the 1970s, but the movement had begun much earlier. It originated in early twentieth-century Protestant fundamentalism, whose adherents focused on keeping evolution out of the nation's classrooms and returning Americans to the "fundamentals" of the Christian faith.[55] During the Cold War, Americans increasingly responded to the movement's message of strong national defenses, limited government, and protection of the nuclear family. Then, in the 1960s, the religious right gained even greater strength. Its clear moral vision, rooted in religious tradition, offered Americans stability during a period when social protests roiled the country.[56] The 1976 presidential campaign, which propelled born-again Jimmy Carter to the White House, drew attention to the increasing role of evangelicals in politics, as well as the nation's religious revival.[57] Indeed, the outsize influence of conservative Christians in national, state, and local elections led *Newsweek* to declare 1976 "The Year of the Evangelical."[58]

One of Christian conservatives' main claims was that the nuclear American family was under attack, an assault that undermined the country's moral fabric.[59] The evangelical emphasis on "traditional family values" encompassed both the idealization of the heterosexual nuclear family and strict adherence to gender roles, leading evangelicals and other conservative Christians to galvanize in response to a variety of political and legal issues, including the Equal Rights Amendment, *Roe v. Wade*,[60] and the gay liberation movement.[61] Of course, nothing symbolized the breakdown of traditional household structures more than ballooning divorce rates, which conservatives blamed on feminist activism.[62] As Christian conservatives attempted to turn back increasingly liberal policies on gender equality, abortion, and queer rights, they used the phrase "family values" to frame political debates over these issues.[63] They also entrenched their opposition to same-sex sexuality by deploying a rhetoric of child protection, language that resonated deeply with the American public as Christian conservatives gained prominence at all levels of government.[64]

By the late 1970s, the religious right presented homosexuality as a choice – one that children might elect if they were not taught that homosexuality was both dangerous and socially unacceptable.[65] Jerry Falwell, the founder of the Moral Majority, one of the largest conservative lobbying groups in the country, explained that allowing gays and lesbians to teach "might be an open invitation for [homosexuals] to subvert our young and impressionable children into their lifestyle."[66] Although Falwell was focused on teachers, his arguments extended with equal force to all queer role models, including parents. Beverly LaHaye, who founded the national lobbying group Concerned Women for America, made a similar claim. She warned that "[e]very homosexual is potentially an evangelist of homosexuality, capable of perverting many young people to his sinful way of life."[67] In these leaders' views, the state had a moral obligation to discriminate against same-sex sexuality. Only by expressing its disapproval through law could it protect children from inadvertently choosing such a harmful path.

The religious right's antiqueer arguments had deep historical roots. For much of the twentieth century, medical, social, and political discourse equated homosexuality with pedophilia, identifying child molestation as both the root cause and the product of same-sex attraction.[68] This theory, which had undergirded the sexual psychopath laws, presented homosexuals as frozen at an immature stage of development. They consequently sought out children of the same gender as sexual partners, abuse that impeded children's own growth and doomed their victims to repeat the cycle of exploitation. The religious right repackaged and modernized these claims, arguing that the danger was psychological, not physical.[69] According to this theory, gay and lesbian adults would serve as role models, causing children to unwittingly adopt their sexual orientation.[70] Evangelicals' expressed fear was thus one of indoctrination, rather than molestation, although many Christian conservatives continued to emphasize that gay men were likely to physically abuse children.

Child protection rhetoric became a hallmark of the religious right's politics in 1977 after conservative Christian activist Anita Bryant launched a voter referendum campaign to overturn Miami's sexual orientation antidiscrimination law.[71] Bryant's "Save Our Children" campaign emphasized the danger of gay and lesbian role models, describing the referendum as necessary to counter "role modeling homosexuals, the ones who aren't openly recruiting, but who don't stay in the closet." The problem, in short, was "the homosexual who is blatant in his profession of his preference and who gives the impression to young people that this lifestyle is not odd or to be avoided, but just an alternative."[72] This campaign rhetoric, which emphasized the supposed danger that gays and lesbians posed to children, resonated with more than just Miami residents. After almost 70 percent of that city's voters approved the law's repeal, other conservative groups launched ballot initiatives around the country.[73] Voters in Wichita, Kansas; Eugene, Oregon; and St. Paul, Minnesota overturned their gay rights ordinances the following year.[74]

The religious right thus made "traditional family values" the centerpiece of its political rhetoric as gays and lesbians were becoming increasingly visible in American society. Gay liberationist and lesbian feminist groups had empowered queer people around the country to be open about their sexuality and assert their rights. These movements inspired even more lesbian mothers, as well as a small number of gay fathers, to make custody claims during the 1970s.[75] Prior to the explosion of gay and lesbian activism, heterosexual parents often blackmailed their homosexual ex-spouses into relinquishing custody. Straight parents would manipulate their former spouses by threatening to disclose their sexual orientation to family, friends, and coworkers.[76] Given widespread social disapprobation, lesbian mothers and gay fathers often kept their sexual orientation quiet for fear of losing their children, jobs, and social support networks.[77] However, gay liberation and lesbian feminism changed the calculus for queer parents by increasing the acceptance of same-sex sexuality in American society. Hundreds of gay and lesbian parents consequently sought custody of their children in court in the 1970s.[78] In 1979, Portland's Community Law Project, a public interest law firm, reported knowing of at least eighty

homosexual parent custody cases in the Portland metropolitan area
that were settled out of court. In its first three years, the Lesbian
Mothers' National Defense Fund (LMNDF), a Seattle-based organization founded in 1974, assisted mothers in 200 cases.[79] Dykes and
Tykes, a New York City lesbian mothers group, received twenty-five
to thirty-five calls a week from lesbian mothers afraid of losing their
children during the first six months of the organization's existence.
The group consequently founded the East Coast Lesbian Mother
Defense Fund in 1976.[80]

As more lesbian mothers and gay fathers came out, queer parent
activist organizations sprang up across the country. The majority of
these were lesbian mother groups, whose members were well-versed
in family law issues as a result of their involvement in feminist
advocacy. In the 1960s, feminists had launched a concerted attempt
to reform the institution of marriage, demanding gender equity
during a couple's relationship as well as an equitable division of
property at divorce.[81] Lesbian feminists expanded this family-
focused work by advocating for queer mothers. Those efforts
included providing emotional support during the contentious court
battles, connecting women to sympathetic attorneys, and raising
funds for legal fees.[82] Lesbian feminist groups sometimes also
helped women go underground, providing them with false identification documents and financial assistance so they could flee with
their children.[83] Although activists viewed this as an option of last
resort, women in Philadelphia helped between fifteen and twenty
lesbian mothers along their "underground railroad" in the 1970s,
connecting them with lesbian feminist community networks all
around the country.[84]

Lesbian mother organizations also publicized the plight of their
members to the wider lesbian community, emphasizing that queer
nonparents should understand custody rights as central to the broader
gay and lesbian rights project.[85] For many in the gay liberation and
lesbian feminist movements, the connection between parenthood and
queer rights was not immediately obvious. In 1977, when one lesbian
mother distributed flyers about her custody case at a lesbian concert,
she received few positive responses from the women in attendance.
By the end of the decade, however, lesbian mother rights had become
central to radical lesbian politics.[86]

FIGURE 6 Dykes and Tykes protest, New York City, 1978. Lesbian mother groups like Dykes and Tykes drew attention to the plight of queer parents, as well as provided crucial support to members fighting custody battles. Photo by Bettye Lane. Courtesy of Schlesinger Library, Harvard Radcliffe Institute.

Gay fathers also created their own groups, which were similar to their lesbian mother counterparts. They assisted their members with their custody disputes and provided a space to share concerns about raising children, but they devoted significantly less time and energy to fundraising.[87] Gay fathers were often in a different economic position than lesbian mothers. Sexist hiring practices, along with the gender pay gap, meant that women who left heterosexual marriages often struggled financially. For lesbian mothers, filing for divorce thus meant facing the threat of both a protracted custody battle and a life of poverty.[88] These issues were particularly concerning for women of color, whose wages were typically lower than those of white women. Gay fathers groups also had fewer members who needed financial support because gay fathers were less likely than lesbian mothers to pursue custody in the first place.[89] Although judges applied a gender-neutral custody standard, they tended to favor mothers. That fact, when combined with judicial prejudice against homosexuality, meant that gay fathers expected to lose custody suits, such that many did not try. Instead, they focused on negotiating with their ex-wives for increased visitation rights.[90] Those who pressed for custody of their children often tried to keep their sexual orientation hidden, living in two worlds. They were sometimes fathers and sometimes gay men, but could rarely be both at once.[91] Most of the queer parent custody cases thus involved lesbian mothers, rather than gay fathers.[92]

As these lesbian mother and gay father organizations grew, they encouraged more queer parents to demand the right to raise their children. Once embroiled in litigation, these mothers and fathers had to address judges' fears about same-sex sexuality, which were rooted in the religious right's arguments. The gay liberation and lesbian feminist movements may have galvanized parents and spurred them to file suit, but the religious right's child protection claims would frame the courts' decisions. Lesbian mothers and gay fathers would consequently have to address courts' concerns about their children's future sexual orientation to secure custody.

Courts' Concerns

In 1973, a judge placed Carol Parrott's two daughters in foster care in Kelso, Washington, a seventeen-hour bus ride away from their mother.[93] Because of Parrott's limited income from her job at Nichols Turkey Breeding Farm, she struggled to pay the $54 round-trip ticket to visit them.[94] At the hearing, child welfare officers argued that the children needed to be in foster homes to ensure "proper adjustment to a 'dominantly heterosexual society.'"[95] Three years earlier, Parrott had lost custody of her two other daughters.[96] In that case, the court reasoned it could not allow the children to live with a lesbian, whose conduct was both illegal and abnormal.[97] The court could not have made its hostility to same-sex sexuality clearer than when it ruled that a foster placement was a better option for children than a home with their lesbian mother. Given this starting point, it was remarkable that custody law transformed at all. Yet the custody context did change dramatically – and quickly.

Gay liberation and lesbian feminism had inspired parents like Parrott to demand their rights. Lesbian mother and gay father groups then supported the men and women as they pressed their claims. But another factor made queer parents increasingly likely to go to court: a statutory change in the early 1970s, which made it more likely that these parents would win their custody battles. In the early and mid-1970s, legislatures replaced a maternal preference in custody awards with a gender-neutral standard that focused on the child's best interests. That shift came about after states introduced no-fault divorce regimes, which allowed couples to divorce without proving misconduct on the part of either spouse. By making divorce much easier to obtain, these laws gave rise to more marital dissolutions – and more child custody disputes. As increasing numbers of litigants went to court to fight for their children, political pressure grew to eliminate the discriminatory custody standard.[98] Feminists argued for reforms because they objected to the ways in which sex-based custody laws reflected and reinforced gendered divisions of labor. At the same time, the growing father's rights movement challenged the judicial custody standards that favored mothers at the expense of fathers. Both political movements lobbied state legislators to enact gender-neutral custody rules, to great effect.[99] By the middle of the 1970s, states across the country had adopted the "best interests of the child" standard, which required judges to specify why they were denying a parent custody rights.[100] Given that the APA had declassified homosexuality from the DSM, courts no longer had a categorical basis for casting homosexual parents as inherently unfit. Instead, judges required evidence that connected the parent's homosexuality with harm to the children. Litigants who opposed queer parents' custody rights thus had to demonstrate a "nexus" between same-sex sexuality and child welfare.

The first appearance of the "nexus" standard in a custody case was in a 1973 decision from Michigan, *People v. Brown*. Unlike most queer parent cases, this lawsuit did not arise from a divorce, but rather a neglect and abuse proceeding. Upon learning that Mae Brown and Arlene Smith, a lesbian couple, were living together with their eight children, the state petitioned to remove the children from the women's "immoral atmosphere."[101] In the state's view, a home headed by a lesbian couple was inherently abusive. The probate judge ruled that the mothers could retain custody of their respective children so long as they separated their households. When the court later learned that the couple and their children were once again living under the same roof, the judge placed the children in foster care. After two years of legal battles, the women won their appeal. The appellate court held that the mere fact of the women's same-sex relationship was an insufficient basis for ruling that the household was unfit for the children.[102] The state would have to show that their sexual orientation harmed the children. Upon receiving the decision, the prosecuting attorney dismissed the cases against the two women, which allowed the children to return to their mothers' home.[103]

Because the nexus standard required courts to conduct an intensive fact-based determination as to the preferable custodian, heterosexual spouses raised a host of objections to gay- and lesbian-headed households.[104] One common argument was that the children would suffer stigma as a result of their homosexual parents' sexual orientation. In 1978, Lynn Ransom's ex-husband made this argument when he petitioned for custody of their two children, 9-year-old Vanessa and 11-year-old Damon.[105] Ransom, an African American woman, lived with her partner, Georgia, at the time.[106] The court-appointed child custody evaluator recommended that the father be given permanent custody because of the stigma associated with Ransom's sexual orientation.[107] The judge disagreed with that conclusion after hearing from several experts, including Wardell Pomeroy, a psychologist who had coauthored the Kinsey reports on male and female sexual behavior.[108] Ransom was not the only lesbian mother who had to contend with this argument. Stigma was such a common refrain that, at a rally for a lesbian mother in San Francisco, one child carried a sign that read: "We're proud, not stigmatized."[109]

In 1984, a United States Supreme Court case undermined courts' ability to consider stigma in queer parent cases. In *Palmore v. Sidoti*, a Florida court had granted custody to a white father after his white ex-wife began living with a Black man, whom she later married. The Supreme Court reversed the decision, noting that "[p]rivate biases may be outside the reach of the law, but the law cannot, directly or indirectly, give them effect."[110] Some lower courts refused to apply the Supreme Court's reasoning to lesbian mother and gay father custody cases, continuing to deny the petitions of homosexual parents because of the stigma their children might face.[111] As the North Dakota Supreme Court reasoned when it upheld a change of custody to the father and the denial of visitation to the lesbian mother: "it is not the function of the courts 'to use these children as the tool of enlightenment to convince society of the error of its beliefs.'"[112] Courts were nevertheless hard-pressed to ignore the Supreme Court, such that stigma became less of a driving force in the disputes. While most cases from the 1970s mentioned the stigma that children would face, that argument rarely appeared by the mid-1980s.

Another claim that frequently arose in queer parent cases was that homosexual adults were likely to molest their children. That argument, which more often appeared in gay father disputes, was rooted in a popular explanation for same-sex attraction: that it was the result of childhood sexual abuse. The idea that homosexuals actively recruited children to homosexuality through molestation was a pervasive notion that dated at least to the 1920s, becoming a common explanation for why gay men's psychosexual development had stopped at preadolescence. As a result of this theory, many people equated homosexuality and pedophilia. By the late 1970s, the claim that homosexuals had the propensity to commit child abuse had mostly disappeared from lesbian mother cases, but the issue continued to be debated for much longer in cases involving gay fathers. As late as 1982, some ex-spouses and experts continued to allege that homosexual parents were "recruiting" the children through sexual abuse.[113] Court decisions made clear that the question of sexual abuse continued to be part of custody battles, as they frequently noted that a lesbian or gay parent, or their same-sex partners, had not molested the child.[114]

Although stigma and molestation peppered court filings, the most consistent concern – and the one used most frequently to deny gay and lesbian parents custody – was that the children would learn to be homosexual from their custodial parent.[115] The APA's declassification of homosexuality had removed a significant barrier to queer parents' claims in custody cases. Courts could no longer dismiss gays and lesbians as mentally ill, which meant they were not categorically unfit to care for their children. However, the APA's decision left unanswered a question that many family court judges considered central to a custody determination: where did same-sex sexuality come from? If it was a learned behavior, as many believed, then granting gays and lesbians custody meant that their children would grow up to be homosexual themselves, a result many judges would not countenance.[116] If it was innate, as lesbian mothers and gay fathers argued, then the sexual orientation of the parents was irrelevant to a court's decision. There could be no nexus between queer parents and harm to the children if homosexuality was an inborn trait.

By the late 1970s, most custody cases turned on debates over the origin and nature of same-sex sexuality, with courts attempting to protect children from the fate that had befallen their parents. The religious right's talking point thus became the central issue in custody battles, as courts were hesitant to permit queer parents the opportunity to transmit their sexual orientation to their children. The fear of homosexual role models explains why, when the LMNDF sought nonprofit status in 1976, the IRS conditioned its tax exemption "on the understanding that none of your educational activities are designed to proselytize or influence any individual's sexual orientation."[117] Whereas earlier notions of recruitment turned on predatory behavior and child molestation, the lesbian mother and gay father custody cases revealed the fear that homosexuality was taught by example. Because of courts' concerns, lesbian mothers and gay fathers necessarily had to emphasize that homosexuality was an inborn and unchangeable trait. Gay liberationist and lesbian feminist groups, which provided crucial support to the mothers and fathers fighting for custody, were ideologically opposed to basing queer rights on same-sex sexuality's biological origins. They wanted the law to recognize individuals' freedom to explore and express their sexual desires, regardless of their source. However, lesbian mothers and gay fathers could not avoid this framework and still hope to maintain custody of their children.

Courts were particularly afraid that a child would grow up to be homosexual when their queer parent was in a relationship, as this would expose the youth to same-sex sexual intimacy. The parent's relationship status often also gave rise to the dispute in the first place. Heterosexual fathers who had been aware of their ex-wives' lesbianism frequently only filed suit for custody upon learning that the women had begun serious relationships or were living with their partners.[118] Some courts denied homosexual parents in romantic relationships custody or visitation, but more often judges imposed restrictions to cabin the possible effect on the children.[119] These court-ordered limitations ranged from prohibiting lesbian mothers and gay fathers from showing any physical affection to their partners while the children were in the home, to conditioning custody and visitation on the partner moving out completely.[120] Judges adjudicating cases involving heterosexual parents, however, only imposed these restrictions if they received proof that the relationships adversely affected the child.[121]

One of the first cases that addressed role modeling involved Bruce Voeller, who helped found the NGTF. In the 1974 decision, the judge reasoned that it was impossible to know what impact Voeller's sexual orientation would have on his children, but that "the immutable effects" of the parent-child bond were such that judges needed to be careful in permitting children's exposure to a potentially harmful environment.[122] The court's visitation restrictions prevented Voeller from "involv[ing] the children in any homosexual related activities," which included attending gay rights marches, meeting Voeller's partner, or even discussing homosexuality with their father.[123] Voeller's case illustrated the problem that lesbian and gay parents faced. The nexus requirement dictated that courts consider lesbian mothers and gay fathers to be presumptively fit parents. Yet many courts undermined the test by considering vague, speculative allegations of unidentified harms that would befall children being raised by gay men and lesbians.[124] At the same time, the nexus requirement allowed homosexual parents to introduce specific evidence that could rebut these claims. The problem for these litigants was that, in the mid-1970s, there was not yet any objective proof that they could marshal. For that to change, experts on the subject would have to emerge.

Experts Emerge

In 1976, Susan Golombok was a graduate student in Child Development at the University of London when she happened upon an article about lesbian mother custody disputes. That piece, which appeared in the feminist magazine *Spare Rib*, detailed the difficulties that lesbian mothers faced in court and stressed the need for social science research to support the women's custody claims.[125] Golombok wanted to help. She contacted Action for Lesbian Parents, the advocacy group mentioned in the article. For her master's thesis, Golombok conducted a study of the lesbian mothers and children she met through the organization.

That study launched Golombok's career – and helped countless lesbian mothers in both England and the United States.[126] When renowned child psychiatrist Michael Rutter learned of Golombok's research, he offered to find funding so she could expand her work as a doctoral dissertation project. Rutter had testified as an expert witness in a number of lesbian mother custody cases and recognized the need for social science research to support the women's claims.[127] In 1983, Golombok published her findings, which concluded there were no differences in the gender identity, sex role behavior, or sexual orientation of children raised in lesbian and heterosexual single mother households.[128] She quickly became a leading researcher on parenting and development in the United Kingdom.

Golombok's career exemplified how custody cases shaped researchers' agendas. Because of judicial concerns, lesbian mothers, gay fathers, and their lawyers sought evidence to establish that same-sex attraction was not something that parents transmitted to their children. Scientists like Golombok conducted studies to address this issue, often with the explicit aim of helping gay and lesbian parents maintain custody of their children. These researchers uniformly concluded that children raised by gay and lesbian parents were not more likely to become homosexual than children raised by heterosexual parents.[129] Their studies thus countered the notion that same-sex sexuality was dangerous to children because it could be passed from parent to child. These scientists also helped to reshape scientific conceptions of homosexuality. Until researchers published these studies, many mental health professionals assumed that parental sexual orientation influenced children's psychosexual development. Logically, then, homosexual parents were more likely to raise homosexual children. The custody disputes thus served as a crucible for scientific research on same-sex sexuality's etiology, extending their impact beyond the lives of the litigants.

Ten years before Golombok set to work, a psychiatrist named Richard Green began examining the effect of parents' homosexuality on their children's future sexual orientation. Green had focused his career on the study of sexuality and gender identity, prompted by his teenage fascination with Christine Jorgensen, an ex-GI who made headlines in 1952 after undergoing gender confirmation surgery in Denmark.[130] Upon entering medical school, Green immediately began working with John Money, a scientist known for his research on intersex conditions and gender identity.[131] Together, they conducted studies that examined the need for parents to model traditional gender roles to avoid "gender role anomalies," which they concluded were ingrained very early in a child's life.[132] A decade after finishing medical school, Green became a crucial player in efforts to declassify homosexuality from the DSM. He was one of the first psychiatrists to publish an article in a peer-reviewed journal arguing for declassification and later became a leader in the 1973 declassification debates.[133] He also connected declassification directly to the issue of child custody, explaining that "the struggle to remove homosexuality from the APA's list of mental disorders was directly linked to the assertion that having lesbian or gay parents was not necessarily contrary to the 'best interests of the child.'"[134]

Green's research had always focused on sexual orientation and gender roles, but he undertook a study of lesbian mothers and their children specifically because courts were asking what effect parental homosexuality had on children's future sexual orientation.[135] Knowing that a longitudinal study that traced the children's development over many years would come too late for many lesbian mothers, Green decided to predict the children's future sexual orientation based on their conformity to gender norms. At the time, psychological thinking linked "inappropriate" or "atypical" gender role behavior in childhood with homosexuality in adulthood. According to this line of thought, preadolescent boys who exhibited "atypical gender-role behavior" were "prehomosexual" and thus needed psychiatric treatment.[136] The gender roles that children exhibited indicated what their adult sexual orientation would be.[137] Therefore, if Green could demonstrate that children raised by gay and lesbian parents conformed to traditional gender roles, he could use that behavior as a proxy for future heterosexuality.

Green debuted his methodology when testifying on behalf of a lesbian mother in 1974. In that case, *Hall v. Hall*, Green testified that the mother's lesbianism would not affect the sexual orientation of her daughter because of the child's conformity to gender stereotypes. Green stressed that the girl played with Barbie dolls and donned a wedding gown when dressing up.[138] Green also made it clear that the mother and her live-in partner encouraged the child to develop along gender normative lines, testifying that they primarily provided the girl with dresses and feminine toys.[139] He predicted that the girl "will be a female feminine heterosexual lady."[140] After the trial, the father withdrew his petition to transfer custody away from the mother.[141] In the research that Green conducted in the years after the *Hall* case, he used the same approach to conclude that parental homosexuality did not generally affect the future sexual orientation of children. In a study of thirty-seven children of lesbian and transgender parents, he examined children's toy, game, and clothing preferences; composition of friend groups; drawings; and career aspirations. Most of the girls favored playing with dolls and wanted to become nurses, whereas the boys generally identified cars as their favorite toys and selected the male-dominated professions of firefighters, police officers, and doctors.[142] Green's landmark studies uniformly concluded that a parent's sexuality had little effect on that of their children, since the youth followed traditional gender roles.[143]

Lesbian mother custody cases inspired other researchers, who all came to similar conclusions as Green.[144] Psychiatrist Martha Kirkpatrick and her colleagues at the University of California at Los Angeles published their study in 1981, which also determined that parental homosexuality did not affect children's future sexual orientation.[145] Like Green, Kirkpatrick's team drew its conclusions based on the children's gender conformity and the lesbian mothers' emphasis on raising heterosexual children. They reinforced both points when describing one study participant: "Mother states she hopes Sara is heterosexual in adult life. Sara enjoys dressing up as a princess in mother's high heels and negligee and plays the Mommie in imaginary games."[146] The mother thus promoted Sara's heterosexuality by furnishing her with the stereotypical trappings of femininity, demonstrating how the mother also identified gender conformity and heterosexuality as interrelated.[147]

While Kirkpatrick and Green were both psychiatrists, researchers in other disciplines – including nurses, social workers, and anthropologists – soon added to the literature on the subject. They all also pointed to judicial questions as the impetus for their research.[148] In 1982, Ellen Lewin, an anthropologist at the University of California at Berkeley, published her comparison of eighty divorced lesbian and heterosexual mothers, concluding that the households were structured similarly.[149] Her research suggested that parental sexual orientation did not affect how the mothers raised their children. Lewin, a lesbian active in the queer community, began her research in 1977 after hearing about Risher's custody battle. She later explained that she undertook her work with the "fantasy that [she] would be called upon to be an expert witness in some of these cases."[150] Her research proposal and design, funding applications, interviews, and preliminary analysis all aimed to help lesbian mothers litigating custody rights.[151] Lewin funded some of her work with a grant from the National Institute of Mental Health (NIMH), which provided legitimacy to a project in which she had a personal stake.[152] Although certain colleagues expressed discomfort with the general subject of her research, none questioned the appropriateness of "a lesbian researcher working on a lesbian topic" as she prepared her grant proposal.[153] She nevertheless made one change to the grant request, at the suggestion of a senior staff member of the NIMH: she removed the "L-word" from the title and the abstract to avoid attracting the attention of politicians who might object to spending taxpayer money on such subjects.[154]

Most of the research in the late 1970s and early 1980s focused on lesbian mothers, who were the primary litigants in queer parent cases. Gay fathers, however, were also the subject of scholarly inquiry. That research had a different focus because, in these cases, arguments about the psychological impact of gay and lesbian role models often overlapped with claims concerning sexual abuse. For example, in *J.L.P.(H) v. D.J.P*, a case from 1982, the Missouri appellate court flatly dismissed expert testimony that homosexuals rarely molested minors. The court stated that every appellate judge knew that this type of crime occurred more frequently than its heterosexual counterpart.[155] It then upheld the strict restrictions that the trial court had imposed on the father's visitation, which the lower court described as necessary to prevent activities that were "seductive in nature." The "seduction" at issue involved the father introducing his teenage son to his gay friends and sexual partners, as well as taking the teenager to a church with many homosexual members. The court identified the father's actions as harmful because they provided the child with queer role models.[156]

Given courts' dual concerns, the first study on gay fathers and their children addressed both role modeling and molestation. It came from sociologist Brian Miller of the University of Alberta, who published his work in 1979.[157] Miller's study indicated that "second generation homosexuals are rare"[158] and that neither gay fathers nor their homosexual friends molested children. Miller noted that the father-child relationships he studied improved after the parents' divorce, as the fathers left unhappy marriages and began to live openly gay lives.[159] Miller's study remained the sole academic investigation of gay fathers for almost a decade.[160] However, the idea that gay men were likely to molest children shaped conservative counter-research, which argued that gay men were inherently dangerous to children. These articles, which claimed that gay men committed child sexual assault at disproportionately high rates, emerged in the mid- and late 1980s. Most were the work of psychologist Paul Cameron, whose initial research focus was on the health effects of secondhand smoke.[161] He had learned from those studies that the most effective way of discouraging smoking was by educating nonsmokers on the dangers of cigarettes. They would then pressure their family members and friends to change their habits. He applied this same approach to homosexuality, arguing it was necessary for Americans to take a strong stance against gay and lesbian rights to prevent others from becoming homosexual.[162]

Cameron based his arguments about molestation on data from a methodologically flawed questionnaire that he created and distributed in 1983 and 1984. The document contained 550 questions and required an estimated seventy-five minutes to complete.[163] Given its length, few respondents completed the self-administered survey in full. Those who did encountered questions that often suggested the answers that Cameron sought. For example, after being asked to identify as heterosexual, bisexual, or homosexual, respondents had to identify why they believed they "became this way." Forty-two choices followed, including "one of my parents was a homosexual" and "I was seduced by _____."[164] Despite the study's limitations, Cameron relied almost exclusively on the data it produced, using its results to argue that gays and lesbians were more likely to molest children and commit incest.[165] Cameron's virulent antihomosexual bias was so obvious that the American Psychological Association expelled him and the majority of the scientific community ignored his work, which was published only in low-ranked and non–peer-reviewed journals.[166] Indeed, the publication in which Cameron's articles most often appeared, *Psychological Reports*, required authors to pay a publication fee.[167] Of course these significant problems with both Cameron and his work did not dissuade conservative organizations from routinely citing his research when they argued against gay and lesbian rights.[168]

Cameron's study aside, by the mid-1980s, psychologists, psychiatrists, and other social scientists had produced numerous research studies that all concluded that parental homosexuality had no impact on the sexual orientation of children. What this work indicated was that children did not learn to be gay or lesbian from the adults in their lives, one of the main explanations for same-sex sexuality at the time. Although homosexuality's origins remained unclear, this research implied that same-sex attraction was an innate characteristic, rather than a behavior that developed over time. The studies thus undermined Christian conservatives' arguments that the state needed to restrict gays' and lesbians' rights to ensure children would not have homosexual role models.

This research was crucial for lesbians and gay men seeking custody, but this formulation of same-sex sexuality created important tensions between the interests of the plaintiffs and the larger queer community. Gay liberationist and lesbian feminist groups were adamantly opposed to basing rights claims on homosexuality's immutability. In their view, discussions of same-sex sexuality's origins missed the point, because individuals should simply have the freedom to express their homosexual desires, regardless of their origins.[169] A second, larger problem was that the studies promoted the idea that homosexuality was a harmful developmental outcome.[170] These scientists did not assert, as later researchers would, that a child's future sexual orientation was irrelevant to custody because heterosexuality and homosexuality were matters of benign difference. Rather, because researchers were crafting studies that gay and lesbian litigants could use to bolster their custody suits, they by necessity mirrored courts' views as to heterosexuality's inherent superiority. Like litigants, these scientists were constrained by a legal system that encouraged moderate arguments.[171] To protect the rights of gays and lesbians, they paradoxically helped to perpetuate the notion that homosexuality was an aberration that needed to be avoided.[172] Promoting queer rights, in other words, required denigrating queer identity.

Queer rights thus depended on evidence that presumed there was something wrong with the parents' sexuality. The mothers and fathers who benefited from the researchers' findings recognized the double bind that came with relying on studies that identified them as inferior. In one sociological study, a lesbian mother noted that "in order to keep my children I've had to agree to bring them up to be heterosexual, whatever that means, and I ask myself what does that say about being gay, which I am."[173] However, queer parents knew that courts adjudicating custody cases were not interested in changing social norms, but rather serving the interests of the children who lived in a society that considered same-sex sexuality reprehensible. As a result, lesbian mothers and gay fathers had few options but to introduce studies that took homosexuality's undesirability for granted.

Despite being rooted in antiqueer assumptions, the research studies provided courts the opportunity to weave a narrow path between gay liberationists' demands for sexual freedom and the religious right's admonitions that same-sex sexuality would harm society. By emphasizing the scientific issue of what effect parental sexual orientation had on children, litigants could urge decisionmakers to step outside of the political debate over whether Americans should accept or reject homosexuality. Instead, queer parents could focus courts' attention on the fact that parental sexual orientation did not affect children. Whether courts would be willing to do so, however, was an open question.

Convincing Judges

Jeanne Jullion had met Gianfranco Ceccarelli, the man she would later marry, while studying abroad in Florence, Italy during her junior year in college.[174] After the couple separated in 1977, their 4-year-old lived with her in California, while their 9-year-old moved to Italy with his father. However, after Jullion became concerned about how her ex-husband was raising their older child, she petitioned for custody of both sons.[175] Ceccarelli, for his part, filed for sole custody, claiming that Jullion's lesbianism rendered her an unfit parent. He then forced his ex-wife to answer detailed questions about her sexual habits and subpoenaed her past partners.[176] Jullion's parents, who objected to their daughter's sexual orientation, submitted affidavits on Ceccarelli's behalf.[177] The trial court granted Ceccarelli's petition, but the appellate court reversed that decision.[178] In its opinion, the judge explained that sexual orientation was irrelevant to the custody decision, colorfully remarking that he did "not care if the mother's love object was a sewing machine."[179] Jullion's grueling ordeal ended with her obtaining custody of her younger son and visitation with her older child.[180]

By the time Jullion's case concluded, she had spent approximately $12,000 in attorney and expert witness fees.[181] That was a startling sum, but only a fraction of the more than $40,000 that Mary Jo Risher spent on her case.[182] Part of Risher's budget went to hiring psychologists to testify as to her children's emotional and psychological health.[183] As these figures indicate, litigation costs could be crushing. In highly contested cases, lesbian mothers might pay tens of thousands of dollars for attorney and court fees, as well as thousands more for expert testimony.[184] And yet, by the early 1980s, expert testimony had become all but necessary to winning these custody disputes. Without this evidence, queer parents could not address judges' concerns about their children's future sexual orientation. With expert help, however, queer parents had a fighting chance of securing custody of their children.

Both Risher and Jullion were able to hire experts with the support of women around the country, who responded to their pleas for financial assistance by sending personal checks and holding events to generate more funds.[185] Other women turned to lesbian mothers' groups for help in defraying the legal costs. The LMNDF solicited donations from its members by reminding them that "no matter what time of the day, or what month of the year it is, there is a lesbian mother somewhere in this country wondering how she can raise the money to keep her child."[186] In 1976, the group sent $400 to a lesbian mother in Indiana who, the organization explained, had a "$90 a week job, and an ex-husband who has not paid child support in a year."[187] The expense of hiring attorneys and experts added yet another barrier for low-income women, who already struggled to make ends meet. The high costs of litigation also help explain why so few lesbian mother cases involved women of color. Given racial income disparities, it was particularly difficult for these mothers to afford the legal fees.

Case after case demonstrated the key role of experts in convincing judges to grant lesbian mothers custody. Rosemary Dempsey, for example, secured custody of her 10- and 11-year-old daughters in 1980, after Richard Green testified about the future sexual orientation of children with homosexual parents. Dempsey, who was active in the lesbian-feminist movement, had lived with her partner, Margaret Wales, and Wales's three daughters for five years. This was the first case in which a New Jersey court awarded custody to a lesbian mother living with her partner. It also constituted a striking departure from how the jurisdiction had approached Bruce Voeller's custody battle six years earlier. Similarly, a Massachusetts appellate court ruled in favor of a lesbian mother in 1983, citing the testimony of four unidentified psychologists. The opinion focused primarily on one expert, whose study comparing the children of heterosexual and homosexual parents revealed no difference in the future sexual orientation of the children.[188]

Expert testimony also benefited gay fathers, who likewise used evidence that their homosexuality would not influence their children's future sexual orientation to win their custody petitions. In 1982, the Oklahoma Supreme Court granted a gay father custody of his twin 11-year-old sons, relying on psychiatric expert testimony about the children's sexual orientation. The father had also reassured the court that he "never encouraged the boys to adopt his own sexual preference and, indeed, prefers that they have the normal sexual orientation."[189] This father's statement reflected the agonizing predicament that queer parents faced. Lesbian mothers and gay fathers had to disparage themselves to maintain custody of their children. Some might have also internalized society's hatred for homosexuality, leading them to believe that same-sex attraction was undesirable. Regardless of what motivated the parents, the end result was tragic. To maintain rights to their children, queer parents had to reinforce the inferior status of same-sex sexuality.

Parents also convinced judges to rule in their favor by introducing research studies, rather than calling experts to testify. In *Blew v. Varta*, for example, a Pennsylvania appellate court relied on the Green and Kirkpatrick studies to grant Beth Blew and her partner partial custody of 8-year-old Nicholas. The court explained that "a variety of psychological studies indicate that lesbianism does not correlate negatively with the ability to raise a healthy, normal child."[190] Likewise, in the 1987 case of *Conkel v. Conkel*, the Ohio Court of Appeals relied upon Green's work in granting a gay father overnight visitation with his 7- and 10-year-old boys.[191] Green's research, the court found, undermined the mother's claim that the father's homosexuality would influence his children's sexual orientation.

Because of the key role of psychiatric research, queer rights groups did their best to disseminate information about experts, psychiatric studies, and their influence in court. Some organizations assisted queer parents by sharing the news of victories and defeats in their newsletters, an important contribution given that few cases produced published opinions on which other judges could rely. Because of these groups' efforts, the knowledge that one case generated consequently became part of a custody battle in another part of the nation. The NGTF went further, preparing a "Gay Parent Support Packet" that provided statements of support from leading mental health organizations and listed psychiatric studies on parental homosexuality.[192] It also contained letters from ten nationally recognized experts, including Green, Money, and Pomeroy.[193] The NGTF packet additionally contained a statement from Benjamin Spock, the most famous pediatrician of the era. Spock's contribution emphasized that there was no evidence linking parental homosexuality to children's sexual orientation, which he argued was logical given that most gays and lesbians had heterosexual parents.[194]

Experts relied on the NGTF's information as much as litigants did. In a 1980 case in Arizona, involving a lesbian couple who met in prison and sought to recover custody of their children after their release, the court required the attorney general's office to provide expert testimony on "homosexual lifestyles." The state presented Dr. Dean B. Mitchell, a Phoenix psychologist, who testified for two and a half hours as to whether lesbian women were competent parents, the stability of lesbian relationships, whether lesbians abused children, the likelihood that being raised by a lesbian couple would prevent a child from being heterosexual, and the pressures that the children would face from their peers.[195] Mitchell based his testimony on his clinical experience working with homosexual clients and the information contained in the NGTF Gay Parent Support Packet. As he wrote to the NGTF, the combination of these two sources of information allowed him "to present a cogent presentation before the Juvenile Court."[196] Based on his testimony, the court awarded the mothers custody. Mitchell was not the only expert who consulted the scientific studies that the NGTF distributed when forming their opinion. Most custody cases did not feature the researchers themselves, but rather local psychiatrists, psychologists, and social workers, whom lawyers selected as their experts because they were known to and respected by the family court judges.[197]

Of course, not all courts found expert evidence convincing. Some judges were reluctant to rely on expert testimony because of the studies' limited scope. In the 1980 case of *Hulett v. Hulett*, a Kansas court denied a lesbian mother custody after determining that the scientific evidence she had presented was inconclusive due to its "preliminary nature."[198] The court focused on the lack of longitudinal studies, a problem that child development specialists readily conceded. Kirkpatrick herself stated that the lack of long-term research limited the conclusions that could be drawn from studies of homosexuals and their children.[199] Other courts simply considered the expert evidence irrelevant, focusing instead on the children's exposure to "immoral behavior" or the problem of allowing "children to be placed in a home where the felony of sodomy is committed at least twice a week."[200] Queer parents were far more likely to win their cases in Northeastern or Western courtrooms than in the South or Midwest, where judges were less willing to consider the scientists' conclusions.

Even on the coasts, some lesbian mothers struggled to have courts accept expert recommendations. The 1974 case of Sandra Schuster and Madeleine Isaacson, who had met at their Pentecostal church and moved in together with their six children, illustrated judges' hesitancy in trusting even court-appointed psychiatrists. In that case, Dr. S. Harvard Kaufman opined that there was no need to remove the children from their mothers' custody because any knowledge they gained about same-sex sexuality "need not predispose them to become homosexuals."[201] Although the trial judge said he was "particularly impressed" by the psychiatrist, he nevertheless ordered the women to separate their households.[202] The women complied by moving into adjacent apartments, but the financial burden of running two homes led them to move back in with one another. The Washington Supreme Court later ruled that the women could continue to live together as same-sex partners and raise their children jointly.[203] The case, which was one of the first lesbian mother victories before a state supreme court, garnered nationwide publicity. *People* magazine even ran a sympathetic three-page story on the couple that featured a photograph of the women snuggled tight, holding hands.[204]

Despite these dissenting voices, many judges accepted the scientific studies. By 1985, not only were ever-greater numbers of lesbian mothers going to court, but most of them were winning their petitions.[205] In these cases, judges repeatedly cited researchers' work to explain why they were granting queer parents' petitions.[206] Scientists had produced their studies to help lesbian mothers and gay fathers fight for custody – and they did. Thanks to this research, gay men and lesbians did not invariably have to choose between their sexual identity and their children. Importantly, these custody awards did more than affect the lives of lesbian mothers, gay fathers, and their children. They also gave rise to a new type of family that offered Americans an alternative vision of queer life. Being gay or lesbian did not necessarily mean challenging social conventions and defying tradition. It could also encompass being a loving mother or caring father. These households, which scientific studies had made possible, helped same-sex sexuality appear more familiar, and therefore less menacing, to straight society.

* * *

A little more than a decade after the photograph of Mary Jo Risher's pained expression appeared in newspapers around the country, the legal landscape had changed dramatically. Family court perspectives on same-sex sexuality had shifted so much that, by the early 1980s, many queer parents were leaving the courthouse with custody rights. In one case, the judge described a gay father's home as a "wholesome environment" that provided his son with much-needed stability.[207] That characterization was a striking contrast to earlier judicial decisions, which had cast the homes of gays and lesbians as dens of iniquity and sites of pathological danger.

The custody cases produced hundreds of legally recognized gay- and lesbian-headed families. These households, in turn, gave rise to a new type of queer visibility, one that focused on child-raising and domestic life. Lesbian mothers and gay fathers went to court at a time when the religious right was railing against gays and lesbians as dangerous to children and harmful to the moral order. At the same time, gay liberation was emphasizing the importance of sexual freedom. Unlike lesbian mothers and gay fathers, who emphasized their adherence to convention, queer radicals demanded the right to deviate from established norms. The parents in these custody cases consequently presented an image of what it meant to be queer that was entirely different from either of those two visions. These mothers and fathers were open about their sexual orientation, thereby aligning themselves with the queer rights movement. Yet, they emphasized the importance of family, the religious right's talking point. They understood sexual liberty to include the freedom to embrace the middle-class, nuclear family structure. Their insistence that homosexuality and family could coincide consequently helped to inaugurate a new vision of same-sex sexuality.

These custody awards would not have happened without research studies that eased judges' fears about the origins of homosexuality. The experts' findings that same-sex sexuality was not a behavior that children learned from parents opened the door to custody awards, even as they reinforced biases against gays and lesbians. Their studies presumed that same-sex attraction was harmful and abhorrent, forcing gay and lesbian parents to present arguments that denigrated their own identities. Researchers were trying to provide litigants with the tools they needed to succeed in court, rather than transform society's deep-seated prejudices. Yet each custody award mattered, because every one of these queer households undermined the religious right's argument that gays and lesbians were inherently dangerous to children. Of course, when spread over the fifty states, these new types of households were few and far between. Given that judges on the coasts were the ones most likely to grant custody, queer families simply did not exist in large swaths of the country. Moreover, the decisions did not eliminate fears of same-sex sexuality, which many courts continued to frame as abnormal and dangerous. Nevertheless, the decisions generated profound legal change by giving rise to visible gay- and lesbian-headed households. Custody cases might be the most local of actions, but they began the process of reframing the nation's understanding of the family.

As queer parents gained legal ground, a crisis was beginning to roil the queer community. In the early 1980s, a mysterious new disease had emerged, one that would quickly become a devastating epidemic. As the AIDS crisis unfolded, the gay and lesbian rights movement began focusing its attention on securing legal recognition for same-sex couples. The custody cases had started to reshape popular under-standings of same-sex sexuality by establishing that gays and lesbians were dedicated and caring parents. The next rights battle, which emphasized that same-sex couples were devoted and loving partners, would likewise help to change derogatory narratives of gays and lesbians as self-centered, profligate, and dangerous.

3

Recognizing Relationships

Corporate and Municipal Domestic Partnership Programs during the AIDS Crisis

Mark Morgan was not alone as his partner of four years, Jack Harris, lay dying of AIDS in a Raleigh, North Carolina hospital. He had help from Harris's mother, who joined Morgan in spending nights by the side of the man they both loved.[1] But those moments of unity disappeared as soon as Harris passed away. Harris's mother immediately challenged her son's will, which left his entire estate to Morgan, producing a competing document that named her as her son's sole beneficiary. Morgan was shocked to learn that she had arranged for Harris to sign the new will in the hospital, at a time when he was no longer coherent.[2] The Harris family's attacks on the men's relationship only escalated from that point onward. On the day of the funeral, Harris's family had the men's phone line disconnected. Morgan spent that afternoon wrangling with utility companies, rather than mourning his loss. Forty-eight hours after the service, when Morgan returned to the home he had shared with Harris, the family accused Morgan of trespassing and threatened to have him arrested. Alarmed by these developments, Morgan's friends established a legal defense fund on his behalf.[3]

Morgan's experiences were all too common. Throughout the 1980s and early 1990s, as the HIV/AIDS epidemic swept the country, thousands of gay men perished from AIDS-related infections.[4] Many were estranged from their families as a result of their sexual orientation.[5] These biological relatives' rights nevertheless trumped those of long-term partners, who often found themselves excluded from medical decision-making, banned from hospital rooms, left out of funeral planning, and fighting for inheritance rights.[6] Like so many others, Morgan was crestfallen that Harris's family did not allow him to sit with them at the funeral service, despite the men having been life partners.[7] Battles over end-of-life decisions, burials, and estates were only the tip of the iceberg. Countless other rights turned on relationship recognition. Unmarried couples could not always visit one another in the hospital, nor were they typically permitted to take sick leave to care for their partners. If the worst should happen, they were not entitled to funeral or bereavement leave. Same-sex couples, because they could not marry, also suffered significant financial consequences. Access to health insurance benefits, disability insurance disbursements, pension payouts, tax exemptions, and inheritance rights all depended on marriage.

The AIDS crisis made all too clear the serious practical consequences that came with the state's refusal to recognize gay and lesbian relationships. As the epidemic raged with no end in sight, obtaining legal rights for same-sex couples became increasingly urgent. Over time, gay and lesbian rights groups' efforts to protect queer relationships came to concentrate on securing domestic partnership programs, a concept that advocates had developed long before anyone had heard of HIV. The epidemic, however, prompted the movement to turn more of their attention to developing these policies. Domestic partnership programs were not uniform in the benefits they conferred, but they all extended some of the rights associated with marriage to same-sex couples.

It was this connection to marriage that made domestic partnerships so controversial. For Christian conservatives, treating gay and lesbian couples as if they were spouses was appalling. Accepting same-sex couples as equivalent to different-sex relationships implied that homosexuality was morally equivalent to heterosexuality, a prospect that the religious right could not countenance. The debate over domestic partnerships thus turned on different issues, and proceeded from a different starting point, than battles over custody. Those cases were fought over homosexuality's origins and transmissibility, with lesbian mothers and gay fathers forced to concede that homosexuality was an undesirable developmental outcome. Those involved in contests over domestic partnerships, on the other hand, insisted that same-sex sexuality was neither harmful nor deviant. They also maintained that society should accept queer couples as families. These were more radical claims than queer parents had made, but advocates' willingness to push the boundaries of social convention only went so far. Even as same-sex couples insisted that their families deserved respect, they also emphasized how queer relationships mirrored traditional marriages. The end result was that domestic partnership programs offered an alternative to marriage that reinforced the primacy of the marital relationship.[8]

Efforts to secure domestic partnership rights inaugurated a new debate over the meaning and nature of family. That was not, however, what initially inspired advocates to work on the issue in the late 1970s and early 1980s. For queer liberationists, domestic partnership benefits were not a matter of redefining the nuclear household. They were simply a question of obtaining workplace equality.[9]

Obtaining Workplace Benefits

Jeff Weinstein's distinguishing feature was his self-described "gender fuck drag" – women's clothing, long hair, and a beard. He adopted the style after the Stonewall riots of 1969, when he came out of the closet in two ways: personally, as a gay man, and politically, as a socialist feminist. Before he moved to California for graduate school in 1968, the native New Yorker had not been involved in any political causes. That changed in the early 1970s. While living in Southern California, he organized on behalf of farmworkers, protested the Vietnam War, and became involved in gay liberation groups. It was during this time that he first began thinking about domestic partnership benefits, but he quickly dismissed the idea as an impossible dream. His journalism career took him back to New York, where he began working for a weekly paper called the *Village Voice*. Then in 1979, he learned that his employer provided health insurance to his straight colleagues' unmarried partners. He reasoned that, if the *Voice* was willing to extend benefits to heterosexual domestic partners, then it might consider doing the same for its queer employees.[10]

Weinstein initially raised the issue with union leaders, then with the rest of the paper's staff, all of whom were overwhelmingly supportive of the change. There was little antiqueer sentiment at the *Voice*, the nation's first alternative newspaper. Consequently, during the next set of contract negotiations, which were finalized in 1982, one of the union's primary demands became health insurance for same-sex partners. When the newspaper agreed to provide health benefits to "spousal equivalents," its lawyer asked the union to keep the deal quiet to avoid employees at other workplaces demanding similar programs. Upon hearing that request, Weinstein responded by sending out a press release announcing the change to the world.[11]

The *Voice* quickly became known around the country for having broken new ground, and in the years to come would be cited as an example for other institutions considering domestic partnership benefits.[12] It was one of a handful of employers on the coasts that began offering health benefits to employees' same-sex partners in the early and mid-1980s, typically in response to union demands. For these unions, the benefits were a concession they could gain for their queer members. For the gays and lesbians who lobbied to put the benefits on the unions' agendas, it was part of a larger effort to secure equal rights.

The workplace had historically been a perilous site for members of the queer community. In the mid-twentieth century, gays and lesbians routinely lost their jobs when their sexual orientation became known, with government employers actively trying to root out queer civil servants.[13] At the federal level, officials reasoned that, since gays and lesbians were susceptible to blackmail, they constituted security risks.[14] State and local governments focused their efforts on purging gay and lesbian staff from schools, where they might "recruit" children to their ranks.[15] Private employers took a more passive approach. As long as employees were discreet, most employers did not look too closely into workers' private lives.[16] But as gay liberation took hold in the 1970s, more queer employees resisted the pressures of this implicit bargain. Unions helped facilitate these individuals' growing openness about their sexual orientation at work because employees at most unionized workplaces could only be fired for misconduct, which typically did not include homosexuality.[17] For that reason, gays and lesbians could feel some measure of safety when they were out on the job. As more of these community members became visible in their professions, they were sometimes able to form caucuses within their unions or create employer-recognized resource groups.[18] In addition to promoting the interests of gay and lesbian workers, these assemblies served as a beacon to others, inspiring fellow employees to come out.[19]

In the late 1970s and early 1980s, gays and lesbians increasingly pressed their unions to demand benefits for their unmarried partners. In 1979, Tom Brougham, a clerical employee for the City of Berkeley, approached his union about obtaining medical and dental coverage for his longtime partner, Barry Warren.[20] Brougham, who coined the term "domestic partner," found the city's refusal to extend benefits to same-sex partners particularly galling given that Berkeley had enacted a sexual orientation antidiscrimination law in 1978.[21] The union agreed with domestic partnership benefits in principle, but it was unwilling to prioritize the issue.[22] The attention that Brougham drew to the topic, however, made waves across the bay.[23] In San Francisco, the city's public employee unions put domestic partner benefits on their bargaining table, sparking years of back-and-forth with the city's health services department.[24]

The effort to secure domestic partnership benefits in San Francisco quickly expanded beyond union negotiations. When Bill Kraus, a gay political activist, heard about the unions' demands, he began lobbying for a municipal domestic partnership registry.[25] In his thinking, a program that recognized devoted same-sex couples would counter the widespread stereotype that gay men were debauched hedonists. In 1982, the Board of Supervisors approved the domestic partnership ordinance, which allowed unmarried couples to memorialize their commitment if they shared in "the common necessaries of life," a legal term of art for spousal obligations. However, Mayor Diane Feinstein vetoed the program.[26] Publicly, Feinstein expressed concern that people who registered as the domestic partners of city employees might try to claim medical benefits, thereby imposing ruinous costs on the City.[27] Privately, she took a more censorious tone. She communicated to the city's gay leaders that she was not going to endorse a policy that sanctified meaningless and fleeting relationships.[28] Feinstein's decision outraged gays and lesbians around the country – even though most had never heard of domestic partnerships before she rejected the bill.[29] The debate in San Francisco publicized the concept of domestic partnership programs, as well as reverberated back across to Berkeley, where the East Bay Gay and Lesbian Democratic Club took up the cause.[30] In 1984, the City of Berkeley became the first municipality to offer domestic partner benefits to its employees.[31] Brougham and Warren were the city's first registrants.[32]

Unions typically led the charge on domestic partner benefits, demanding them during contract negotiations with employers. However, gays and lesbians in positions of power sometimes took the initiative to put the benefits on the bargaining table. In Santa Cruz, California, openly gay Councilmember John Laird wanted his city to offer its employees domestic partner benefits. He consequently approached the unions, asking them to make it part of their 1986 negotiations.[33] The politician decided on the strategy after seeing voters in nearby San Jose and Santa Clara repeal their sexual orientation antidiscrimination laws through ballot referenda.[34] He reasoned that, since labor contracts could not be put to popular vote, domestic partner benefits would be protected if the unions requested them. He then instructed the city's labor negotiators to agree to the benefits without demanding any compromises in exchange.[35] The union was thrilled at the win-win that Laird had devised, which allowed Santa Cruz to become the third city in the country to offer domestic partner benefits.[36] Just one year earlier, West Hollywood, California, had become the second.[37]

Although unions were essential to securing domestic partnership rights in the early 1980s, they were not always at the forefront of change. They only demanded these benefits if gay and lesbian employees pressed for them – which meant that domestic partnerships only made it onto the union agenda in places with queer employees who were open about their sexual orientation. Even in the few workplaces that met those conditions, queer workers like Tom Brougham sometimes fought alone. Others had to battle against their unions. In 1982, the American Civil Liberties Union (ACLU) represented Lawrence Brinkin, who sued his union and his employer, the Southern Pacific Railroad, after the company denied him bereavement leave to attend the funeral of his partner of eleven years.[38] Adding insult to injury, Southern Pacific gave Brinkin's coworker leave to attend the funeral of a stepmother he had never met.[39] Under the union contract, employees were entitled to three days of leave upon the death of "immediate family," which the city interpreted to mean a legal relative.[40] Since gays and lesbians could not marry, the ACLU argued that the city's position violated San

Francisco's antidiscrimination law, which prohibited discrimination based on both sexual orientation and marital status.[41] Brinkin, like many others, lost his case.[42] The judge expressed her sympathy, but ruled that Brinkin's only solution was to convince the legislature to amend the marriage code.[43]

For the few unions who took up the call for domestic partner plans, the main challenge they faced was convincing employers that their health benefits costs would not skyrocket.[44] Decisionmakers reasoned that the people most likely to need the insurance coverage were gay men suffering from AIDS. As a result, they assumed the benefits would primarily be used for catastrophic claims, a significant expense.[45] Insurers consequently warned that the programs would require employers to spend substantially more on premiums. A second, related concern that insurance companies expressed was that employees would abuse the program – which would then increase the price tag for employers. Longtime labor attorney Allen Berk explained that, without an easy means of verifying the relationship, employees could fraudulently enroll sick friends who needed coverage, which would then lead costs to spiral out of control.[46] He consequently described domestic partnership plans as "one of the most insane ideas I ever heard."[47]

Because of these assumptions, officials tasked with predicting the costs of the programs gave astronomically high estimates. San Francisco's Task Force, for example, concluded that the city would have to expend more than $1 million per year to extend benefits to the domestic partners of municipal employees.[48] Similarly, Maryland's insurance provider claimed the program would cost the state an additional $12 million a year.[49] Most insurance companies did not even give an estimate – they simply refused to underwrite domestic partnership policies.[50] Sixteen companies turned down the city of West Hollywood when it sought to expand its coverage to domestic partners. The city's only option was to self-insure its employee health benefits.[51] Indeed, insurance companies' unwillingness to extend coverage also led to the demise of the first domestic partner benefits program in the country. Although the *Village Voice* typically receives credit for having pioneered the concept, the paper was not in fact the first company to offer domestic partner benefits to its employees. The first program began at Workers' Trust, a small insurance carrier in

Eugene, Oregon, in 1980.[52] Six years later, the company ended the program when it could no longer find a larger carrier to underwrite its domestic partner policies.[53]

To help convince insurers to offer the benefits, companies devised a way of verifying the relationships: they required employees to sign an affidavit attesting that they were in a spouse-like relationship with their domestic partner.[54] These affidavits were designed as an administrative solution to avoid fraud, but they had an important effect on queer family visibility. The documents made clear that domestic partnerships were relationships that mirrored marriage under the law.[55] The programs only extended to unrelated adults who lived together, shared day-to-day living expenses, and planned to remain together indefinitely.[56] Employers made domestic partnerships similar to marriage in another way. They imposed a waiting period between the time an employee ended one domestic partnership and registered another, based on the state's waiting period between divorce and remarriage.[57] Together, these provisions framed same-sex couples as akin to spouses, reflecting how many, but not all, gay and lesbian partners structured their lives.[58] The administrative decision thus elevated one type of queer household, in the process obscuring the many same-sex relationships that did not fit the nuclear family model. It also meant that domestic partnerships would not become a mechanism for securing benefits for alternative households. However, that was the cost of obtaining the programs, which at the time were a radical departure from the marital norm.

As it turned out, fears about the programs' expense were overblown.[59] In part, that was because few people took advantage of the policies.[60] Applying for domestic partner benefits meant coming out at work, which was a risky proposition. Even if unions protected their jobs, gays and lesbians might still have to endure hostility, bias, and disdain from their colleagues.[61] Another reason was that AIDS treatments were significantly less expensive than care for other common medical conditions, such as high-risk pregnancies, heart disease, and cancer.[62] Unfortunately, few medications were available to treat HIV, and those that were on the market typically did not prolong patients' lives for long.[63] Because the costs of domestic partnership coverage were so low, West Hollywood's decision to self-insure turned out to be a financial boon. Instead of paying

$100,000 for a commercial carrier to provide its health insurance for six months, it only spent $35,000 in premiums.[64] Other workplaces, which had secured insurance underwriting by agreeing to surcharges, were quickly able to negotiate an end to the extra payments.[65]

Thus, by the mid-1980s, a handful of small employers had begun offering domestic partner benefits to their employees. These programs were limited in number, but they were nevertheless consequential. Until these companies began offering domestic partnership benefits, no institution recognized same-sex couples' relationships. Moreover, most of these employers were municipal governments. As a result, their programs did more than offer gay men, lesbians, and their partners access to medical insurance. They also opened the door to other claims for state relationship recognition, which became all the more pressing as the AIDS epidemic swept through queer communities.

The Need for Relationship Recognition

Miguel Braschi murmured words of love and devotion as Leslie Blanchard took his final, agonizing breaths. Braschi and Blanchard had met at a queer bar in San Juan, Puerto Rico, in December 1975. Braschi, who grew up on the island, was home from college for the winter break. Blanchard was on vacation, taking a few days away from running his successful hair salon, where his clients included Mary Tyler Moore, Robert De Niro, and Meryl Streep. Six months later, they were living together in Blanchard's rent-controlled apartment in New York City. On their first anniversary, they exchanged kisses, pledges of fidelity, and Cartier love bracelets to mark their commitment.[66]

In May 1986, Blanchard came down with what at first seemed like a bad flu. When his symptoms did not subside, he went to a doctor, where he received a devastating diagnosis: he had AIDS. As gay men in New York City, Blanchard and Braschi had spent years living with anxiety and fear as the disease ravaged their community. The worst had now come to pass – one of them was now afflicted with the deadly virus.[67] Although the men hoped that Blanchard would survive, they knew the mortality rate was extraordinarily high. The first FDA-approved treatment for the disease, AZT, was still a year away.[68] Blanchard, like so many gay men at the time, quickly succumbed to the virus. Four months after his initial diagnosis, the 52-year-old was in the hospital. That was where he would spend the last ten days of his life, with Braschi at his side.[69]

In the weeks that followed, Braschi struggled to put together the pieces of a life without Blanchard. Then, one month after Blanchard's death, Braschi received a notice to vacate the apartment the men had shared.[70] The landlord hoped to remove the unit from the city's rent control program, which would allow him to raise the rent significantly. Under New York City law, owners could do so if no surviving family member lived in the home. Since the men were not biologically or legally related, the landlord maintained that Braschi did not qualify as family and therefore could not take over the lease.[71] When the letter came, Braschi found himself not just grieving the death of his partner, but also about to lose both his affordable housing and the most tangible reminder of their life together.

Eviction was only one of many legal problems that gay men like Braschi had to face during the AIDS crisis. Because a host of rights turned on relationship recognition, the epidemic put into stark relief the harms that befell same-sex couples due to the state's refusal to recognize their unions. As grief-stricken partners grappled with definitions of family that excluded them, the push for domestic partnerships took a new turn. The project had begun in the workplace, as a means of obtaining equal benefits for gay and lesbian employees. By the mid-1980s, its scope had expanded, encompassing both employment benefits and the legal rights that municipal governments offered spouses. The AIDS crisis thus added urgency to the problem of family recognition, which gay and lesbian rights groups attempted to solve with domestic partnership programs.

The epidemic did more than change advocates' priorities – it reshaped the gay and lesbian rights movement as a whole, launching a new era of queer rights advocacy. What began as a handful of mysterious symptoms in 1981 had become an urgent crisis within a few short years.[72] By the end of the decade, more than 100,000 people in the United States had died of the debilitating disease.[73] Before AIDS emerged, gay men and lesbians had largely been organizing in distinct political movements. Lesbian feminists had separated themselves from gay liberation to focus on women's needs and desires, which they accused gay men of ignoring.[74] The HIV/AIDS epidemic changed the political calculus. The emergence of an existential threat to gay men prompted lesbians to put aside their different policy priorities.[75] The extent of the crisis was simply so massive that it overcame divisions in the community, particularly in the face of the government's indifference to the suffering of the epidemic's victims and the devastation the virus wrought on the gay community. Gays and lesbians consequently united in anger. Together, they demanded research funding and support for those suffering from the fatal virus.[76] They also organized for protections from discrimination in employment, housing, and public accommodations, which skyrocketed as the epidemic continued with no effective treatments in sight.[77]

Then, in 1986, a Supreme Court ruling added fuel to the already raging fire. In *Bowers v. Hardwick*, the Court upheld Georgia's consensual sodomy statute in an opinion that communicated the justices' outright contempt for same-sex sexuality.[78] At the time, police rarely enforced the remaining prohibitions on consensual sodomy, but gay and lesbian rights leaders focused their energies on eliminating the provisions because they served as "the bedrock of legal discrimination against gay men and lesbians."[79] These advocates had known that the Court was unlikely to declare that the U.S. Constitution protected the queer community from discrimination, so they argued that the document safeguarded consenting adults' right to privacy in their homes.[80] That strategy, however, ultimately backfired. The case turned on the vote of Justice Powell, who had initially joined four others in voting down the laws as unconstitutional. But the justice later changed his mind – and his crucial fifth vote. The key issue for Powell was that he could not reconcile the idea of privacy in the home and same-sex sexuality. Home, he thought, "usually connotes family, husband and wife, and children."[81] In a draft of his concurring opinion, he wrote that sodomy was the "antithesis to family" because civilization depended on procreation.[82] Had Powell recognized that queer families existed, a major Supreme Court defeat might have been a victory. Instead, Powell joined the majority opinion, which derided the queer rights claim as "at best, facetious."[83] His colleague, Chief Justice Burger, penned a concurrence that was even more offensive. There, he described consensual sodomy as a heinous crime more serious than rape.[84]

The hateful opinions shocked gays and lesbians around the country, who quickly mobilized to express their outrage and resentment.[85] Thousands took to the streets in protest, demonstrating at rallies and marches that continued for months.[86] Others responded by digging deep into their pocketbooks. By the end of 1986, contributions to the National Gay and Lesbian Task Force (NGLTF) had increased by 50 percent, while those to Lambda Legal Defense and Education Fund had tripled.[87] These national organizations were consequently able to hire additional staff, expanding their legal dockets in the process.[88] Still other members of the queer community formed new, local organizations, opening up additional fronts in the war over gay and lesbian rights.[89] Advocates used this influx of funds and energy to address the increasingly urgent issue of family recognition.[90] The AIDS epidemic had forced an entire generation of gay men and lesbians to reckon with the painful effects of the law's refusal to recognize their relationships. Most of those afflicted with the deadly virus were people in their twenties, thirties, or forties – people who, before the emergence of HIV, had little reason to think about medical decision-making, estate planning, or burial plans.[91] The epidemic suddenly put these issues at the forefront. Same-sex couples who had built lives together soon learned that hospitals, state agencies, and funeral homes all disregarded their bonds.[92] Biological family members – even those who had rejected their queer kin – had legal rights that lifetime partners did not.

The AIDS crisis produced untold numbers of heart-wrenching tales, creating a burgeoning demand for relationship recognition. It was a tragedy unrelated to the devastating epidemic, however, that brought home just how vulnerable the law made all same-sex couples.[93] That story began in 1983, when Sharon Kowalski suffered extensive brain injuries from a head-on collision with a drunk driver. When her partner of four years, Karen Thompson, heard the news, she raced to the hospital, where she spent two hours frantically trying to find out if Sharon was still alive. As she later recounted, although the women were committed life partners – they had exchanged rings, purchased a home together, and named one another as beneficiaries on their life insurance policies – no one would talk to her because she was not "family."[94] Karen's grueling experience that first night would start an eight-year legal battle to be at Sharon's bedside.

At the time of the accident, neither of the women were out to their families – or anyone at all. When the Kowalskis learned the nature of the couple's relationship, they responded with disgust and anger. For the first few months of Sharon's recovery, Karen did her best to avoid Sharon's parents by visiting at times when she knew they would not be at the hospital.[95] Then, the Kowalskis tried to separate the women by moving Sharon to a nursing home three hours away, even though Sharon repeatedly expressed her desire to see Karen. Five days a week, for more than a month, Karen made the long journey to see Sharon.[96] Sharon's father, Donald, consequently used his legal authority as Sharon's guardian to end all contact between the women.[97] Karen went to court, challenging both Donald's appointment as guardian and his decision to prevent the women from seeing one another. However, she lost those claims.[98] Three years later, when Donald stepped down as guardian, citing his own medical problems, the probate court again denied Karen's request to be appointed in his place.[99] Given the Kowalskis's steadfast opposition to Karen's involvement in their daughter's life, the court considered a neutral third party a better option.

As Karen's case unfolded, it became a rallying cry for gays and lesbians around the country. By 1988, "Free Sharon Kowalski" committees had formed in seventeen cities, with the groups hosting rallies, educational events, and fundraisers to help Karen with the more than $115,000 in legal fees that she had incurred.[100] Supporters responded to the many injustices of the case. Courts typically defer to the wishes of those under guardianship, but the judge disregarded Sharon's clear requests to have Karen by her side.[101] Moreover, the court ignored that Karen had been key to Sharon's recovery. In the months following the accident, before Sharon's father prohibited the women from being in contact, Karen had spent eight to ten hours a day with Sharon, guiding her through physical therapy exercises. Thanks to Karen's efforts, Sharon developed enough finger coordination to be able to type words and phrases.[102] Finally, the courts refused to identify the women as anything other than "roommates," showcasing how little they understood or respected the women's partnership.[103]

FIGURE 7 Karen Thompson in the late 1980s. Karen's struggle to be allowed by Sharon's bedside publicized the need for queer relationship recognition. Photo by Marcy Hochberg. Courtesy of Windy City Times.

The couple's plight – which the national press covered in detail – illustrated clearly how the state's unwillingness to recognize queer families affected all gays and lesbians.[104] By that point, many same-sex couples had learned how few options they had to prevent family members from separating them in moments of calamity. Some were able to forestall hardship through private contracts, such as powers of attorney and wills.[105] But those who did so were few and far between.[106] Many did not know of these legal options, while others lacked access to costly attorneys. Even when couples were able to prepare these legal documents, biological families could – and would – challenge them in court. Some, like Jack Harris's mother, filed competing wills, but others argued that the legal documents were invalid, either because their children lacked the capacity from AIDS-related dementia or because the partner had exerted "undue influence" over their son or daughter.[107]

National organizations mobilized to remedy these injustices, filing suits on behalf of gays and lesbians. The individuals they represented included Braschi, who won his petition before New York's highest court in 1989.[108] The case asked the court to interpret the term "family" in New York City's rent control code to include same-sex partners, as the statute did not include a definition. The court concluded that the term did not turn on "fictitious legal distinctions," but rather should depend on the "reality of family life."[109] Two long-term partners like Blanchard and Braschi certainly qualified. As a result of that ruling, Braschi had a right to remain in the home that he and Blanchard had shared for a decade. Two years later, the Minnesota Court of Appeals took a similar approach when it ruled in Karen Thompson's favor. In the opinion granting Karen guardianship over Sharon, the court held that the trial judge had abused his discretion when he failed to consider that the women were "a family of affinity, which ought to be accorded respect."[110] Fittingly, the court issued the opinion twelve years to the day that the women had exchanged rings and vowed to spend their lives together.[111]

These lawsuits helped individual litigants and created important precedent that assisted others, but they were a piecemeal solution to a wide array of problems. In addition to eviction and guardianship, many other rights turned on relationship recognition, including inheritance, pension payments, medical leave, medical decision-making, and hospital visitation. Advocates consequently turned their attention to securing a new relationship recognition regime: domestic partnerships. The programs they imagined were different from the union-driven efforts of the early and mid-1980s, which focused on obtaining health benefits for members' unmarried life partners. The versions that advocates proposed were broader. They included not just employment rights, but also new government registries that would allow all same-sex couples to record their relationships with the state. Like insurance benefits, the idea for registries predated the AIDS crisis, but the epidemic turned the concept into a movement priority.

Advocates hoped the registries would yield three distinct, but equally important benefits.[112] First, domestic partners would obtain some of the rights associated with marriage. Most marriage-based rights come from federal and state law, but a small number – such as hospital and prison visitation – are municipal. Second, the registries would encourage employers to extend their benefits, including health insurance and sick leave, to domestic partners. Human resources departments often balked at having to create a registration system for employees, which was a time-consuming endeavor. Eliminating the administrative barrier would resolve that practical problem, as well as alleviate companies' underlying concerns about fraud.

Finally, by providing an option for same-sex couples to record their relationships and receive the government's recognition of their union, the programs would communicate that the state identified same-sex couples as akin to their different-sex counterparts.[113] That would help make same-sex couples more visible, which advocates knew was key to obtaining rights. As Lambda Legal argued to its supporters in a 1989 fundraising mailer: "As long as our relationships are invisible, we're vulnerable."[114] Gays and lesbians did not need the state's acknowledgment to know that their relationships were genuine, valuable, and important, but they understood that legal recognition would help straight society come to the same conclusion.[115]

By the late 1980s, the push for family recognition had coalesced into a demand for domestic partnership programs that both provided tangible rights and conferred state recognition on same-sex couples.[116] This demand was part of a broader turn to family law within the queer rights movement. National organizations' legal agendas became so family-law focused that, in 1989, Lambda Legal established a Family Relationships Project to handle its custody, guardianship, and domestic partnership matters.[117] Of course, not all members of the gay and lesbian community agreed that family recognition was worth the movement's attention. At a lesbian forum in Chicago in 1990, many participants argued that community leaders had misidentified the problem. In their view, the issue was not that the state refused to grant same-sex couples the same rights as straight households, but rather that the state allocated benefits based on marriage in the first place. As one attendee explained, rather than arguing that gays and lesbians should have access to spousal medical benefits, community members should spend their time lobbying for a national health care service.[118] When advocates later began pressing for marriage rights, community members would make similar objections.

Yet despite these dissenting views, large swaths of the gay and lesbian community considered domestic partnership programs essential, both for the benefits they conferred on the couples who registered and for their effect on how straight society would view the queer community.[119] These intangible benefits were what made the programs so controversial. Christian conservatives objected to granting same-sex couples even a limited set of rights, but they were particularly outraged at the notion that the state would cast gay and lesbian couples as similar to married spouses. Domestic partnerships consequently became a political lightning rod, with queer rights advocates and Christian conservatives squaring off over how the state would define the family.

Redefining the Family

At the late afternoon ceremony on Valentine's Day, 1991, an announcer introduced each of the couples who descended the stairs of the San Francisco City Hall rotunda. Many held their domestic partnership certificates aloft, proudly displaying their new status to the more than 500 supporters gathered below.[120] The celebration marked the first day that San Francisco offered its unmarried residents the option of registering their relationships. It was also the capstone to an almost ten-year effort to provide the city's same-sex partners some kind of government recognition.

After Feinstein rejected the domestic partnership bill in 1982, advocates lobbied the Board of Supervisors to override her veto.[121] However, an ally of Feinstein's on the Board refused to defy the mayor, such that advocates had to wait until the city elected a different chief executive to try again.[122] In 1989, after Feinstein had left office, the Board of Supervisors unanimously passed a domestic partnership ordinance, which was almost identical to the 1982 version. After the new mayor, Art Agnos, signed it into law, religious conservatives put the legislation on the ballot, asking the city's citizens to repeal the measure. They argued that domestic partnerships constituted an "audacious," "wild," and "presumptuous" assault on marriage. Domestic partnerships, in their view, provided all of the benefits of matrimony, without requiring any of the responsibilities.[123] In the off-year election, few San Franciscans turned out to vote, and most who did cast their ballots against the registries. Despite the electoral results, the Board of Supervisors believed that public opinion was on their side. Consequently, they put domestic partnerships to a popular vote the following year, when a midterm election would drive citizens to the polls.[124] As they expected, San Francisco's citizens approved the proposal, opening the door to the Valentine's Day celebration. More than 300 same-sex couples flooded City Hall that day to register their relationships.[125]

FIGURE 8 Newly registered domestic partners on the first day that San Francisco's ordinance went into effect, 1991. San Francisco, as the first major city to offer a domestic partner registry, helped introduce the concept of domestic partnerships to large swaths of the country. Photo by Darcy Padilla. Courtesy of AP Images.

San Francisco became the first major American city to offer a domestic partnership registry, auguring a change in American law. By the mid-1990s, towns and cities all around the country had followed suit, establishing domestic partnership programs that offered some legal recognition to same-sex couples. At the same time, the tortuous path to domestic partnership rights in the Bay Area indicated just how challenging securing these programs would be. As advocates lobbied cities and states to create domestic partnership registries, Christian conservatives galvanized in opposition. Both sides recognized that the programs would shape Americans' understandings of what it meant to be a family.

For Christian conservatives, the traditional nuclear family was sacrosanct.[126] The Bible taught that families, not individuals, were the centerpiece of society. The ideal household, in turn, comprised a breadwinning father and stay-at-home mother, reflecting their belief that men and women had distinct and fixed gender roles.[127] According to this view, the sexes complemented each other, with both contributing to their children's moral upbringing by providing models of masculinity and femininity. This conception of the family had important implications for public policy. Given that nuclear families formed the bedrock of American society, the state had an obligation to encourage and support traditional households. The family was so crucial to evangelical principles that, in the 1970s, the religious right rose to a renewed national power by making a return to "family values" the centerpiece of its politics.[128] Over the next three decades, the rhetoric of family values would come to dominate national politics, shaping policy debates on both sides of the political aisle.[129]

In light of their worldview, it was unsurprising that Christian conservatives responded to domestic partnership programs with alarm. Any deviation from the ideal nuclear family necessarily constituted a dangerous attempt to reshape society.[130] One of the main objections that conservative leaders lodged was that domestic partnership benefits would have harmful downstream consequences on the institution of marriage. They argued that, by recognizing and conferring benefits on existing unmarried couples, domestic partnership programs communicated to America's youth that heterosexual marriages were no longer the ideal way to structure their lives.[131] Treating unmarried partners as family would therefore discourage the permanent, committed relationships that were essential to raising children. They consequently warned that domestic partnership programs, by denigrating traditional families, would "send shock waves through our society."[132]

Of course, the religious right also opposed domestic partnerships because these programs conferred legitimacy on same-sex sexuality. Conservatives had long identified gays and lesbians as immoral, citing biblical injunctions against sodomy. They additionally cast members of the queer community as depraved, deviant, and destructive, connecting same-sex sexuality to pedophilia and disease.[133] Some went so far as to identify AIDS as divine retribution for gays' and lesbians' immorality.[134] However, it was increasingly difficult for Christian conservatives to press an explicitly antiqueer argument beyond evangelical circles, as the AIDS crisis had shifted the general public's perceptions of homosexuality. Over the course of the 1980s, the public's fear of gays and lesbians had started to wane – as had some of their disdain. In the early years of the epidemic, sensationalist media accounts whipped the public into a frenzy, depicting the queer community as profligate pleasure-seekers who had unleashed God's wrath on the world.[135] By the end of the decade, that image had started to change, with journalists coming to focus on how gay men and lesbians were loving and committed partners who cared for one another in their final, anguishing moments.[136] These reports on the hardships that the queer community suffered helped to generate sympathy for the plight of gays and lesbians, making same-sex sexuality appear less sinister. Reflecting this shift, prime time television shows increasingly featured queer couples, which in turn helped foster the public's growing acceptance of same-sex sexuality.[137] The change in public opinion also stemmed from the fact that the AIDS crisis had pushed many gays and lesbians out of the closet, either because they contracted the disease or because they responded to calls for solidarity.[138] By 1992, 43 percent of Americans reported having a gay friend or close acquaintance, almost double the number that said the same in 1985.[139]

These changes in public opinion reshaped the political ground on which the religious right operated. As one Republican consultant ruefully commented, "[g]ays are just one more thing we've accepted about our political landscape, like long hair and feminists."[140] At the same time, the religious right realized that Americans' tolerance for same-sex sexuality had limits – and one of the lines they drew was at same-sex marriage.[141] Because Americans of all political backgrounds overwhelmingly opposed allowing queer couples to marry, Christian conservatives emphasized that only a small step separated domestic partnerships and same-sex marriage.[142] They consequently warned elected officials and the public more generally not to open the door to marriage rights.

Queer rights advocates countered conservatives' claims with two pointed rebuttals. First, they steadfastly maintained that domestic partnerships were categorically different from marriage. That was a politically expedient argument, as well as one that reflected the views of many gays and lesbians. During this period, a debate over whether the movement should seek marriage rights was roiling the queer community.[143] Some opposed making marriage a goal as a matter of principle, arguing the movement should instead work to unseat marriage as the primary means of allocating family benefits.[144] This camp argued that individuals should not have to mimic heterosexual families to access benefits. Instead, everyone should have the freedom to structure their households in alternative ways. For this group, domestic partnerships were the end goal – an alternative to marriage that would promote justice for those who were different.[145] Other community members insisted that marriage rights were essential for gays and lesbians to enjoy full legal equality, with marriage a test of America's acceptance of same-sex sexuality.[146] It was precisely because of marriage's hallowed status that gays and lesbians needed to have access to the institution. This faction, however, also recognized that opening marriage to same-sex couples was a nonstarter in the existing political context.[147] This group was consequently more than willing to emphasize that the queer community had no designs on marriage rights. The end result was that both camps insisted to the straight world that domestic partnerships and marriage were distinct.

At the time, marriage equality seemed so far-fetched that few Americans believed that domestic partnerships would serve as a stepping-stone to marriage. For that reason, queer rights advocates' second response to conservatives' arguments was much more consequential. What advocates stressed was that conservatives had the issue backwards. The problem was not that the law would change the composition of American families, but rather that the law did not reflect the reality of existing households. The nuclear family model had never been an accurate description of how much of the country structured their households.[148] Furthermore, societal changes in the 1960s and 1970s unrelated to gay liberation had undermined marriage's status as the foundational principle for American households. The rise of no-fault divorce laws had produced soaring rates of marital dissolution, giving rise to more single-parent and blended families.[149] Second-wave feminism, for its part, had expanded women's educational and employment opportunities, which reduced women's financial imperative to marry.[150] The end result was that, by the early 1980s, the number of "traditional" families – comprising two married parents with children – had declined precipitously.[151] The percentage of couples who lived together outside of marriage, on the other hand, had risen dramatically.[152] There was such a growing number of unmarried, cohabitating couples that courts began recognizing their rights to property acquired during the relationship and "palimony" – alimony-like payments following the dissolution of the relationship.[153]

As much as conservatives decried these demographic shifts, municipalities debating domestic partnership programs were hard-pressed to ignore them. A Los Angeles Task Force estimated that almost a quarter of the city's adult population lived with an unmarried partner.[154] In Washington, D.C., the City Council heard that most of the capital's households were composed of single mothers with children, extended families, or unmarried couples – not the nuclear ideal that the religious right lauded.[155] Reports on the changing family noted that most of these unmarried couple households comprised straight men and women, who did not wed for personal, political, or financial reasons.[156] As a result, domestic partnership benefits would primarily benefit heterosexuals, rather than the queer community. Reinforcing that point was data showing that most registrants of existing programs were not same-sex partners, but rather unmarried heterosexual couples.[157] In Seattle, 70 percent of employees taking advantage of domestic partnership benefits were straight. In Berkeley, California, the figure was 84 percent.[158] As much as Christian conservatives argued that domestic partnerships would cause social upheaval by discouraging marriage, it seemed to many that the proverbial ship had already sailed.

The reality on the ground helped queer rights advocates convince more than a dozen municipalities to create domestic partner registries in the early and mid-1990s, which allowed unmarried couples to record their commitment.[159] One of these was Minneapolis, the city where Karen and Sharon had shared their lives, and the site of their protracted legal battle.[160] The first lesbian couple to register in the Twin Cities was Marie Hanson and Ann Monson, two women who had spent years fighting for domestic partnership rights.[161] In 1989, Hanson joined her lesbian colleagues in filing suit against their employer, the Minneapolis Public Library, for refusing to extend health care benefits to their partners.[162] The next year, when the City Council debated a domestic partnership ordinance, both Hanson and Monson testified at the hearings.[163] Hanson argued her relationship was just as valuable as a marriage, noting the couple had been sharing their lives together for longer than any of her married coworkers.[164] After hearing from Hanson, Monson, and others, the Council agreed to create a registry and expand its sick and bereavement leave policies to domestic partners.[165] However, it still refused to extend health insurance coverage to domestic partners, the issue that had prompted Hanson to file suit. It would take another three years for Minneapolis to expand its health care program.[166]

Minneapolis was not the only city that spent years considering domestic partnerships, slowly conferring rights on same-sex couples. In New York, Los Angeles, Seattle, and Washington, D.C., the process was similarly protracted, with elected officials expanding their domestic partner benefits over time.[167] In other locales, the battles were quicker – and more dramatic. In Atlanta, advocates thought they could celebrate after the City Council approved two bills in 1993: one that created a domestic partnership registry and another that extended health insurance benefits to the partners of city employees. The mayor, Maynard Jackson, signed the registry ordinance into law, noting that it would primarily benefit unmarried heterosexual couples.[168] However, Jackson, who was on a business trip in Europe, also faxed a veto of the benefits bill just hours before the provision was set to become law, citing concerns about costs.[169]

Jackson's decision unleashed a torrent of anger from Atlanta's queer community.[170] Gays and lesbians took to the streets, staging a weekend of protests, including one in front of the mayor's home, where demonstrators held signs that read: "Gay Atlanta stabbed in the back by the mayor."[171] Several of the protestors covered their t-shirts in ketchup while shouting that the mayor had "blood on his hands."[172] It was not just the veto that fueled their rage, but also their feeling of betrayal. Jackson had courted the queer vote by pledging his support for domestic partnership benefits, only to go back on his word. The politician seemed surprised by the protests, since he had approved the registry. In Jackson's view, he had kept his promise. However, the ongoing, widespread clamor from the queer community prevented the mayor from turning his attention to his upcoming reelection campaign.[173] To quell the discord, Jackson announced that he would support a domestic partnership benefits program so long as the legislation delineated expected costs and sources of funding.[174] Less than one month after the mayor's veto, the legislature passed a slightly revised domestic partnership benefits bill. Jackson signed it into law, only to have the Georgia Supreme Court rule the ordinance unconstitutional two years later.[175] The Georgia constitution prohibited cities from enacting a "special law relating to the rights or status of private persons."[176] According to the court, this meant that the city had to use the state's definition of dependents when allocating benefits, which did not extend to domestic partners.[177]

FIGURE 9 Activists protest Mayor Maynard Jackson's veto of Atlanta's domestic partnership benefits ordinance, 1993. After the queer community flexed its political muscle, Jackson signed a domestic partner benefits bill into law. © Atlanta Journal-Constitution. Courtesy of Georgia State University Library.

The court's decision may have eliminated the health benefits program, but it left the city's registry intact, such that same-sex partners could still record their relationships.[178] As a result, Atlanta remained among the growing list of cities, towns, and counties that, by the mid-1990s, were offering registries, benefits to employees, or both.[179] Most of the governments offering domestic partnerships were small cities in liberal states, like California and New York. A patchwork of programs consequently dotted the coasts, with domestic partnership policies cropping up in both suburban enclaves and bustling metropolises on either side of the country. In these locales, same-sex couples might be able to register as partners, obtain family benefits if one member worked for the city, or have access to both types of programs. In most of the country, however, they had no rights at all. Even as some major cities began offering domestic partnership registries and benefits, the majority continued to balk at the prospect.[180]

The queer community also sometimes lost the benefits they had fought so hard to establish. In some areas, like Atlanta, that happened after opponents challenged the programs in court. In others, conservatives pushed back by putting the provisions to a popular vote in ballot referenda.[181] Nine months after the Austin City Council created a domestic partnership program, a majority of Austin's citizens cast their ballots in favor of repealing the ordinance.[182] Gay and lesbian rights advocates also struggled to convince state legislators to offer domestic partner benefits, with only a few states creating limited programs in the early and mid-1990s.[183] Massachusetts and Vermont extended domestic partner health insurance benefits to state employees, while Illinois granted domestic partners visitation privileges at hospitals and nursing homes, as well as access to state-subsidized housing. No state created a domestic partner registry that extended all of the rights of marriage to unmarried couples, which would have made all the difference for gays and lesbians fighting over medical decision-making, guardianship, and inheritance rights.

Although most states and municipalities refused to even consider domestic partnership programs, the fact that any government officials were debating the policies provided the queer rights movement with some of the intangible benefits they sought. The very existence of registries and benefits communicated to straight society that gays and lesbians formed committed, long-term partnerships. When the national press reported on these programs, it spread the image of stable queer households to the entire country, helping to make gay and lesbian life appear less different – and less threatening – to many Americans. That was particularly important in the late 1980s and early 1990s, when AIDS had made queer life seem particularly dangerous. Of course, the programs were based on a particular subset of the gay and lesbian community, one that followed conventions around domestic life. As a result, media reports served to make only that part of the queer world visible to straight society. Their focus on partners and caretakers also did little to alleviate the disgust that many Americans felt for same-sex sexual intimacy. Yet the fact that Americans increasingly identified gays and lesbians as dedicated partners was a remarkable shift, one that was unimaginable at the time that advocates began lobbying for domestic partnership benefits.

What helped these devoted same-sex couples become even more visible were changes in the corporate sector. Domestic partnerships had begun with union demands to employers, before becoming a matter of municipal recognition. As these programs continued to proliferate, private sector employees began insisting on similar options. The benefits, they argued, were so essential to recruiting and retaining queer employees that companies should view them as a corporate necessity. In the mid-1990s, an increasing number of businesses agreed.

A Corporate Necessity

There was a certain irony to the Coors Brewing Company's problem. The corporation branded itself as a symbol of the Western frontier spirit, rugged masculinity, and American tradition, descriptors that straight society rarely associated with the queer community.[184] Yet the company was frantically trying to appease gays and lesbians, who had begun boycotting the iconic American beer firm in the late 1970s, when rumors emerged that the company asked invasive questions about applicants' sexuality during the hiring process.[185] To make amends, Coors adopted a sexual orientation antidiscrimination policy, donated hundreds of thousands of dollars to queer community programs, and aggressively marketed its products in lesbian and gay newspapers.[186] By 1993, the company had a lesbian and gay employee group, known by its jocular acronym LAGER, for Lesbian and Gay Employee Resource.[187] Two years later, it announced that it would extend its benefits to employees' same-sex partners.[188]

Coors was one of an increasing number of major American corporations that offered domestic partnership benefits to its employees in the mid-1990s.[189] When the *Village Voice* first announced its program in 1982, the decision was a radical move befitting an alternative newspaper. A little more than a decade later, domestic partnership benefits had become a staid business practice among the Fortune 500, essential to recruiting and retaining employees in several major industries. Many of these companies were headquartered in large cities, but their offices were spread across the country. As a result, these programs extended the geographic range of domestic partnerships far beyond the bounds of progressive metropolises. Like municipal programs, these private sector offerings rankled Christian conservatives, who pressured the businesses to reverse their decisions. However, large corporations maintained their policies because they recognized that discrimination was bad for business – it hampered recruiting, retention, and marketing. That companies resisted conservatives' pressure suggests that same-sex sexuality had become unexceptional in certain segments of American society. At the same time, these corporate policies, which bolstered the visibility of gays, lesbians, and their families in the white-collar workplace, helped to make same-sex sexuality more acceptable in companies around the nation.

Corporate domestic partnership plans emerged soon after municipal programs took hold, largely because the government policies inspired private sector employees to demand similar benefits. Cities' experiences also offered a practical blueprint that demonstrated how businesses could administer the programs, as well as provided important data that eased employers' concerns that these benefits would be extremely costly.[190] Gay and lesbian rights advocates immediately recognized how useful this information would be in efforts to convince other businesses to offer similar programs. They consequently collected and publicized the available data, to great effect.[191] At Lotus, a Cambridge, Massachusetts software firm, management's main objection to domestic partnership benefits was their potential expense. The company approved the program in 1991, after reviewing a study of several municipalities, all of which showed AIDS-related care was less expensive than other catastrophic illnesses.[192]

Lotus was the first Fortune 500 company to offer its employees domestic partner benefits. The firm's decision helped to spark a sea-change in corporate policies, with competitors rushing to conform to the new standard that the software giant had set out.[193] Within several years, more than seventy major corporations had joined Lotus, including Apple, Disney, Genentech, HBO, Levi Strauss, Microsoft, Universal Studios, Viacom, Warner Brothers, and Xerox.[194] Most of the companies were in the entertainment or technology fields, where industry players competed for talented employees in politically liberal, and disproportionately queer, labor markets. Indeed, Lotus adopted its domestic partnership policy largely based on the belief that doing so would make the company the "employer of choice" for progressives in the tech industry.[195] By that point, Silicon Valley companies had developed a host of other benefit offerings to lure bright minds to their offices, including flexible hours and child care programs.[196] For businesses used to innovating to compete, domestic partnership benefits likely seemed like less of a departure from the norm than an extension of existing practices.

These domestic partnership programs became a fact of Fortune 500 corporate life thanks to lobbying from gay and lesbian employee resource groups (ERGs).[197] ERGs developed in the 1960s in response to growing racial tensions in the workplace, with the first such groups offering racial minorities a space to share their experiences and obtain support in overcoming workplace challenges.[198] In the late 1980s and early 1990s, gay and lesbian ERGs had begun dotting the corporate landscape, spurring a change in company policies. Unlike unions, which secured concessions by threatening strikes, ERGs achieved their goals by emphasizing that inclusive policies were good for a company's bottom line.[199]

Gay and lesbian ERGs began their efforts in the late 1980s by asking employers to institute sexual orientation nondiscrimination policies.[200] As they explained to upper-level management teams, queer employees could be more creative and productive if they were not constantly concerned about homophobia.[201] The existence of these policies in one workplace helped spread them to others. At Microsoft, several gay and lesbian employees stayed at the technology firm – even when competitors offered them valuable incentives to leave – because those other companies did not have sexual orientation nondiscrimination protections.[202] To recruit gays and lesbians to their ranks, Microsoft's competitors learned that they had to adopt similar policies. They were not the only ones. By 1994, a quarter of Fortune 500 companies had sexual orientation nondiscrimination provisions.[203] These policies did not create enforceable contract rights for employees, but gay and lesbian ERGs pressed for them because they helped to foster a corporate culture that was more accepting of same-sex sexuality.[204]

In the early 1990s, ERGs presented domestic partnership programs as a similarly inexpensive way to recruit and retain queer employees.[205] Gays and lesbians then put pressure on businesses that lacked these benefits by declining to interview for positions at the companies. They simultaneously rewarded those firms that adopted the programs with fierce loyalty.[206] A marketing associate for HBO described her employer's domestic partnership benefits as a "validation of sorts" that made her want to remain at the media company.[207] Domestic partnership rights consequently generated dividends to employers even though few gay men or lesbians ultimately registered for the benefits.[208] Queer employees often forwent health insurance for their partners because they feared that coming out at work would jeopardize their careers. Companies tried to alleviate these anxieties by making the enrollment process confidential and limiting who had access to the affidavits of spousal equivalency.[209] Yet even at businesses with a small number of registrants, the existence of the programs mattered. As one gay employee explained: "I don't intend on *using* them, but it really makes me feel I'm paid equally to every other employee. It was symbolic, which meant more to me than the monetary value of the benefit."[210]

Domestic partnership benefits, like nondiscrimination policies and diversity programs, helped change white-collar corporate culture to be more supportive of queer employees. Those shifts, in turn, allowed gay and lesbian employees be more open about their sexual orientation to their colleagues.[211] At Microsoft, the company's initiatives changed the workplace atmosphere enough that Don Pickens, a product manager for the software program Word, could joke freely with his coworkers about his sexuality. When a colleague sent an email that she would be at a meeting from "eight until ten straight," he did not think twice about replying that he would "be there from eight until ten too, but definitely not straight."[212] Gay and lesbian employees often credited queer-inclusive policies – which increasingly encompassed both nondiscrimination policies and domestic partnership benefits – with making their work environments more open and welcoming.[213] As a result, they were more willing to be out on the job, thereby increasing the visibility of gays and lesbians at companies across the country. Of course, these policies did not eliminate the rampant discrimination that queer employees continued to face. However, they began the process of making corporate spaces more inclusive.

Similarly, ERGs did not convince all employers that inclusivity was good for business. At AT&T, the gay and lesbian group – known as LEAGUE, for Lesbian and Gay United Employees – struggled to secure the media giant's support.[214] Since LEAGUE's inception in 1987, members had been the targets of harassment and abuse from their coworkers.[215] Backlash spread beyond the company's walls in 1991 after the *New York Times* featured LEAGUE in an article on gays and lesbians in the workplace, noting that AT&T paid for speakers on gay and lesbian issues, sponsored workshops on queer rights, and designated a week in June for "Gay Awareness."[216] AT&T panicked when Christian radio stations began criticizing the company, leading the corporation to withdraw its sponsorship of Pride events.[217]

LEAGUE also struggled to obtain a domestic partnership policy at AT&T.[218] The issue rose to the forefront in 1990, after the company denied survivor's benefits to Sandra Rovira, the partner of a deceased lesbian employee named Marjorie Forlini.[219] The women's relationship had all the hallmarks of marriage: they had exchanged vows, purchased a home, and raised children together. Their union ended after twelve years, when Forlini died of cancer in Rovira's arms.[220] However, AT&T maintained that the benefits were only available to legal spouses, a position that angered its queer employees and exacerbated the already deep tensions between the telecommunications firm and its workforce.[221] Rovira filed suit against the company, arguing that AT&T violated its own sexual orientation and marital status antidiscrimination policies. She lost, but queer employees kept pressing the issue at the company. AT&T began offering domestic partner benefits in 1998.[222]

AT&T's history illustrates both how reluctant companies came to embrace domestic partner benefits, as well as the effect of conservative opposition on corporate practices. Much like the communications company, many businesses began offering domestic partner benefits after a lawsuit. Some companies were defendants in the cases, but others revised their policies because they feared being taken to court like their competitors.[223] Middlebury College, for example, rapidly approved a domestic partnership policy after employees at the University of Vermont won their suit before the Vermont Labor Relations Board in 1993.[224] The two schools joined the growing number of academic institutions that began providing domestic partner health benefits to faculty and staff in the early and mid-1990s.[225]

Lawsuits also spread domestic partnership programs beyond healthcare benefits for employees, prompting some businesses to change how they defined families across the board. That was because, in addition to employees and their families, gay and lesbian consumers increasingly objected when corporations discriminated against same-sex couples. In many instances, a company's refusal to equate a partner to a spouse inflicted significant financial harm, rendering gays and lesbians ineligible for auto loans, mortgages, or insurance coverage.[226] By the late 1980s, National Gay Rights Advocates, a legal defense fund based in San Francisco, was filing at least a dozen suits a year against life insurance companies.[227] The underwriters typically rejected the applications of gay men who listed their domestic partners as beneficiaries, using the information to avoid insuring individuals likely to have AIDS.[228] In each of these cases, the plaintiffs argued that the actions discriminated against sexual orientation and marital status, in contravention of state statutes, local ordinances, or the companies' own written policies.

Gays and lesbians also pressed for domestic partner rights even when there was little money on the line. They demanded family rates for pool memberships, partner benefits for frequent flier miles, and spousal discount cards at stores, also citing state and local antidiscrimination laws.[229] The injury in these cases was mostly symbolic, with the policies implying that queer relationships were somehow lesser than marriage. Yet that was harm enough for gays and

lesbians to go to court.[230] The results of the lawsuits were mixed –
some companies settled the cases, agreeing to change their discriminatory practices, while others fought in court to the bitter end.
Regardless of the outcome, these lawsuits indicate how much the
movement for domestic partnership rights had changed since the
mid-1980s, when these benefits emerged as a mechanism for meeting
the needs of the sick and dying. By the early and mid-1990s, they had
become a way for middle-class gays and lesbians to assert that their
relationships both existed and deserved social recognition.

These new, queer-inclusive corporate policies generated significant
controversy. Much like when municipalities announced domestic partnership programs, Christian conservatives protested the decisions.
AT&T was not the only company to suffer the wrath of the religious
right. Conservative leaders threatened to boycott Levi Strauss, which
both offered same-sex couples health benefits and withheld donations
to the Boy Scouts because of the group's prohibition on openly gay
members.[231] Individuals staged their own protests. When Lotus began
offering domestic partner benefits, some customers mailed back their
discs to the tech firm, noting that they would never use the company's
software again because Lotus was "supporting Satan."[232] Elected
officials sometimes also joined the fray, communicating their outrage
by inflicting substantial costs on the corporations. In 1992, a Texas
Board of Commissioners voted to deny Apple $750,000 in tax abate-
ments because the company offered domestic partner health
benefits.[233] Other legislative actions were more symbolic, but no less
noteworthy. In Florida, fifteen lawmakers circulated an open letter to
the Walt Disney company, condemning their domestic partnership
program for endorsing an "unhealthy, unnatural, and
unworthy" lifestyle.[234]

Disney, like the other large companies, remained steadfast in its
support for domestic partner benefits.[235] For most of these corporations, the pressure to keep up with competitors outweighed political
concerns.[236] Industry experts often noted that domestic partner benefits had become crucial to attracting and keeping valued employees.
There were thus financial costs to refusing to offer domestic partner
benefits, ones that could be higher than the expense that came from
backlash to the plans.[237] As one financial consultant explained, concerns about recruitment and retention were such that "[c]ompanies are

more influenced by whether competitors have such policies than by what happens in the local political sphere."[238] The result was that, despite conservatives' opposition, many Fortune 500 corporations revised their policies in the mid-1990s to recognize the domestic partnerships of both their employees and customers. These tended to be some of the largest companies in the country, thereby making domestic partnerships available to many employees. At the same time, these programs were only available at a small subset of American businesses. In most workplaces, queer employees simply did not have access to these benefits.

Despite their limited numbers, the corporate domestic partnership programs, like the municipal policies, had both practical and symbolic effects. In addition to providing valuable benefits to gay and lesbian employees around the country, these firms turned domestic partnership programs into a fact of corporate life for major companies. By the mid-1990s, the private sector was at the vanguard of the fight for queer equality, providing more rights than many government entities.[239] That, in turn, contributed to the rise of visible queer employees in the white-collar workplace. Domestic partnerships had come a long way from Weinstein's radical activism. Over a decade and a half, domestic partnerships had become a staid human resources policy, one that reinforced the ways in which gay and lesbian couples conformed to traditional family life.

* * *

When the AIDS crisis began, no institutions recognized same-sex partners. By the time the epidemic had started to wane in the mid-1990s – thanks to the development of protease inhibitors – the legal landscape had changed dramatically. Domestic partnerships were not available everywhere, but they were increasingly an option for queer couples in cities on the coasts and at major companies. Domestic partnership programs granted important concrete benefits to gays and lesbians, which members of the queer community urgently needed. They did not offer all of the rights of marriage, many of which depended on state and federal laws beyond the programs' reach. But they did help to remedy some of the harms that came from the state's refusal to treat same-sex couples as family.

As importantly, domestic partnership programs conferred essential intangible benefits. They promoted the social acceptance of gay and lesbian families by demonstrating the ubiquity of same-sex couples and imparting a crucial message: that these families deserved state recognition. The public and private sector programs thus helped to make same-sex couples more visible and helped to reinforce that gay and lesbian couples were unexceptional. That was a particularly important shift given that the AIDS crisis had made the queer community appear different and dangerous. Domestic partnership programs recast gays and lesbians as members of traditional households, rather than a population apart. Of course, domestic partnership policies only extended to queer couples who fit the marital mold. Concerns about administrative burdens and fraud meant that advocates could only secure the benefits for those who were in spouse-like relationships. The end result was that domestic partnership policies raised the profile of one type of queer family, obscuring other types of households. But the fact that any city or state recognized same-sex couples as family was a remarkable change.

Because of the essential practical and symbolic effects that came with domestic partnership recognition, gay and lesbian rights advocates fought long and hard for these programs. Union leaders and queer ERGs, rather than lawyers or judges, were at the forefront of the effort to convince businesses and municipalities to change their policies regarding family benefits. These individuals did not necessarily see their work as law reform projects, but their advocacy helped change legal definitions of family to include queer households. Domestic partnership programs did not exist everywhere, but each policy helped publicize the concept, helping it to spread to other businesses and municipalities. Even where political and corporate leaders declined to institute the programs, debates over domestic partnerships drew national attention. As a result, discrete advocacy projects helped to make queer families more visible across the country.

That fact was particularly troubling for Christian conservatives, who fervently opposed any efforts to recognize same-sex couples as family. These battles over domestic partnerships were especially worrying for the religious right given that, at the same time as some same-sex couples were fighting for domestic partnership recognition, other gays and lesbians were demanding the right to create families in a different manner: through foster care and adoption. In the 1980s, their battles to foster and adopt made gay and lesbian parenting even more contentious than it had been in the custody disputes that had come before. It was one thing to allow gay and lesbian parents to raise their own children. It was quite another to place other people's children in the homes of queer couples. The country thus became embroiled in a national controversy over whether gays and lesbians were inherently dangerous to children. The outcome of the debate would have a significant effect on Americans' understandings of same-sex sexuality.

4

Adopting Change

Social Workers, Foster Care, and the Expansion of the Queer Family

Sue Pavlik and Millie Jessen had been dating for five years when they agreed to foster Eric, an HIV-positive infant. Eric was born prematurely in June 1987, only a few months after the FDA had approved the first drug to treat AIDS.[1] Doctors warned the women that they did not expect their foster son to live to see his first birthday. Eric survived, but spent the first two years of his life in and out of hospitals, battling pneumonia and a life-threatening bacterial blood infection.[2] After the couple nursed him through those trying periods, he grew into a playful and happy child.[3] When the women sought to adopt him, however, the California Department of Social Services (CDSS) opposed their petition.[4] Several years before Eric was born, the CDSS had developed a policy against joint adoptions by unmarried couples, a rule the agency designed to prevent same-sex couples from becoming adoptive parents.[5] As a result, although social workers agreed that the adoption was in Eric's best interests, they could not endorse the women's petition.[6] CDSS policy might have constrained child welfare officers, but it did not tie the court's hands. The judge granted the adoption, thereby making the trio a legal family.

California was not the only state that tried to prevent gays and lesbians from fostering or adopting during the mid-1980s and early 1990s. During this period, a growing number of queer couples petitioned for foster care licenses and adoption orders. Unlike the prior generation of gays and lesbians, these individuals had come out earlier in their lives. They were thus less likely to have had children through different-sex relationships. Instead, they primarily became parents

FIGURE 10 Sue Pavlik and Millie Jessen with their 2-year-old son Eric, 1989. In the late 1980s, the state increasingly turned to queer couples to provide loving and nurturing homes for hard-to-place children. Photo by Paul Sakuma. Courtesy of AP Images.

through foster care and adoption. This surge in gay and lesbian foster and adoptive parenting sparked national controversy over states' policies. The religious right insisted – as it had for almost a decade – that gay and lesbian parents harmed children because they served as role models for homosexuality. That political talking point had played an important role in the custody disputes, informing how judges responded to the petitions of gay fathers and lesbian mothers. Yet the stakes of the foster care and adoption debates were different than the custody context. Indeed, they were much higher.

Unlike the custody cases, gays and lesbians were not asking for parental rights over their own children. Instead, the state would be housing other people's children in the homes of gays and lesbians. Accordingly, by making these placements, the state seemed to be increasing the queer community's reach. Children who might otherwise never come into contact with gays and lesbians would find themselves living with same-sex parents. Moreover, by certifying gays and lesbians as foster parents, the state was explicitly granting these homes its seal of approval. Thus, these debates were about more than just whether an agency would license any particular parent. Because foster care was a state service, agencies that reviewed the applications of queer parents necessarily had to take sides on the religious right's child protection argument and decide whether to recognize queer households as families.

Foster care, as well as adoptions of foster children, was only one dimension of a larger fight that was brewing over parental rights in the 1980s. During this period, as some gays and lesbians became parents through foster care, others created their families through assisted reproduction.[7] The problem for these lesbian couples was that only the birth mothers were the child's legal parent. The nonbirth parents, known as the intended mothers, had no rights unless the court allowed them to adopt their children as stepparents. However, state laws only permitted these types of adoptions if a couple was married – an option unavailable to same-sex partners. The law's refusal to recognize intended mothers as parents imposed significant harms on queer families. The couples' children were ineligible for their intended mothers' employer-sponsored family benefits, such as health insurance and college tuition programs. If the parents ended their relationship, the children might be separated from their intended mothers, who had no right to custody or visitation. If the biological parent passed away, the children could find themselves in foster care, rather than with their other parent. Just like in the domestic partnership context, the state's refusal to recognize queer couples had serious practical consequences.

Lesbians and gay men thus were clamoring for two types of adoption rights – adoption out of foster care and stepparent adoption – at a time when many Americans viewed homosexual parents with skepticism, if not outright hostility. What helped change the legal landscape was that the foster care system was overloaded. There were ever-more children needing to be placed with families, which meant that social workers were desperate to find more homes. That crisis provided a window of opportunity for would-be gay and lesbian parents, who offered a solution to child welfare workers' problem.

An Overloaded System

When Sharon Kahn was a teenager, she resolved that she would someday be a foster parent. Her experience volunteering at a children's shelter in Queens, New York, had shown her how important it was for children to have loving, nurturing homes, a fact that also inspired her to become a licensed therapist who specialized in childhood trauma.[8] In 1984, she and her partner, Irene Lewis, began fostering 3-year-old Jennifer and 5-year-old Nathan, physically and sexually abused siblings who had entered the child welfare system after police officers found them alone at night on a traffic island.[9] Sharon and Irene became the siblings' third set of foster parents, taking in Jennifer and Nathan after their first two foster families withdrew because they were unable to control the children's erratic behavior. Social workers struggled to try to find a new home for Jennifer and Nathan, as most prospective parents declined when they heard how challenging the children were. The CDSS had run out of options when Sharon and Irene volunteered.[10]

Sharon and Irene were only two of the many queer adults who provided foster homes for children during the mid-1980s and early 1990s. During this time, the foster care system was in crisis – and had been for more than a decade. In the early 1970s, the number of children in foster care increased dramatically because of new mandatory child abuse reporting laws.[11] Foster care was meant to provide a temporary home for abused or neglected children. If the children could not be reunited with their parents, then they would become eligible for adoption. The overburdened system, however, neither returned the children to their families nor placed them with adoptive parents. Instead, children languished in temporary homes, with no permanent arrangements in sight. The foster care situation only grew worse in the 1980s. At the start of the decade, Congressional funding alleviated some of the pressure on the system, but the stagnant economy and the crack cocaine and HIV/AIDS epidemics quickly took their tolls.[12] By the mid-1980s, the number of children in foster care was again on the rise, as was the average length of stay in temporary homes.[13] By 1992, there were 54 percent more children in foster care than there had been just six years earlier.[14]

Gays and lesbians, who desperately sought to care for children, seemed to offer a solution to states in dire need of foster parents. However, social workers were initially hesitant to accept help from the queer community. Like courts adjudicating custody cases, they feared that these parents would serve as role models for homosexuality. Because of these concerns, in the 1970s agencies limited their placements with queer parents to self-identified gay and lesbian teen-agers.[15] In 1973, the head of the Illinois Department of Children and Family Services explained that the agency would not consider putting younger children in the homes of gays and lesbians because such a placement "would be too great to risk unless we are quite sure of a lifelong pattern of such behavior." He further stressed that gay and lesbian homes were "far from an ideal solution" and used only "as a last alternative."[16] Child welfare agencies nevertheless had to turn to same-sex parents because finding families willing to foster openly queer youth was so challenging. In 1975, Washington social workers placed 16-year-old Bob with a same-sex couple after multiple group homes rejected him because of his sexual orientation.[17]

Despite being limited to self-identified gay and lesbian teens, these placements were controversial. In Bob's case, the judge reviewing the placement chastised social workers for encouraging "deviant behavior." He ordered the state to house the teen in a juvenile detention center until they could find a heterosexual couple willing to take him in.[18] Opposition also came from agency officials, some of whom proposed regulations banning queer adults from serving as foster parents.[19] Despite efforts to curtail these placements, social workers' practice of housing self-identified queer teens with same-sex parents continued through the 1980s. Before Sharon and Irene took in Jennifer and Nathan, they had already served as foster parents to a 15-year-old self-identified lesbian named Marie. They too heard grumblings that they were harmful role models for the children in their care. Marie's therapist, for example, described a camping trip that the women took with Marie and her girlfriend as "double-dating."[20]

In the 1980s, social workers expanded their placements beyond queer teens, housing ever-more children in the homes of same-sex couples. Often, these were so-called "special needs" children, meaning those who were older, or who had developmental delays, psychological issues, or physical disabilities.[21] Sharon and Irene were not the only queer parents who took in traumatized children, providing them with the love and support they needed to thrive. Social workers assigned special needs children to gay and lesbian families so frequently that the *Advocate*, a queer community magazine, ran an article provocatively headlined: "Homes of Last Resort: Is America Dumping Its Unwanted Children on Gays Hoping to Adopt?"[22] The piece cited adoption experts who admitted that gay and lesbian parents would often be given "harder children," including "crack babies" and infants with AIDS, because social workers considered their homes a final backstop.[23]

Social workers could have turned to gay and lesbian couples earlier, when the foster care system first became overloaded. What made them more willing to accept these households in the 1980s were shifting ideas about same-sex sexuality. The same research studies that convinced judges to grant custody to lesbian mothers and gay fathers also persuaded the scientific community that homosexual foster parents were not dangerous to children. By the mid-1980s, scientific consensus had coalesced to the point that both the APA and the National Association of Social Workers (NASW) issued statements denouncing discrimination against gay and lesbian foster and adoptive parents.[24] The NASW also amended its code of ethics to prohibit discrimination on the basis of sexual orientation.[25] Of course, not all social workers complied with the NASW's directive. Those who personally objected to gay and lesbian foster parents subjected them to closer scrutiny, hoping to find a reason other than their sexual orientation to reject their applications.[26] But the professional organizations' consensus likely made more social workers amenable to placements in gay and lesbian households.

The scientific studies also led some states to institute antidiscrimination provisions in their foster care and adoption regulations. In 1982, New York became the first state to bar social workers from rejecting applicants based solely on their homosexuality. The guidelines explained that gays and lesbians did not influence the sexual orientation of children, nor were homosexuals more likely to molest children than heterosexuals.[27] New Jersey, New Mexico, and Vermont quickly followed suit.[28] As a result, for some social workers, placing children with gay and lesbian foster parents became a legal requirement in addition to a professional imperative. During this time, only one state – Florida – explicitly prohibited gays and lesbians from adopting. Its legislature had passed the law after Anita Bryant's successful 1977 campaign to repeal Miami's antidiscrimination ordinance.[29]

Most states' laws remained silent on the issue of queer foster parents, neither permitting discrimination nor endorsing placements in gay and lesbian households. State agencies filled the regulatory void with unofficial policies, which were as likely to oppose placements with gays and lesbians as they were to support them.[30]

Administrative law empowers civil servants to exercise their discretion, so that they can apply their expertise in the absence of specific statutory requirements.[31] As a result of that flexibility, policies could vary within states. For example, in California, the Sacramento office of the Adoption Operations Bureau approved openly queer applicants, while its Los Angeles counterpart did not.[32] In other units, employees had discretion over whether to approve gay and lesbian parents. That could divide colleagues, as social workers in San Francisco's adoption office discovered. In 1986, one caseworker matched a 3-year-old child with Steven Fritsch Rudser, a gay man. The child's social worker refused to read the Rudser home study, suggesting that the placement would result in the child growing up gay.[33] When she finally visited his home, she avoided touching anything, giving Rudser the impression that she feared contracting a disease from the surroundings. Despite her opposition, the adoption unit ultimately approved the placement.[34]

By the mid-1980s, many child welfare agencies had begun relying on gay and lesbian parents. Some social workers believed that queer adults did not harm children, but others turned to these homes simply because they had no other options. Without regulations opposing such placements, caseworkers could exercise their discretion without much oversight. As a result, a growing number of gay and lesbian couples fostered or adopted children, thereby increasing the number of visible queer families around the country. Because these couples often took in children with special needs, the placements helped to frame queer parents as particularly compassionate and devoted to protecting children. Moreover, by licensing queer homes, social workers undermined the religious right's narrative that gays and lesbians were harmful to children. That said, given Christian conservatives' long-standing child protection rhetoric, these placements were extremely controversial. Indeed, by the middle of the 1980s, their increased use had generated a political backlash that produced calls to ban the practice.

Foster Parenting Bans

Donald Babets was a Sunday school teacher who worked for the Boston Fair Housing Commission. His partner of nine years, David Jean, was a church musical director and business manager of a home for single mothers.[35] The men underwent an eleven-month review and six weeks of training before becoming foster parents.[36] They were the first openly gay couple that the Massachusetts Department of Social Services (MDSS) licensed.[37] Like many other child welfare agencies at the time, the MDSS originally planned to limit their placements in the men's home to gay and lesbian adolescents. However, like its counterparts in other states, the MDSS struggled to find families for hard-to-place children, particularly siblings and those who had suffered trauma. As a result, when a social worker needed to foster two physically abused boys, the agency had few options other than the queer couple.[38]

Two weeks later, that decision became a matter of national controversy after the *Boston Globe* printed an article questioning the placement. In the piece, the newspaper quoted community members who described the decision as "crazy" and a "breakdown" of society's "values and morals."[39] That afternoon, the MDSS removed the children, explaining they were concerned that the publicity would be harmful to the boys' well-being.[40] Rather than temper public outcry, the MDSS's actions fanned the flames of the debate. The *Globe*'s short article on the placement – buried in the middle of a Wednesday paper – quickly became the leading story around the country, turning a local issue into a national event.[41] Reporters and camera crews descended upon the Babets and Jean home, which became a target for angry youth, who pelted the men's house with rocks, bottles, cans, and rotten vegetables.[42] In California, Sharon and Irene were so alarmed when they heard the news out of Massachusetts that the women asked the Lesbian Rights Project to help them with their own adoption petition.[43]

The placement triggered outrage because so many Americans considered gays and lesbians inherently harmful to children. Although scientific research had convinced many judges deciding custody cases that children did not learn to be gay or lesbian from the adults in their lives, the studies' conclusions were not widely known. As a result, when Americans learned that gays and lesbians could legally foster and adopt children in all but one state, many demanded that officials take action to prevent these families from forming.[44] The debates that followed would help disseminate researchers' findings more broadly, in the process contributing to a shift in Americans' understanding of homosexuality.

In Massachusetts, the tumult intensified two weeks later, when the MDSS issued guidelines that all but banned gay and lesbian foster parents in the state. The rule required social workers to place children with relatives or a married couple. In theory, single parents and unmarried couples could foster children, but only if the Social Services Commissioner approved the placement in writing.[45] The MDSS then imposed administrative barriers, including onerous paperwork requirements, to prevent social workers from even trying to secure approval.[46] Supervisors also discouraged social workers from attempting to place children with gays and lesbians.[47] The MDSS was thus able to secure a ban on gay and lesbian foster parents without ever mentioning sexual orientation in the formal policy.[48]

The debate over Massachusetts's new law was ongoing when New Hampshire entered the fray. A month after the initial *Globe* article, a New Hampshire newspaper revealed that its state's child welfare agency, the Division of Children, Youth, and Families (DCYF), had knowingly licensed a gay man as a foster parent.[49] To temper public outcry, the legislature pressured the DCYF to institute a categorical prohibition on gay and lesbian foster parents. When the DCYF refused, New Hampshire's legislature enacted a ban.[50] Elected officials' debate over the state's foster care policy centered on the same questions and concerns that courts had addressed in the queer parent custody disputes. The law's sponsor, Representative Mildred Ingram, claimed that gays and lesbians would model homosexuality, passing it on to their children. Leading New Hampshire Republicans agreed. Former state Supreme Court Justice Charles Douglas analogized same-sex sexuality to other types of learned behavior, explaining: "A friend tells me that if you speak French at home around young children, they grow up learning how to speak French ... . I think that same principle applies to young children who are raised by foster parents ... ."[51] Ingram also maintained that homosexuals were predators who were more likely to molest children than heterosexuals. State Senator Jack Chandler drew a vivid picture to illustrate this point. He compared child placements with gay and lesbian parents to "putting a pound of roast beef in a cage with a lion. You know it's going to get eaten."[52]

The bill's opponents, by contrast, argued that the discriminatory law's prohibition on gays and lesbians would harm children by making fewer foster homes available.[53] New Hampshire was facing such a critical shortage of foster care facilities that the state had started to run classified ads for foster parents.[54] Given that there was no evidence that gays and lesbians influenced the sexual orientation of the children in their care, the law's opponents argued that the state was needlessly eliminating potential homes.[55] Like the custody disputes, these debates assumed that homosexuality was an undesirable developmental outcome. They differed, however, because they highlighted that gays and lesbians were willing to care for children that no one else would. The religious right may have insisted that children needed to be protected from same-sex sexuality, but queer adults were among the few opening their doors to children in need.

In both Massachusetts and New Hampshire, social workers became leading opponents of bans on gay and lesbian foster parenting. In Massachusetts, child welfare officers criticized the policy at length and emphasized that it was based on bias and unsubstantiated fears, rather than clinical evidence. One social worker compiled seventy-five studies that undermined the policy, then submitted the three-inch stack to the governor's office.[56] That clinical evidence physically dwarfed the two pages of a book on childrearing that the governor's office used to justify the regulation.[57] Representatives from the state's leading mental health organizations and child welfare agencies also met with Governor Michael Dukakis to urge him to reverse course.[58] When the Dukakis administration refused to yield, the Massachusetts Association of Social Workers joined Babets and Jean in a lawsuit against the state. It quickly became clear to officials that they had no chance of succeeding in the trial court, even though the judge ruled that the plaintiffs' Equal Protection claim was subject to rational basis review, a standard that typically results in governmental policies being upheld. In its opinion denying the state's motion to dismiss, the court described the policy as "blatantly irrational" given the exceptional care that Babets and Jean had provided to the boys they fostered.[59] Rather than engage in prolonged litigation, which would invariably require an appeal, the Dukakis administration settled the dispute in 1990. It replaced its ban with a regulation that divided applicants into one of two categories – those with and without parenting experience.[60] It also allowed social workers to place children with inexperienced parents with the approval of a local supervisor.[61] As a result of this change, Massachusetts's law no longer prevented gays and lesbians from serving as foster parents, such that social workers were once again able to place children with same-sex couples.

FIGURE 11 Don Babets and David Jean, standing in the center, flanked by their attorneys, 1986. The state's decision to place foster children in the men's home drew national outcry and generated sustained attention to gay and lesbian foster and adoptive parenting. Photo by Paul Benoit. Courtesy of AP Images.

In New Hampshire, DCYF employees took a more subtle and subversive approach. Since the statute prohibited placements in homes with homosexual adults, social workers got around the law by simply not asking prospective foster parents about their sexual orientation.[62] As DCYF Director David Bundy later described the situation, "we came up with 'don't ask, don't tell' way before Clinton," a reference to the military policy that the forty-second president instituted, which allowed gays and lesbians to serve in the armed forces so long as they did not disclose their sexual orientation.[63] In New Hampshire, social workers could not place children in homes where gays and lesbians revealed their sexual orientation to DCYF, but they otherwise ignored the statute.[64] What this meant was that gays and lesbians had to remain silent about their sexual orientation when interacting with DCYF employees, but could nevertheless foster and adopt children.[65] The child welfare agency's workaround allowed members of the queer community to become parents, even as the law condemned gays and lesbians as harmful to children.

New Hampshire's social workers were not the only ones who found creative ways to circumvent laws that discriminated against queer parents. In Florida, the only other state that banned same-sex adoption, agency officials also disregarded their statute.[66] In 1987, reporters covering the New Hampshire controversy wondered how the Sunshine State enforced its prohibition. They consequently interviewed Gloria Walker, the director of Florida's adoption agency.[67] Walker confessed that Florida's adoption forms did not ask applicants about their sexual orientation. As a result, gays and lesbians were able to adopt children despite the official ban.[68] In reporting this fact, Walker appeared unconcerned about the prohibition, blithely explaining that she "knew little about the law" or why the Florida legislature had enacted it.[69]

New Hampshire's ban was on the books for more than a decade.[70] Florida's lasted even longer.[71] Nonetheless, during that time, both states became home to a rising number of gay- and lesbian-headed households. Some same-sex couples were likely circumspect when it came to publicly identifying as queer, given the states' restrictive policies. However, the statutes did not require them to be completely invisible – only that they not disclose their sexual orientation to adoption officials. For that reason, these households proliferated in both states, which made it easier for their communities to see that queer parenting was not harmful to children. Moreover, as lawmakers considered their states' adoption policies, Americans learned through media reports that professionals in the field – psychologists, psychiatrists, and social workers – all considered sexual orientation irrelevant to child welfare. These debates simultaneously challenged the religious right's talking point and helped make queer families a reality. As a result, the public could see for themselves that gays and lesbians raised happy, well-adjusted children. These events likewise revealed that the queer community was a group that helped children in need, a fact that also undermined conservatives' claims that the state needed to protect children from homosexuals. Relatedly, journalists' accounts of the queer community's altruism provided an important counternarrative to Christian conservatives' framing of gays and lesbians as hedonists whose selfishness had unleashed AIDS on American society.

As these debates unfolded, many gays and lesbians were able to become foster and adoptive parents. Some queer community members, however, found themselves turned away by biased adoption officials. To create the families they wanted, these couples turned to a different option: artificial insemination.[72] In fact, so many lesbian couples took advantage of assisted reproduction in the 1980s that experts began to speak authoritatively of a "lesbian baby boom." This phenomenon gave rise to a set of novel legal issues, the resolution of which further increased the visibility of queer families.

The Lesbian Baby Boom

Four years after exchanging vows in a small backyard ceremony, Natalie and Rita were expecting their first child. The women had initially wanted to adopt a baby, but the agencies they contacted were discouraging. Nothing in Arizona law expressly prohibited same-sex couples from adopting, yet the women learned that state officials were unlikely to place a child in their home. To form their family, Natalie and Rita realized that they would have to find another option. In August 1988, Rita looked in the Yellow Pages under "S" for sperm, where she found a list of Phoenix fertility clinics. Six months and $2,500 in out-of-pocket costs later, Natalie was pregnant. The women were jubilant, as were their families. Natalie's mother immediately began knitting a baby sweater.[73]

Natalie and Rita were only one of thousands of lesbian couples who became parents using assisted reproduction in the 1980s. Many lesbians and gay men had had biological children before this period, but until the lesbian baby boom, they typically did so when they were in relationships with people of a different sex. The lesbian baby boom thus represented an entirely different paradigm: one in which women lived openly as lesbians and did not ever need to be involved with a man to give birth to a child.[74] What made these families distinct was that they were lesbian households from their inception – and that raised a host of new legal issues. Primary among them was what parental rights, if any, the nonbiological mother would have. Intended mothers did not fit the traditional family law framework, which assumed that a child had one mother and one father.[75] The law also presumed that a child's legal parents were the birth mother and her husband.[76] Lesbian couples, however, comprised two mothers and they could not marry. Since their relationships existed outside of family law's doctrinal contours, these women ran the risk that courts would not recognize the intended, nonbiological mother as a legal parent. If the birth mother died, or the couple separated, the intended mother would have no legal right to ever see her children again.

Securing legal protections for intended parents became a pressing issue as ever-greater numbers of lesbian couples availed themselves of artificial insemination in the 1980s. Insemination techniques had existed long before this time, with reports of artificial insemination dating to shortly after the Civil War. Unmarried women, however, often could not access these services.[77] In 1977, a survey of fertility doctors revealed that 90 percent refused to work with single women.[78] Many lesbians in the late 1970s consequently relied on self-insemination, obtaining sperm through informal networks of helpers who connected them with anonymous donors.[79] Insemination at home, with the aid of a syringe or baster, allowed lesbians to avoid discriminatory medical clinics.[80] An added benefit of relying on these types of go-betweens was that they cost a fraction of what fertility doctors charged for their services, even if the results were less successful.[81] In the late 1970s and early 1980s, artificial insemination became more widely available thanks to feminist organizations, which mobilized to expand women's reproductive choices. In 1979, three different feminist collectives published guides on self-insemination.[82] Then, in 1982, the Oakland Feminist Women's Health Center opened a sperm bank with the explicit goal of helping unmarried women – both straight and gay – become pregnant.[83] Within three weeks, the bank received between 700 and 800 inquiries from women around the country, including many lesbians.[84] A year into the program, 20 percent of the bank's recipients were lesbians. By 1989, lesbians accounted for almost half of the bank's clientele.[85]

In the 1980s, two developments prompted lesbians to increasingly turn to clinics for insemination.[86] The AIDS crisis had prompted public health officials to warn that self-insemination was dangerous, as clinics were the only ones able to test the specimens for sexually transmitted infections.[87] Self-insemination also became a less appealing option as it became clear that states' laws only terminated donors' paternity rights when licensed physicians performed the insemination.[88] Since women who inseminated at home risked having the donors later granted visitation with the children, lesbians increasingly demanded the services of medical professionals. When doctors refused, some women turned to the courts, filing lawsuits for marital status discrimination.[89] Slowly, fertility clinics around the country began opening their doors to lesbian couples, who eagerly engaged their services.[90]

Once created, these families then had to confront a legal system that did not recognize that children could have two mothers. There was no precedent for recognizing a lesbian coparent's rights until 1983, when Linda Loftin filed a custody suit against her former partner, Mary Flourtnoy.[91] Loftin and Flourtnoy had started their relationship in 1977, marrying in a religious ceremony in Dublin, California, later that year.[92] When the couple decided to have children, Loftin's brother donated his sperm, which the women used to inseminate Flourtnoy. They gave their daughter the Loftin family name and listed Loftin as the "father" on the birth certificate. After the couple broke up in 1980, however, Flourtnoy refused to allow Loftin any visitation with their daughter.[93] It took Loftin years to secure supervised, five-and-a-half-hour visits with her daughter every other Thursday.[94]

Loftin's custody battle set off alarm bells for lesbian mothers around the country, who learned that their rights could be in jeopardy. Before Loftin's case, the Lesbian Rights Project of San Francisco received few calls from lesbians interested in the legal dimensions of donor insemination. In 1984, however, the group received an average of thirty-five calls a month from lesbians seeking advice on the issue.[95] By 1989, that number had quadrupled.[96] The organization's legal director began holding workshops on the legal implications of artificial insemination, which hundreds of women attended.[97] The LMNDF similarly became inundated with letters from lesbians seeking advice. Some of the writers came from places with large queer communities, such as New York and Massachusetts, but the lesbian baby boom had become so widespread that letters came from states like Indiana, Montana, New Mexico, and Wisconsin, which were not known for their queer populations.[98] Women in rural areas, suburban towns, and urban enclaves all wrote to the organization, asking for information and assistance.

In the early 1980s, these women had few options available to protect their families. A birth mother could nominate her partner as the child's guardian, but courts were not required to follow that recommendation. The mothers could enter into a coparenting agreement, but these documents were not enforceable contracts.[99] The legal landscape was so bleak that, when the National Center for Lesbian Rights (NCLR) published a guide for lesbian mothers considering insemination in 1984, it could only offer dire warnings for the intended parents. Should the partners separate, it concluded, the intended mother was unlikely to have any legal rights. It consequently cautioned intended mothers that their partners could legally preclude them from ever seeing their children again.[100] The NCLR's pessimism was well-warranted. In the 1980s, many lesbian mothers tried to follow Loftin's lead by filing for custody of their children after separating from their partners. Most, however, lost.[101]

Michele G. was one of the women who spent years unsuccessfully fighting to establish her parental rights. She and her partner, Nancy S., had had two children together by means of artificial insemination during their sixteen-year relationship. They listed Michele as the father on the children's birth certificates and gave both Michele's surname.[102] After the women's relationship ended, they shared custody for three years, until a dispute over scheduling led Michele to petition for a formal order in 1988. Her attorneys from the ACLU, Lambda Legal, and NCLR urged the court to identify Michele as a parent by equitable estoppel, a legal doctrine that courts had developed to protect the custody rights of unmarried and nonbiological fathers.[103] In these cases involving different-sex couples, courts conferred legal parenthood on unmarried fathers who, at the urging of the children's mothers, acted as parents. They also recognized that married fathers, who had children using sperm donors, were legal parents regardless of the fact that they were genetically unrelated to their sons or daughters.[104] Lawyers for lesbian mothers, like those in Michele's case, argued that courts should approach same-sex couples the same way, focusing on conduct and consent, rather than marriage or biology.[105] In their view, just as the law had adapted in response to the lived reality of different-sex households, so too should it recognize queer families.

Courts overwhelmingly rejected these arguments, requiring either marriage or a biological relationship to the child.[106] They were concerned that opening the door to other parental claims would create havoc. Nancy's attorney stoked those fears, arguing that marriage served as an important gatekeeper, without which the court would be inundated with custody claims from babysitters, nannies, and childcare workers, all of whom could "get very attached."[107] The lawyer went so far as to declare: "wet nurses don't get parental rights."[108] In its ruling, the California Court of Appeals agreed with the lawyer's argument, although it adopted a very different tone. The court went to great pains to emphasize that Michele was a mother in every practical sense of the word, and that the children would suffer from losing their relationship with the woman they called "mom." It concluded, however, that the law did not consider Michele a parent. The problem, according to the court, was that there was no principled way to distinguish between lesbian coparents and other types of people involved in raising children. As a result, conferring legal rights on Michele could lead to custody and visitation suits from extended relatives, close friends, or longtime caregivers.[109]

The court ignored that Michele and Nancy were spouses in all but name. The women had even had a private marriage ceremony in 1969.[110] Had it identified the women as married, Michele would have been the children's legal parent.[111] However, the court did not even consider analogizing Michele to a husband. Since courts were unwilling to recognize the mothers' rights after their relationships dissolved, lawyers searched for a way to protect the relationships while the families were still intact. They soon realized that adoption would allow them to do just that.

Second-Parent Adoptions

Not long after their 1983 commitment ceremony, Laura and Victoria joined a "baby maybe" support group for lesbians who were considering having children.[112] In 1985, Laura gave birth to Tessa Kate, whom she conceived through artificial insemination. Four years later, Victoria expanded their family when she adopted a toddler from Nicaragua named Maya Jo.[113] In 1991, the women filed petitions with the District of Columbia, asking for each to be declared the legal parent of the other's child. The adoption orders they secured made all the difference two years later, when Victoria died after a tree branch fell through her car windshield. Because Victoria had adopted Tessa Kate, Tessa Kate received the same social security benefits as her sister. Thanks to Laura's adoption of Maya Jo, Maya Jo was not a legal orphan who risked being taken away from the only family she had ever known.[114]

Laura and Victoria were able to protect their family through "second parent" adoptions, a legal tool that lesbian rights advocates developed in the mid-1980s to establish lesbian coparents' rights. They were a variation on stepparent adoptions, which allowed stepparents to adopt the child of their new spouse.[115] Traditionally, children could only be adopted if they had no legal parents, as adoption severed the existing parent's rights. Stepparent adoptions were the one exception to that rule, allowing the biological parent to maintain their legal relationship following the adoption. Second-parent adoption petitions asked courts to identify women like Laura and Victoria as akin to stepparents. Although courts had been unwilling to extend the rights of married couples to lesbian coparents petitioning for custody, they overwhelmingly took the opposite view in the adoption context. Courts broadened a legal doctrine that was limited to married couples, allowing lesbian coparents to become the legal parents of their partners' children.

The first second-parent adoptions took place in 1985, when trial courts in Alaska and Oregon granted lesbian couples' petitions.[116] Neither judge issued written findings, making it impossible to determine what had led them to extend the stepparent exception. That also meant the cases had little utility for attorneys looking to convince courts in other jurisdictions to approve second-parent adoption petitions.[117] The decisions were important, however, because they convinced advocates that their novel legal strategy was worth pursuing. Attorneys with the Lesbian Rights Project, the ACLU, and

Lambda Legal Defense and Education Fund all began urging courts to recognize second-parent adoptions, efforts that reflected the organizations' increasing focus on family rights in the 1980s.[118] As ever-more gays and lesbians became parents during this period, these groups organized day-long conferences that addressed custody and visitation rights, adoption and foster parenting, and legal protections for domestic partners.[119] They also launched projects devoted to the rights of gay and lesbian families, which included litigating for second-parent adoptions.[120]

These advocates soon got the second-parent adoption precedent they needed, when a California court issued a published opinion granting a second-parent adoption.[121] That case involved Donna Hitchens, the founder of the NCLR. She had been with her partner, Nancy Davis, for seven years when they decided to start a family. Hitchens adopted three-year-old "K." in 1984 as a single mother, then the women jointly adopted a second daughter. In 1986, Davis filed a petition to also adopt K. so that both of their children would have the economic and emotional security that came with two legal parents.[122] Adoption officials were initially divided on how to respond to Davis's case. They scrawled notes on the paperwork that the situation was a "hard call" because Davis was not "truly a stepparent."[123] The California agency found itself in a difficult position – its leaders did not want to endorse gay and lesbian adoptions, but they were also unwilling to explicitly discriminate based on sexual orientation.[124] The CDSS consequently developed a policy whereby social workers would only recommend adoptions by single individuals or married couples. However, the agency's employees, like their counterparts in New Hampshire, quickly developed a work-around. To encourage courts to grant the adoptions that they could not formally endorse, social workers stressed the suitability of the parents and explained that their negative recommendation was solely due to departmental policy.[125] Trial courts were able to deduce that they should grant the second-parent adoptions.

Hitchens's victory influenced the decisions of courts around the country, helping to produce a new legal regime. By 1992, over 200 lesbian couples had secured second-parent adoptions in seven states and the District of Columbia.[126] Just three years later, the number of states with second-parent adoptions had grown to eighteen.[127] Many of these cases involved women who had formed families through assisted reproduction, although they also featured women who had adopted children as single parents, rather than as a couple, because of unofficial antiqueer policies and biased child welfare agents. Second-parent adoption allowed same-sex couples to avoid the prejudice of some social workers and sidestep discriminatory regulations. Indeed, California judges' constant willingness to approve lesbian mothers' second-parent petitions rendered the discriminatory CDSS rule meaningless, exactly as social workers hoped.[128] Judicial oversight, like New Hampshire's "don't ask don't tell," became another way that same-sex couples were able to circumvent antiqueer laws.

The rapid success of second-parent adoptions was striking in light of courts' unwillingness to expand parentage doctrines to include lesbian mothers. The difference may have been that adoption petitions did not seem to open the door to the same range of custody and visitation claims as those of lesbian coparents. The spread of second-parent adoptions was also surprising given that the plain language of every state's law reserved stepparent adoptions for married couples. Courts therefore could easily have dismissed the women's claims – and some did. Judges often balked at second-parent adoptions, rooting their decisions in a textual analysis of the adoption statute.[129] Many others, however, devised various ways to make second-parent adoptions fit within their states' frameworks. Some focused on the ways in which lesbian couples were married in all but name. In one case from Indiana, a judge granted the petition of Janet Moor and Deborah Hentgen after finding that they "were an espoused couple." The court highlighted that the women had married in a church ceremony and changed their last names to "Hentgen-Moore."[130]

Few courts were willing to rule that lesbian couples were married for purposes of the state's adoption statute, but some were willing to eschew a strict textual analysis, focusing instead on the undeniable existence of these families. Judges recognized that, regardless of whether they granted the petitions, two women would continue to raise the children. The question was therefore whether granting the petitions would serve the children's best interests. As one New York court explained, in In re *Adoption of Caitlin*, the issue "was not whether, in the abstract, it is in the best interests of children to have two mothers, as opposed to a single mother or a mother and a father." Instead, the question before the court was whether, "given the realities of the relationships between the children and the petitioners and between the petitioners and the biological mothers, would the children herein be better or worse off if the adoptions were approved?"[131] When framed in that way, the answer was clear. The court granted the adoptions. Notably, the *Adoption of Caitlin* case arose three years after New York's highest court had rejected lesbian mothers' claims to parentage under equitable estoppel.[132] Second-parent adoptions had therefore become the only way for lesbian mothers in the state to protect their children.

Like in New York, judges in other parts of the country recognized that second-parent adoptions promoted the statutes' intent, which was to strengthen the emotional and financial security of children. Formally recognizing the relationship between parent and child would reinforce their psychological bond.[133] Additionally, adoptions conferred important legal rights on children, including inheritance and social security benefits in the event of a parent's death or disability. Both factors were central to the decisions. In one case, the trial judge commented that the child would be able to take advantage of the petitioning mother's generous employer-sponsored medical and education benefits.[134] The judge also noted that the adoption would confer important emotional benefits, describing those as "perhaps even more crucial than the financial."[135] Courts thus interpreted the language of the statutes broadly because the adoptions promoted the children's interests. Even if the women were not technically stepparents, judges determined that they were close enough.[136]

In their decisions, courts rarely addressed whether same-sex parents would affect the children's future sexual orientation. A few judges cited studies concluding that gay and lesbian parents were not more likely to have homosexual children.[137] However, courts were just as likely to discuss the children's welfare in general terms, noting that these children did not suffer any inherent disadvantage from having same-sex parents.[138] Judges may have been convinced that parents simply did not serve as role models for their sexual orientation, but their decision to sidestep the question may also have been pragmatic. Courts recognized that, even if they denied the adoptions, the children would still live with two mothers.[139] As a result, whether the court approved of the women's relationship was irrelevant to the child's daily life. The only question was whether the child was better off having two legal parents. The answer was invariably yes.

In ordering the adoptions, judges recognized that they were endorsing a different – and controversial – household arrangement. But they concluded that these families were simply one variation among many. As one New Jersey court remarked, "families have always been complex, multifaceted, and often idealized" and judges should not "continue to pretend that there is one formula, one correct pattern that should constitute a family."[140] Like cities and towns considering domestic partnership programs, the judges were aware of the changing composition of the American family. From their position on the bench, it was clear that family life was diverse, with more children being raised by unmarried partners, single mothers, and extended family members than ever before. By the early 1990s, households increasingly diverged from the traditional nuclear family model, which assumed different-sex spouses raised their biological children. For that reason, courts denied that they were creating a new type of family, insisting instead that they were only protecting ones that already existed.

Judges were correct that the adoption orders shielded the families of the lesbian baby boom. When tragedy struck, the children still had a legal parent. If a couple separated, the children were able to continue to see both parents. But the courts' decisions did more than recognize reality. They also shaped social conceptions of the family by expressing that genetic ties were not what made people parents. That expressive effect became increasingly important as ever-more queer families formed, becoming a visible presence in communities around the country. Greater numbers of Americans were consequently confronting same-sex sexuality in their day-today-lives, a fact that would require them also to decide what it meant to be a family.

Queer Family Visibility

Judy Jenkins's three children liked to sing a jingle about their two moms, which they adapted from the children's show *Barney and Friends*. On television, the purple dinosaur sang: "I love you, you love me. We're a happy family." Their version went: "I love you, you love me, homosexuality." The siblings would continue with the lines: "People think that we're just friends, but we're really lesbians." The children occasionally belted out the tune while grocery shopping in their hometown of Ypsilanti, Michigan, where they felt comfortable talking about their family life. Having two moms was so unremarkable in their community that, at show and tell, Jenkins's third grader could talk about the gay and lesbian parents' convention that he attended with his moms.[141]

Jenkins's family was one of a growing number of queer households that was out and proud in the early 1990s. By this time, the queer family's profile had risen significantly. Gay fathers and lesbian mothers had seized upon their roles as parents, hosting preschool picnics, volunteering at school functions, and running for the PTA.[142] Their efforts helped them become more visible as heads of households, as did the custody awards, foster care placements, and adoption orders. Once courts granted custody to queer parents and ruled in favor of their adoption petitions, other institutions had to recognize both partners as parents. Schools were required to give both fathers access to the child's records. Doctors had to involve both mothers in medical decision-making for the child. Medical plans and insurance companies had to offer family benefits to queer households.[143] In other words, the court orders helped make the queer family a more prevalent part of American society by giving gay and lesbian parental relationships the force of law. In the course of their interactions with queer households, some straight community members would come to agree with the courts that these were families like any other. Others, however, would try to push back against the growing wave of queer households.

FIGURE 12 Queer Made Family, March on Washington, 1993. In the early 1990s, queer households became increasingly visible throughout the country. Cathy Cade Photograph Archive, BANC PIC 2012.054–PIC, Box 8. © The Regents of the University of California, The Bancroft Library, University of California, Berkeley.

Queer families did not exist in all parts of the country, but they became nationally known in the early 1990s when the mainstream press suddenly "discovered" lesbian families created through assisted reproduction. Journalists from major outlets began publishing regularly on the lesbian baby boom, informing their readers of the rising numbers of legally recognized queer families.[144] In 1992, the *New York Times* ran a front-page article on the subject, complete with a photograph of a happy gay family playing a board game before football practice.[145] The story noted that so many queer families had formed in the 1980s that numerous organizations had sprung up to support them, offering picnics, barbecues, dances, rodeos, and conferences where lesbian mothers, gay fathers, and their children could meet others with similar households.[146] The largest of these groups was a national organization called COLAGE, for Children of Lesbians and Gays Everywhere, which held conferences, distributed resources, and connected members looking for pen pals.[147]

Social acceptance of these legal families came in fits and starts. When Soji Bargeron's family moved to Northern Virginia in the mid-1980s, she endured so much bullying for having a lesbian mom that she would run away from school crying. After almost a decade, she continued to hear derogatory comments, but her teachers were supportive and many of her friends thought it was "cool" that her mother was queer.[148] In nearby Columbia, Maryland, Jan Nyquist's neighbor refused to allow her daughter to play with Nyquist's two sons because Nyquist was a lesbian living with a woman. Nyquist went to the neighbor's home to introduce herself. As she later explained, once the neighbors knew her personally, they allowed the children to play together and her sexual orientation was "no big deal."[149] Across the country, in the Bay Area, Sharon and Irene's relationship barely registered to those in their children's lives. When Jennifer told people she had three mothers and one father, people typically assumed her family was Mormon.[150]

The growing visibility of households headed by gays and lesbians sparked a new set of debates over the place of same-sex sexuality in American society. As the experiences of Bargeron and Nyquist illustrated, not all towns were as welcoming as Yspilanti. However, community members who objected to same-sex sexuality could do little about the existence of these households. Queer parents had legal rights, which institutions were required to respect. What dissenters could do was register their disdain, as well as express their views that these gay and lesbian households were both different and dangerous. One way they did so was by leading efforts to censor books on queer households, which publishers began producing in the late 1980s. In 1989, *Heather Has Two Mommies* hit bookstores around the country, telling the story of Mama Jane and Mama Kate, who had a child named Heather through artificial insemination.[151] The next year, the same publisher released *Daddy's Roommate*, a story about a boy, his father, and the father's partner, Frank.[152] The goal of these books was to support the growing number of children with gay and lesbian parents, but the texts soon became targets of antiqueer animosity.

Those battles began in 1992, when community members in Goldsboro, North Carolina, tried to have *Daddy's Roommate* banned from the public library.[153] Karen Grant, who led the opposition, discovered the book after her 6-year-old began looking at its colorful pictures. Grant was enraged to see a character in the book explain that being gay "is just one more kind of love and love is the best kind of happiness."[154] Although Grant described the passage as "anti-family," other Goldsboro residents disagreed. Chief among them was a 17-year-old named Matt, whose parents had divorced several years earlier when his father came out as gay. Matt told the library board that having had access to the book would have helped him to better navigate a difficult moment in his life. Matt's testimony introduced members of his community to queer households, as well as helped to convince the library's board of trustees to keep the book on the shelves.[155]

Debates over *Daddy's Roommate* and *Heather Has Two Mommies* continued to divide towns all around the nation for years to come. In 1993, attempts to censor the stories were so common that the texts topped the American Library Association's list of most targeted books.[156] To avoid outright bans, library boards in Georgia, Missouri, New Jersey, North Carolina, and Virginia reclassified the texts as "adult non-fiction," often requiring patrons to request copies by name.[157] In other communities, residents expressed their outrage by stealing the books from the library shelves. Larceny was so widespread that the books' publisher offered free replacement copies of *Heather*

Has Two Mommies to the first 500 libraries that reported the theft.[158] The company also produced other texts, including *Gloria Goes to Gay Pride* and *How Would You Feel if Your Dad Was Gay?*, thereby providing additional resources to support the children of queer parents.[159] Importantly, not all libraries ceded to pressure to withdraw the books. The Louisville, Kentucky public library, for example, retained *Heather Has Two Mommies* despite vocal protests.[160] Its director reminded critics that, although some objected to same-sex sexuality, others did not, and the library needed to serve everyone. If parents did not want their children to read the books, that was their choice – but it was not the role of the state to limit a resource that reflected the wide variety of household arrangements that existed around the country.

These censorship battles were minor fronts in communities' wars against queer families. Of course, for gay and lesbian parents who had to fight their neighbors, the events were demoralizing. Yet the fact that these debates emerged at all was a marker of how much more visible the queer family had become. When Mary Jo Risher fought for custody in 1975, queer parents were unheard of in most of the country. Just two decades later, that was no longer true. Custody disputes like Risher's had given rise to new scientific conceptions of same-sex sexuality, which in turn had helped convince social workers and judges to approve foster placements and adoption petitions. The parents who, like Risher, went to court for custody rights had been fighting for their families. But the scientific studies that their lawsuits had produced had a much broader effect, making it possible for other gay men and lesbians to become parents through foster care and adoption.

The debates over foster care and adoption had helped queer households form all around the country. Queer families lived in large cities, mid-size towns, and small rural areas. By 1993, studies estimated that at least 2 million children had at least one gay or lesbian parent.[161] Some of these children were born to lesbian mothers and gay fathers in different-sex relationships, who came out after their sons and daughters were born. However, as gay liberation spread, more of these parents created families with their same-sex partners. The foster care and adoption battles of the 1980s, which gave rise to foster placements, adoptions out of foster care, and second-parent adoptions, helped to reshape the American family. By the early-1990s, queer households had become

commonplace, so much so that family-centered policies became a movement priority. These families also changed the backdrop for debates
over queer rights more generally. Gays and lesbians were no longer
fighting as individuals, who were vying for sexual freedom. Instead, they
were battling as committed couples and heads of household, who were
arguing for the rights of their families.

* * *

In 1993, Tim Fischer, a gay man who was raising two children with his
partner in Montclair, New Jersey, told the *New York Times* that life
had changed dramatically for queer families. As he explained, "We
used to say we were invisible, but no longer."[162] If anything, Fisher's
assertion was an understatement. By the time the article appeared,
queer families – formed through custody cases, foster care placements,
and adoption orders – could be seen in playgrounds and at schools
around the country. These households helped to shift popular understandings of same-sex sexuality. Media images of queer life were no
longer limited to furtive assignations in dingy bars or lonely nights
spent cruising for strangers. Instead, journalists increasingly associated
gays and lesbians with playgrounds, schools, and minivans. That
vision of queer life was not an accurate representation of many – or
even most – members of the queer community. However, the fact was
that a growing number of same-sex couples were raising children.

Social workers had helped to make that shift possible, through
foster care placements and adoption home studies that had given rise
to ever-larger numbers of households headed by gays and lesbians.
Community members interacted with these families at schools and
playgrounds, or came across depictions of them in children's books
at the libraries. Librarians and social workers are not the typical agents
of law reform, but they served those roles in state and local battles over
foster care, adoption, and censorship. The families they helped create
and publicize contributed to a change in many Americans' conceptions
of same-sex sexuality. That, in turn, aided gay and lesbian rights
advocates in combatting Christian conservatives' opposition to the
community's rights.

The religious right had long succeeded in opposing queer rights by
claiming that gays and lesbians were harmful to children. However,

adoption orders and foster care licenses maintained that the opposite was true, with each one undermining Christian conservatives' antiqueer stance. Second-parent adoptions, which framed intended mothers as stepparents, had a similar effect. In addition to helping recast gay and lesbian couples as akin to married spouses, the decisions identified the women as so devoted to their partners and children that they affirmatively took on a legal obligation of care. The orders conveyed a powerful expressive message to American society, communicating that the state approved of same-sex parents and their homes. Like foster care placements, adoption decrees helped to make the queer family a legal and social reality.

By the early 1990s, the queer family had become an increasingly common part of American life. But even as gay and lesbian parents gained legal ground, securing rights to custody, foster care licenses, and second-parent adoptions, same-sex sexuality continued to be highly controversial. For many Americans, gays and lesbians were not loving family members, but rather dangerous vectors of disease. The queer community had long suffered at the hands of bigoted assailants, whose prejudice all too often manifested in violence. As gay and lesbian rights advocates struggled to stem the tide of hatred, the queer family would come to play an essential role in combatting bias. This time, however, the queer family did not only comprise same-sex couples and their children. It now included the parents of queer children, who rushed to assist their gay sons and lesbian daughters.

Part II

Straight Parents, Queer Children

In the spring of 1987, doctors at the Mayo Clinic in Rochester, Minnesota told Dean Lechner that the reason for his wheezing and coughing was not bronchitis, as they had previously thought. It was AIDS. Upon hearing the devastating diagnosis, Dean called his family to tell them he was not returning home to Waseca. A few months earlier, the 34-year-old had moved back to the small farming community in southern Minnesota, hoping to start a business with his brother. When he fell ill, he stayed in bed for two weeks, until his neck tightened to the point where he could no longer breathe. At that point, he called for an ambulance, which rushed him to the hospital for evaluation.

The news Dean received at the clinic upended his life. At the time, AIDS was a death sentence. Dean knew that the disease would ravage both his body and mind. He could not imagine putting his family through the pain of seeing him deteriorate. Dean also did not want them to endure the stigma that came from having a family member with HIV. He was well aware that, in other small towns around the country, schools, restaurants, and swimming pools had made it a point to exclude people suffering from the disease. Dean consequently thought it better to return to San Francisco, where he had spent most of his adult life, working at a political fundraising company. His sister, Barbara, immediately disabused her brother of his plan, telling Dean: "Dogs go off to die, Dean – and you're no dog .... You're a son; you're a brother. And you are loved."[1]

Barbara, a church organist, knew all about sickness and stigma. In 1948, five years before Dean was born, their brother contracted polio. The state health department nailed a sign to the family's front door, warning others to stay away from the white clapboard house on the nameless country road. The family quarantined for six weeks. When they emerged, 12-year-old Barbara began protecting her younger sibling from the boys who would knock him down and throw his crutches into the snow. Barbara was prepared to fight for Dean just as ferociously. So was their mother, Elvira. After Dean returned home, the 68-year-old wrapped her frail arms around her son. She then began watching over him day and night, making sure that he ate and took his medicine. She stopped attending bingo so she could be by his side constantly. Years earlier, she had been similarly supportive when she learned that Dean was gay. Elvira had gone to visit him in San Francisco shortly after he relocated to the Bay Area. Dean had not known how to come out to her before she arrived, so he simply let her see that he lived in a one-bedroom apartment with another man. In response, Elvira had stammered, initially unable to express her feelings. But the message that Dean took away from her was clear: "You are my son, and I love you."[2]

The Lechner family did more than help Dean face a terrifying and debilitating illness. Through their unconditional love and support, they also helped form a foundation for broader social change. Elvira, Barbara, and other straight family members allowed their communities to see that gays and lesbians were an integral part of American society, rather than members of a shadowy, separate world.[3] The men and women who, like Dean, braved societal prejudice, communicated to their neighbors, colleagues, and communities that gays and lesbians were no different from everyone else. Their parents, grandparents, and siblings then disseminated this message more widely, capitalizing upon their ability to reach mainstream Americans who were distrustful of queer rights advocates. Their heterosexual identity offered a powerful strategic advantage, one that these straight family members eagerly leveraged to promote gay and lesbian rights. Additionally, these relatives made explicit what the fights for gay and lesbian parental rights had only suggested: that same-sex sexual attraction was an innate, benign, and widespread characteristic. Queer adults had once been queer children, raised in conventional households. That fact demonstrated that same-sex sexuality was not a difference to be repressed, but rather an ordinary aspect of traditional families.

Many of these straight family members began their advocacy efforts after seeing the harassment and violence that their gay and lesbian relatives suffered because of their sexual orientation. Dean may have grown up with a supportive family, but his peers ridiculed their classmate for being gay. When he was 17, the abuse he endured turned violent. At a school dance, someone hit him over the head with a beer bottle. After he picked himself off the floor, Dean got into his car, but his attackers pursued him, trying to run him off the road. Dean made it home, but not to safety. After he closed the garage door, he left the motor running while he debated whether life was worth continuing. Years later, when the AIDS diagnosis made him once again face death, Dean wondered how his hometown would react. His fear that Waseca would close its doors to him never materialized. Instead, after the town's newspaper printed a headline announcing his condition, community members welcomed Dean back with open arms – literally. Many stopped him on the street to offer hugs. Almost 200 well-wishers also sent cards, books, poems, and prayers. At the high school reunion he attended, Dean's former tormentors approached him, one by one, to apologize.[4]

In the 1980s, few places responded to AIDS sufferers in the same way as Waseca. Neighbors were more likely to turn their backs on members of the queer community than they were to embrace gays and lesbians. Parents often rejected their children, rather than supporting them in their dying days.[5] Indeed, prejudice and intolerance against the queer community increased as HIV became a national crisis. Violence against gays and lesbians soared, creating what advocates described as an epidemic of hate.[6] The queer community mobilized in response, pressing for police reform and hate crimes legislation. But gays and lesbians struggled to convince Americans that bigotry, hatred, and violence were more dangerous than same-sex sexuality. It took parents of queer children, like Elvira, to reframe the debate. Their efforts helped the country see that the queer family was more than same-sex partners and their children. It also comprised straight parents, who loved their gay sons and lesbian daughters. This image of the queer family would prove crucial to combatting the attitudes that all too often turned deadly.

5

Combatting Violence

Protecting the Queer Community on the Streets and in the Schools

The attack began near San Francisco's Buena Vista Park, a well-known queer cruising site.[1] A group of teens descended upon a gay man, punching him in the face, kicking him in the back, and striking him with a bottle – all in front of fifty onlookers. The attackers seemed untroubled by having so many witnesses to their crime. As it turned out, their indifference was justified. Not a single person tried to help, not even the police. The man made desperate attempts to flag down first a patrol car, then two motorcycle officers, as the teens chased him down the street. The police ignored his cries. The man was finally able to find refuge in a neighborhood bar, which offered him shelter until it was safe for him to go back outside.[2]

The teens' assault was brutal, brazen, and entirely unexceptional. It was just one of more than 1,700 attacks on gay men and lesbians that queer groups documented in the first eight months of 1983.[3] Community United Against Violence (CUAV), a San Francisco queer antiviolence organization, included a lone paragraph on the incident when describing a recent spate of attacks on gays and lesbians in a community newspaper. It was one of the few places where CUAV provided detail on the incidents that it recorded. Violent attacks indelibly marked the lives of the victims, leaving them with emotional – and often physical – scars. However, there were simply too many acts of violence for the organization to go into depth on any single event. As a result, CUAV typically limited its reports to aggregations of data, cataloging whether the victim was harassed, threatened, or assaulted.[4]

During the 1980s, the queer community was under constant attack. Gays and lesbians had long been the targets of violence, but the AIDS crisis unleashed a new torrent of animosity against the queer community. As hatred rose, so too did physical assaults.[5] Passersby often shouted slurs at gay men and lesbians. Others threw glass bottles. Still other assailants punched, kicked, or stabbed queer victims, selecting their targets because of their sexual orientation. These perpetrators, who would descend into gay and lesbian neighborhoods to express their contempt for same-sex sexuality, often used such force that victims had to be hospitalized.[6] The gay and lesbian community was not even safe off the streets, as queer bars, clubs, and community centers became the targets of bomb threats.[7] Even queer-friendly religious institutions were attacked. In Jacksonville, Florida, the situation was so dire that one such church had to have bulletproof windows installed.[8] These acts of violence sent a shudder of fear through the queer community, reminding its members that they could become the target of hate at any time.[9]

Most of these attackers were teenagers, who knew little about the queer world other than the prejudice they had learned from the adults in their lives.[10] Because so many assailants were adolescents, rates of violence rose sharply when school let out, only to decline just as dramatically when classes reconvened in the fall.[11] Of course, straight youth did not just torment queer adults – they also directed their anger and hatred at their peers. Gay and lesbian teens, as well as youth suspected of being queer, endured rampant rejection, harassment, and violence from their classmates, which reinforced the hateful messages they received from teachers, parents, and community members. As a result, a substantial percentage of queer youth dropped out of school, abused alcohol and drugs, and considered ending their despair with their own hands.[12] Indeed, by the end of the 1980s, suicide had become the leading cause of death among gay and lesbian adolescents.[13] There were thus two types of violence that marked the lives of queer youth: assaults from peers, as well as harm that the teens inflicted on themselves.

Gay and lesbian rights advocates knew they needed to act. Members of the queer community could not go out in public without risking harassment, physical attacks, and even death, which made it impossible for gays and lesbians to be open about their sexual orientation. Until the violence abated, the price of being out was far too high. But how to combat the danger was a difficult question to answer, leading advocates to adopt various approaches to resolving the problem. Some focused on preventing attacks on the streets. Others, typically teachers and parents of queer children, focused on creating support systems in schools, so that gay and lesbian teens would not give up hope for a better future. Efforts to shape educational policies may seem like matters of politics rather than law. Educational materials and programs, however, are governed by state and local administrative regulations.[14]

Together, these campaigns helped to make visible the high rates of violence that gays and lesbians suffered.[15] The projects did not end violence against queer adults, nor did they stop gay and lesbian youth from committing suicide at alarming rates. Indeed, both problems continue to be pervasive. These campaigns were nevertheless consequential. They demonstrated to straight society that antiqueer bigotry could have dangerous effects. They also made visible the straight parents of gay and lesbian children, who would become crucial advocates for queer rights. These family members would help many Americans recognize that gays and lesbians were an integral part of traditional households, which made queer rights appear less threatening. Moreover, by focusing on the safety of gay and lesbian children, these parents furthered a different goal that was fundamental to the establishment of queer family rights in the United States. Their campaigns helped to transform the meaning of child protection in the context of same-sex sexuality. By arguing that same-sex attraction was an inherent attribute rather than a learned behavior, these parents suggested that children did not need to be protected from gays and lesbians. Instead, it was queer youth who needed protection – from harassment, bigotry, and violence.

When advocates began these campaigns in the early 1980s, they initially turned to the police for help. However, too many officers saw gays and lesbians not as the victims of crime, but rather as its perpetrators. Advocates' first task would therefore be to convince law enforcement that antiqueer violence was a problem. As they focused on that work, they also took protection into their own hands, patrolling the streets of queer neighborhoods to make the streets safer for their community. The slogan of one of the groups, "queers bash back," was as sincere as it was campy. Gays and lesbians had had enough.[16]

Unsafe Streets

Their fuchsia berets marked them as members of San Francisco's Street Patrol. Every Friday and Saturday night, they walked the streets of the Castro in groups of five, armed only with two-way radios, handcuffs, and notebooks to jot down the license plate numbers of assailants. At the sound of whistles, which community groups had distributed by the tens of thousands, they came running, hoping to detain attackers until the police could take them into custody.[17] In the late 1980s and early 1990s, gay and lesbian street patrols formed around the country to deter violence, support victims, and assist law enforcement in investigating crimes.[18] The Streetcats monitored the West Hollywood district of Los Angeles, the Q Patrol safeguarded Houston's Montrose neighborhood, and the Pink Angels marched through Chicago's North Side.[19] In New York, the Pink Panthers patrolled Greenwich Village, at least until MGM sued the group for copyright infringement.[20] Similar groups sprang up in Boston, Dallas, Kansas City, Philadelphia, and Seattle, all dedicated to the same cause: allowing gays and lesbians to walk in queer neighborhoods and socialize in queer establishments free of harassment, abuse, and violence.[21]

The patrols helped make streets safer, but they did not solve the broader problem of violence that was tormenting queer communities around the country. In the mid-1980s and early 1990s, as the AIDS epidemic raged with no end in sight, rates of bias-motivated crimes against gays and lesbians soared.[22] To obtain relief from the urgent problem of violence, advocates lobbied law enforcement to address the rise in antiqueer crime. That was easier said than done. Despite their mandate to protect the public, the police rarely took violence against gays and lesbians seriously. The challenge for advocates was convincing law enforcement that the queer community deserved protection. For that, the police needed to see gays and lesbians as the victims of crime, rather than its perpetrators. Framing the queer community as victims was in some ways a risky decision. Casting an identity group as a population apart, even to extend legal protections, often stigmatizes its members.[23] However, in the context of queer rights, advocates did not have much to lose. To many Americans, gays and lesbians already seemed dangerous, deviant, and diseased.

When queer rights advocates began their work, they had no trouble identifying the cause of the uptick in violence. While violent crime had risen across the nation in the 1970s and 1980s, assailants began targeting gays and lesbians in particular due to the community's increased visibility.[24] There was a deep irony to this fact, given that the gay liberation movement had emphasized "coming out" in the 1970s as a means of reducing bias and prejudice.[25] As it turned out, queer visibility was a double-edged sword. The decriminalization of consensual sodomy and the elimination of vagrancy laws had made it easier for gays and lesbians to be open about their sexual orientation, but these changes had not consistently translated into greater acceptance. If anything, the community's increased visibility made it easier for assailants to find victims. Gays and lesbians who were open about their sexual orientation frequently became targets of hate. The NGLTF put the problem most bluntly: "As growing numbers of us who choose to live openly as lesbians and gay men, the numbers of those who want to bludgeon us back into the closet also grows."[26]

The connection between visibility and violence only increased over the course of the 1980s, as the AIDS epidemic brought more attention to queer communities. The widespread association of homosexuality with the fatal disease exacerbated already entrenched biases against gays and lesbians. As Randy Schell, one of CUAV's co-founders, explained: "People are getting the message that gay equals AIDS, that it's OK to hate these people and it's OK to do something about it."[27] David McKirnan, a psychologist at the University of Illinois at Chicago, put the connection in different terms. Homophobia was based on the idea that gays and lesbians would "do something" to straight people. AIDS seemed to provide a tangible illustration of the harm that same-sex sexuality posed to society.[28] In 1992, a survey by the National Association of People with AIDS revealed that more than 20 percent of respondents had been victimized because of their HIV status.[29] CUAV consequently began speaking of both homophobia and "AIDS-phobia" as the cause of violence against gays and lesbians.[30] Attackers, for their part, often explicitly tied their crimes to AIDS, making clear that the deadly disease had motivated their hate. As they descended on members of the queer community, some would scream invectives like "You faggots gave us AIDS" or "Here come the AIDS carriers, let's get them!"[31] In Superior, Wisconsin, an assailant confessed that he had stabbed a gay man to death because homosexuals "spread AIDS."[32] Other AIDS-related crimes were not violent, yet nevertheless terrifying. One HIV-positive New Yorker came home to find "Faggot with AIDS" scrawled on his apartment door and a puddle of gasoline in his entryway.[33]

As the AIDS epidemic continued, assaults against gays and lesbians around the nation did not just become more frequent – they also became increasingly severe.[34] In 1987, CUAV documented that a greater percentage of victims in San Francisco were requiring medical attention, hospitalization, and surgery than ever before.[35] All too many members of the queer community died at the hands of bigots, perishing in brutal ways. As Schell chillingly expressed, when asked to describe attacks on gays and lesbians, "[a]nything you could imagine being used to desecrate another human being has been used."[36] Year after year, CUAV, the National Violence Project, and other antiviolence organizations reported appallingly high numbers of violent crimes, from all corners of the country.[37] These groups collected data from more than thirty states and the District of Columbia to paint a bleak picture of queer life in America. Some of those increases may have been the result of more victims reporting the crimes, but it seemed clear to advocates that violence itself was on the rise.[38] Violence became so rampant that antiviolence groups described it as having "reached epidemic proportions."[39]

The queer community, which had to live with the constant fear of attacks, was all too familiar with the problem. The challenge for advocates was that the violence was often invisible to the straight world. Although gay and lesbian community papers regularly printed accounts of the crisis in the mid-1980s, the information was largely absent from the mainstream press. Because of the AIDS epidemic, gays and lesbians typically appeared in newspaper pages as dangerous vectors of disease, not as victims of crime. In 1986, the *New York Times* published the first major mainstream media article on the scope and extent of antiqueer violence.[40] That article – which only appeared on page thirty-six of the paper – almost never made it to print. The journalist drafted the piece using statistics and reports from gay and lesbian antiviolence advocates, but the editor rejected that data as biased. He initially insisted on corroboration from state or national law enforcement, but ultimately relented because that information simply did not exist.[41] At the time, few law enforcement agencies tracked hate crimes against gays and lesbians – or anyone at all. Cash-strapped police rarely had the resources to invest in these kinds of efforts. Instead, they used their limited funds for other priorities.[42]

Because police did not collect this data, officers were as unaware of the violence as the general public. That fact was especially worrying for queer rights advocates, for two reasons. First, police could not investigate crimes they did not know about, which further emboldened assailants.[43] Attackers struck in broad daylight, with streets full of witnesses, like the incident near Buena Vista Park. The assaults demonstrated that perpetrators had little fear of arrest or prosecution.[44] As a representative from the Philadelphia Gay and Lesbian Task Force explained, attackers viewed members of the queer community as "easy targets" because police were unlikely to ever hold these assailants accountable for their crimes.[45] The second problem was that, since police departments did not understand that a crisis was underway, they refused to dedicate resources to combatting antiqueer crime. Indeed, despite advocates' evidence to the contrary, major police departments flatly denied that bias crimes against gays and lesbians were on the rise.[46]

If convincing the police to collect data and investigate the crimes was not enough, advocates had yet another challenge to confront: a reluctance on the part of victims to disclose the assaults. The information that antiviolence groups had been gathering since the late 1970s and early 1980s consistently showed that more than 75 percent of the victims never reported the attacks to law enforcement.[47] Victims had various reasons for keeping silent. Some feared that filing police reports would out them to their families, colleagues, and neighbors.[48] Although more members of the queer community were open about their sexual orientation in the 1980s, being out continued to be a risky proposition. Gays and lesbians often lost their jobs, homes, and families, such that many men and women were understandably reluctant to have their sexual orientation become known. Others refused to report the crimes because they were afraid of the reception they would receive at the police station. Law enforcement officials often treated queer victims with indifference, if not outright hostility.[49] When Michael Cameron, a professor of music at the University of Illinois, approached a patrol car to report the beating he had suffered on a Chicago street, the officers drove away.[50] That was a better response than what a Raleigh, North Carolina, bar owner named Warren Kilby experienced. When Kilby tried to report that a man had stabbed him during their tryst, the police warned Kilby that they would arrest him for sodomy if he insisted on pressing charges.[51] Those reactions were cruel, but not surprising. Police officers shared in the antiqueer biases that plagued society. If anything, law enforcement's role in enforcing vagrancy and antisodomy laws had likely deepened some of the officers' prejudices.[52]

Gay and lesbian rights groups consequently recognized that, for any data-collection efforts to show the true extent of the violence, they would first need to increase reporting. Advocates therefore pressed law enforcement agencies to institute wide-ranging reforms, some of which they had been seeking since the 1970s.[53] They demanded that departments require sensitivity training, appoint liaisons to the gay and lesbian community, and hire openly queer officers.[54] The gay and lesbian community pressed for these changes at every opportunity. When the Los Angeles Police Department (LAPD) held a meeting to address concerns about violence in the queer neighborhood of Silver Lake, attendees quickly focused the discussion on the biased attitudes of some police officers, emphasizing that the LAPD needed to make changes to training and recruitment.[55] The queer community's ability to secure change depended in large part on the political clout they wielded.[56] In Houston and Seattle, the relationship between gays, lesbians, and the police improved significantly after the queer community helped elect a sympathetic mayor. In Washington, D.C., Mayor Marion Barry rewarded gay and lesbian rights advocates for their assistance with his first mayoral election by involving them in the selection of the new chief of police.[57] The man who the committee chose for the role subsequently appointed a liaison to the gay and lesbian community. He also made clear to rank and file officers that the department would no longer tolerate antiqueer attitudes.[58]

Over the course of the 1980s, as gays and lesbians became more involved in local politics, many major police departments implemented the changes that the queer community demanded. In Washington, D.C., the department set up a recruitment booth at the city's Pride festival.[59] In Philadelphia, after the city's Lesbian and Gay Task Force met with the police commissioner, he endorsed the need for sensitivity training "for cultural, ethnic, racial and sexual differences."[60] His department later announced it would form an antibias unit to handle complaints of antiqueer crime.[61] In New York, where the police department already had a special unit to investigate hate crimes based on race and religion, the commissioner extended its mandate to address antiqueer violence.[62] These changes were uneven, with attitudes often varying by city, precinct, and officer.[63] In Minneapolis, one gay man joked that, if he were ever badly beaten, he would crawl his way into St. Paul, where officers were known to be a bit more respectful toward the queer community.[64] Given the extensive bias of police officers, antiviolence groups continued their work for decades.[65] Yet, by the late 1980s, the relationship between queer communities and the police had improved significantly in many major cities.[66]

Advocates had been able to secure important reforms, but the changes were slow, small, and scattershot. Antiviolence groups had data going back to the 1970s that showed police bias was a major problem, yet they had only been able to make inroads in a small percentage of police departments. The queer community knew that, to prevent violence from happening, they had to find a broader and more comprehensive solution to the problem. Gays and lesbians needed Americans to understand that antiqueer prejudice was far from harmless. On the contrary, bias could quickly become harassment, violence, and murder. Combatting violence thus required that the public see the link between hate and crime. Fortunately for gay and lesbian rights advocates, states were in the midst of debating laws that could help them do just that.

Legislating against Hate

Leo Treadway had two distinguishing features: a bushy white beard and a clerical collar.[67] In 1981, the openly gay Vietnam War veteran had helped found the Wingspan Ministry, which provided pastoral care to Minneapolis's queer community.[68] Wingspan was a program of St. Paul-Reformation, a Lutheran congregation. Treadway had first encountered the parish in the late 1970s, when Anita Bryant came to St. Paul to campaign against the city's sexual orientation antidiscrimination law. The pastor of St. Paul-Reformation had contacted Treadway to ask how his congregation could support the gay and lesbian rights ordinance.[69] When Treadway later had the idea for Wingspan, he knew exactly which church would offer a welcoming home.

Because of Treadway's long-standing work with the Minneapolis queer community, the Minnesota governor approached him in 1987 to serve on a newly formed Task Force on Prejudice and Violence.[70] The purpose of the Task Force was to collect data on bias-motivated violence in the state, which advocates hoped would convince legislators to enact a hate crimes law.[71] Elected officials had previously blocked a proposed hate crimes statute, which included protections based on "affectional or sexual orientation." One of the main arguments against the bill was the absence of evidence that perpetrators targeted individuals because of their sexuality.[72] These legislators simply did not see gays and lesbians as the victims of crime. The invisibility of the violence had thus prevented Minnesota's queer community members from obtaining the legal protections they desperately needed.

To address elected officials' objections, the Task Force quickly set to work gathering data. Its members spent thirty-six hours listening to nearly 150 witnesses at eight public hearings around the state.[73] Almost a quarter of the testimony addressed crimes based on sexual orientation, thanks largely to the calls that Treadway had put out to the queer community.[74] In drafting its findings, the Task Force supplemented the close to 1,300 pages of testimony with 200 pages of published sources, including studies from the NGLTF's Anti-Violence Project and reports of attacks on gays and lesbians in the press.[75] The efforts of the Task Force paid off. In 1988, the legislature enacted a hate crimes law that included protections based on sexual orientation.[76]

Minnesota was not the only state to enact a hate crimes statute in the late 1980s and early 1990s. Hate-motivated offenses were an age-old problem, but it was during this period that the concept of "hate crimes" emerged. That new theoretical lens helped make the issue appear more urgent, as well as made additional legal solutions available to solve the problem.[77] The hate crimes laws that advocates devised took various forms.[78] Some statutes created new criminal provisions, while others enhanced the penalty for existing offenses, created private rights of action for victims, or required law enforcement to track hate crime incidents.[79] The laws were often called anti-intimidation and antiterrorism bills, and they defined hate crimes differently. Typically, though, they addressed perpetrators who committed unlawful actions because of their prejudice toward the victim's social group.[80]

The movement to enact hate crimes protections, which grew during these years, provided an opportunity for gay and lesbian rights advocates. Hate crimes protections would publicize that violence against the queer community was on the rise, thereby making gays and lesbians visible as victims of crime. Criminologists warned that the laws could be counterproductive. Hate crimes statutes implicitly acknowledged that assailants targeted gays and lesbians for their difference, which could have the harmful effect of reinforcing the queer community's outsider status.[81] However, these arguments had little effect on a community that was struggling to make clear the dangers of antiqueer bigotry. At the time, few Americans recognized that bias was the problem they had to guard against. To the contrary, between Cold War depictions of gays and lesbians as security threats, the religious right's assertion that same-sex attraction constituted a physical threat to children, and the association between the queer community and AIDS, most identified the main peril as homosexuality itself.

Queer rights advocates were not concerned with promoting any specific type of hate crimes statute. Most also did not stop to consider the racialized effects of expanding the criminal justice system.[82] Instead, their focus was on making sure that any hate crimes law included protections for sexual orientation, in order to make the violence against gays and lesbians visible. Attaining that goal was an uphill battle, as the first wave of these statutes only addressed crimes based on race, ethnicity, and religion.[83] As more states debated these new types of laws, gay and lesbian antiviolence organizations lobbied to link hate violence and queer victimhood.

Over the course of the 1980s, these groups made some gains. In 1984, California began requiring its police to collect data on sexual orientation-motivated offenses.[84] Three years later, Wisconsin became the first state to impose additional penalties for sexual orientation-based crimes.[85] Cities like Atlanta, Columbus, St. Louis, and Seattle also enacted hate crimes laws that included protections based on sexual orientation.[86] Despite these successes, sexual orientation-inclusive hate crimes protections were few and far between. By 1990, half of the states had some type of hate crimes law, but only five states and the District of Columbia had extended their statute's provisions to sexual orientation.[87] Legislators balked at including sexual orientation in the bills for the exact same reason that gay and lesbian advocates pressed for its inclusion.[88] As one elected official explained, he opposed a sexual orientation-inclusive hate crimes law because it created "a powerful, symbolic message" that the state considered same-sex sexuality acceptable.[89]

In 1990, the legal landscape changed decisively. That year, Congress enacted the Hate Crimes Statistics Act, which required the attorney general to collect and publish data on hate-motivated crimes, including those spurred by antiqueer bias.[90] Federal officials had first introduced the law, which initially only extended to racial, ethnic, or religious prejudice, in 1985. When the Senate failed to consider the bill before the legislative session adjourned, the NGLTF saw an opportunity.[91] The group convinced openly gay Congressman Barney Frank to amend the bill to include sexual orientation within the list of protected characteristics, and then joined a coalition of groups advocating for the bill's passage.[92] This change to the proposed law's purview generated heated debate. Although members of Congress were enthusiastic about combatting prejudice, some opposed equating same-sex sexuality with race and ethnicity.[93] Others, like Congressman George Gerkas of Pennsylvania, feared that the law would serve as "a subtle but a significant step toward normalizing homosexuality."[94] In the Senate, Jesse Helms shared a similar view. He consequently tried to scuttle the law by proposing a series of amendments, including one that read "[t]he homosexual movement threatens the strength and the survival of the American family as the basic unit of society."[95]

During other political moments, these objections might have torpedoed the bill. However, in the late 1980s and early 1990s, a series of scandals had left the religious right in shambles, reducing its power over national politics.[96] In 1985, members of the Moral Majority began leaving in droves after the group's president, Jerry Falwell, loudly defended the white apartheid South African government.[97] Two years later, a young woman alleged that popular televangelist Jim Bakker had drugged and sexually assaulted her, then purchased her silence with church funds.[98] Others soon added their own claims of impropriety against the minister, including charges that Bakker had engaged in same-sex activities.[99] Given the turmoil surrounding the religious right, Republican voters unsurprisingly spurned more conservative candidates for U.S. president in 1988.[100] They rejected a bid by Pat Robertson – a religious broadcaster and ordained Baptist minister – in favor of George H.W. Bush.[101] Unlike his predecessors, Bush made no effort to solicit the evangelical vote during the election, reasoning that Christian conservatives were unlikely to support his Democratic opponent, Michael Dukakis.[102] Once in office, Bush dashed what was left of evangelicals' low expectations when he selected a pro-choice doctor to lead the Department of Health and Human Services.[103]

The religious right would ultimately manage to rise from these ashes, but not before Congress had debated and passed the sexual orientation-inclusive Hate Crimes Statistics Act.[104] The statute was the first piece of federal legislation to recognize the problem of antiqueer violence. Moreover, when President Bush signed the bill into law, he conferred an important symbolic victory on the queer rights movement – he invited gay and lesbian rights advocates to the ceremonial signing, marking the first time that movement leaders had been welcomed to the White House for such an event.[105] Gay and lesbian rights advocates consequently celebrated the passage of the law, even as they recognized its limitations.[106] The legislation did not create a new category of crime, increase punishments for hate offenses, or provide a private cause of action for victims. Although the statute required the attorney general to issue an annual report on hate crimes, states did not have to collect any information or transmit their data to the federal government. Because of these limitations, many advocates later criticized the government's publications for underreporting hate violence in America.[107] The law was problematic for another reason. Although the religious right's influence over Congress had waned, Christian conservatives still held enough sway that lawmakers agreed to compromise on the language of the bill. They amended the statute so that it read "[n]othing in this Act shall be construed ... to promote or encourage homosexuality."[108] The law thus simultaneously protected gays and lesbians and denigrated them.

The statute nevertheless constituted a significant milestone, as well as an important victory for the queer community, because it conferred legitimacy on same-sex sexuality.[109] It suggested that gays and lesbians were akin to racial, ethnic, and religious minorities, groups entitled to heightened legal and constitutional protections. The law thus implied that homosexuality was immutable, like the other protected traits. This formulation of same-sex sexuality would have been anathema to gay liberationists and lesbian feminists, who in the 1970s rejected efforts to base rights claims on homosexuality's status as an innate and unchangeable trait.[110] By the 1980s, however, this was not the position of the legal advocacy groups that had come to dominate the movement. These organizations believed that emphasizing immutability and analogizing their community's civil rights struggles to those of racial and ethnic minorities was a more effective strategy than focusing on sexual freedom and social revolution.[111] In part, the AIDS crisis had made arguments about sexual freedom appear unreasonably dangerous. Also important was the fact that courts were more likely to strike down discriminatory laws if they targeted individuals because of their innate and unchangeable traits. Queer rights attorneys were well aware that the Civil Rights and feminist movements had secured important judicial victories by emphasizing the immutability of race and sex.[112] Finally, the public was more accepting of characteristics that they saw as inborn. Indeed, that was one of the reasons why the queer rights movement's opponents emphasized that same-sex sexuality was a behavioral choice. All three factors meant that framing homosexuality as immutable was key to securing legal rights.[113]

By including sexual orientation among the other protected characteristics, the statute had other benefits. The Hate Crimes Statistics Act framed gays and lesbians as part of the polity, rather than a population apart. The law communicated a clear message that violence against gays and lesbians was a problem and that the government had a responsibility to rectify this harm. According to the law's framing, the danger to society was not gays or lesbians. Rather, Americans needed to protect themselves from the biases that produced antiqueer violence. Additionally, by helping to make the epidemic of antiqueer violence visible, it prompted state-level officials to act. In the year after Congress passed the Hate Crimes Statistics Act, eight additional states enacted hate crimes statutes that included sexual orientation as a protected characteristic. As a result, by 1992, twenty-one states had sexual orientation-inclusive hate laws.[114] These states were concentrated on the coasts, but some – like Florida, Iowa, Texas, and Wisconsin – were in the South and Midwest.[115]

These hate crimes laws did not end antiqueer violence. Yet the statutes were an important step forward in the fight for gay and lesbian rights. They helped advocates reframe same-sex sexuality, which many Americans saw as a danger to society. Instead, gays and lesbians became victims who deserved compassion and protection. Relatedly, the laws helped demonstrate that antiqueer animosity had tangible, harmful consequences. Many straight Americans may not have accepted same-sex sexuality, but most recoiled at the thought of individuals suffering physical violence because of their sexual orientation. The statutes consequently helped Americans start to face the deadly consequences of hate, in the process helping to convey that homophobia, not homosexuality, was the problem that the country needed to address.

Antiviolence groups had pressed for hate crimes laws to forestall the violence that made it so perilous to be queer. As this part of the gay and lesbian community lobbied legislatures, another set of advocates were working to reduce attacks against gays and lesbians in a different manner. Rather than focus on violence in the streets, these groups concentrated their efforts on the schools. The same individuals who committed crimes against queer adults directed their anger toward their peers, making every school day excruciating for gay and lesbian youth. This abuse often had deadly consequences, as too many children decided to end their suffering by committing suicide. Advocates knew they had to act to prevent queer adolescents from succumbing to virulent antiqueer attitudes. Otherwise, these children might never live to see a better future.

Unsafe Schools

Jamie Nabozny dropped out of school in eleventh grade. He simply could no longer stand the abuse he suffered every day at the hands of his classmates. On the bus, his peers spat on him and threw pencils at his head. At school, they would taunt him with derogatory names. Some took their hate further. In seventh grade, two boys wrestled Jamie to the floor and pretended to rape him while the rest of the class looked on and laughed. During Jamie's freshman year, classmates knocked him to the floor and urinated on him. The next year, a group of ten teens attacked him in a school hallway. They kicked him in the abdomen so many times that he needed surgery. School officials dismissed Jamie's complaints, coldly remarking that gays and lesbians should expect to be treated with disdain and animosity.[116] By the time Jamie was 16, he had attempted suicide three times.[117]

Jamie was not the only queer adolescent whose experiences left him feeling so hopeless that suicide seemed like the only option. In the 1980s, a series of reports revealed that gay and lesbian youth attempted suicide at disproportionate and shockingly high rates.[118] Queer teens endured rampant rejection, harassment, and violence from their peers and teachers. Some coped by abusing alcohol and drugs. Others dropped out of school to avoid the torment. Still others tried to stop the pain once and for all by attempting suicide. By the end of the decade, queer adolescents were more likely to die at their own hands than from any other cause.[119] That was a sobering fact not just for members of the queer community, but also for the parents of gay and lesbian youth. Many mothers and fathers became all too familiar with how painful teenage years could be for their children, as they witnessed firsthand the torment and anguish that their sons and daughters suffered. These experiences ultimately led straight parents of gay and lesbian children to mobilize against violence. The campaigns they launched did more than combat hate violence. They would also change the face of queer rights advocacy.

In the early and mid-1980s, parents of queer children began organizing under the banner of Parents and Friends of Lesbians and Gays (PFLAG). They lobbied public schools to educate teachers and students about same-sex sexuality, hoping that, if schools corrected common misconceptions about homosexuality, educational environments would become more supportive spaces for gay and lesbian youth. PFLAG had limited success in changing schools, but the organization's work had a significant impact on the evolution of queer rights. These relatives would ultimately help Americans understand that queer households did not just include gay men, lesbians, and their children, but also the queer community's straight families of origin. PFLAG's advocacy was important for another reason. The group helped reframe homosexuality as a matter of benign difference, an unremarkable attribute that some members of every community possessed. That was not how all members of the queer community understood their sexual orientation. It was also not the argument that all advocates wanted to use to pursue rights claims. However, this formulation of same-sex sexuality was key to securing legal protections for gays and lesbians.

PFLAG was not originally a political advocacy group. The organization dated back to 1972, when Jeanne Manford witnessed an attack on her gay son Morty at a Gay Activist Alliance (GAA) protest. The GAA had gathered at New York City's Hilton Hotel to protest media portrayals of homosexuality. During the melee that ensued, the president of the Uniformed Firefighters Association kicked and punched Morty while the police looked on, refusing to defend a victim of violence.[120] Outraged by the experience, Jeanne published a letter of support for her son in the *New York Post* and, at the city's next Pride parade, displayed a sign that read "Parents of Gays Unite in Support of Our Children."[121] Mothers and fathers of queer children flocked to Jeanne at the event. She and a group of twenty other parents later banded together to form a support group, which initially met in the basement of a Greenwich Village church.[122] By 1979, parent support groups had sprung up around the country. They joined forces to establish an umbrella organization, which eventually became called Parents and Friends of Lesbians and Gays, or PFLAG.[123] In the early 1980s, PFLAG expanded from a source of support for parents to an advocacy organization, quickly taking on a unique role in the queer rights movement.

FIGURE 13 Jeanne Manford marching in New York City's fifth Pride parade, 1974. Manford inspired other parents to become advocates for their gay sons and lesbian daughters. Photo by Fred W. McDarrah/MUUS Collection. Courtesy of Getty Images.

When the parents who founded PFLAG began their efforts, they recognized that their support mattered a great deal to their children. What they were not expecting was how influential they would be to those outside of the gay and lesbian community. Individuals who rejected queer advocates' arguments as propaganda had a more open mind when listening to a PFLAG parent.[124] As one PFLAG mother later explained, "I'm a parent. Other parents will respond to me as [a] *parent.*"[125] PFLAG parents were able to "build a bridge" between the gay and straight worlds because its members explicitly framed themselves as part of the mainstream.[126] The group presented its members as devoted parents and relatives, who exemplified the traditional values that Christian conservatives argued were under attack. This appeal to respectability allowed PFLAG to have a different – and broader – reach than many gay and lesbian rights groups. In the 1970s, gay liberationists and lesbian feminists had challenged social conventions around gender and sexual orientation. During the AIDS crisis, queer rights advocacy had taken a more militant turn. Groups like ACT UP, which were known for their theatrical protests and confrontational demonstrations, were effective in generating attention to the plight of people with AIDS.[127] In the process, however, they alienated many onlookers.

PFLAG provided a more comforting image by refocusing public attention from same-sex intimacy to the queer community's straight families of origin. Unlike other branches of the queer rights movement, PFLAG parents adopted a staid approach. They emphasized that they were socially conservative individuals who opposed radical efforts to change society. Jeanne, for example, described herself as a "quiet, retiring sort of person" who would never so much as "cross the street against a traffic light."[128] Mainstream media echoed this portrayal, describing her as a "prim, bespectacled woman" whose family could be featured in a "Disney movie, rated 'G.'"[129] PFLAG members recognized that they held a unique place within the movement precisely because of their respectability. As one PFLAG chapter put it, the group was "the 'warm fuzzy' image that the media doesn't mind showing to their viewers or their readers."[130]

By reassuring a public that identified same-sex sexuality as both different and dangerous, PFLAG parents knew they could help make society a better place for their children. The problem, however, was that there were not enough of them. Many mothers and fathers simply could not accept that they had gay sons or lesbian daughters. These parents described themselves as entering their own type of closet when their children came out as queer, one in which they spoke less frequently about their sons and daughters.[131] The parents' sorrow and silence stemmed from their deep fear that they had caused their children's homosexuality – or, at the very least, that they would be blamed for having done so.[132] Some parents were anxious that they had neglected to protect their children from predators. Others, however, were concerned that they had failed in their roles as mothers and fathers. Since the 1960s, psychoanalytic theories of homosexuality had emphasized the role of parents in producing queer children.[133] According to those conceptions of homosexuality, adults engaged in same-sex relationships to fulfill their unmet emotional needs from childhood.[134] A son or daughter coming out as gay or lesbian thus suggested that the parents were as deviant as their children.[135] Moreover, since the 1970s, political debates over queer rights had reinforced the notion that adults were responsible for a child's homosexuality. The religious right, after all, had come to a renewed national power by arguing that children needed to be protected from queer adults, who served as role models for the "gay lifestyle." That rhetoric implied that parents had failed to protect their children from harmful influences.

PFLAG learned early on that emphasizing homosexuality's status as an innate and unchangeable trait helped to alleviate parents' fears, thereby making it more likely that they would accept their queer children. As one PFLAG father explained, "[a]fter learning, with total surprise, that one of our sons was gay, I initially felt some comfort in attributing a biological cause to his sexual orientation, thereby lessening some of the irrational guilt I harbored."[136] Although biological theories of homosexuality seemed to implicate both parents equally, some interpreted them to put the responsibility primarily on mothers. One father at a support group for parents of queer children laughed with relief upon hearing that homosexuality was an inborn trait, believing that his wife was responsible for their son's homosexuality because she was the one who carried him in utero.[137] To convince these parents to accept their queer children, PFLAG consequently emphasized homosexuality's biological origins. Doing so was strategically useful for other reasons. Individuals who identified homosexuality as immutable were more likely to support gay and lesbian rights. Moreover, by suggesting that sexual orientation was an immutable characteristic, like race, the argument could help to secure constitutional protections against discrimination. Indeed, these political and legal considerations were why other national gay and lesbian rights groups stressed that same-sex sexual attraction was an inborn trait.[138]

Given the numerous benefits that came from accentuating homosexuality's biological origins, PFLAG consistently emphasized that homosexuality was both natural and normal. One of the group's first publications, "About Our Children," centered on these two points. [139] The booklet explained that same-sex sexuality was not uncommon, given Kinsey's studies, which showed that gays and lesbians constituted 10 percent of the global population.[140] As a result, a community like Des Moines, Iowa, likely had 20,000 queer residents and 50,000 immediate family members of those gay men and lesbians.[141] The document also noted that, although no one knew where sexual orientation originated, it was clear that homosexuality was an innate trait.[142] Gays and lesbians, the group maintained, had no choice in their attractions. Their only decision was to live openly and honestly, or endure a stifling existence in the closet.[143] PFLAG parents distributed this pamphlet widely, hoping the information would reduce prejudice against queer individuals – and therefore avoid the violent attacks that their children suffered.[144]

PFLAG was particularly eager to disseminate this information in schools, which were bleak environments for queer youth. Survey data revealed that half of the gay male and a significant percentage of the lesbian respondents had been harassed or physically assaulted in school because of their sexual orientation. Almost a third of the survey participants had dropped out because of the abuse.[145] Studies of high school juniors and seniors similarly showed that almost a third had witnessed acts of violence against students or teachers who were suspected of being queer.[146] The authors of research studies on gay and lesbian youth suicide uniformly emphasized the need for educational reform, which included making curricula more inclusive, combatting peer harassment, and offering counseling or support groups to sexual minority youth.[147] PFLAG parents took up their call for change, offering to educate teachers and students alike that same-sex sexuality was an unremarkable variation in human development.

But the group's efforts were extremely controversial. Parents of queer children were not the only ones to believe in the revolutionary potential of educational policies and materials – their opponents similarly identified the extent to which materials within the classroom's four walls could reshape American society.[148] Since conservatives believed that same-sex sexuality was a mutable characteristic that children learned, they objected to any attempts to inculcate tolerance for gays and lesbians. Christian conservatives feared that children would become homosexual if schools did not condemn gays and lesbians. In their view, schools had an obligation to emphasize homosexuality's harm, to prevent youth from electing the "gay lifestyle." Even neutral information about same-sex sexuality ran the risk of "recruiting" children.

The challenge for PFLAG was that, even though the religious right's national influence had waned, the political movement continued to hold inordinate power over local educational policies. Christian conservatives had been cultivating that influence since the 1950s, when they mobilized to oppose racial desegregation and what they saw as public schools' increasingly secular bent.[149] They framed their arguments in terms of parents' right to educate their children based on Christian moral absolutes, claiming that public education was leading children away from God, the Church, and scripture.[150] In the early 1980s, the religious right redoubled its attention to public schools. The movement was following the call of Robert Simonds, an influential evangelical minister, who urged Christian conservatives to focus their energies on school board elections, where he saw a golden opportunity to advance their interests. In 1983, he founded Citizens for Excellence in Education (CEE) – a group devoted to upholding the "Christian World View in a secular humanist society" – for this purpose.[151] When he began his work, there were over 15,000 public school boards across the country, 94 percent of which were composed of elected members.[152] Simonds emphasized that, given low voter turnout in local elections, conservatives could easily influence the political makeup of school boards. By doing so, Christian conservatives could further their political and spiritual agenda. After all, school boards approved curricula, selected textbooks, and made hiring and firing decisions.[153] Simonds's strategy was remarkably successful. Within a decade, CEE had 1,200 "active parents' chapters" across the country.[154] In 1992, the group claimed credit for the election of 3,611 conservative parents to school boards.[155]

Once in place, conservative Christian school board members pushed their agenda on a number of issues, including supporting school prayer, replacing lessons on evolution with creationism, and prohibiting books with allegedly anti-Christian content, such as witchcraft or mysticism.[156] However, in the mid-1980s, no topic commanded more attention than sexuality education, especially the questions of AIDS and homosexuality.[157] These related issues became increasingly important as the national conservative movement focused its attention to fighting gay and lesbian rights, a central plank of its family values politics.[158] Christian conservatives, who feared that presenting homosexuality as normal and acceptable would lead children to elect a "gay lifestyle," opposed any efforts to provide students with fact-based, neutral information about same-sex sexuality. School districts across the country were thus embroiled in debates over whether and how to depict homosexuality – a topic that reliably drove conservative Christians to the polls – when PFLAG parents approached teachers and administrators.[159]

Given this political environment, administrators were understandably hesitant to engage with PFLAG parents. PFLAG's first president, Adele Starr, spent years trying to meet with teachers in the Los Angeles school district to educate them about same-sex sexuality. In the early 1980s, she wrote to all of the district's school principals, asking to present at in-service meetings. Not a single one responded.[160] In 1984, she convinced the Los Angeles Board of Education to approve PFLAG as a provider of faculty workshops, but that yielded a lone invitation to present at a teacher training session.[161] Starr kept writing to school administrators, pleading her cause. Although she reminded California administrators that a dozen PFLAG chapters stood ready and willing to provide workshops free of charge, Starr made little headway.[162] Around the country, other PFLAG parents likewise struggled to get the attention of educators. In Denver and St. Louis, chapter members reported sending outreach letters to local high schools, but only a handful of teachers responded by inviting PLFAG parents to speak to their classes.[163] When Denver public schools finally agreed to offer a training session for teachers that corrected myths and stereotypes about same-sex sexuality, the backlash came swiftly. Christian conservatives decried the program as "homosexual indoctrination," telling parents that their tax money was "being spent to try and convince children – maybe even your own – that they should consider homosexuality."[164]

Because of the pernicious political environment, most school administrators were unwilling to consider PFLAG's offer to help educate teachers and students. They instead told PFLAG that homosexuality was simply not a topic that educators could broach.[165] The religious right's influence thus often prevented PFLAG from making inroads into the classroom. The resistance that PFLAG faced was enormous, creating an imposing challenge for gay and lesbian rights advocates. Given that they could not provide teachers or students with even limited facts about homosexuality, they had little chance of making these spaces safer for queer youth. The advocacy environment was grim, but parents of queer children were not the only ones attempting to reshape students' experiences. As PFLAG parents mobilized, so too did a teacher in Los Angeles. From her position within the school, she was able to develop a program that would help queer youth throughout the country.

Supporting Queer Teens

Virginia Uribe was unprepared for the deluge of calls that followed her appearance on Sally Jessy Raphael, a nationally syndicated daytime talk show. In 1988, the show had invited Uribe, a teacher at Fairfax High School in Los Angeles, to discuss Project 10, a program she had designed to support gay and lesbian teens.[166] Named after Kinsey's estimate that 10 percent of the population was homosexual, Project 10 provided drop-in counseling for students, outreach to parents, and training sessions for teachers.[167] Uribe's program aimed to reduce the pressures that gay and lesbian teens faced by emphasizing that same-sex sexual attraction was not shameful. Homosexuality was a variation in human sexuality, not a deviant or immoral behavioral choice. The day the episode aired, sixty schools called Uribe for more information. Even more parents of queer children dialed her number, many of whom had lost their sons or daughters to suicide. Uribe later described these conversations as "gut wrenching," but her exchanges with the mothers and fathers reinforced the importance of her work.[168]

Uribe, like PFLAG parents, believed it was essential for schools to be supportive environments for queer youth. Schools could not meet their educational mission if they failed to address the needs of all of their students – including gay and lesbian pupils. However, teachers and administrators rarely acknowledged that this population even existed.[169] Uribe set out to change that fact, so that schools would truly promote all children's welfare. She was much more successful than PFLAG parents, even though her efforts were just as controversial as theirs. Like PFLAG, Uribe directly challenged Christian conservatives' arguments that schools needed to forestall homosexuality. She insisted that preventing same-sex sexual attraction was a futile effort, because homosexuality was an immutable characteristic. As a result, rather than fight against the existence of queer youth, schools needed to inculcate acceptance of them. The difference between Uribe and PFLAG was that Uribe did not frame her work as an effort to instill tolerance. Instead, she emphasized that she was reaching out to gay and lesbian adolescents, to keep them from dropping out. She was not trying to change the beliefs of straight teens. She was simply trying to protect and nurture queer youth.

Uribe came up with Project 10 in 1984, after a group of gay and lesbian students came to her to discuss the discrimination and harassment they suffered at school and within their families.[170] One student, named Chris, was 14 when he told his parents he was gay. After they forced him out of the house, he spent a year sleeping on the streets. If his living situation was bad, his experiences at school may have been worse. Chris's fellow students harassed and physically assaulted him, and teachers compounded the problem by making snide remarks about his sexuality. Chris attended five different high schools within the Los Angeles Unified School District, including Fairfax, but the attacks continued everywhere he went. He eventually dropped out of school entirely.[171] Chris's experience was all too common. Other students told Uribe of experiencing similar ordeals. To dull their feelings of isolation, alienation, and inadequacy, some of the students turned to drugs and alcohol. Others attempted suicide.[172]

FIGURE 14 Virginia Uribe with students in her Los Angeles high school classroom, 1987. Uribe's Project 10 program, which emphasized that same-sex attraction was a natural variation in human sexuality, provided crucial support to queer teens. It also helped educate straight students about gays and lesbians. Photo by Kent Garvey. Courtesy of ONE Archives at the USC Libraries.

The gay and lesbian students who approached Uribe did not realize it, but their teacher already knew how difficult it was to grow up as a queer teen. After all, she had been one herself. The daughter of Italian immigrants had been raised to believe that lesbianism was immoral – so much so that, in her twenties, she married a man, hoping that the relationship would "cure" her of her own homosexuality.[173] Within a few years, she had divorced her husband, fallen in love with a woman, and come out to close family members and friends.[174] By the time she developed Project 10, Uribe was living with her partner of fourteen years, but she continued to keep her sexual orientation hidden at work. When the *Los Angeles Times* reported on the program, it divulged her secret to all of its readers, abruptly forcing her out of the closet. Uribe ultimately described the event as "personally liberating" and helpful to her students.[175] The existence of an out lesbian teacher sent a clear message to them: there was nothing shameful about same-sex sexuality.

Uribe offered her queer students advice and encouragement, letting them know they were neither deviant nor depraved. She delivered the same message to teachers, administrators, and parents, emphasizing that individuals had no choice in their sexual attractions. Although no one knew where homosexuality originated, Uribe noted that the "overwhelming evidence in scientific literature" was that individuals could not alter their sexual orientation. For that reason, homosexuality was "not something that can be promoted."[176] By eliminating one of the main explanations for homosexuality's origins, Project 10 made it seem more likely that same-sex sexuality was an inborn fact, the product of biology or genetics. According to Project 10, homosexuality was just like heterosexuality – a matter of mere difference that American society needed to accept.

Uribe knew how controversial these arguments about homosexuality would be, given that the religious right had long opposed queer rights on the basis that same-sex sexuality was a behavioral choice and a "lifestyle." To try to sidestep political arguments, Uribe emphasized that Project 10 was "not an advocacy program." Instead, it was "an attempt to relieve some of the pressures on gay kids so that they can go on to graduate instead of dropping out."[177] How Uribe framed her program was essential. School administrators had balked at the overtures of PFLAG parents, who seemed to be bringing trouble to their doors. Uribe, on the other hand, was solving a problem that schools had to address. She made it clear that Project 10 served officials' interests.[178] Indeed, by affirming the worth and dignity of gay and lesbian students, Project 10 changed many teens' lives dramatically. Greg Cartwright, for example, transferred to Uribe's school to join Project 10 after suffering so much harassment from his peers that he began abusing alcohol and drugs. At Fairfax, he thrived, graduating as valedictorian.[179] The experiences of students like Greg seemed to provide proof that the experts were right. Districts that created supportive environments for queer students could have a positive impact on their lives. Because of Project 10's success at Fairfax, the program quickly spread to other Los Angeles schools. District officials enthusiastically supported Project 10, a fact Uribe found puzzling until she later discovered how many of the decisionmakers had queer family members.[180]

Uribe might have insisted that Project 10 merely supported gay and lesbian students, but the program did much more than that. By making it possible for openly gay and lesbian teens to stay in school and be a visible part of their communities, it also helped to make same-sex sexuality an unremarkable aspect of everyday life for their peers. Changing the educational experiences of queer youth thus necessarily influenced the perceptions of straight teenagers, whose exposure to same-sex sexuality in schools was no longer limited to admonishments about AIDS. It was this effect on other students that Christian conservatives feared – and why they launched a concerted attack on the program. Louis Sheldon, president of the Traditional Values Coalition, excoriated Project 10 as a "homosexual recruitment program," as did Beverly LaHaye, the founder of Concerned Women for America.[181] Sheldon was an evangelical minister who left his pulpit for months at a time to work for conservative causes.[182] A self-described "lobbyist for the Lord," Sheldon became one of the most influential figures in the religious right, reaching the height of his influence when Republicans gained control of Congress in the 1994 midterm elections.[183] In the late 1980s, he led the charge against Project 10, which he described as a "sodomy class" that put teens on "the path to [their] death with HIV infection."[184] He argued that Project 10 rested on the faulty assumption that homosexuality was "a permanent condition," rather than "a disorder from which a victim needs to be healed."[185] Since Sheldon and other conservatives cast same-sex sexuality as a choice, rather than an immutable characteristic, they argued that an individual who identified as gay or lesbian could become heterosexual through counseling.[186]

At Sheldon's urging, California legislators introduced a series of bills to eliminate Project 10. Assemblywoman Marion LaFollete first proposed a law prohibiting new funding for the Los Angeles school district unless it eliminated the program.[187] When that failed, she introduced a budget amendment to require written parental consent for any teacher to talk to any student about homosexuality. Violations would have been punished by denying administrative salary funding to the offending teacher's school district for one year, but the Assembly likewise defeated the proposal.[188] The Senate rejected similar bills, as well as a resolution that linked counseling programs for gay and lesbian youth to the spread of AIDS.[189] Although unsuccessful, each proposal received unanimous support from Republican legislators, demonstrating how decidedly conservatives opposed Project 10.[190]

Outside of California, Project 10 was just as much of a political lightning rod. In state after state, Christian conservatives used Project 10 to argue against queer-inclusive educational policies. After hearing about the program, the Texas legislature required instructional materials to emphasize that "homosexual conduct is not an acceptable lifestyle."[191] In Colorado and Oregon, conservatives cited Project 10 as a justification for their 1992 antiqueer ballot measures. Colorado's citizens enacted Amendment 2, which prohibited the state from protecting gays, lesbians, and bisexuals from discrimination on the basis of their sexual orientation, while voters in Oregon narrowly defeated a similar measure.[192] In both states, campaign organizers stoked parental fears by proclaiming that schools were already using Project 10 to indoctrinate children into homosexuality.[193] In Oregon, the measure's sponsors took special pains to attack the program. They described Project 10 as an effort to send "practicing homosexuals into the classroom," who would inform students that "1 in 10 of them are homosexual and that they need to be identified."[194]

Ironically, conservatives' opposition led to Project 10's expansion. The publicity prompted schools around the country to contact Uribe for information on starting their own versions the program.[195] Uribe wryly commented that she had to "thank Lou Sheldon" for making her small program known nationally.[196] Additional attention came after the National Education Association endorsed Project 10 in 1989, with the organization resolving that "every school district should provide counseling for students who are struggling with their sexual/gender orientation."[197] By 1993, Uribe had distributed 3,000 copies of the "Project 10 Handbook" to school districts all over the country. Cambridge, Massachusetts, launched its own version of Project 10, as did Richmond, Virginia.[198] In Los Angeles, almost half of the city's high schools had Project 10 programs, teachers at all school levels had received Project 10 training, and libraries across the district had lesbian and gay themed books available to students.[199] The Los Angeles school board also publicly recognized Uribe's work and courage in promoting the interests of queer students.[200] Uribe received accolades from the Los Angeles City Council, Los Angeles Board of Education, and the California Legislature.[201] Uribe also received support from PFLAG, whose leaders lauded Project 10. They lobbied the Los Angeles School District to release Uribe from all of her classes so that she could focus her energies on expanding her program.[202]

Project 10 did not make inroads into every school. For every administrator and teacher who implemented the program, more refused. Yet Project 10 and programs like it were extremely consequential.[203] In addition to changing some students' lives, they helped reframe narratives around same-sex sexuality. Project 10 never attempted to pinpoint homosexuality's origins, but the program assumed that gays and lesbians did not choose their sexual orientation. As a result, it implicitly argued that same-sex sexuality was an innate and fixed trait. Moreover, by emphasizing the plight of queer youth, programs like Project 10 insisted that gays and lesbians were not predators, but victims. That, in turn, helped reshape what child protection meant. For decades, conservatives had presented themselves as children's defenders. Through programs like Project 10, gay and lesbian rights advocates challenged their opponents' claim of moral superiority.

No one expressed their concern for child welfare more effectively than Uribe. When asked to comment on the opposition that Project 10 engendered, she would calmly reply: "Who wouldn't want a child to succeed in school, and to receive an education, and to become productive in life?"[204] Uribe's retort demonstrated how, by trying to change the pernicious environments for queer youth, advocates helped undermine the long-standing political narrative of gays and lesbians as dangerous to children. Instead, they argued that it was Christian conservatives who endangered children through their bigoted policies and attitudes, which stigmatized queer youth and made them targets of ridicule and torment.

* * *

By the early 1990s, educational initiatives had become a central pillar of the queer rights movement's antiviolence efforts. Advocates only influenced a small percentage of the nation's schools, but their efforts were nevertheless significant because of how they reformulated child protection arguments. Christian conservatives had long based their opposition to gay and lesbian rights on the premise that homosexuality was dangerous to children. Although individual gay men and women had challenged this claim in custody cases, as well as by fostering and adopting children, the political battles over school policies were the first large-scale, public attacks on the fundamental belief of those who wished to limit the rights of queer Americans. Through educational policies, gay and lesbian rights advocates emphasized that they were the ones defending children. What youth needed was protection from the religious right's bigotry. Programs like Project 10 may have been local initiatives, designed by nonlegal actors, but the message they communicated influenced national debates about queer rights.

Gay and lesbian rights groups' efforts to secure hate crimes protections had a similar effect. Like the schools-based programs, these laws identified same-sex sexuality as an immutable, biological fact, like race, ethnicity, and gender. That fact undermined traditional notions that homosexuality was a "lifestyle choice" that innocent children could somehow be "recruited" into. Same-sex sexuality was not, as Christian conservatives claimed, a destructive behavioral choice, but rather an inborn trait that individuals could not change. Hate crimes statutes were premised on this view of homosexuality, thereby giving it the government's imprimatur. The laws were significant for another reason: they marked a decisive shift in how the state addressed same-sex sexuality. For most of the nation's history, penal codes punished queer conduct, defining gays and lesbians as felons. In the 1960s, states had begun decriminalizing consensual sodomy, but that was a far cry from identifying gays and lesbians as individuals worthy of respect. Hate crimes protections communicated that gays and lesbians were citizens like any other, and as such deserved the state's protection.

Advocates' efforts to secure hate crimes protections and support queer youth were particularly important because they came at a time when the AIDS epidemic had become the dominant image of gay and lesbian life. Christian conservatives had seized upon the health crisis to argue that it provided clear evidence that same-sex sexuality was both dangerous and immoral. Yet, each one of the queer community's multiple law reform projects undermined this claim. Campaigns to secure domestic partnerships highlighted the loving relationships that same-sex couples shared. Foster care and adoption battles demonstrated that gays and lesbians were devoted parents, thereby providing another counterpoint to the religious right's claims. Unlike these legal disputes, the efforts to combat antiqueer violence were not projects that were inherently about families. However, they had the effect of promoting queer family visibility. Attacks on gay men and lesbians inspired straight parents to become advocates for queer rights. These relatives' increased visibility sent a clear message: same-sex sexuality was part and parcel of "conventional" family life. Additionally, like the custody, domestic partnership, and adoption campaigns, antiviolence advocates helped to show that threats to "traditional American values" did not come from gays and lesbians. The queer community had, after all, fought for the right to create nuclear families. Instead, the danger to social stability came from those whose prejudice led them to attack their fellow citizens. Antiviolence laws and policies allowed the straight world to see that antiqueer prejudice all too often turned into physical harm. That, in turn, caused many members of the public to identify gays and lesbians not as dangerous predators, but rather as victims who deserved support and sympathy.

By the late 1980s, gay and lesbian rights groups had helped to make antiqueer violence visible, but attacks continued at an alarming rate. School environments were still so perilous for queer youth that suicide rates remained startlingly high. Advocates had long recognized that both dilemmas had the same root cause: prejudice on the part of young adults. Trying to inculcate tolerance among America's youth was a daunting proposition. Project 10 had met extreme resistance, even though it focused on reaching self-identified gay and lesbian youth. Although this required straight teens to respect their homosexual peers, heterosexual youth were not the program's focus. By the late 1980s, however, advocates realized that they had to face teens' antiqueer attitudes head-on. They consequently sought to change what schools taught about homosexuality. Their efforts would put the queer family at the front and center of the movement to combat violence.

6

Teaching Tolerance

The Queer Family Comes Out against Hate

On a sweltering August day in 1992, Mary Griffith pushed to the front of a crowded California Board of Education meeting. Once she had the floor, the president of the Diablo Valley, California chapter of PFLAG shared her family's tragedy: her son had killed himself by jumping from a freeway overpass because, as he wrote in his diary, he believed his homosexuality made him "no good to anyone, not even God."[1] Griffith implored the Board to adopt the proposed educational guidelines, which would make schools a more welcoming place for people like her son. The policy under consideration would have required schools to teach students that, in addition to traditional families with two married parents, people also lived in households headed by grandparents, siblings, foster parents, and same-sex parents. Griffith argued that this information would reduce queer children's sense of difference, which could prevent them from contemplating suicide.[2]

David Llewellyn, the director of the Western Center for Law and Religious Freedom, urged the Board to not be swayed by stories like the ones that Griffith recounted. Gays and lesbians who committed suicide were responding to "personal guilt."[3] The state had an obligation to promote traditional families, not treat all kinds of families as equal.[4] Louis Sheldon, the influential conservative minister, added that the guidelines constituted "recruitment par excellence" because they identified same-sex sexuality as normal and acceptable.[5] Like Llewellyn, Sheldon dismissed the disproportionately high rates of queer youth suicide with the blithe explanation that "[k]ids are not committing suicide because of actions against homosexuality but because they know within themselves that it is not normal."[6] These arguments swayed the California Board of Education, which sent the guidelines back to a committee for revisions.

The California Board of Education was not the only executive agency considering whether and how to teach students about same-sex sexuality during this period. In the early and mid-1990s, debates over these issues swept the nation, engulfing towns, cities, and states across the country. In the years leading up to the California hearing, queer rights groups had tried to combat violence by legislating against hate and supporting gay and lesbian students in schools. However, these projects did not address the root of the violence – the prejudice and contempt that children learned at an early age. To forestall hate crimes, queer rights advocates demanded that schools combat bias against same-sex sexuality by teaching all students that gays and lesbians deserved the same dignity and respect as other members of society.

The California Board of Education hearing exemplified the competing concerns over curricular reforms that made the topic so contentious. Like Griffith, gay and lesbian rights advocates emphasized the harms that queer people of all ages suffered at the hands of prejudiced youth. School officials, they insisted, had to take action to prevent this harm. They maintained that, rather than shrouding homosexuality in moral judgment, teachers should identify same-sex sexuality as an unexceptional variation in human sexuality. These advocates also pressed for materials that introduced school-age children to gay and lesbian families. Through these curricular reforms, advocates hoped to shift the dominant images of same-sex sexuality from danger, disease, and depravity, to community, care, and compassion. The changes they suggested were minor, yet they were enough to draw the ire of Christian conservatives. The religious right insisted that presenting the queer community as unobjectionable was the wrong lesson for educators to draw from stories of violence and suicide. Teaching students to accept homosexuality did not protect children or society. Rather, children needed to be protected from becoming queer in the first place. These arguments resonated deeply with many members of the public, who felt torn between their growing tolerance for same-sex sexuality and their visceral discomfort with queer life. The religious right's widespread appeal limited the arguments that gay and lesbian rights advocates could make, as well as reduced the movement's ability to secure change.

The California hearing was representative of the battles over queer rights in another important way: it marked a notable shift in gay and lesbian rights advocacy. By the time Griffith appeared before the Board of Education, she was one of tens of thousands of parents of gay and lesbian children who had come out loudly and publicly. PFLAG had formed in the late 1970s and started its educational reform efforts in the early 1980s. However, the organization's numbers grew dramatically in the late 1980s and early 1990s. As droves of parents began mobilizing on behalf of their queer children, they turned an antiviolence campaign into a movement for gay and lesbian family rights. These mothers and fathers made clear that queer families were more than simply gay- and lesbian-headed households – they also included straight adults who had gay sons and lesbian daughters. Christian conservatives had long argued that they opposed gay and lesbian rights to protect both children and the American family. The parents of queer children insisted that the religious right's claims were flawed. After all, many traditional, nuclear American families included gay sons and lesbian daughters. Promoting families thus necessarily required supporting queer rights. These parents' efforts presented gays and lesbians as integral members of American society, rather than a population apart. The queer community consequently appeared more familiar, and less frightening, than it ever had before. These parents' advocacy, which shifted the terms of the debate over queer rights, had another significant effect: it would also make it possible for a tragedy that struck in 1998 to change American society decidedly.

Griffith, like others working to secure curricular reform, began her efforts knowing that inculcating tolerance for gays and lesbians was bound to be controversial. After all, when members of PFLAG first attempted to speak to teachers in the early 1980s, they made little headway. What made their advocacy so challenging was both the power of the religious right and the ongoing AIDS crisis. Christian conservatives eagerly pointed to the epidemic as evidence of homosexuality's danger. That argument made school administrators even more reluctant to introduce policies that would inculcate tolerance for same-sex sexuality. Given the opposition of the religious right, gay and lesbian rights advocates anticipated that the Reagan administration would strenuously resist their efforts. The president was callously indifferent to the plight of the queer community, repeatedly refusing to fund AIDS programs.[7] However, his surgeon general, the evangelical Dr. C. Everett Koop, became an unexpected and influential ally. His work created a window of opportunity for educational reform, which gay and lesbian rights advocates quickly seized upon.

A Window of Opportunity

In the 1979 film, *Whatever Happened to the Human Race?*, Koop appeared on a peninsula bordered by the Dead Sea, where he claimed the ancient city of Sodom had once thrived. Surrounded by hundreds of plastic dolls face down in silt – to represent the millions of fetuses aborted since *Roe v. Wade* – he intoned: "Sodom comes easily to mind when one contemplates the evils of abortion and the death of moral law."[8] The film was not the pediatrician's first antiabortion crusade. In 1975, he had joined Billy Graham and other evangelical leaders to form the Christian Action Council, which had a singular focus: lobbying Congress to curtail abortion access.[9] The film turned Koop into a leader in the Christian pro-life movement, prompting Reagan to tap him to serve as surgeon general. The nomination was an easy way for Reagan to repay the political debt he owed to evangelicals for their support during his presidential campaign.[10] But, once confirmed to the country's top medical post, Koop disappointed his fellow coreligionists by refusing to take an active stance against abortion. He reasoned that "the law of the land said abortion on demand was legal" and it was not up to him "to lead an insurrection within the government against the Supreme Court."[11] Koop had clear moral principles that led him to consider abortion an abomination. However, he distinguished between his personal views and his professional obligations, considering the two entirely distinct.[12]

The line that Koop drew between his religious convictions and his scientific post also led him to dash evangelicals' expectations with respect to same-sex sexuality. Koop flatly refused to adopt a moralizing perspective on AIDS. He personally considered homosexuality unacceptable, but his task as surgeon general was to stem a deadly epidemic.[13] Koop knew this could only happen if people understood the risks of unsafe sex.[14] As a result, in a report he issued in 1986, Koop urged schools to candidly address sex practices and provide students information on both straight and queer relationships.[15] He also recommended that schools instruct students on condom use, arguing that "[y]ou can't talk of the dangers of snake poisoning and not mention snakes."[16] At the time the surgeon general issued his recommendations, many sex education materials stigmatized same-sex sexuality, presenting it as unacceptable, if not criminal. Their homophobic content contributed to the disproportionately high rates at which queer adolescents contracted HIV.[17] As one researcher explained, the discrimination, verbal abuse, and physical attacks that gay and lesbian adolescents experienced drove some teens to seek companionship in the streets, where they engaged in unsafe sex practices.[18] Between 1990 and 1992, AIDS diagnoses among teenagers and young adults had increased by almost 70 percent, a surge that a House of Representatives Committee attributed to the "hushed or moralistic tones" of sex education.[19]

Koop's decision to champion comprehensive, fact-based AIDS education enraged his evangelical compatriots. Phyllis Schlafly denounced the surgeon general for advocating the "teaching of safe sodomy in public schools."[20] At the time, prominent conservatives identified AIDS as a marker of God's judgment, if not a fitting punishment for immoral behavior.[21] Congressman Newt Gingrich, then an emerging conservative leader, recognized the political opportunity that AIDS offered the Republican Party. He noted that AIDS would "do more to direct America back to the cost of violating traditional values, and to make America aware of the danger of certain behavior than anything else we've seen."[22] Whether due to political pragmatism or moral principle, the Reagan administration remained conspicuously silent during the early onslaught of the epidemic. The president only spoke the word "AIDS" in public in 1986, by which time 25,000 people had already perished from the disease.[23]

Koop's insistent appeals filled the void that the president's silence had created, spurring lawmakers into action.[24] Although schools had begun offering sex education at the turn of the century to prevent venereal disease, by 1985, only three states and the District of Columbia mandated the subject.[25] Five years later, that number had increased to twenty-three, with thirty states and the capital also requiring AIDS education.[26] The actual information that students received varied widely, as local school boards determined the content of their districts' sex education classes. They could select any materials that would satisfy the state's regulations. However, many districts began instructing students on safe sex practices. By 1991, 74 percent of sex education curricula mentioned condom use.[27] Some districts also began distributing condoms to students.[28]

Of course, not all states adhered to the fact-based, queer-inclusive model that Koop promoted. That was no surprise, given that, by 1994, 60 percent of candidates aligned with or backed by Christian conservative groups were winning elections at the local, state, and federal levels.[29] Additionally, several states' sex education laws explicitly marginalized queer students and increased the stigma associated with same-sex sexuality.[30] For example, Alabama and Texas both required that sex education programs emphasize that homosexuality was an unacceptable lifestyle and a criminal offense.[31] Moreover, schools in these and other states often relied upon abstinence-only curricula, which instructed students that they needed to refrain from sexual intercourse until marriage. Because no state recognized same-sex unions, these lessons implied that gays and lesbians needed to live entirely celibate lives. That position was implausible, but it reinforced the notion that same-sex sexuality was far outside the norm. These curricular materials also typically presented homosexuality in a negative light by only mentioning same-sex sexuality in connection to AIDS.[32] One of the most popular programs, *Sex Respect*, went even further, identifying the AIDS epidemic as "nature's way of 'making some kind of comment on sexual behavior.'"[33]

Koop's recommendations nevertheless sparked a sea change in school curricula, which provided gay and lesbian rights advocates an important opportunity to foster educational environments that destigmatized same-sex sexuality. Gay and lesbian children around the country were suffering, and that torment too often led to suicidal despair. Advocates realized that they could transform the lives of queer youth if schools would teach children that same-sex sexuality was a matter of benign difference, rather than cast gays and lesbians as immoral, deviant, and diseased. Protecting gay and lesbian youth thus required providing children with a different vision of same-sex sexuality. Queer youth needed to know that their future was not just illness and death, but rather a fulfilling life like the ones their straight peers enjoyed. That reframing would also affect how heterosexual youth understood homosexuality, as they would learn same-sex intimacy was more than a pathway to AIDS. Advocates consequently hoped that educational reform would reduce the bigotry that too often led to hate violence against queer adults.

That potential for change was what made the educational materials so controversial. To Christian conservatives, they seemed like attempts to "convert" vulnerable children to homosexuality. Moreover, even many parents with more liberal politics were uncomfortable with some of queer rights advocates' initiatives. The other issues associated with creating gay and lesbian families – custody awards, domestic partnership registries, foster care licenses, and adoption orders – did not affect their children directly. Curricular changes, on the other hand, did. The religious right consequently received support from parents of all political stripes on education issues, even as conservatives were losing the larger cultural war over gay and lesbian rights. In the late 1980s and early 1990s, Americans had become increasingly tolerant of same-sex sexuality. In 1977, only slightly more than half of Americans believed gays and lesbians should have equal employment rights. By 1992, that number had soared to approximately 80 percent.[34] Lawmakers in cities and states around the country acted in response to these changing opinions, decriminalizing consensual sodomy and enacting antidiscrimination protections in employment, housing, and public accommodations.[35]

Even as Americans were growing more comfortable with gays and lesbians, that tolerance had limits. The same individuals who opposed discrimination against the queer community in employment balked at the idea of their children having contact with gay and lesbian adults.[36] A majority of parents surveyed in a 1992 national poll stated that they would not want their children to have a gay or lesbian elementary school teacher, would not allow their children to watch television shows with queer characters, and would refuse to let their children play at the home of a friend with same-sex parents.[37] Undergirding their fear was the idea that had been so central to debates over custody, foster care, and adoption – that homosexuality was a learned behavior that children might pick up from their surroundings. A 1993 poll showed that Americans were evenly divided on whether homosexuality was an immutable characteristic or a choice that individuals elected.[38] Parents did not want their children to grow up to be queer, which many viewed as a dangerous aberration that would only lead to early death from HIV.

Conservatives' child protection rhetoric, which insisted that schools could forestall same-sex sexuality by instructing children that homosexuality was an immoral and abnormal choice, thus resonated with Americans all along the political spectrum. As school districts increasingly debated whether and how to change their school curricula, concerns about homosexuality's origins infused the conversations, limiting the arguments that queer rights advocates could make. That was true even in progressive New York City, where advocates launched the first campaign to teach all students – queer and straight – about gay and lesbian families.

Curricular Reform Controversies

Heather started to cry when she thought she was the only one of her preschool classmates without a father. However, her teacher Molly assured her that not everyone's family was the same. To illustrate the point, Molly instructed the class to draw pictures of their families. Many of the children created pictures of nontraditional households: a mother and sister, a mother and stepfather, two fathers, and a family in which none of the children looked alike because they were adopted. Heather, for her part, depicted her two mothers. After Molly hung the drawings around the room, she told the children that love was what defined a family.[39]

So went the story in *Heather Has Two Mommies*, a book that garnered broad attention – and generated significant controversy – after New York City cited the book in its first-grade teaching guide, *Children of the Rainbow*. Heather may have been fictional, but her story reflected a real change in American families. As a result of custody disputes, foster care policy battles, and the lesbian baby boom, increasing numbers of queer couples were raising children. In fact, the author of *Heather Has Two Mommies*, Lesléa Newman, wrote the story after a lesbian acquaintance bemoaned that there were no books she could read to her daughter about a family like theirs. The comment resonated with Newman, who as a child had been frustrated that she never saw her Jewish home reflected in the stories she read.[40] The queer author therefore decided to write the book to reduce the isolation that the children of lesbian mothers felt. The New York City curriculum set out to do the same, which is why it included *Heather Has Two Mommies* in its list of recommended reading. But the goals of *Children of the Rainbow* extended beyond providing support to the children of queer parents. By making gay- and lesbian-headed families visible to their peers, the city also hoped to instill tolerance for same-sex sexuality at an early age, thereby reducing the harassment, abuse, and violence that queer teens and adults endured.

Gay and lesbian rights advocates pressed schools to introduce materials like *Children of the Rainbow* precisely to prevent children from developing antiqueer attitudes. During this period, the limited information that students received about same-sex sexuality tied gays and lesbians to the spread of AIDS, which taught students to fear and hate the queer community. Educators' focus on children's households would help make families the main symbol of gay and lesbian life, rather than AIDS. Students would therefore identify gays and lesbians as integral parts of the social fabric, rather than dangerous vectors of disease. Curricular reform was also strategically important, as it provided another counterpoint to the religious right's child protection rhetoric, thereby continuing the reframing that advocates had begun with school counseling programs. Child protection claims insisted that the state had to protect children from gays and lesbians. Advocates of curricular reform maintained the opposite. Instead, it was gays, lesbians, and their children who needed protection from bigotry, harassment, and violence.

The debate over what it meant to protect children was what rendered *Children of the Rainbow* so controversial. New York City published the guide in 1991 as part of a broader multicultural education reform effort, spurred by the violent death of a 16-year-old in Bensonhurst, Brooklyn.[41] Yusef Hawkins, a Black student at Stephen Decatur Junior High, was walking with three friends in the predominantly working-class, Italian-American neighborhood when they were attacked by a group of white teenagers carrying baseball bats and brandishing handguns.[42] The New York City Board of Education responded by mandating a curriculum that promoted tolerance based on race, religion, national origin, sex, age, physical handicaps, and sexual orientation.[43] The Board included sexual orientation because of the rising levels of antiqueer violence, much of it the product of many teenagers' virulent hatred of gays and lesbians.[44] Despite the Board's clear directive, *Children of the Rainbow* barely referred to queer individuals. The document referenced same-sex parents on just three of its 443 pages.[45] These few passages were nevertheless important. They emphasized the need for teachers to help children develop a positive attitude toward gays and lesbians to forestall later homophobic discrimination and violence.[46] The guide also urged teachers to discuss the value of every type of family household, "including two-parent or single-parent households, gay or lesbian parents, divorced parents, adoptive parents, and guardians or foster parents."[47] At the time of the *Rainbow* guide's publication, family structures had become more diverse. Indeed, only one in five married couples with children in the U.S. had a breadwinning husband and a homemaker wife.[48] Because of the many variations in family types, the document reminded teachers that children raised by single mothers or lesbians could feel left out of Father's Day activities.[49]

Most districts in the City approved the guide with little discussion or fanfare, but even the document's limited mention of gays and lesbians outraged Mary Cummins, the president of Queens' District 24 school board.[50] She quickly launched a campaign against the curriculum.[51] Cummins was a devout Catholic who was committed to conservative causes.[52] Under her leadership, the District 24 school board had banned its teachers from mentioning abortion or birth control.[53] For Cummins, the *Rainbow* curriculum's decision to incorporate gay and lesbian families at all was appalling. Presenting these households as unobjectionable was even worse.[54] She fanned the flames against the guide by claiming, absurdly, that it was part of a larger plan to mandate explicit instruction in same-sex intercourse. In a letter to the district's 22,000 parents, she stated that fourth grade teachers would soon be required to "refer[] to anal sex" while demonstrating "how to use condoms and creams."[55] She also helped to create and disseminate videos, posters, and pamphlets that identified the curriculum as a "gay recruitment campaign."[56] Cummins did not wage her battle against the *Rainbow* curriculum alone. She received help from national Christian right organizations, who helped infuse the debate with inflammatory rhetoric.[57] To generate wider opposition to the guide, Pat Robertson's Christian Coalition joined forces with the Archdiocese of New York, creating a coalition that also brought together Orthodox Jews and Latino and African American Christians to create one of the city's largest cross-cultural religious lobbies.[58]

At these organizations' urging, many parents took to the streets, participating in six public demonstrations, including a rally outside the Board of Education that drew 2,000 attendees.[59] At a protest in City Hall park, almost 200 parents rallied against the curriculum, some holding signs that read "Homosexuality Is Not Normal."[60] As the controversy unfolded, Schools Chancellor Joseph Fernandez received two death threats.[61] The arguments reached such a fever pitch that shoving broke out at school board hearings in Brooklyn and Queens.[62] The Board of Education was willing to have districts delay introducing same-sex families until sixth grade, to alleviate parents' concerns that the material could influence children's sexual orientation.[63] That fact became lost as a vocal contingent of parents and school board members launched an assault on the *Rainbow* curriculum. A mere three references to same-sex couples had led the entire city to erupt in anger and acrimony. As the *New York Times* remarked, "[o]nce opponents had transformed Mr. Fernandez into a Hitler and the curriculum's lessons about families into the ABC's of sodomy, it no longer really mattered what the curriculum actually said."[64]

FIGURE 15 Opponents of the *Children of the Rainbow* guide protest outside the New York City Board of Education headquarters, 1992. The New York City teacher's guide made national headlines, generating heated debate over what students should learn about same-sex sexuality in school. © Donna Binder.

To quell the discord, the Board of Education ultimately eliminated the requirement that schools inculcate tolerance for gays and lesbians.[65] But by that point, the *Rainbow* curriculum had captured national attention, such that its very mention served as shorthand for queer rights issues. Elected officials around the country mobilized in response to the *Rainbow* controversy. In Elizabethtown, Pennsylvania, the school board approved a policy affirming that the district would never tolerate or accept "pro-homosexual concepts on sex and family."[66] One of the board members, Thomas A. Bowen, explained that the resolution was necessary in light of the *Rainbow* curriculum: "I think parents in New York wish they'd taken preemptive action before the superintendent introduced textbooks that present homosexuality as an approved alternative lifestyle."[67] As a result of the resolution, the town's administrators and music teachers prohibited the school band from performing "YMCA," as both the song and the Village People were "associated with the gay lifestyle."[68] The 1979 hit was not the only pop culture casualty in the fight to keep homosexuality out of schools. In Sawyers Bar, California, the school principal had to review episodes of Sesame Street before they could be shown to kindergarten classes after a parent objected that Bert and Ernie "promote homosexuality."[69] Questions about the fuzzy puppets' sexuality generated so much attention that the show's producers eventually issued a press release denying that Bert and Ernie were dating.[70]

Although many communities opposed implementing a queer-inclusive curriculum, that was not the case everywhere. In Fairfax County, Virginia, the school district had previously embraced a comprehensive approach to health education, requiring instruction on contraception, abortion, masturbation, and homosexuality.[71] In 1990, the school board unanimously approved a requirement that ninth graders watch a film entitled *What If I'm Gay?* and discuss the lesson with their parents.[72] The board dismissed critics' objections that the video could lead students to become homosexual, although it did give parents the option of having their children excused from class during the screening. Only approximately 1 percent of parents exercised that right.[73] These positive changes continued in the years after the *Rainbow* debacle. In 1992, after rejecting the queer-inclusive heath education framework that Mary Griffith had championed, the California Board of Education reversed course. The policy it adopted mandated the inclusion of all students, regardless of sexual orientation, and referenced families headed by same-sex parents.[74] The textbook the Board later unanimously approved based on this framework had an entire section on homosexuality.[75] Queer rights advocates provided trainings around the state to help teachers use the material in their classes.[76] Similarly, in 1993, the Massachusetts Board of Education recommended that all school districts incorporate "gay studies" into their curriculum.[77] That same year, the state enacted a prohibition against sexual orientation discrimination in public schools.[78]

Other localities voted out school board members who championed intolerance, demonstrating the communities' support for queer-inclusive curricula. Earl Kielley, an incumbent member of the Madison, Wisconsin school board, lost reelection in 1990 by a large margin because he opposed a ninth grade education goal that read: "[students] will be accepting of an individual whose sexual orientation is different from his or her own." Kielley argued that the proposal promoted homosexuality.[79] Community members responded similarly in Merrimack, New Hampshire. In 1995, the town's school board passed a sweeping policy that banned any activity or instruction that had "the effect of encouraging or supporting homosexuality as a positive lifestyle alternative."[80] Chris Ager, the board's chairman, described the move as necessary "to keep our Merrimack schools free from promoting homosexuality."[81] To not violate the ban, teachers removed canonical works, including Shakespeare's *Twelfth Night*, from the curriculum; eliminated instructional materials, such as one that referenced Walt Whitman's homosexuality; and stopped teaching students how to prevent AIDS.[82] The policy prompted student protests and a lawsuit; conservatives lost their majority at the next election, at which point the newly constituted school board rescinded the policy.[83]

Community members in some parts of the country therefore challenged opposition to the *Rainbow* curriculum, leading the pendulum to swing back in favor of queer-inclusive curricula. As a result, despite the significant resistance that the guide engendered, some municipalities began introducing materials that promoted tolerance for gays and lesbians. Students in these schools began learning that queer-headed households were a common part of society. By highlighting how same-sex couples formed families like everyone else, these lessons presented children with an understanding of gay and lesbian life that focused on conventional relationships, not sexual hedonism and disease. While this portrait of queer family life did not capture the diversity of the community's households, it did reflect the genuine beliefs of many advocates, who identified gay and lesbian families as indistinguishable in every meaningful way from households headed by heterosexuals. These advocates also had strategic reasons for emphasizing the similarities between queer and straight families. Doing so was a politically expedient way of tempering the controversies associated with even limited portrayals of gay and lesbian life. Indeed, even this strategy had only limited success. Because of the strident opposition that the reforms engendered, queer-inclusive curricula only spread to a small number of schools around the country. Yet the fact that any district instituted these lessons marked a seismic change in American society. After all, just a decade earlier, school district officials had uniformly rejected PFLAG's calls to educate students about same-sex sexuality.[84]

Perhaps more important than the limited change on the ground was the efforts' significant discursive effect. The educational reform initiatives may not have changed the curricular content of most schools, but they allowed gay and lesbian rights advocates to continue refuting the religious right's child protection arguments. Doing so was essential, given how often Christian conservatives wielded child protection rhetoric to impede queer rights advocacy. Through curricular reform battles, gay and lesbian rights organizations communicated that the key problem was not protecting children from gays and lesbians. Homosexuality, after all, was a common, unremarkable, immutable trait. Instead, schools had to focus on the needs of children with gay and lesbian parents, as well as the welfare of gay and lesbian youth, by combatting antiqueer bias. In other words, what children needed to be protected from was not the queer community, but rather homophobia.

Queer rights advocates met with intense resistance when they began lobbying schools to change what students would learn about same-sex sexuality, a fact that constrained their ability to secure even the limited reforms they sought. What would ultimately change the social and legal landscape was not just the continuing efforts of gays and lesbians themselves, but also the advocacy of their families of origin. In the late 1980s and early 1990s, unprecedented numbers of straight mothers and fathers of queer youth came out of the closet, so to speak, revealing themselves to be loving, supportive parents of gay and lesbian kids. In doing so, they introduced many Americans to a different kind of queer family. These parents would quickly become the key players in the fight to combat prejudice and violence.

A Different Queer Family

Karen struggled to explain why she had become estranged from her lesbian daughter, Nick. The two were airing their differences on a 1992 episode of the *Oprah Winfrey Show*, on "parents who can't deal with the fact that their children are gay."[85] Part of Karen's distress stemmed from not knowing the origins of her daughter's homosexuality. When Oprah asked Karen if she thought that Nick had been molested, Karen demurred, saying only that she "had certain reasons to believe that maybe she was a victim at one time." Nick rolled her eyes and shook her head, explaining that she had no idea what her mother was referencing. To bridge the gap between the women, Oprah assured Karen that same-sex sexuality was a natural variation in sexual orientation. To make her point, the talk show host offered the analogy of stepping into a field of clovers. Although most clovers are three-leaved, a few have four foils. She then exclaimed: "Every time I see a four-leaf clover, I say, oh, that's a gay clover!"[86] Oprah's audience laughed and cheered, delighted by their host's wit. Oprah's quip, however, did little to assuage Karen's deep discomfort with same-sex sexuality.

Karen was far from the only parent who had difficulty accepting her child's sexual orientation. The AIDS crisis had brought some parents closer to their gay sons and lesbian daughters, but the epidemic also exacerbated the rifts between many straight parents and their queer children.[87] Indeed, PFLAG had struggled throughout the 1970s and 1980s to convince parents like Karen to accept and support gays and lesbians. Yet, soon after Karen appeared on *Oprah*, PFLAG experienced a period of tremendous growth. Tens of thousands of parents flocked to the organization, swelling its ranks and allowing the organization to launch a concerted campaign against antiqueer violence. As PFLAG publicized the dangers of hate and bigotry, the group also helped change public perceptions of same-sex sexuality. Queer life did not just comprise gays and lesbians – it included their straight family members. That reframing of same-sex sexuality would help many Americans embrace queer rights.

PFLAG became a major player in national battles over gay and lesbian rights in the early 1990s, after a series of scientific studies emerged on homosexuality's origins. Until that point, PFLAG had struggled to recruit members. In part, the organization had difficulty addressing parents' anxieties that they were responsible for their children's homosexuality. The group knew that framing same-sex sexuality as innate was key to convincing parents to join their cause. However, PFLAG had so little scientific evidence to draw upon that, in 1988, the group conducted a survey of leading researchers to try to establish that homosexuality was innate.[88] Although the organization's president asserted that science was "laying to rest the myth that persons 'choose' to be homosexual," the researcher's statements were much more equivocal. Most agreed that sexual orientation was linked to genes and hormones, but they also maintained that psychological and "social factors" played a role.[89] The organization used the studies to prepare a pamphlet entitled "Why Is My Child Gay?," recognizing that many parents needed to answer this question before they could accept their child's sexual orientation.[90]

Then, beginning in 1991, a series of scientific studies made headlines for having identified homosexuality's biological origins. In a short article in *Science*, one of the leading peer-reviewed journals in the natural sciences, a neuroscientist named Simon LeVay reported that the hypothalamus of gay men's brains was much smaller than that of straight men, and about the size of straight women's. These differences indicated that there might be a biological underpinning to homosexuality. Only a few months after LeVay made headlines with his research, another scientific journal published evidence that homosexuality might be genetic. That work revealed that identical twins were more likely to both identify as gay than fraternal twins or adopted brothers.[91] A few years later, a third scientific report indicated that sexual orientation was fixed in the strands of human DNA. That study showed that 82 percent of gay brothers shared a DNA marker on the tip of their X chromosome.[92]

None of these researchers came close to establishing that same-sex sexuality was innate. In fact, all of the studies had profound methodological flaws.[93] LeVay, for example, did not verify the subjects' sexual orientation, but instead simply assumed that men who had died of AIDS were gay.[94] The studies' limitations were so significant that, when advocates tried to use them in court, many judges refused to credit the research with establishing homosexuality's immutable nature.[95] PFLAG nevertheless seized upon the science, knowing it was key to convincing parents to accept their children. At its annual convention in 1991, it tapped a medical researcher to discuss the findings in a keynote speech.[96] The organization also invested heavily in disseminating the scientific findings.[97] To publicize the research, the group used a $25,000 gift from an anonymous donor to create a "homosexuality and biology education fund."[98] As part of that project, it created a thirty-three page pamphlet, entitled "Why Ask Why?," which parsed the technical language of the studies.[99] The group explained that, since the science demonstrated that same-sex sexuality was a biological trait, parents should not feel "guilty" or "to blame" for their children's sexual orientation.[100]

PFLAG knew these arguments were crucial to convincing many parents to support their queer children, but the organization's emphasis on homosexuality's biological origins raised concerns among some members of the gay and lesbian community. In the 1970s, gay liberationists and radical feminists had been adamant that rights should not depend on homosexuality's origins. In the early 1990s, John D'Emilio, historian and founder of the NGLTF Policy Institute, drew renewed attention to their objections. At a NGLTF board meeting in 1993, he urged the organization to reconsider relying on arguments that gays and lesbians were "born this way."[101] He conceded the political utility of the argument and admitted that many members of the queer community believed that their sexual orientation was innate. But he noted that not all gays and lesbians agreed that they were born queer. In his view, the movement should be capacious enough to include everyone, not just those who agreed with the majority. Moreover, D'Emilio cautioned that the "born this way" argument could prove to be strategically harmful, rather than emancipatory. Science, in his words, was "a thin reed."[102] If researchers later disproved homosexuality's biological origins, the foundation on which the community's rights were based would crumble.[103] He consequently urged skepticism, asking movement leaders to consider why they felt compelled to "ask why."[104]

D'Emilio was not the only one to raise these objections, but most gay and lesbian rights organizations ignored these concerns about biological arguments.[105] PFLAG, like other groups, conceded that having to rely on homosexuality's immutable nature to secure rights could be problematic. It also agreed that, in principle, gays and lesbians should not have to justify their sexuality any more than straight individuals.[106] However, the organization recognized that biological arguments were what resonated most with conflicted parents. PFLAG's audience therefore limited the group's ability to focus on other claims. Political developments in the late 1980s also pushed PFLAG and other gay and lesbian rights groups in the direction of making immutability arguments. More specifically, advocates had to respond to the religious right's new tactic for opposing queer rights.

After losing the foster care fights, the religious right expanded its antiqueer rhetoric beyond its traditional claim that the state needed to protect children from homosexuals who would "convert" them to the "gay lifestyle," either through abuse or role modeling. Instead, it began asserting that gays and lesbians were inappropriately claiming "special rights" that society only owed to individuals who were discriminated against due to immutable characteristics, like race, ethnicity, or sex.[107] According to this framing, since homosexuality was a behavioral choice, gays and lesbians did not constitute a "legitimate minority" deserving of legal protections.[108] This argument took the focus away from children, all while doubling down on the claim that homosexuality was a chosen characteristic. The religious right's new mutability argument proved decisive to a range of queer rights debates, from battles over hate crimes protections to antidiscrimination laws.[109] It also generated renewed attention to whether same-sex sexuality was a biological fact or a behavioral choice.

PFLAG's intuition that these scientific studies would transform queer rights battles was correct. In the wake of widespread media accounts touting homosexuality's biological origins, political liberals increasingly identified gays and lesbians as "born that way."[110] Accounts of the research did not convince moderates or conservatives at the same rate, leading political scientists to conclude that Democrats were ideologically predisposed to accept the studies' findings and conclusions.[111] Regardless of why progressives more readily identified same-sex sexuality as innate, the result was the same: they became more supportive of queer rights.[112] That, in turn, had a significant – and rapid – effect on national politics. In 1988, Democrats selected Massachusetts Governor Michael Dukakis as their nominee for president, a candidate that gay and lesbian rights advocates reviled for having instituted a ban on same-sex foster parents.[113] Dukakis's apparent homophobia led one queer community magazine to compare him to Anita Bryant, the evangelical singer who had led the 1977 effort to repeal Miami's sexual orientation antidiscrimination law.[114] Four years later, however, all five Democratic presidential hopefuls aggressively courted the gay and lesbian vote.[115]

The studies also helped fuel PFLAG's explosive growth. Over the course of the 1990s, the organization expanded to more than 400 regional chapters, which collectively boasted more than 80,000 members.[116] Some parents came to the organization already accepting their queer sons and daughters. Others, like Mary Griffith, became involved only after losing their children. Her family's ordeal made her both reconsider her moral opposition to same-sex sexuality and become an advocate for queer youth.[117] But other new PFLAG members were parents who were unsure about homosexuality's origins and needed the organization's assurance that they had not inadvertently harmed their children. PFLAG was increasingly able to do this by pointing to the scientific studies of the early 1990s. PFLAG's larger size allowed the organization to become an even more effective and important advocacy group. It no longer simply helped parents accept the sexual orientation of their children – it transformed them into activists. The organization emphasized that parental love and advocacy went hand in hand. Parents' private support of their queer children was not enough. They additionally had to show their love by becoming vocal activists.[118] As one chapter put it, "We think of advocacy as support gone public."[119] PFLAG also framed gay and lesbian rights advocacy as a way of repaying the organization. One regional group, for example, reminded parents that "when you no longer need PFLAG, PFLAG needs you."[120]

With the organization's encouragement, by the mid-1990s, large numbers of PFLAG parents had come out of the closet.[121] The group's members attended Pride parades, contacted elected officials, and spoke at public events, using their stories to make their queer families increasingly visible.[122] That change was significant. When the parents of queer children took up the fight for their sons' and daughters' rights, they helped Americans see that support for gay and lesbian rights and support for traditional families was one and the same. Ironically, PFLAG's efforts succeeded by shifting the focus of queer rights from gays and lesbians themselves to their straight family members. Members of the public could therefore support civil rights for the queer community because they sympathized with parents, all while continuing to oppose same-sex sexuality, which many did. Indeed, most Americans continued to identify same-sex sexuality as immoral even as they increasingly backed sexual orientation antidiscrimination protections.[123] Of course, PFLAG parents fought against that disconnect, insisting on not just tolerance, but acceptance. The group made the then-radical argument that there was nothing wrong with being queer.[124] At the time, gays and lesbians were fighting for the right to raise children by emphasizing that they would not transmit their sexual orientation to their sons or daughters. That framing allowed these men and women to win custody battles, obtain foster care licenses, and secure adoption orders. However, it assumed that homosexuality was an undesirable outcome, one that society should avoid. PFLAG parents asserted the opposite. They did not love their children despite their sons' and daughters' same-sex attractions. They loved their children, full stop.

FIGURE 16 Three women marching in Pride parade, carrying signs that read "I celebrate my lesbian grandaughter," "3 generations celebrating true family values," and "I celebrate my lesbian daughter." The straight relatives of gays and lesbians, who became increasingly visible in the mid-1990s, helped change public perceptions of same-sex sexuality. Cathy Cade photograph archive, BANC PIC 2012.054, Box 10, © The Regents of the University of California, The Bancroft Library, University of California, Berkeley.

By the mid-1990s, PFLAG's growth and visibility on the national scene had allowed the group to take on new advocacy projects. One of these campaigns was aimed at preventing antiqueer violence. That issue had always mattered a great deal to PFLAG members, who lived with the constant fear that harm would befall their children because of their sexual orientation.[125] The only question for the organization was how to best address the problem. By this point, gay and lesbian advocacy groups had been working for decades to curb antiqueer violence by appealing to legislators and law enforcement. Given its unique ability to reach mainstream audiences, PFLAG tried a different approach: it took the issue directly to the public. In 1994, after debates over antiqueer ballot measures and whether gays and lesbians should be permitted to serve in the military revealed the depth of Americans' misconceptions about same-sex sexuality, PFLAG launched a public education campaign called "Project Open Mind."[126] The organization began by surveying residents of Atlanta, Houston, and Tulsa to devise a media strategy.[127] What they discovered shocked them. Despite advocates' decades-long efforts to publicize hate crimes, few respondents were aware of the epidemic of violence that the queer community confronted.[128] In Tulsa, only 6 percent identified violence against gays and lesbians as "very serious."[129] Americans were also unfamiliar with the disproportionately high rates of queer teen suicide, despite increasing federal attention to the problem.[130] In 1989, the Department of Health and Human Services's Task Force on Youth Suicide had issued a study revealing that queer youth were two to three times more likely to attempt suicide than their heterosexual counterparts. The document also reported that 30 percent of gay and lesbian teens had attempted suicide at least once.[131]

Project Open Mind consequently set out to educate the public on the twin issues of violence and suicide. In 1995, PFLAG debuted an ad that alternated between the image of a young woman, frantically searching through a room, and leaders of the Christian Right, intoning against homosexuality.[132] As Jerry Falwell, Pat Robertson, and Jesse Helms preached that "homosexuality is a moral perversion and is always wrong" and "God hates homosexuals," the woman found what she was searching for: a gun. The clip concluded with a sobering fact: "It is estimated that thirty percent of teenage suicide victims are gay or lesbian."[133] Within two years, Project Open Mind commercials had reached approximately 6 million households in four mid-sized cities.[134] Even more Americans heard about the advertisements than saw them, thanks to conservative commentator Pat Robertson. His threats to sue any broadcaster airing the commercials generated so many newspaper articles and editorials that PFLAG pocketed an estimated $5 million in free media attention.[135]

The campaign complemented the commercials with print ads and billboards.[136] In 1996, the Houston chapter spent $40,000 to put up sixteen signs on major freeways. After one of them was defaced, media coverage on antiqueer violence in the city skyrocketed.[137] PFLAG members used the opportunity to speak to newspaper and television reporters, which generated even more public attention, leading the Houston City Council to invite gays and lesbians to testify about hate crimes.[138] Project Open Mind also succeeded in making violence more visible in other parts of the country. In towns and cities across the nation, PFLAG speakers received invitations from civic organizations, business groups, educators, and faith communities.[139] PFLAG credited Project Open Mind with expanding its reach beyond its traditional community partners, producing relationships with national and international groups like the U.S. Department of Justice and the International Olympic Committee.[140] In each of these exchanges, PFLAG helped spread the message that hate violence targeted members of the queer community because of who they were. Sexual orientation, like race and sex, were immutable characteristics that no one could change.

Project Open Mind maintained that Americans should understand antiqueer violence as a significant problem, one rooted in bigotry and hatred. The danger to American society, PFLAG insisted, was not homosexuality, but religious intolerance. The organization was working to communicate this message when newspapers began reporting on a brutal assault in Laramie, Wyoming. The tragedy would send shock waves through the country – and the rest of the globe. It would also completely change the debates over antiqueer violence.

Matthew's Message

At first, Aaron Kreifels thought he was looking at a scarecrow. The University of Wyoming freshman had been riding his mountain bike on the outskirts of Laramie on October 7, 1998, when an errant rock sent him careening toward the figure. As Kreifels approached it, he realized with horror that he was not looking at a stuffed mannequin, but a person lashed to a split-rail fence. Kreifels, who had been a track star in high school, ran half a mile to the nearest house to call for help.[141] Kreifels later learned that he had stumbled upon 21-year-old Matthew Shepard – Matt, to his friends and family – also a student at the University. Matthew, who was 5 foot 2 and 105 pounds, had met his assailants the night before at a campus bar, where two men decided to target him because he was gay. After luring Matthew into their pickup truck with a promise of a ride home, they drove him out of town and tied him to the bottom of a wooden ranch fence. The men then tortured Matthew as he begged for his life, using a pistol to shatter his nose, cut his face, and crack his skull in four places. They ultimately abandoned Matthew in the near-freezing temperatures. He would spend the next eighteen hours alone, strung up on the desolate plain. When help finally arrived, first responders noted that Matthew's face was covered in blood, except in two spots. There, his tears had washed the red stains away.[142]

The barbarity of the attack shocked the country. The brutal hate crime became front-page news as journalists from all over the world descended on Laramie.[143] The hospital where Matthew was put on life support received so many calls that it began posting twice-daily updates on its website. Within days, those reports had logged more than 800,000 views.[144] When Matthew passed away six days after the assault, having never regained consciousness, thousands of Americans attended rallies, marches, and vigils.[145] In nearly every part of the country, cities, towns, and villages hosted demonstrations, processions, or memorials in honor of the slain student. The response to Matthew's death was unprecedented in American history. Only a few years earlier, parents had taken to the streets to protest the mere mention of gay and lesbian families in schools. In those confrontations, many members of the public insisted it was more important for educators to protect children against the danger of being queer than prevent violence against gays and lesbians. For these Americans, bigotry and hatred seemed less of a danger than the homosexual "lifestyle." By the time Matthew took his last breath, PFLAG parents had helped to shift perceptions of same-sex sexuality. Then, as the country grieved for the young man, advocates seized upon the opportunity to reshape the national conversation around antiqueer violence. In the process, they argued that violence against gay and lesbian individuals was also an attack on the family.

There were several reasons why Matthew's death had a marked influence on American society. The blond-haired sprite, who had just enrolled at the University, exemplified youthful innocence.[146] The press reveled in his privileged upbringing, which included a boarding school education in Switzerland, where he learned multiple foreign languages and skied during breaks.[147] Once reporters – at activists' urging – began describing his position on the split-rail fence as a crucifixion, Matthew became a martyr.[148] The religious iconography became even more explicit in the months after Matthew's murder, framing the choice as one between good and evil. In 1999, as the case against Matthew's assailants unfolded, a group of Matthew's friends appeared outside of the courthouse dressed as angels. They used their oversized wings to block the signs of the Westboro Baptist Church, a fundamentalist congregation that gained notoriety in the early 1990s for its public protests of Pride parades and military funerals.[149] The church had previously picketed Matthew's funeral, displaying signs that read "God Hates Fags" and "Matt in Hell."[150] Angel wings soon appeared around the country to counter antiqueer protestors.[151]

FIGURE 17 Photograph of Matthew Shepard, 1998. The torment that Matthew suffered produced a national reckoning, leading many Americans to understand the danger of antiqueer violence. © Gina van Hoof.

The media attention to Matthew's death helped many Americans finally understand that violence against gays and lesbians was a significant problem that the country had to address.[152] Journalists immediately connected Matthew's death to widespread antiqueer attitudes, thereby framing Matthew's murder not as an isolated incident of violence, but as just one example of a societal epidemic that the country had failed to contain.[152] Their articles, which drew on federal and state hate crimes data, emphasized that, like race and sex, sexual orientation was an immutable characteristic.[153] Advocates' earlier antiviolence efforts consequently helped journalists convey the extent of antiqueer violence. These reporters' arguments seemed to resonate with many Americans. Polls from after Matthew's death showed that 75 percent of respondents identified violence against gays and lesbians as a serious problem.[154] That figure was a striking increase from what PFLAG had discovered when it launched Project Open Mind.

Many tragic events quickly fade into the background, leaving society unchanged. But gay and lesbian rights advocates had spent decades publicizing the dangers of antiqueer bigotry. Because of their efforts, when the news of the attack on the young man swept the nation, America was prepared to understand hate crimes against gays and lesbians in a different way than ever before. What also helped Matthew's ordeal have an enduring effect was the work of his mother, Judy. Soon after Matthew's death, she began spreading her son's gospel, maintaining the public's focus on antiqueer violence. Judy was unlike many PFLAG parents. She did not bat an eyelash when her son came out, let alone grieve for a perceived loss. She had long assumed homosexuality was innate, reasoning that it was unlikely that anyone would choose such a stigmatized identity. Given society's homophobia, Judy knew that Matthew would need support from his parents to navigate the world.[155] But Judy was all too uncommon in her perspective. Many gays and lesbians, who had suffered the heartache of familial banishment, wished for the relationship with their parents that Judy had with Matthew.[156] When the brutal assault on Matthew propelled the Shepard family into the national spotlight, Judy immediately began communicating the clear, powerful message that parents should accept and love their queer children. In a statement issued shortly after Matthew died, she urged parents to hug their children and not "let a day go by without telling them you love them."[157] Judy thus explicitly connected antiqueer violence and the family in ways few Americans had seen before. In the years following Matthew's death, parents contacted Judy to ask how she had been able to readily accept her son's homosexuality. Those questions enraged Judy, who wondered how parents could ever consider rejecting their children.[158]

Since Judy never struggled with her son's sexual orientation, she did not become involved with PFLAG – or any other gay and lesbian rights organization – until after Matthew's death. But she quickly became a major figure in the movement to end bullying and antiqueer violence. In 1999, Judy filmed a PSA for the Gay, Lesbian, and Straight Education Network, which was lobbying for gay-straight alliances in high schools.[159] The clip began with images of young men in a locker-lined hallway, shouting derogatory epithets like "homo" and "fag." Judy then appeared, imploring viewers: "the next time you use words like these, think about what they really mean." To reinforce the point, the screen turned to an image of Matthew, with the years of his birth and death, followed by the words: "Murdered because he was gay."[160] The spot aired on MTV, where high school students were most likely to see it.[161] That same year, Judy also filmed a PSA for the Human Rights Campaign, which began with home video clips of Matthew as a child. Those soon faded to images of Matthew's killers and the wooden fence on which he spent his last moments. Judy then explained to viewers: "In a perfect world, if your child is gay, you don't worry about their safety, you just worry about them being happy. I loved Matt just the way he was."[162] In the first month of the ad's release, it appeared 525 times in thirty-eight states, reaching major markets like Dallas, Philadelphia, Los Angeles, and Seattle. It also appeared on screens in smaller localities like Albuquerque, New Mexico; Eau Claire, Wisconsin; and Burlington, Vermont.[163]

Judy's advocacy kept Matthew's story – and the effect of antiqueer violence on American families – in the national spotlight long after journalists and camera crews had decamped from Laramie. Through the Matthew Shepard Foundation, which the Shepard family created on what would have been Matthew's twenty-second birthday, Judy helped spread her son's story to promote acceptance for gays and lesbians.[164] In addition to PSAs and speaking engagements, the Shepard Foundation promoted *The Laramie Project*, a play that told the story of Matthew's life and death.[165] It quickly became one of the most-performed plays in the United States, appearing on hundreds of professional and high school stages shortly after its release in 2000.[166] Matthew became such a powerful symbol that, when Congress enacted a federal hate crimes prevention statute in 2009, the legislation bore his name.[167]

FIGURE 18 Judy and Dennis Shepard at the funeral for their son, Matthew, 1998. Judy's advocacy helped make clear that antiqueer bigotry harmed families. Photo by Steve Liss. Courtesy of Getty Images.

The country's reckoning with antiqueer cruelty had a tangible impact on the law, albeit an unexpected one. Advocates hoped that Matthew's death would convince elected officials to enact hate crimes protections, but those legislative efforts quickly stalled.[168] Hate crimes laws had always been controversial because they seemed to punish individuals not for their actions, but for their underlying thoughts. For many, the line between criminalizing hate and punishing speech was far too thin, particularly since prosecutors often used a perpetrator's language to prove they had been motivated by hate.[169] The brutal torture that Matthew suffered did not change the fact that, for the laws' detractors, hate crimes provisions extended the reach of the state in problematic ways. Legislators consequently focused on other, less contentious, means of protecting gays and lesbians from bias. In the years following Matthew's death, municipalities across the United States increasingly considered and enacted sexual orientation antidiscrimination ordinances.[170] These statutes conferred tangible rights on gays and lesbians, while also identifying the queer community as akin to other persecuted minorities, like racial and ethnic groups. The laws consequently offered many of the same benefits of

hate crimes laws without entering the debate over whether the provisions policed thoughts rather than actions. Moreover, the public
tended to approve of these provisions. Even though half of
Americans polled after Matthew's death believed homosexuality was
morally wrong, 82 percent said the government should treat people
equally, regardless of their sexual orientation.[171] As a result, when
conservatives launched ballot measure campaigns to repeal the
antidiscrimination laws, citizens overwhelmingly rejected their
efforts.[172]

In the wake of Matthew's death, schools also increasingly undertook efforts to protect queer youth and inculcate tolerance for same-
sex sexuality.[173] In California, the legislature responded to Matthew's
assault by outlawing harassment of gay and lesbian students and
teachers in public schools.[174] In Laramie, elementary school children
wore yellow cardboard badges, which displayed their pledge to never
hurt someone because that person was different.[175] Advocates had
long argued that schools could forestall violence by emphasizing tolerance. In the aftermath of Matthew's murder, policymakers and community members increasingly agreed. These changes showed how
much American society had changed from just over half a decade
earlier, when many rejected the *Children of the Rainbow* guide.
Of course, that did not mean that all schools changed their curricula.
Most did not. Similarly, hate violence against the queer community did
not end. Far from it.[176] But Matthew's ordeal did have a significant
influence on Americans' opinions, making them recognize that
antiqueer prejudice could lead to physical harm. The brutal attack he
suffered brought unprecedented attention to the problem of antiqueer
violence, helping make the issue visible. And that, advocates had long
recognized, was key to stemming the epidemic of violence.

* * *

By the time that news of Matthew's torture emerged out of Laramie,
gay and lesbian rights advocates had been working for decades to
inculcate tolerance for the queer community. They may have been
unable to prevent the horrors that Matthew endured on the
Wyoming plain, but their efforts nevertheless had a significant effect.
The police reforms that queer rights groups had secured in major cities

around the country helped victims come forward to report violent crimes. Because of the federal hate crimes legislation, the public increasingly became aware of these attacks. Also important was that some schools around the country had started teaching their students that gays and lesbians were committed partners and loving parents, exactly like straight couples. Children additionally learned that homosexuality was a matter of difference, not deviance. Those lessons helped to generate greater acceptance for gays and lesbians by providing a essential counter to the religious right's claims of homosexual "indoctrination." Advocates' state and local antiviolence educational policy initiatives thus allowed Americans to respond to Matthew's murder with unprecedented grief and outrage. In other words, Matthew's death marked a turning point for the country largely because of the campaigns that the queer rights movement had undertaken in the years preceding his murder.

Matthew's death also had an enduring effect because of his mother's advocacy efforts. Judy would not let Americans forget that her son's fate was all too common. She kept the issue of antiqueer violence in the national spotlight, as well as helped many Americans realize that the gay and lesbian community was not a separate population. She reinforced that queer individuals were cherished sons and daughters who formed an integral part of American households and communities. Moreover, Judy was not the only parent who communicated this message. The thousands of mothers and fathers who joined PFLAG in the 1990s all insisted that support for queer rights was a traditional family value. By sharing their love for their children, these mothers and fathers offered a crucial rejoinder to religious conservatives' talking point. They also countered the rhetoric of fear that permeated debates over gay and lesbian rights. During battles over domestic partnerships, foster care licensing, and adoption rights, gays and lesbians had begun reframing this narrative by demonstrating that they were committed partners and doting parents. PFLAG parents continued this effort, insisting that the queer community was not a population to be feared, but rather embraced.

Of course, not all gays and lesbians had supportive relatives. Many members of the queer community were estranged from their parents, who rejected their sexual orientation. Yet the lesson that PFLAG tried to teach the country was that opposition to same-sex sexuality meant harming both children and their families. That framing was important, allowing individuals who considered same-sex sexuality immoral to nevertheless support queer rights because they sympathized with straight mothers and fathers. What this meant was that, even where PFLAG parents were unsuccessful in cultivating acceptance for same-sex sexuality, their efforts still opened the door to queer rights advances.

Presenting gays and lesbians as members of conventional nuclear households made the queer community appear more familiar to straight America than it ever had before. What the public saw were parents who cherished children who happened to have been born queer. That framing would prove essential in the years to come, as gay and lesbian rights advocates became embroiled in a new legal battle: the fight for marriage equality. The struggle for marriage rights began after decades of advocacy on behalf of queer families, who needed state recognition to protect partners and parents. The AIDS crisis had made clear just how many rights turned on marriage. So too had the lesbian baby boom, which had produced thousands of mothers who were not their children's legal parents. Marriage equality offered a solution to these problems, such that same-sex couples increasingly demanded the right to wed. The country consequently became engulfed in debates over marriage equality, with Americans considering the nature of the queer family with an unprecedented intensity. By this point, gays, lesbians, and their straight families had all come out of the closet. Gays and lesbians had become visible as sons, daughters, parents, and partners. The question that remained was whether, given these changes, the country would be willing to accept same-sex couples as spouses.

Part III

Queer Families

As a child, Sonya Harry dreamt of the beautiful white dress she would wear on her wedding day. She was so excited about the party that her family and friends would attend that a family friend promised to bake Sonya a tiered cake for the occasion. Of course, Sonya did not just want a wedding. It was part of a broader vision of her life, which would include a loving partner and two children.[1] Because of Sonya's childhood hopes for the future, her parents initially struggled when their daughter later came out as a lesbian. For Tom and Jan, who were co-pastors in the United Methodist Church, the problem was not Sonya's sexuality. Instead, they were anxious about the barriers and hostility that their daughter would face as a queer woman in a prejudiced society. They also worried that Sonya's dreams of marriage and children would never materialize.[2]

Two years after disclosing her sexual orientation to her parents, Sonya put those fears to rest. In 2002, she and her partner, Alison, exchanged promises of lifelong commitment at a ceremony in her parents' backyard, adapting the vows that Tom and Jan had used at their wedding decades earlier. The family friend provided the promised cake, which fed the crowd of over 100 attendees who had gathered to celebrate the couple.[3] The event was not entirely joyous, marred in part by the reactions of some of the neighbors, who told the Harry family that they would stay away on the day of the wedding to prevent their children from being exposed to same-sex marriage.[4] Other neighbors, however, approached the family to express their support, in the process sharing stories of a queer brother, aunt, or other family member. Several same-sex couples also spoke to Jan and Tom about the event, wistfully remarking: "we wish we had lived in a time when we could have done that."[5]

The women's ceremony marked the LGBT rights movement's progress – as well as the distance it still needed to travel. Even as their family and friends celebrated the women's happiness, Sonya and Alison remained unmarried in the eyes of the law. When they wed in 2002, no state recognized same-sex unions. Eleven years later, the women traveled to New York to be legally married, but their home state of Ohio refused to treat them as family.[6] Because of the state's position, the boys who Sonya and Alison were raising lacked the security of having two legal parents. Tom and Jan's hearts ached at knowing that the state did not treat their daughter the same as their straight son. They communicated this hurt to the Supreme Court in an amicus brief that PFLAG submitted in support of the plaintiffs in *Obergefell v. Hodges*, which asked the Court to hold that laws prohibiting same-sex marriage violated the United States Constitution. Sonya, Alison, and their children, the Harrys told the Court, deserved better.[7]

The Harry family's story, like the many others that the Court heard as it considered *Obergefell*, emphasized that same-sex couples were no different than straight ones. Sonya and Alison were conscientious and devoted parents, who volunteered at their children's school and encouraged their sons' connection to their church.[8] The women were emblematic of the thousands of queer parents who had become visible and integral members of their community through custody decisions, foster care placements, and adoption orders. Not all gay men or lesbians had become parents, nor did most of the queer community fit the idealized vision of domestic life that Tom, Jan, and the marriage equality movement put forward. However, as the political and cultural battle over same-sex marriage heated up in the 1990s and 2000s, advocates discovered that highlighting the experiences of this segment of the LGBT community was necessary to attain marriage rights. Consequently, advocates underscored how gay men and lesbians were beloved members of straight families, who felt the pain of having the law define their relatives as lesser simply because they were born queer.

That was not how the movement initially framed its arguments. When advocates began their efforts to legalize same-sex marriage, they emphasized the Constitution's mandate of equal protection under the law. The government, they argued, was discriminating against individuals because of their status as members of a minority group, which was patently unjust. The movement quickly learned, however, that these legalistic arguments did not resonate with most judges, lawmakers, or voters. Securing marriage equality required a different strategy. Rather than focusing on equal treatment and antidiscrimination, advocates discovered that centering the values traditionally associated with marriage – love, commitment, and the desire to care for children – was the most effective way to promote marriage equality. The key was not to demand that Americans reject laws that discriminated against people because they were queer. Instead, what advocates discovered was that they should insist on same-sex couples' rights to marry so that gays and lesbians could express their dedication to one another and promote the interests of their children. Accounts of loving partners and parents like Sonya and Alison would consequently prove crucial to securing marriage equality. In fact, all of the legal changes that allowed for the creation of queer families and their increasing visibility in American society were indispensable to the rise of same-sex marriage rights. They served as the foundation upon which marriage equality was built.

Indeed, it was no coincidence that Tom and Jan, the parents of a lesbian, were the ones conveying their daughter's story to the world. Over the course of the 1990s and early 2000s, the families of gays and lesbians had become indispensable advocates for the queer rights movement. The arguments that Tom and Jan made – which echoed those of other marriage equality advocates – would ultimately convince the Supreme Court to rule in favor of marriage equality. That decision was a significant marker of legal change, one that the queer rights movement had spent more than half a century working to make possible. Because of those previous rights battles, the *Obergefell* decision did not serve as a harbinger of a new era in queer legal advocacy. Instead, it was the culmination of a broader social and legal transformation, one that could not have happened without decades of family-centered strategies.

7

More Perfect Unions

Marriage Equality, Public Opinion, and the Queer Family

Jackie Young was quick to emphasize that the fight for marriage equality was not a queer rights issue. Instead, it was a battle to vindicate a basic constitutional principle: the government should not discriminate against minority groups.[1] Young was a speech pathologist turned feminist activist, who had served two terms in the Hawaii legislature. In 1998, she led Hawaii's Protect Our Constitution, one of the country's first campaigns for marriage equality.[2] Same-sex marriage rights had become a matter of national controversy in 1993, after the Hawaii Supreme Court ruled in favor of gays and lesbians demanding the right to marry.[3] Five years after the decision, opponents of marriage equality had put the issue to the popular vote in the Aloha State, asking Hawaii's citizens to decide same-sex marriage rights for themselves. Protect Our Constitution, with Young at its helm, mobilized to protect the rights of gays and lesbians to wed.

With the help of the Human Rights Campaign, Protect Our Constitution raised more than $1 million dollars to fight the proposed ban on marriage equality.[4] It used those funds to develop and air almost a dozen television ads that highlighted the dangers of amending the state's constitution to exclude any minority group.[5] In one, a veteran civil rights activist, who had fought alongside Dr. Martin Luther King, Jr., reminded viewers that his rights "wouldn't exist today" if they had been put to a vote.[6] In another, the head of the League of Women Voters of Hawaii was even more direct about the dangers of allowing the government to discriminate against disfavored minorities. She warned voters that the state legislature had never before taken away rights from a group after a court ruled in their favor. "If they succeed," she asked rhetorically, "who is next?"[7] Ad after ad focused not on queer rights, but on the broader harm that governmental discrimination inflicted on society. The campaign highlighted how discrimination had injured Hawaiians in the past and created a dangerous precedent for the future. The measure's sponsors, the group explained, had singled out a minority because of a trait over which they had no control.[8] Such government behavior had to be condemned regardless of the identity of the minority group.

Protect Our Constitution's appeals to equal treatment and antidiscrimination principles failed to convince Hawaiians. On November 3, 1998, 69 percent of voters cast their ballots to restrict marriage to different-sex couples.[9] In Alaska, the other state where same-sex marriage was on the ballot, 68 percent voted to amend their constitution to ban same-sex unions.[10] These ballot measures on marriage rights – the first of dozens to come – took place during a tumultuous period for the LGBT rights movement. Voters cast their ballots less than a month after Matthew Shepard's brutal murder. That tragedy had produced an outpouring of grief from every part of the country, leading many to recognize that bigotry had deadly consequences. By that point, more Americans had also come to appreciate that same-sex attraction was not inconsistent with their values. However, a large gap remained between the public's willingness to reject intolerance and their readiness to accept same-sex marriage. For most Americans, marriage equality was a bridge too far.

Over the next seventeen years, the country would debate same-sex marriage rights with an intensity like never before. Marriage equality would appear on the ballot in thirty-six different states, sometimes more than once. In these electoral campaigns, LGBT rights groups suffered setback after setback. Advocates also experienced a host of legislative losses as elected officials mobilized against marriage rights for gays and lesbians.[11] But the marriage equality movement ultimately managed to stem the tide of defeat and change the course of the law. Courts began recognizing same-sex couples' right to marry and states started to enact laws enshrining marriage equality into their statutory codes.[12] By 2011, Gallup polls indicated that a majority of Americans supported marriage rights for same-sex couples.[13] The following year, voters for the first time adopted marriage equality at the ballot box.[14] When the Supreme Court ruled in 2015 that the U.S.

Constitution protected queer couples' right to marry, thirty-eight states already recognized these unions.[15]

What helped change the movement's fortunes was a major shift in strategy – one that was more than three decades in the making. When the fight for marriage equality began, advocates made arguments like Jackie Young's, which were rooted in logic and abstract legal principles. They insisted that marriage equality was simply a matter of treating similarly situated individuals alike. In their framing, gays and lesbians were just another minority group defined by an immutable characteristic, against which the government could not legally discriminate. As a result, queer couples deserved the same rights as their straight counterparts. Any other outcome constituted an unacceptable infringement of individual liberty. As compelling as these arguments may have sounded, advocates would discover, time and time again, that they failed to persuade their fellow citizens. Most people viewed marriage as much more than a state institution. It was not just a formal legal status, but rather a social tradition with deep emotional resonance. The result was that abstract arguments about equality and analogies to other forms of governmental discrimination simply did not connect with voters. Moreover, as in past battles over gay and lesbian rights, opponents of marriage equality quickly focused their arguments on child welfare, suggesting that same-sex marriage would be harmful to children. Appeals to abstract constitutional principles had trouble making inroads against the fears of child endangerment that marriage equality's opponents stoked.

LGBT rights advocates were only able to gain legal ground when they too appealed to emotion, likening their cause to the same attributes of traditional marriage that their opponents claimed to be defending. Marriage equality groups began to emphasize love, commitment, and the well-being of children. They did so by highlighting how discrimination harmed long-standing, devoted same-sex couples, the children they raised, and the straight parents who cherished them. They often relied on the parents of queer children to communicate this message, a practice advocates had developed years earlier. These straight relatives helped to reinforce the movement's emphasis on family life. By shifting their focus to love, commitment, and child-rearing, advocates framed marriage equality as consistent with traditional family values.[16] This approach riled many members of the queer community, who wanted advocates to pursue rights for those who bucked tradition, rather than those who embraced conformity.

The political landscape, however, prevented the marriage equality movement from taking that more radical stance.

Marriage equality groups were able to stake these claims because more than 100,000 gay- and lesbian-headed households already existed, thanks to years of family-centered strategies.[17] Over the course of the 1980s and 1990s, the LGBT rights movement had secured domestic partnership benefits, custody awards, foster care placements, and adoption orders. These families made clear to straight Americans that gays and lesbians formed committed couples, who then raised children. In the 1990s, the parents of queer children had come out to combat violence against their sons and daughters. Their work highlighted that gays and lesbians were part and parcel of traditional families. All of these changes transpired long before organizations put same-sex marriage rights on their advocacy agendas. Yet these decades of work on behalf of the queer family were what ultimately made marriage equality possible.

Earlier battles for family rights also influenced the fight for same-sex marriage by helping advocates learn crucial strategic lessons, namely the importance of working with nonlegal actors. Custody awards had depended on social scientists, domestic partnership benefits on unions and human resources personnel, foster care licenses and adoption orders on social workers, scholastic policies on teachers, and antiviolence projects on the media. Since marriage rights were so often decided through ballot measure contests, one of the movement's most important legal venues became the court of public opinion. As a result, the marriage movement found itself relying on pollsters, marketers, and designers. Campaign advertising became as important to the fight for marriage as briefs, statutory language, and administrative codes – if not more so. Television commercials and radio ads are not typical legal tools. And yet, for the LGBT movement, pressing for rights using nontraditional methods had become another crucial tool in a well-worn playbook. These commercials disseminated the movement's message that same-sex marriage was not a shocking break with tradition, but rather a reasonable extension of Americans' long-standing values.

Convincing the public took time. When the battle over marriage rights began, Americans were so dead-set against marriage equality that movement leaders did their best to dissuade same-sex couples from challenging the discriminatory laws.[18] The issue was simply too contentious. But not every member of the queer community agreed with that approach. In 1990, a Hawaiian activist named Bill Woods took matters into his own hands. He identified three same-sex couples who wanted to marry, then alerted local media as to when they would be applying for marriage certificates. Woods expected the men and women to make newspaper headlines. Instead, they made history.[19]

Mobilizing around Marriage

Ninia Baehr and Genora Dancel had been dating for less than three months when Dancel proposed. The pair met after Baehr's mother pointedly remarked that her beautiful coworker was a lesbian and urged her daughter to introduce herself. Baehr quickly fell in love with Dancel, a Filipina American broadcast journalist. Two weeks after their first date, Baehr told her mother that she had a feeling they would be together for the rest of their lives.[20] Less than three months later, the women were engaged. At the time, neither expected to be able to legally marry. For Baehr and Dancel, the proposal simply marked an emotional commitment to spend their lives together.[21] That would quickly change. Within a year, they had become the lead plaintiffs in the lawsuit challenging Hawaii's marriage laws.[22] Their case would spark the marriage equality movement, which did not exist prior to Woods setting the events in motion.[23] Although plaintiffs had filed for marriage rights before, and movement leaders had long been debating whether to pursue marriage equality, the movement would only coalesce in the wake of the Hawaii Supreme Court's decision in the women's favor. That ruling would also generate outcry, outrage, and legislative backlash all across the country, setting the stage for more than two decades of mobilization.

The women's involvement in the push for marriage rights, like their relationship, unfolded rapidly. A few days before Woods's planned action, Baehr had called the Gay and Lesbian Community Center in Honolulu to ask if there was any way for her to be covered under Dancel's medical insurance. Woods, who answered the phone, explained that discriminatory marriage laws prevented her from obtaining this type of workplace benefit. He then invited Baehr and Dancel to join the two other couples he had lined up to take a stance for justice by applying for marriage licenses. The idea appealed to Baehr, but she wanted Woods to speak to Dancel directly. When Woods contacted Dancel, he gave her twenty minutes to decide, since he had to dash off the press release.[24] The next day, after the state refused to grant them the licenses, Woods led the group to the Hawaii headquarters of the ACLU, where they applied for representation.[25]

Woods had a much easier time convincing couples to be involved in the lawsuit than he did persuading a lawyer to take the case. The ACLU, like many other organizations fighting for queer rights, refused to be involved in marriage advocacy.[26] For many movement leaders, the problem was practical. They recognized that discriminatory marriage laws served as a barrier to achieving equality, but they also believed the claims were unlikely to succeed.[27] Moreover, they thought that pursuing marriage equality was bound to provoke a backlash that would undermine efforts to secure antidiscrimination laws, hate crimes protections, and queer-inclusive educational policies.[28] Other gay and lesbian rights advocates opposed these lawsuits for ideological reasons. They agreed that marriage conferred a host of material benefits on couples, including tax deductions, social security payouts, and access to family health insurance plans. These advocates likewise recognized that marriage would bestow an insider status that would reflect society's acceptance of same-sex sexuality.[29] That privileged position, however, was the problem. For these advocates, the movement's focus should not be helping gays and lesbians conform to the mainstream. Instead, they believed that queer rights advocates should be promoting liberty. In their view, movement organizations should pursue the right to be different – to reject conventional marriage without penalty.[30] As a result, rather than opening up marriage to same-sex couples, this camp wanted community organizations to focus on redefining the family beyond nuclear, marital households.[31] Legal recognition for many types of family forms would have the benefit of opening the state's resources to a greater variety of households, which would create a more equitable welfare state.

Given these internal conflicts, it was no surprise that movement leaders kept marriage off their legislative agendas. In 1991, when the NGLTF provided its members with a list of issues to rank in order of preference, the group did not even include marriage as an option.[32] However, the movement's priorities would change after the Hawaii Supreme Court ruled in favor of the plaintiffs in 1993. In *Baehr v. Lewin*, the court held that the state's discriminatory marriage law was subject to strict scrutiny, which required the state to articulate a compelling justification for discriminating against same-sex couples.[33] Though this type of holding typically results in a statute's invalidation, the court did not declare same-sex marriage legal in Hawaii. Instead, it remanded the case back to the trial court to evaluate whether the state could meet the standard.[34] Despite the court's tentativeness, the decision caused a sensation around the country, as Americans – queer and straight – began to seriously think about marriage equality.[35]

FIGURE 19 Genora Dancel and Ninia Baehr in 1996. The women's lawsuit in Hawaii sparked a national marriage equality movement. Photo by Dennis Cook. Courtesy of AP Images.

The *Baehr* decision changed the queer community's thinking about same-sex marriage. For the first time, marriage equality seemed like something that advocates might plausibly achieve. Gays and lesbians who had never previously imagined getting married suddenly clamored for that right, knowing it would allow them to access essential, tangible benefits.[36] The queer community had learned all too well the importance of marriage during the AIDS crisis. Although corporate and municipal domestic partnership programs had made some spousal benefits available to same-sex couples, and second-parent adoption had granted lesbian mothers and gay fathers parentage rights, there were still a host of legal benefits that were only available to couples in state-recognized marital unions. What also motivated members of the queer community were the expressive gains that would come with legal marriage. The state's refusal to solemnize same-sex relationships communicated that gay and lesbian couples were lesser than their different-sex counterparts. Access to marriage would thus affirm the dignity and fundamental humanity of gays and lesbians.

For the movement's attorneys, who had been debating marriage rights for years, the decision was significant for another reason. Until the ruling, marriage rights appeared to be as difficult to secure as alternative family rights, which some advocates had been championing. However, the Hawaii court's opinion changed the movement's calculus. It created an obvious approach to achieving marriage equality, which was not the case for those who wished to disconnect the benefits of matrimony from the institution of marriage. That path forward was based on a legal doctrine called "comity." The doctrine of comity required states, in most instances, to recognize and give effect to the laws and judicial decisions of other states. That principle was why a marriage legally entered into in one jurisdiction was valid and binding in every part of the country.[37] Thus, because of comity, the *Baehr* case could do more than change the law in Hawaii. Since all states would have to recognize the Hawaiian unions, it had the potential to put marriage equality within reach nationwide. Lambda Legal Defense and Education Fund, which had declined to represent the *Baehr* plaintiffs, quickly shifted gears, making marriage rights one of its priorities.[38] The comity doctrine became the cornerstone of Lambda Legal's plan, which the group would put into place once the Aloha State began issuing licenses.[39] Lambda Legal would urge gay and lesbian rights organizations to focus their energy on getting couples to Hawaii, where they would legally wed. Lambda Legal would then litigate to have those unions recognized in their home states.

The decision generated as much attention from the queer community's opponents, who became particularly anxious about the future of marriage rights when they saw Lambda Legal's memo detailing its planned maneuver.[40] Someone had leaked the document. To defend traditional marriage, a coalition of conservative leaders devised a three-pronged approach. They would pursue a constitutional amendment in Hawaii to nullify the court's decision. They would also seek federal legislation to protect states from having to recognize same-sex marriages entered into in other states. Finally, they would lobby for state laws limiting marriage to different-sex couples.[41]

The constitutional amendment in Hawaii, which conservatives secured in 1998, was what took the longest. By that time, Congress had enacted the Defense of Marriage Act (DOMA). DOMA defined marriage under federal law as a union of different-sex couples and released states from their obligation to recognize same-sex marriages from other jurisdictions.[42] In the hearings on the 1996 law, DOMA's supporters wielded Lambda Legal's memo to emphasize the looming danger that the Hawaii case posed.[43] It was clear to federal officials that they needed to act quickly. Once the House Judiciary Committee had sent the bill to the full House, Speaker Newt Gingrich put the law on the fast track. Within three days, DOMA had passed the House with an overwhelming majority.[44] DOMA made its way through the Senate just as rapidly, landing on President Clinton's desk in September 1996. Clinton had supported gay and lesbian rights in his run for the country's highest office, but he had always drawn a line at same-sex marriage. Given that his efforts to change the military's policy on queer servicemembers had been a public relations fiasco, his advisors cautioned that a veto would jeopardize his chances of reelection.[45] Clinton may have been torn, but political pressures made clear that he only had one option. Late one night, he quietly affixed his signature to the bill, making DOMA the law of the land.[46]

Federal officials were not the only ones who responded to the Hawaii court ruling with legislation banning same-sex marriage. All across the country, state representatives became embroiled in debates over "defense of marriage" laws that defined marriage as different-sex

unions and refused to recognize same-sex marriages from other jurisdictions.[47] To support their efforts, conservative organizations distributed an explosive video entitled *The Ultimate Target of the Gay
Agenda: Same Sex Marriage.*[48] The video warned that, if Hawaii
started issuing marriage licenses to same-sex couples, a "legal night-
mare" would ensue. Other states would have to recognize the unions,
which would normalize same-sex sexuality.[49] The video made the
stakes clear: elected officials were not just voting to prevent gay and
lesbian marriage rights, but to forestall society's acceptance of same-
sex sexuality. That argument galvanized elected officials around the
country. By 1997, twenty-three states had passed "defense of marriage" statutes that banned same-sex unions.[50] In Hawaii, where the
supreme court had based its decision on the state's constitution, the
legislature approved a measure to amend the document, which voters
ratified in 1998. By that point, Baehr, Dancel, and the other plaintiffs
had taken their case back to the trial court, which had ruled in their
favor. The constitutional amendment, however, meant they could not
legally marry. The couples' lawsuit consequently did not open the door
to marriage equality nationwide.

But by that point, the events in Hawaii had inspired advocates on
the other side of the country, giving rise to the next chapter in the
marriage equality saga. The fight for legal marriage had begun with
couples who wanted to express their commitment to one another.
It would soon focus on the children they raised.

Litigating for Children

Susan Murray had been practicing law in Vermont for six years when
she heard about a troubling custody case. In the summer of 1989,
Susan Hamilton, Susan Bellemare, and their son Collin were driving
down a back road when a speeding truck hit them head-on. Hamilton
died at the hospital. While Bellemare was recovering from a fractured
hip, broken collarbone, and bruises to her heart and lungs, Hamilton's
parents secured temporary custody of 14-month-old Collin, who was
Hamilton's biological child. After Bellemare recovered, they sued for
permanent custody, arguing that blood relatives living in a "traditional
marriage setting" would offer the boy a more stable home.[51] Murray
volunteered to represent Bellemare and was quickly able to reunite the

family.[52] The "Case of the Three Susans" made Murray the go-to lawyer in Vermont on gay and lesbian family law issues.[53]

Murray thus had her finger on the pulse of Vermont's queer community when she attended a meeting at the Boston office of Gay and Lesbian Advocates and Defenders (GLAD) in 1994. GLAD had invited attorneys from all over New England to discuss the future of marriage equality in light of the ongoing case in Hawaii.[54] During that session, Mary Bonauto, GLAD's primary litigator, asked the group if GLAD should open another front in the battle for marriage rights by filing a lawsuit on the East Coast. Many in the room decried the option as reckless, but Murray thought Vermont was ready.[55] She had helped persuade her state's supreme court to rule in favor of second-parent adoption rights, a legal change that the legislature had then codified.[56] Vermont had been receptive to queer rights in other contexts as well. It had robust hate crimes protections and included sexual orientation in its nondiscrimination statute.[57]

In 1997 – as states around the country were enacting marriage bans – GLAD and Murray filed *Baker v. State* in Vermont on behalf of three same-sex couples.[58] That lawsuit would mark a new era in debates over marriage equality. In the wake of the *Baker* case, the justifications for restricting same-sex marriage would come to focus on child welfare. That shift was in many ways unsurprising. For decades, Christian conservatives had succeeded in restricting queer rights by arguing that gays and lesbians were harmful to children. At the same time, queer rights advocates had undermined those claims first through custody cases, then foster care placements and adoption orders, then finally through educational reform. Each of these rights contests reinforced that gays and lesbians were dedicated parents who nurtured their children, rather than harmed them. These legal developments would make all the difference in the marriage equality context.

That the case would turn on the welfare of children was not evident from the outset. The plaintiffs argued that the state's marriage law unlawfully discriminated against same-sex couples, in violation of the Vermont constitution's Common Benefits Clause. For the law to survive, the government had to establish that the law bore "a reasonable and just relation" to a governmental objective.[59] That standard required judges to weigh the plaintiffs' interests against the state's articulated goals. To help the courts appreciate the magnitude of the law's harm, GLAD vetted the plaintiffs carefully, selecting individuals whose lives would evoke judicial sympathy. Stan Baker, for example, was descended from a Revolutionary War leader, a fact that reinforced how marriage rights were consistent with the country's founding values of freedom, liberty, and equality.[60] Lois Farnham was a seventh-generation Vermonter who ran a Christmas tree farm, an occupation that offered a wholesome image of queer life.[61] GLAD selected Nina Beck and Stacy Jolles to highlight the practical problems that the discriminatory law created. When Beck gave birth to the couple's son, hospital officials challenged Jolles's right to be present because the couple was not married.[62]

GLAD's decision to include queer parents as plaintiffs in the case would turn out to be crucial, because the lawsuit – like many of the cases that followed – would hinge on the role of marriage in fostering children's development. The legislative blitz to ban same-sex marriage had produced a long list of reasons to limit the right to different-sex couples, including the need to protect religious beliefs, defend a traditional institution, and prevent courts from overruling the will of the majority. In *Baker*, the Vermont attorney general put forward two different arguments, both of which related to child welfare. The first, which became known as the "responsible procreation" claim, was that limiting marriage to different-sex couples furthered the connection between marriage and childrearing. According to this argument, the state offered the structure and benefits of marriage to encourage parents to enter into a permanent relationship, which gave rise to more stable family structures for children. Same-sex couples, who could not have unplanned pregnancies, did not require marriage in the same way as different-sex couples. The second argument was that children fared best in households with both a male and female role model.[63] This became known as the "optimal childrearing" claim.

Although these arguments would come to dominate lawsuits over same-sex marriage, the Vermont Supreme Court readily dismissed both. In the court's view, the responsible procreation argument was simply illogical. Numerous same-sex couples were raising children as a result of custody awards, foster care placements, and adoption orders. As the court explained, excluding these households from marriage did nothing to reinforce the link between marriage and childrearing.

Instead, it simply punished existing families, thereby harming children.[64] Thus, much like courts evaluating second-parent adoption petitions, the Vermont Supreme Court based its decision on the reality on the ground. Same-sex parenting already existed, and the law needed to recognize that fact. The state's second argument fared no better. The court described the idea that different-sex parents were, categorically, better role models than same-sex parents as "fundamentally flaw[ed]." The court noted that the state legislature had itself rejected this argument when it permitted same-sex couples to adopt.[65] The state could not claim that same-sex parents were good role models in one instance and bad ones in another. The adoption battles of the late 1980s thus made it possible for marriage equality advocates to counter the state's second argument. Because the state licensed queer couples as foster parents, it was clear to the court that the state had already determined that children could thrive in the care of gays and lesbians. The Vermont attorney general consequently could not justify discriminating against same-sex couples in the context of marriage.

Even though the court dismissed the substantive justifications that the state put forward for its discriminatory regime, it did not mandate marriage licenses for same-sex couples. Instead, the judges reasoned that crafting an appropriate remedy was a legislative prerogative.[66] In part, the court was persuaded by the state's argument that a sudden change to the marriage laws could have a "destabilizing" effect. The judges concluded that elected officials would need to provide guidelines defining the status and rights of same-sex couples to avoid confusion and disruption in government services. As a result, they ruled that the legislature would have a "reasonable period of time" to correct the discrimination that same-sex couples faced. The state could do so through any legal framework that offered same-sex couples the statutory benefits and protections of marriage.[67]

The court's compromise ruling offered the legislature an opportunity. Elected officials could comply with the mandate by offering same-sex couples civil unions, rather than expanding marriage rights.[68] Even this legislative option was extremely controversial, leading to what one commentator described as "one of the most intensely personal, deeply emotional, soul baring and heart wrenching debates ever held" in the state senate.[69] After both chambers narrowly approved the civil unions proposal, the governor signed the bill into law behind closed doors, explaining that he was eliminating the typical fanfare to avoid further exacerbating divisions among Vermonters.[70] The absence of a bill signing ceremony did not dampen the spirits of gay and lesbian rights advocates, who recognized that they had won a significant victory. Civil unions were not marriage, but the legislative scheme provided queer couples with the same state benefits as legal spouses.[71] Thousands of gays and lesbians flocked to Vermont to gain the rights that the state was offering.[72] Among them were Bonauto, who had led the Vermont litigation, and who was raising twin girls with her long-time partner.[73] Bonauto later described the outcome of the case as bittersweet. She had made a legal breakthrough, but she was disappointed that she had not secured the right to marry for the queer community.[74] Within a few years, she would make a second attempt at marriage equality, this time in Massachusetts.[75]

The lawsuit she filed in 2001, *Goodridge v. Department of Public Health*, unfolded in much the same way as the Vermont litigation. Like before, Bonauto spent a great deal of time on plaintiff selection, knowing that sympathetic and relatable figures would help persuade the judges to rule in their favor.[76] The complaint she filed was likewise based on the state's constitutional guarantees of liberty and equality, which were broader than those of the federal Constitution.[77] The Massachusetts constitution protected both "freedom from" government intrusions into protected spheres, as well as "freedom to" partake in state benefits.[78] In response to the complaint, Massachusetts made the same arguments that Vermont had, namely that restricting marriage was necessary to promote responsible procreation and ensure "the optimal setting for child rearing."[79] The state hoped that this case would yield a different outcome than in Vermont, but when the Massachusetts high court handed down its decision, its reasoning mirrored the *Baker* opinion. Like in Vermont, the Massachusetts court dismissed both of the state's arguments, highlighting their irrationality given the "sizeable class" of same-sex parents raising children as a result of custody suits, foster care licenses, and adoption petitions.[80] In fact, the state facilitated these families, both by permitting same-sex couples to adopt and by mandating that insurance companies cover assisted reproductive technologies.[81] The Massachusetts court additionally noted that "[n]o one disputes that the plaintiff couples are families, that many are parents, and that the children they are raising ... need and should have the fullest opportunity to grow up in a secure, protected family unit."[82] Like the Vermont ruling and the second-parent adoption cases that had come before, the decision was rooted in the reality of family life. Regardless of whether the state allowed gay and lesbian couples to marry, their households would still exist. If the state refused to extend the benefits of marriage to queer parents, it would only harm the children that it was claiming to protect.

Where the cases diverged was in their remedy. Unlike its neighbor, the Massachusetts court rejected the notion that civil unions were equivalent to marriage.[83] To comply with its constitutional obligations, the state would have to offer same-sex couples marriage licenses. Elected officials, knowing their constituents opposed marriage equality, responded by voting to amend the state's constitution. Unlike other jurisdictions, however, Massachusetts required a series of three votes over a multiyear period before a constitutional amendment could go into effect.[84] Until the process was complete, clerks had no choice but to issue licenses to same-sex couples. On the first morning that the ruling went into effect, Bonauto accompanied three sets of the *Goodridge* plaintiffs to Boston's City Hall to file their paperwork. Since Massachusetts typically requires applicants to wait three days before receiving their licenses, Bonauto then walked the men and women to Probate and Family Court to request a waiver of the waiting period. When asked for a justification, she explained: "They've waited seventeen years. They'd like not to have to wait an additional three days."[85] The judge granted the petition, allowing all three couples to wed that day. At the first ceremony, Bonauto broke down in tears upon hearing the officiant declare the couple married "[b]y the power vested in me, by the Commonwealth of Massachusetts."[86] For a lawyer who had been fighting for marriage rights for a decade, knowing that the state recognized the couple's union felt like "the cage had been lifted off, and it was just a different world from that point forward."[87] She was right. Within a year, approximately 6,000 same-sex couples had wed in Massachusetts, changing the face of marriage in that state.[88]

These unions shifted the terms of the political debate in Massachusetts. When the legislature met a year later for the second set of votes on the constitutional amendment, the provision failed.[89]

One of the officials who changed his mind was Republican minority leader Brian Lees, who had coauthored the original amendment. As he explained: "Gay marriage has begun and life has not changed for the citizens of the Commonwealth, with the exception of those who can now marry who could not before."[90] Other lawmakers and many Massachusetts residents had changed their minds as well. Immediately following the *Goodridge* decision, public opinion polls showed wide disapproval for the judicial opinion and strong support for a constitutional amendment.[91] One year later, citizens' views had shifted dramatically – so much so that voters returned to office those lawmakers who had endorsed same-sex marriage and elected more marriage equality supporters to the state legislature.[92]

Some members of the voting public, like Lees, had seen that marriage equality did not change society. Others had come to terms with same-sex marriage as a result of exchanges with their queer family members, friends, neighbors, and colleagues.[93] Over the course of the 1990s, increasing numbers of gays and lesbians, many of whom were parents, had come out, helping their community members become more familiar with both same-sex sexuality and the existence of queer families. Still others may have been influenced by larger social, political, and cultural shifts, which informed the debates over same-sex marriage.[94] Regardless of what prompted any person to change their views, the shift in public opinion helped to convince the state's lawmakers to leave marriage equality intact. As a result, same-sex marriage remained legal in Massachusetts.

Much like the events in Hawaii, the decision of one court in a single state would take the nation by storm. Those debates had already reached a fever pitch when, in February 2004, the newly elected mayor of San Francisco took matters into his own hands.

Responding to Marriage Rights

By national standards, Gavin Newsom was a liberal politician. In the famously progressive Bay Area, however, the Irish Catholic lawmaker had been the conservative choice for voters.[95] During San Francisco's mayoral election, Newsom had not given any indication that same-sex marriage rights would be on his legislative agenda. That changed after President George W. Bush's 2004 State of the Union address.

As Newsom walked out of the event, where Bush had lambasted "activist judges" and called for a constitutional amendment limiting marriage to different-sex couples, he overheard a couple denouncing the "homosexual agenda." The president's exhortations and the attendees' hostility disturbed the mayor, who immediately got on the phone with his staff to devise a plan of action.[96]

Three and a half weeks later, on February 12, 2004, Newsom announced to an incredulous press that his administration would start issuing marriage licenses to same-sex couples on Valentine's Day.[97] He explained to reporters that he had taken an oath of office, which required him to uphold both the United States and California constitutions. The *Goodridge* decision had convinced him that both mandated marriage equality. Newsom expected that courts would quickly shut him down. After all, the role of a mayor was to implement existing laws, not create new ones. But the "Winter of Love," as the press called this period in which queer partners could marry in San Francisco, lasted for twenty-nine days.[98] By the time a California court issued an injunction, more than 4,000 same-sex couples had traveled to San Francisco's City Hall to celebrate their marriages.[99]

The photographs and videos of queer couples clamoring to marry their long-term partners helped to change debates over same-sex marriage. For some, the images challenged popular perceptions of marriage equality as an assault on tradition. What the nation saw were men and women who sought to mark their devotion to one another in much the same way as their heterosexual counterparts. Many witnessed the couples' commitment, as well as the families they were raising, and became more supportive of marriage equality.[100] For others, however, the events in San Francisco made the danger of same-sex marriage more tangible – and immediate. To prevent elected officials from following in Newsom's footsteps, as well as to forestall additional decisions like *Baker* and *Goodridge*, opponents of marriage equality rushed to secure state constitutional amendments that banned same-sex marriage. Gay and lesbian rights advocates' victories thus produced a significant and sustained backlash, which impeded the marriage equality movement just as it was beginning to build momentum.

The first queer couple to be married in San Francisco were lesbian rights pioneers Phyllis Lyon and Del Martin, who had been together since that fateful night in Seattle when they confessed their feelings to one another.[101] Advocates bestowed the distinction upon the "founding mothers" of the movement in recognition of their long relationship and decades of advocacy for queer rights.[102] Honoring the couple was also a strategic choice. The women had been together for more than half a century, drove a Honda, and regularly got their hair done. Marriage equality advocates knew these facts would help undermine their opponents' stereotypes of gays and lesbians as philandering iconoclasts.[103] Lyon and Martin, for their part, never expected to be married. As lifelong feminists, the institution held little appeal for them. But when Newsom pronounced the couple "spouses for life," both women wept.[104] It was a moment of social and legal progress that neither had expected to see in their lifetimes.

The media soon flooded the country with images of ebullient gay and lesbian pairs, who waited for hours in the cold and rain for the legal right to wed their partners.[105] Many, like Lyon and Martin, were white-haired, older couples who had spent decades in committed relationships.[106] To show their support, Americans around the country donated money for local florists to give out bouquets to the brides and grooms.[107] The media attention inspired elected officials around the country, from Sandoval County, New Mexico, to New Paltz, New York, to issue licenses to same-sex couples, although judges shut down their efforts almost immediately.[108] The issue before the courts was not whether same-sex couples had a constitutional right to marry, but rather whether mayors and other city officials had exceeded their authority in answering that question on their own, rather than waiting for legislative action or a judicial order.[109] Since the role of the executive was to enforce the law, rather than to create or interpret it, the courts ruled that the local officials had infringed upon legislative and judicial prerogatives.

All across the nation, conservatives responded to these events by sponsoring more than a dozen ballot measures to restrict same-sex marriage. Unlike most of the initiatives that had come before, these were not statutory bans on marriage equality, but rather amendments to state constitutions. Changing the constitutions would keep mayors like Newsom from claiming they were obligated to recognize same-sex marriage rights. It would also prevent judicial decisions like those in Vermont and Massachusetts, which were based on interpretations of the states' constitutional provisions. Conservative groups put so many measures on state ballots that, by the 2004 election cycle, the LGBT rights movement simply did not have enough time, energy, or money to go around. Many of the ballot initiatives were in the South or Midwest, where local advocacy groups had never before worked on an electoral campaign.[110] As a result, there was little infrastructure in place to fight for marriage rights, which most local activists considered less of a priority than employment nondiscrimination laws and hate crimes protections.[111] These LGBT rights advocates were nevertheless forced to turn their attention to marriage because of the measures that their opponents had sponsored.[112]

In the Vermont and Massachusetts court cases, LGBT rights attorneys had won by focusing judicial attention on the queer families that formed as a result of custody cases, foster care placements, and adoption orders. However, movement organizations did not seize upon these arguments in the 2004 ballot box battles. They followed a different path, one that another set of advocates had set out years before debates over marriage equality had gripped the country. In the late 1980s, Christian conservatives had sponsored a series of ballot measures to restrict gay and lesbian rights.[113] In those campaigns, queer rights organizations had convinced voters to support their cause by arguing that the measures inscribed inequality into the law. These campaigns explained that discriminatory statutes inflicted tangible harms, because they meant that gays and lesbians could lose their jobs simply for being queer.[114] Moreover, gay and lesbian rights advocates underscored that allowing the government to target any minority group created a dangerous precedent for all citizens.[115]

These prior campaigns served as a model for groups fighting for marriage rights at the ballot box. During the 2004 election cycle, marriage equality organizations implored citizens to vote against marriage laws if they opposed discrimination. In Oregon, where voters had repeatedly cast their ballots to protect queer rights, the marriage equality campaign highlighted the many benefits that same-sex couples could not access without marriage, including the ability to make medical decisions for one another, visit their partners in the hospital, and collect pension benefits.[116] These advocates also noted that, with a ban on same-sex marriage, the state's constitution would no longer treat all citizens equally, which undermined one of the country's foundational principles.[117] In Oregon, like every other state with marriage on the ballot that year, the campaign explicitly avoided asking voters to endorse same-sex sexuality. Time after time, viewers heard that they were not voting in favor of queer rights, but rather were casting their ballots against discrimination.[118] They were ensuring equal treatment, which formed the cornerstone of American law. To reinforce the point, most of the campaigns used titles that emphasized nondiscrimination, like Equality Florida or the Fair Wisconsin Committee.[119]

Advocates' appeal to antidiscrimination principles and equality failed. Every state considering same-sex marriage rights approved a constitutional ban.[120] Once the votes were tallied, the legal devastation of the election was clear: the number of states with constitutional bans on same-sex marriage had jumped from six to nineteen. To make things worse, the nation had reelected a Republican president opposed to LGBT rights.[121] Advocates were stunned by the wave of defeats. Before Election Day, they had been buoyed by their successes in Vermont and Massachusetts, where the courts had concluded that marriage restrictions were discriminatory, harmful, and irrational. However, it was clear that the public did not agree. The electoral rout led even the most ardent of marriage equality supporters to think queer rights advocates had tried to attain too much, too fast. Some movement leaders wanted to deprioritize marriage rights in favor of different issues.[122] Others, however, urged their colleagues to remain steadfast and simply reevaluate the movement's advocacy strategies.[123]

Those who argued for staying the course prevailed. To determine what messages would resonate with voters, LGBT rights organizations set about testing various frameworks for talking about marriage.[124] Over the next several years, they conducted focus group research, which revealed that there was a way for the marriage equality movement to convince the public.[125] What these studies uncovered was that moderate Americans did not view marriage as a legal institution.[126] For many of those casting their ballots, marriage was about validating relationships, not obtaining rights or benefits.[127] For that reason, messages about abstract legal principles, like equality, fairness, and nondiscrimination, were bound to fail. Instead, the marriage equality movement needed to emphasize the emotional dimension of marriage: care, commitment, and love.[128]

Marriage equality advocates may have sought out this data, but they found themselves hesitant to adopt such a radical shift in strategy. Although the movement had weathered substantial losses in this period, its approach had also generated important gains. By 2008, six states had created domestic partner registries,[129] two additional state supreme courts had recognized marriage equality,[130] and public opinion polls registered steady yearly increases in support for both same-sex marriage and domestic partnerships.[131] These gains indicated that emphasizing legal rights and principles could yield results. Changing the campaigns' focus to commitment and sacrifice, on the other hand, might not necessarily be more successful. Moreover, the new approach ran the risk of exacerbating a rift within the queer community. Since the late 1980s, advocates had been divided on whether to seek marriage rights, with many dismissing marriage equality as an assimilationist goal that betrayed the movement's principles. For this camp, marriage was a patriarchal institution that limited who could access important state rights and benefits, which ranged from inheritance and parentage, to pension payouts and healthcare plans. The campaign for marriage rights thus only served to reify an unjust system. If the movement switched strategies to emphasize conformity, tradition, and family values, it would be embracing an assimilationist approach to an assimilationist goal.[132]

Because of these concerns, LGBT rights advocates were still debating strategy when Christian conservatives put another marriage ban on the ballot. That fight, in California, would finally convince the marriage equality movement to take the ideological risk and emphasize the traditional family. What this meant was that California's Proposition 8 would become a major turning point for the movement – and for marriage equality more broadly.

Strategic Turning Points

Mayor Newsom had expected courts to shut down his act of civil disobedience. However, he had not anticipated that his actions would lead the California Supreme Court to recognize the marriage rights of same-sex couples. Once he began issuing licenses to gay and lesbian partners, plaintiffs rushed to get courts involved. Some of the litigants opposed marriage equality and asked judges to enforce the state's 2000 statute prohibiting same-sex marriage. Others were supportive of queer rights. They demanded that the courts declare Newsom's interpretation of the state and federal equal protection clauses correct and enshrine marriage equality into law. The California Supreme Court settled all of the cases at once, ruling in 2008 that the state's ban on same-sex marriage violated the California constitution's Equal Protection Clause. After determining that sexual orientation was an immutable trait, and therefore deserved the same protections as race and sex, it applied strict scrutiny, which required the state to demonstrate that the restriction was necessary to serve a compelling state interest.[133] The attorney general's argument, that the law was required to protect the traditional institution of marriage, was insufficient to meet this exacting standard.[134] As the court wryly noted, limiting marriage to different-sex couples was unnecessary to protect the interests of straight households given that "[t]here are enough marriage licenses to go around for everyone."[135] Preventing same-sex partners from marrying, on the other hand, imposed "a real and appreciable" harm upon their families.[136] Together, these facts demonstrated that the state did not have a compelling interest in prohibiting same-sex marriage.

The court's ruling did not end the debate over marriage equality in the Golden State. That was because, even before the ruling came down, groups who opposed same-sex marriage had been circulating initiative petitions to amend the constitution.[137] They succeeded in putting Proposition 8 on the November 2008 ballot. By the time the campaign over Proposition 8 began, queer rights advocates had faced thirty ballot measures on marriage rights in nearly as many states. But the California contest was different. All of these other measures had been preemptive. They were efforts to keep marriage equality from coming to those states. Proposition 8, on the other hand, would eliminate the existing rights of hundreds of thousands of queer Californians.[138] Because the fight was so important, the campaigns for and against marriage equality spent a combined total of approximately $85 million, making the Proposition 8 campaign the most expensive ballot measure contest in U.S. history up to that time.[139] The more than $43 million that marriage equality groups spent, however, was not enough to preserve marriage equality in California.[140] Proposition 8 passed with 52 percent of the vote.[141]

At the same time, the experience would teach the LGBT movement an important lesson, one that would ultimately make marriage equality possible nationwide.

When opponents of marriage equality launched Proposition 8, their victory was far from assured. In fact, few thought the measure would succeed given the state's progressive politics. Even though Californians had approved a statute banning same-sex marriage in 2000,[142] early polls showed voters defeating Proposition 8 by wide margins.[143] But the measure's sponsors were dedicated to their cause. They hired consultants to conduct voter surveys and convene focus groups to identify what messages their campaign should highlight. What that research revealed was that, although Californians were generally tolerant of gays and lesbians, voters would be willing to prohibit same-sex marriage if the measure's sponsors could establish that failing to do so would impose tangible harms.[144] Supporters of Proposition 8 used this information to develop a game-changing commercial. In it, a pigtailed girl ran into the kitchen, excited to tell her mother about what she had learned in school that day. She handed her mother a book, explaining it told the story of "how a prince married a prince, and *I* can marry a princess!"[145] As the mother's eyes opened wide, a professor from the Pepperdine School of Law – an institution in southern California that emphasized teaching "Christian values" – appeared on the screen to explain that this was not a hypothetical scenario.[146] In Massachusetts, schools were "teaching second graders that boys can marry boys."[147] To make matters worse, the professor explained, Massachusetts's highest court had ruled that parents could not object. Without Proposition 8, the same events could unfold in California.[148] A follow-up ad featured the parents from the Massachusetts lawsuit, who provided viewers with a firsthand account of how marriage equality had undermined their parental authority.[149]

Neither commercial ever explained why teaching children about same-sex marriage was harmful. Neither needed to. Christian conservatives had spent decades arguing that mere exposure to same-sex sexuality would result in children learning to be gay or lesbian. As a result, viewers understood what the commercial was insinuating.[150] Most Americans had come to believe that same-sex sexuality was innate, but many were still fearful that it was not – and they were unwilling to risk their own children's futures.[151] Not surprisingly, a post-election report concluded that the "princes" ad was especially effective in persuading parents with school-age children to vote for the constitutional amendment.[152] Within a week of the ad's airing, poll numbers showed Proposition 8 in the lead by four percentage points, whereas before it had been trailing by fourteen to seventeen percentage points.[153] The television spots did more than reinforce the child protection arguments that had been present in so many battles over queer rights. They also addressed a second, growing concern among conservatives that had begun to percolate as public opinion turned in favor of marriage equality: that same-sex marriage would be forced on conservative institutions and communities.[154] Devout individuals feared that they might have to participate in activities that violated their religious principles. Even if the law protected their conscience-based objections, religious Americans would likely be vilified as bigots.[155] Christian conservatives worried that the wrath of the secular majority would ultimately reduce their ability to take a moral stance against same-sex sexuality.

Marriage equality advocates, for their part, were also furiously churning out ads to reach voters. Despite the wave of electoral defeats, which had only continued since the 2004 election, campaign leaders were convinced that appeals to antidiscrimination and other legal principles would resonate in their state. As a result, they prepared commercials that followed the same playbook as previous campaigns. The ads analogized the constitutional amendment to institutionalized racism, including Jim Crow and Japanese internment, much like the campaign in Hawaii had done.[156] The California groups also aired a humorous parody of the then-ubiquitous "Mac versus PC" commercials, where "No on Prop 8" took the place of the hip Mac and "Yes on 8" became the uptight, out-of-touch PC. In the ad, Yes on 8, dressed in a suit and clad with a gladiator helmet and shield, explained that he was protecting a different-sex couple from gay and lesbian marriages. In response, the couple expressed their support for marriage equality, noting that "same-sex marriages have been legal here for months and nothing's happened."[157] The ad, like the ones that emphasized antidiscrimination principles, appealed to logic. It asked voters to distinguish between their personal views on marriage and the practical effect of recognizing marriage equality. Marriage rights for same-sex couples, the campaign insisted, had little tangible effect on straight Californians, but had a significant impact on the day-to-day lives of queer individuals.

The campaigns' approaches could not have been more different. Marriage equality advocates appealed to reason, emphasizing the need to treat same-sex couples like their different-sex counterparts. Their opponents, on the other hand, played on viewers' emotions, capitalizing on their anxieties that marriage equality would harm children and devout parents. On Election Day, fear won out. A majority of voters cast their ballots in favor of the constitutional amendment, rescinding same-sex couples' marriage rights.[158] For movement advocates, losing the fight over Proposition 8 was devastating.[159] If they could not preserve marriage equality in California, they seemed unlikely to succeed anywhere else. The defeat did, however, produce a piece of data that would be instrumental to the movement's ultimate victory. It came from a nonprofit organization called Let California Ring, which had conducted a small-scale advertising experiment during the Proposition 8 campaign.[160] Its findings provided real-world confirmation of researchers' conclusions that a change in messaging could convince Americans to support marriage equality.

Let California Ring's experiment was as simple as it was ingenious. To test the success of appealing to love and commitment, Let California Ring developed a commercial that showed a bride facing a series of physical obstacles to meet her groom at the end of the wedding aisle. Her veil snagged, her heel broke, she tripped and fell. The commercial ended with a simple question for viewers: "What if you couldn't marry the person you love?"[161] The group aired the clip in the Santa Barbara media market, then compared polling results in that region to those of Monterey, a city in Northern California with a similar population. What it found was striking: levels of support for marriage equality rose by eleven points in Santa Barbara after the ad aired. In Monterey, where they did not broadcast the commercial, it stayed the same.[162] On Election Day, Santa Barbara was the only county in Southern California to vote down Proposition 8.[163] That outcome would likely have been the same without the ad, given that Santa Barbara citizens reliably voted for progressive causes. It was an outlier in a region known for propelling the contemporary conservative movement to national power.[164] The key data point for advocates was thus not the electoral result, but rather the jump in the polls after the ad aired. The experiment seemed to prove the value of appealing to emotion and emphasizing the conservative ideals of commitment, love, and family, rather than making logic-based arguments that depended on the abstract notions of antidiscrimination and equal treatment.[165]

With that lesson in mind, marriage equality advocates got to work revising their messaging. Freedom to Marry, a national organization for marriage equality, led the charge by creating videos with this new message for its partners to distribute across the country.[166] In one, a lesbian couple and their daughter laughed as they shared pizza and sang together at a church service. The women explained that marriage meant that "every child can feel good about the home they come from."[167] The commercial emphasized that many same-sex couples were parents, a fact that custody decisions, foster care licenses, and adoption orders had made possible. In another, a heterosexual couple, who had just celebrated their twenty-fifth wedding anniversary, told viewers that they wanted their gay son to "have what we have – a happy marriage."[168] This ad relied on parents, who had been such effective messengers in the antiviolence movement, to reinforce that gays and lesbians were part of loving, traditional families.[169] In a third, Freedom to Marry featured a mother discussing the parenting skills of her lesbian daughter Sarah, as well as the harm she had seen Sarah suffer as a result of the marriage laws.[170] This video combined the themes of the other two, both illustrating that gays and lesbians raised children and reminding viewers that queer adults came from straight households. The goal of every ad was to help viewers realize that same-sex marriage did not undermine their values. To the contrary, marriage equality was consistent with what they already believed.

By the time this new public education campaign was ready to debut nationwide, the social backdrop to the legal movement had begun to change. Public opinion had slowly become more accepting of same-sex marriage, especially as more gays and lesbians came out.[171] The increasing presence of queer television characters also helped. By the early 2000s, *Will & Grace*, which featured two openly gay men, including one in the titular role, had become one of the highest-rated shows on prime time television.[172] As Americans became more familiar with same-sex sexuality, they also became more open to marriage rights for queer couples. In 2011, for the first time, public opinion polls showed a majority support for same-sex marriage.[173] The next year, the political atmosphere had changed enough that then-Vice President Joe Biden announced he was in favor of marriage equality.[174]

It remained to be seen whether societal shifts in favor of same-sex marriage rights, combined with advocates' new messaging, would be enough to change the movement's fortunes at the ballot box. However, advocates were optimistic – so much so that a marriage equality group in Maine put a measure on the state's 2012 ballot, asking citizens to approve marriage rights for same-sex couples.[175] The way that advocates structured their campaign illustrated just how much the movement's strategy had shifted. Just three years earlier, the state's voters had adopted a statutory ban on same-sex marriage.[176] During that 2009 battle, LGBT rights advocates used their original strategy, appealing to logic and abstract legal principles. They argued that the proposed restriction was discriminatory and enshrined inequality into the law.[177] In 2012, the campaign changed its emphasis – and accordingly, its name. Equality Maine became Mainers United for Marriage (MUM). MUM then worked with Freedom to Marry to create a set of commercials featuring parents and grandparents, who spoke from large, light-filled homes and verdant, well-tended yards. These men and women explained that they had enjoyed long and loving marriages, and they wanted their gay and lesbian children and grandchildren to be able to have the same opportunity.[178] As one set of parents remarked, they did not dream of a civil union when they were young – they wanted to get married, and the two were not equivalent.[179] These mothers and fathers continued the tradition of parents advocating for their children, which the movement had learned was so effective at convincing political moderates to support queer rights. The ads emphasized love, family, and fidelity, with one describing marriage as "a commitment that comes from your heart."[180] The commercials' copy thus reinforced the visual image of same-sex marriage as a traditional family value, one consistent with support for conventional households.

On Election Day in 2012, the movement's new strategy paid off. Maine became the first state to approve same-sex marriage by popular vote. In Maryland, Minnesota, and Washington, the three other states with marriage on the ballot, the marriage equality movement was also victorious.[181] LGBT rights groups' complete sweep surprised everyone – advocates included. After suffering so many defeats, advocates had not dared hope that they could attain so much, so fast. That night's victory celebrations were only some of the markers of the movement's immense strides. By that point, twelve states and the District of Columbia recognized same-sex marriage as a result of court victories, legislative enactments, and successful ballot measures. Moreover, polling showed that the majority of Americans supported the right of same-sex couples to marry.[182] Many changes in American society had contributed to these shifts, including cultural, social, and political developments. But what had produced the electoral results was a change in strategy, one in which advocates emphasized the love that queer families shared. That approach may have further antagonized some members of the queer community, particularly those who did not want advocates to prioritize marriage rights. However, it allowed the marriage equality movement to secure legal gains that benefited countless queer households.

The advocates celebrating the electoral results could not have known it, but the movement's complete triumph was just around the corner. The person who would help to unlock the last door was an 84-year-old platinum blond named Edie Windsor. Her case, which the Supreme Court heard in the spring of 2013, would change how courts across the country approached debates over marriage rights.

Winning Marriage

Instead of a diamond ring, Thea Spyer gave Windsor an engagement pin that she could wear without raising questions about her private life. When Spyer proposed in 1967, Windsor was not out as a lesbian at IBM, where she worked as a computer programmer. Eight years later, Windsor retired from the technology company, hoping to spend more time traveling with Spyer.[183] However, Spyer was soon diagnosed with multiple sclerosis, which first required her to use a cane, then crutches, then a wheelchair, all of which made their journeys increasingly difficult. Toward the end of Spyer's life, Windsor became Spyer's caretaker, helping her into bed at night and assisting her with the oxygen mask she needed to sleep safely.[184] One of the women's last trips was to Ontario, Canada, which recognized same-sex marriages. They wed there in 2007, after being engaged for forty-two years. When Spyer died, she left her entire estate to Windsor, who had to pay more than $350,000 in taxes even though spouses are typically entitled to inherit the estates of their husbands and wives tax-free. Because of DOMA, the federal government did not recognize the women's union as a legal marriage.

Windsor sued.[185] Her case challenging the discriminatory law made it to the Supreme Court, producing a monumental decision. She asked the Court to review the validity of a federal statute, not rule on whether same-sex couples had a constitutional right to marry. Yet the Court's reasoning in that case would transform the legal landscape. Like the court cases that had preceded the lawsuit, it too would turn on the welfare of children and the queer families that already existed around the country. For that reason, the changes that the LGBT rights movement had secured to family law doctrines would make all the difference. The fights for domestic partnerships, custody, adoption, and foster care had created the families that helped convince the Supreme Court to recognize same-sex marriage rights. The battles that the parents of queer children had waged also helped the Court see that marriage equality was a continuation of tradition, rather than a break from the accepted norm.

In *United States v. Windsor*, the Court struck down DOMA after concluding that the statute inscribed inequality into the law. The federal provision, it ruled, inflicted a dignitary harm, demeaning the couples that some states had chosen to protect through their marriage statutes. Moreover, it introduced instability into marital relationships, burdening households by creating different standards for marriage under federal and state laws.[186] Although the Court's decision focused on equality, dignity, and the integrity of the marital relationship, the most consequential part of the opinion was its short mention of how the law harmed children. As the Court explained, the federal ban on same-sex marriage "humiliates tens of thousands of children now being raised by same-sex couples." It also noted that the law "makes it even more difficult for the children to understand the integrity and closeness of their own family and its concord with other families in their community and in their daily lives."[187]

FIGURE 20 Edie Windsor acknowledges supporters as she leaves the Supreme Court, 2013. Windsor's victory produced a sea change in American law. Within two years of the Court's decision in the *Windsor* case, the number of states recognizing same-sex marriage had jumped from twelve to thirty-eight. Photo by Chip Somodevilla. Courtesy of Getty Images.

   These references to children and parents were appropriately brief, given that Windsor was one of the few marriage equality plaintiffs who did not have children.[188] Yet those two sentences of the opinion would prove crucial. Since the lawsuits in Vermont and Massachusetts, legal arguments over same-sex marriage bans in the courts had continued to focus on children. In the eighteen cases that were appealed to federal Circuit courts or state high courts after *Goodridge*, fifteen were based on child protection claims, with opponents of marriage equality arguing that the laws were necessary to promote responsible procreation, optimal childrearing, or both.[189] Because of their emphasis on children, one judge aptly concluded that, although the marriage equality cases were formally about discrimination against gays and lesbians, "at a deeper level ... they are about the welfare of American children."[190] In these lawsuits, courts were focused on the children's emotional health, social adjustment, and educational outcomes. That was a very different inquiry from the custody disputes of the late 1970s and early 1980s, when judges concentrated on whether a parent's homosexuality would affect their children's future sexual orientation. That courts had moved away from that issue, which assumed homosexuality was an undesirable developmental outcome, indicated just how much more accepting American society had become of same-sex sexuality.

Because the cases turned on child welfare concerns, the legal disputes – like the custody cases of decades prior – centered on evidence from psychiatrists, psychologists, and other social scientists. In case after case, the American Psychological Association, American Psychiatric Association, and American Academy of Pediatrics filed briefs that attested that there was "no scientific evidence that parenting effectiveness is related to sexual orientation."[191] Expert witnesses reinforced this point, repeatedly testifying that there was no difference in the developmental outcomes of the children of same-sex and different-sex parents.[192] They also submitted lists of the approximately 150 studies that demonstrated that the children of gay and lesbian parents fared as well as those raised by heterosexual parents, research that the growing numbers of queer families had made possible.[193]

This social science research convinced many judges around the country that marriage bans did not protect children, but rather harmed them. Before the Court issued its opinion in *Windsor*, marriage equality advocates had registered a string of victories around the country.[194] The outsize influence of social science research on marriage equality cases, which overwhelmingly supported same-sex marriage rights, convinced conservatives to generate their own data.[195] In 2009, the Witherspoon Institute, a conservative think tank, tapped Mark Regnerus, a sociologist at the University of Texas, to conduct the research. With almost $800,000 in grant funds from conservative groups, Regnerus gathered a random sample to test the effects of same-sex marriage on children.[196] In 2012, he published his findings in *Social Science Research*, a leading academic journal.[197] Regnerus claimed to have shown that children of queer parents fared less well than those raised in straight households. However, the methodology he used to analyze the data was so deeply flawed that more than 200 social scientists signed a letter protesting the publication.[198] Among other problems, the sociologist ignored the effect that separation, divorce, and remarriage had on children, attributing any negative outcomes to their parents' sexual orientation rather than the instability they experienced. Regnerus's work did not just generate outrage within his profession. It proved equally controversial in the Michigan court where conservatives first introduced it. The trial court flatly refused to give it any credence, dismissing the sociologist's testimony and research as "entirely unbelievable and not worthy of any serious consideration."[199]

Debates over Regnerus and his conclusions quickly receded into the background after the *Windsor* decision. The opinion changed the political and legal valence of child protection claims. The Supreme Court had implied that gay and lesbian parents did not harm children – opponents of same-sex marriage did, by supporting discriminatory laws that stigmatized the daughters and sons of queer couples. Its formulation of the issue, in turn, provided a way for courts to circumvent social science debates regarding children's welfare. Most of the courts that issued their decisions after the *Windsor* ruling consequently did not address social science at all.[200] Instead, they emphasized how *Windsor*'s logic led them to rule in favor of the plaintiff couples.[201] Only two high courts balked at what had become a clear trend in favor of marriage rights for gays and lesbians.[202] In the two years after *Windsor*, the number of states that recognized same-sex marriage jumped from twelve to thirty-eight.[203] The legal landscape thus looked much different when the Supreme Court decided *Obergefell v. Hodges* in 2015 than it had in 2013, when it ruled on Windsor's case.

Child protection had only appeared in passing in the *Windsor* opinion, but it was central to the *Obergefell* ruling. In that decision, which held that the federal Constitution protected same-sex couples' right to marry, the Court dwelled on what it only mentioned briefly in *Windsor*: that gays and lesbians were loving, supportive parents.[204] The Court recounted the lives of April DeBoer and Jayne Rowse, a couple who exemplified the virtues of love, devotion, and sacrifice. The two nurses had adopted three children out of foster care, including a premature infant who required twenty-four-hour care and a baby with special needs.[205] The problem for these women, and what had led them to file suit, was that Michigan's restrictive laws only permitted adoption by different-sex married couples or single adults. The women consequently challenged Michigan's ban on same-sex marriage both because they wanted to solemnize their commitment and also to give their children two legal parents. Attorneys had selected these women as plaintiffs knowing their story would resonate with judicial decision-makers – and it did.[206] The Court emphasized how, should tragedy befall the couple, the children would have no right to remain with their other parent. The decision also noted that DeBoer and Rowse were only two of the many queer parents who sought marriage rights to protect their children.[207] By the time the Court heard arguments in *Obergefell*, approximately 690,000 same-sex couples were raising children. They lived in all fifty states and in 93 percent of American counties.[208] The Court emphasized that states and municipalities had made many of these families possible through foster care and adoption rights, as well as other family law doctrines. Yet, marriage laws harmed the same households that the state had helped to form.[209]

With that framing, the Court's opinion turned Christian conservatives' long-standing child protection rhetoric on its head. The purpose of the law was no longer to protect children *from* gays and lesbians. Instead, the state had a responsibility to protect the children *of* gays and lesbians. Queer rights advocates had been making this argument since the educational policy battles, when they lobbied for curricular materials that included gay- and lesbian-headed families. They may not have succeeded in transforming school policies in the early 1990s, but their argument resonated with the Supreme Court when it decided marriage equality rights. The *Obergefell* decision also emphasized the themes that had become so central to the ballot measure campaigns – responsibility, love, and commitment. Queer rights groups had learned that this was how the American public understood marriage, leading advocates to underscore these claims in their messaging. They did the same before the Supreme Court, where the justices responded in much the same way as voters. In its conclusion, the *Obergefell* opinion noted that "[n]o union is more profound than marriage, for it embodies the highest ideals of love, fidelity, devotion, sacrifice, and family."[210]

The framework that the movement had struggled to develop thus turned out to be the key to unlocking marriage at both the ballot box and the Supreme Court. The plaintiffs in the *Obergefell* case, much like the many other couples who fought for marriage rights, had not needed a state certificate to become a family. They had already done that on their own, by sharing in day-to-day joys, sorrows, and challenges. All of these couples had become spouses in every way that mattered, a fact that had helped the Supreme Court conclude that they should have the right to marry. Their love did not just make them a family. It also helped to change the law.

* * *

Four hours after the Supreme Court issued its ruling in favor of marriage equality, the hashtag #LoveWins had appeared in over 6 million tweets.[211] Revelers rejoiced in the streets, hugging, kissing, and waving Pride flags at rallies across the country.[212] That night, the West Wing joined the festivities by illuminating the White House with rainbow colors.[213] Executive staffers had been planning the visual celebration for weeks, hoping the Court would decide in favor of the gay and lesbian litigants.[214] Around the country, cities from San Juan to Niagara Falls also suffused their landmarks with rainbow lights to mark the historic day.[215]

The Supreme Court's ruling in 2015 did not just end twenty-five years of controversy over whether the Constitution encompassed marriage rights for same-sex couples. It also marked a decided shift in how Americans understood same-sex sexuality. Over the course of more than two decades, Americans had come to understand that gays and lesbians were not self-indulgent hedonists, as they had been portrayed at the height of the AIDS crisis. Instead, they were caring and devoted partners, as well as the children of straight parents who loved them. Moreover, the public had learned that many same-sex couples were heads of household, who raised children all around the country. It was not just that gays and lesbians had become more visible – they had become more visible as *mothers* and *fathers*.

Promoting that image of queer life was a deliberate strategy on the part of marriage equality advocates, who realized that they needed to make same-sex marriage appear as unthreatening as possible to straight Americans. They consequently featured attractive, successful queer couples and their straight parents in television ads around the country.[216] Lawyers representing marriage equality plaintiffs instructed their clients to refrain from publicly talking about sex in order to maintain the movement's focus on a wholesome image of families.[217] Movement leaders also selected a disproportionate number of mothers and fathers to serve as plaintiffs in their cases, to highlight the effect of the discriminatory laws on children.[218] Advocates' choices thus explicitly excluded less mainstream movement members, like flamboyant drag queens and sexual nonmonogamists, who drew attention to the ways in which members of the LGBT community defied convention. Of course, many of those individuals would not have volunteered to litigate for marriage rights, which they identified as subverting the movement's interests. But they also were not welcome to join the lawsuits. Marriage equality, the movement's leaders realized, could only be won by emphasizing the queer family's conformity with the conventional family. Advocates had to contend with the clear limits to what the movement could achieve. They had confronted these constraints time and time again, both at the ballot box and over the course of many court battles, which turned on the ability of advocates to convince judges that queer parents were no different than married, different-sex couples.

Movement advocates did not have to look far to find these families, which had formed between the late 1970s and 1990s through custody awards, foster care placements, and adoption decrees. By 2015, these households existed in almost every part of the country. Each and every one of these families illustrated the harm of discriminatory marriage laws, which demeaned queer couples and injured their children. The parents of gay sons and lesbian daughters made clear that same-sex marriage bans inflicted harm on not just the couples themselves, but also their relatives. It was the experience of all of these types of queer families that allowed courts to recognize that marriage inequality needed to end. Marriage might mark the start of many families, but not in this instance. The existence of queer families was both what led advocates to press for marriage rights and what made the *Obergefell* ruling possible. Marriage equality might have become the law of the land because of a Supreme Court decision interpreting the Constitution, but the foundation for the opinion came from changes at the state and local levels, which allowed queer families to form.

On the night of June 26, 2015, movement advocates could bask in the glow of having won a tremendous victory. Bill Woods, whose activism twenty-five years earlier had sparked a national movement, was not alive to savor the moment. However, he had been able to marry his partner, Lance Bateman, in British Columbia shortly after the Canadian province legalized same-sex marriage in 2003.[219] As he explained to a journalist, the couple had decided "long ago, if it's ever really, truly legal someplace, we'd do it."[220] Even as they traveled to formalize their commitment, Woods and Bateman realized that not everyone would accept their union. While in Vancouver, the men braced themselves for protests upon their return home from their wedding. The response was quite different from what they expected. The American Association of Retired Persons issued them co-memberships, while the men's title and insurance companies readily listed them as spouses.[221] The state of Hawaii might not have recognized their marriage, but their community did.

When Woods passed away in 2008, the *Honolulu Advertiser* printed an obituary that listed Bateman as his spouse.[222] Woods was buried in Decatur, Illinois, the town where he had been raised. The obituary that his family placed in the local paper noted that "[t]he best memorial to Bill would be to become or remain active in serving your community."[223] The simple statement reminded readers that ordinary people could change the world, just as Bill had. Marriage equality, like other queer family rights, became possible throughout the country because everyday Americans had taken a stance for equality in their towns and cities. Like Bill, these individuals likely had no idea how consequential their efforts would be. However, each one of them contributed to the transformation of American law.

Epilogue

Paula Ettelbrick, Lambda Legal's Legal Director, was known for her loud and pointed opposition to the movement's focus on marriage rights. But shortly before she died of ovarian cancer in 2011, Ettelbrick changed her mind. She was still concerned that prioritizing marriage equality ignored the needs of vulnerable members of the queer community. But she had also come to appreciate just how enormously the freedom to marry had empowered gays and lesbians.[1] Kate Kendell, who led the National Center for Lesbian Rights for twenty-two years, had a similar change of heart. In the early 1990s, she had discouraged organizations from taking marriage equality cases because she considered marriage an impediment to gay liberation. She eventually became convinced of the opposite. Marriage was not the problem – its denial was. True freedom required living in a world where the law did not discriminate against the queer community.[2] Kendell put her beliefs into action in 2008. During the window in which same-sex marriage was legal in California, she married her longtime partner, Sandy Holmes.[3]

As Ettelbrick and Kendell recognized, marriage equality was a significant victory. The movement for marriage rights secured legal rights for hundreds of thousands of queer households, who obtained access to essential benefits they desperately needed.[4] The campaign for marriage equality was perhaps even more consequential for its expressive effects. It helped to change many Americans' conceptions of queer life and the family, allowing the public to see gays and lesbians as partners, parents, and community members. That broader impact was one that many queer rights advocates – particularly those who initially opposed organizations' decision to devote time, energy, and resources to securing marriage equality – had not anticipated.[5] Of course, it was not the marriage equality movement by itself that secured these changes. Marriage rights depended on half a century of family-centered advocacy, which made queer households a ubiquitous part of American society. These efforts, which obtained legal rights for same-sex couples and their children, shifted the image of queer life in the minds of many Americans. In the mid-twentieth century, same-sex attraction was an indicator of pathology and danger, and the queer family unthinkable. By the time the Supreme Court ruled in favor of marriage equality, most Americans saw same-sex attraction as a benign variation in human sexuality. Gay- and lesbian-headed households, for their part, had become unexceptional.

The Court's ruling in *Obergefell* thus capped a period of extraordinary legal and social change. At the same time, it did not end battles over LGBTQ+ rights. Marriage equality was an important marker of progress, but the right to marry was only one step along the queer community's path to full legal equality. Indeed, same-sex marriage rights did not protect all queer households. Although the institution of marriage is available to everyone regardless of race, income, or social status, those who are most likely to marry are white, middle class, and formally educated. Because of this phenomenon, the *Obergefell* victory largely benefited the most privileged. Additionally, the movement's strategic concessions in the fight for marriage equality meant that advocates presented a limited vision of queer life to gain legal ground. The movement's messaging around marriage emphasized how same-sex couples promoted traditional family values and middle-class norms. Advocates developed these arguments to resonate with political moderates, but their appeal to conventional domesticity left gender and sexual nonconformists out of the conversation.[6] The LGBTQ+ rights movement is consequently continuing to work to secure the rights of these community members.[7]

As queer rights advocates pursue these goals, they are also contending with backlash to the community's gains. Immediately after the *Obergefell* ruling, Christian conservatives began mobilizing in opposition to marriage equality.[8] Much of this resistance centered around purveyors of goods and services for weddings, who argued that their religious principles prevented them from participating in same-sex marriages.[9] These devout Americans framed their demands narrowly. They did not explicitly challenge same-sex couples' right to marry under the law, but instead asked whether devout individuals could decline to participate in the weddings they found objectionable. That was a different claim – in both scale and scope – than the effort to ban same-sex marriage. At the same time, these refusals circumscribed queer couples' rights by limiting what products and services they could access. They also constituted an assault on the dignity of gays and lesbians, communicating that they and their marriages were somehow lesser than straight individuals and different-sex unions.[10] That was by design. For Christian conservatives, claims to freedom of conscience were meant to do more than simply protect their rights – they were a means of continuing the fight over same-sex marriage.[11]

In 2023, religious objectors secured a decisive victory before the Supreme Court in *303 Creative v. Elenis*. A graphic designer from Colorado filed suit in federal court, asking whether she could legally refuse to work with same-sex couples who wanted to engage her services to create a wedding website. Colorado's law protected against discrimination based on sexual orientation, but the designer considered same-sex marriage an affront to her religious principles. The Supreme Court ruled in the designer's favor. It held that the first amendment prohibited the state from punishing a person for expressing their sincerely held religious beliefs. The Court's decision addressed a relatively narrow situation, as the designer expressed her willingness to work with gays and lesbians on nonwedding-related projects. Her objection was to creating websites for unions that contravened her religious principles.[12] The opinion nevertheless emboldened opponents of LGBTQ+ rights, who took the ruling as an opening for other religious refusal claims, which queer rights advocates will have to combat.[13]

The rights of religious objectors are only one of many ongoing debates over LGBTQ+ rights. As the marriage equality movement advanced, political conservatives discovered that they could effectively use transgender rights as a wedge issue to limit and roll back the civil liberties of the entire queer community.[14] By emphasizing the danger of gender identity protections, conservative groups were able to convince voters to repeal both sexual orientation and gender identity antidiscrimination laws.[15] Conservatives also used fears of transgender individuals to secure a startling number of legislative restrictions on the LGBTQ+ community, including limitations on what students could learn about sexual orientation and gender identity in schools.[16] Additionally, they have successfully lobbied for laws that directly target individuals based on their gender identity, such as statutes that prevent transgender youth from accessing essential medical care.[17] In 2023, the unprecedented increase in anti-LGBTQ+ laws prompted the Human Rights Campaign – for the first time in its more than forty-year history – to declare a "state of emergency" for LGBTQ+ people.[18]

These difficult battles have been demoralizing to the LGBTQ+ community. But during painful periods of social and legal retrenchment, the movement's history provides an essential reminder that marginalized communities can attain meaningful legal change. Between 1960 and 2015, American law and society underwent a dramatic transformation. At the start of this period, the state persecuted gay men and lesbians. By the end, it often worked to affirmatively protect them. Over the course of just over five decades, queer rights advocates secured extensive reforms to statutes and legal doctrines, which helped shift the country's understandings of same-sex sexuality. Protections for same-sex couples and their children raised the visibility of gay and lesbian families, which then inspired others to come out. The prevalence of gay fathers, lesbian mothers, and their children demonstrated that same-sex sexuality and family life went hand in hand, thus undermining conservatives' narratives that gays and lesbians were harmful to children. The straight parents of queer children also contributed to the shifting cultural narrative of same-sex sexuality by showing that gays and lesbians were an integral part of traditional households. Together, these changes helped straight society become more accepting of same-sex sexuality. Decades of work on behalf of queer families thus allowed Americans to see gays and lesbians as partners, parents, and community members.

The movement was able to change how the public envisioned a "traditional" household by appealing to convention. But what also helped advocates press their case was that ideas about the family were shifting during this period. The family had always been a pluralistic institution, but it became more visibly diverse in the last three decades of the twentieth century. The religious right continued to idealize the nuclear household, but unmarried couples, single parents, and blended families became increasingly common as feminist activism upended gender norms, the sexual revolution swept the country, and states instituted no-fault divorce regimes. It was consequently easier for the queer rights movement to depict gay and lesbian families as simply one more variation on household structures. The end result was that, when the Supreme Court ruled in favor of marriage equality, same-sex marriage was no longer a contradiction in terms because Americans understood both homosexuality and marriage differently.[19] Indeed, Robbie Kaplan, who represented Edie Windsor before the Supreme Court, concluded her argument to the justices by urging them to recognize that the country had developed a new "moral understanding" of queer life.[20] Americans increasingly recognized that same-sex couples' relationships were no different than those of straight spouses. The law, she argued, simply needed to catch up to social reality.

The future of LGBTQ+ rights, like its past, will undoubtedly depend in some part on circumstances beyond advocates' control. But the movement's successes have been more than a mere matter of fortunate timing or serendipity. They were also the product of painstaking efforts and deliberate strategies. The queer rights movement secured remarkable changes over a relatively short period of time through small victories at the state and local levels. In these battles, advocates worked with nonlegal actors who helped them appeal to public sympathy. They attained these victories by focusing their efforts on discriminatory laws that affected daily life – first, penal code provisions that allowed gays and lesbians to socialize in public, then family law doctrines that gave rise to visible queer families. The changes to criminal statutes and family law that they secured were central to changing Americans' perceptions of same-sex sexuality, which in turn made additional reforms possible. The crucial players in these fights were not just lawyers, legislators, or judges. Equally important to change were social scientists, social workers, union shop stewards, human resources personnel, teachers, school board members, parents, and media consultants. What this history demonstrates is that advocacy at the state and municipal levels, alongside the work of nonlegal actors, can help transform civil rights law. That is because the divide between law and politics is porous. As a result, there are many opportunities for legal change, which a wide array of individuals can seize upon.

Over the course of fifty-five years, advocates fought extensively for each and every victory. They often had to rely upon arguments that many community members found distasteful, if not offensive. The campaigns for gay and lesbian family rights depended on presenting a sanitized vision of queer life, where advocates emphasized caretaking and affection, while deliberately obscuring gays' and lesbians' sexuality.[21] The movement thus succeeded not by offering an alternative vision to conservatives' conception of American society, as gay liberationists sought, but rather by challenging the exclusion of gays and lesbians from the mainstream. The fervent opposition that the movement encountered constrained its ability to press for change. Consequently, advocates have not yet achieved gay liberation's visions of the future, nor have they attained all of the community's legal goals. That fact, however, does not render their past achievements any less profound. The movement for marriage rights may not have reflected the priorities of all members of the LGBT community, but by eliminating a form of legal discrimination, it nevertheless promoted the rights of all queer individuals. Moreover, the LGBTQ+ rights movement has won victories that advocates thought they could never achieve when they began their work, a fact that should inspire optimism, even in the face of contemporary attacks.

Queer rights advocates secured such significant social and legal changes that many members of the LGBTQ+ community marveled at the transformation they had seen in their lifetimes. Indeed, when activist Tom Brougham looked back on his experiences as a gay man in America, he became extremely emotional. Brougham's voice caught as he described signing Berkeley, California's domestic partnership paperwork in 1984. For Brougham, the moment's significance extended far beyond the fact that the city finally recognized the men's relationship. It was also that queer rights advocates had won an important legal right at a time when their victories were few and far between. When Brougham joined the cause in the late 1970s, he had little expectation of success. As he explained, "when we started out, we thought that every stage was almost impossible, but we were going to fight anyway. It turned out none of them were impossible."[22]

Brougham's reflection provides a crucial reminder that, even at the darkest moments, positive change can happen. The future is never certain, but the gains of the past should inspire a measure of confidence. When Brougham's now-husband, Barry Warren, moved to California in 1975, the state still criminalized consensual sodomy.[23] The couple risked imprisonment as felons, as well as institutionalization as sexual psychopaths, simply for expressing their love for one another. Over the course of the following decades, the men endured taunts, insults, and harassment when they fought for their rights. But the law eventually changed. In 2008, the California Supreme Court ruled that same-sex couples had a right to marry under the state's constitution. Following that decision, the men wed at a small ceremony in their home, then sent an announcement to friends and family. It read: "After a very long engagement, Tom and Barry are married."[24]

Brougham and Warren should never have had to wait so long to be allowed to legally marry. Yet the hardships the couple endured remind us that the law can change in meaningful ways. The law can be cruel, but advocates can secure reform. As scholars, activists, and the public look to the future, the past may seem irrelevant. It is not. Studying the ways in which advocates secured queer family rights reveals that legal movements can achieve shifts in state and local laws that will help reshape society. Perhaps as importantly, the movement's history provides hope for the road ahead. As the LGBTQ+ movement continues to fight for rights, advocates' past successes should reassure minority groups that the law can change society for the better. After all, it already has.

Notes

Introduction

1 Mixner and Bailey, *Brave Journeys*, 12.
2 Rivers, *Radical Relations*, 25, 28.
3 Ibid., 28; Smith-Rosenberg, "The Female World of Love and Ritual," 10.
4 Mixner and Bailey, *Brave Journeys*, 12.
5 Ibid., 9.
6 Ibid., 9–10.
7 Ibid., 10.
8 Ibid., 12–13; Johnson, "A Narrative Life Story of Activist Phyllis Lyon," 59; *No Secret Anymore: The Times of Del Martin & Phyllis Lyon*, dir. Joan E. Biren (San Francisco: Moonforce Media, 2003), Prime Video.
9 Mixner and Bailey, *Brave Journeys*, 13.
10 Ibid.
11 Boyd, *Wide-Open Town*, 61–62.
12 Mixner and Bailey, *Brave Journeys*, 14.
13 Ibid.
14 Ibid.
15 Ibid., 14–15.
16 Ibid., 6–8.
17 Ibid., 6.
18 Ibid., 8.
19 Ibid., 16; Phyllis Lyon, interview by Margie Ada, 2011, www.glsen.org/sites/default/files/2020-06/Phyllis%20Lyon%20Transcript.pdf.
20 Mixner and Bailey, *Brave Journeys*, 16.
21 Ibid.
22 Ibid., 17.
23 Johnson, "A Narrative Life Story," 66.
24 Bullough, *Before Stonewall*, 160–68, 170–77; D'Emilio, *Sexual Politics, Sexual Communities*, 102–03.
25 Johnson, "A Narrative Life Story," 84, 88–89, 99–100; Mixner and Bailey, *Brave Journeys*, 32–33, 54–55.

26 Gilmore, *Groundswell*, 103–04, 117–18; Gilmore and Kaminski, "A Part and Apart," 96–97, 102, 104–07.

27 "Phyllis Lyon & Del Martin," *LGBTQ Religious Archives Network*, https://lgbtqreligiousarchives.org/profiles/phyllis-lyon-del-martin; GLBT Historical Society, Phyllis Lyon and Del Martin Papers, 2022, https://oac.cdlib.org/findaid/ark:/13030/c8fx7hq4/entire_text/.

28 Mixner and Bailey, *Brave Journeys*, 54–55.

29 Love and Cain, "Six Cases in Search of a Decision," 5; William Grimes, "Del Martin, Lesbian Activist, Dies at 87," *NYT*, Aug. 27, 2008.

30 Rachel Gordon, "Lesbian Rights Pioneer Del Martin Dies at 87," *SFC*, Aug. 28, 2008.

31 Grimes, "Del Martin, Lesbian Activist, Dies at 87."

32 Ibid.

33 Canaday, *The Straight State*, 5.

34 Lvovsky, *Vice Patrol*, 98–99; Stewart-Winter, "The Fall of Walter Jenkins," 222–23.

35 Antiqueer discrimination continued to be a fact of life at many workplaces, but over the course of the twentieth century, gays and lesbians could increasingly be out on the job. Canaday, *Queer Career*, 10–12, 261–62.

36 Rachel Gordon, "Couple of 55 Years Ties the Knot – Again," *SFC*, June 17, 2008. The City Hall ceremony was the first of the women's two weddings. The couple married in 2004 after San Francisco began issuing licenses to same-sex couples, but courts later invalidated those unions. They wed again in 2008, after the California Supreme Court ruled that the state constitution protected the rights of same-sex couples to marry. Ibid.

37 Eskridge and Riano, *Marriage Equality*; Frank, *Awakening*; Hirschman, *Victory*; Issenberg, *The Engagement*; Klarman, *From the Closet to the Altar*; Pinello, *America's Struggle for Same-Sex Marriage*; Yoshino, *Speak Now*.

38 Barack Obama, "Remarks by the President on the Supreme Court Decision on Marriage Equality" (speech, Washington, DC, June 26, 2015), https://obamawhitehouse.archives.gov/the-press-office/2015/06/26/remarks-president-supreme-court-decision-marriage-equality.

39 Ibid.

40 Becky Bowers, "President Barack Obama's Shifting Stance on Gay Marriage," *PolitiFact*, May 11, 2012.

41 Hull and Ortyl, "Same-Sex Marriage and Constituent Perceptions of the LGBT Rights Movement," 84–86.

42 NeJaime, "Differentiating Assimilation," 3.

43 United States Government Accountability Office, Defense of Marriage Act: Update to Prior Report, Jan. 23, 2004.

44 Chauncey, *Why Marriage?*, 97–98.

45 "Gay Marriage: A Must or a Bust?," *Out/Look*, Fall 1989.

46 Thomas B. Stoddard, "Why Gay People Should Seek the Right to Marry," *Out/Look*, Fall 1989, 12.

47 Ibid.

48 Paula Ettelbrick, "Since When Is Marriage a Path to Liberation?," *Out/Look*, Fall 1989, 9.

49 Ibid.

50 Ibid., 16.

51 Ibid., 14.

52 Mecca, "Introduction," xi.

53 Adler, *Gay Priori*, 86–89; Franke, *Wedlocked*, 9–10; Warner, *The Trouble with Normal*, 91; Craig Willse and Dean Spade, "Marriage Will Never Set Us Free," *Convergence*, Sept. 6, 2013.

54 Case, "Missing Sex Talk in the Supreme Court's Same-Sex Marriage Cases," 678–84; Franke, "The Politics of Same-Sex Marriage Politics," 239–40; Franke, "The Domesticated Liberty of *Lawrence v. Texas*," 1416.

55 Carbone and Cahn, *Marriage Markets*, 17–19; Infanti, "Victims of Our Own Success," 82–85; Joslin, "The Gay Rights Canon and the Right to Nonmarriage," 445–46; Murray, "*Obergefell v. Hodges* and Nonmarriage Inequality," 1209–10.

56 United States Government Accountability Office, Defense of Marriage Act: Update to Prior Report, Jan. 23, 2004, www.gao.gov/assets/gao-04-353r.pdf.

57 Harvey, *A Brief History of Neoliberalism*, 12.

58 Alsott, "Neoliberalism in U.S. Family Law," 26; Robson, "Assimilation, Marriage, and Lesbian Liberation," 786; Rosenbury, "Federal Visions of Private Family Support," 1867.

59 Issenberg, *The Engagement*, 27–29.

60 Murray, "Marriage as Punishment," 56–60; Polikoff, "The New 'Illegitimacy,'" 722; Robson, "Assimilation, Marriage, and Lesbian Liberation," 800–02; Spade, "Under the Cover of Gay Rights," 84.

61 Wuest, *Born This Way*, 55–58.

62 Ibid., 58; Radicalesbians, "The Woman-Identified Woman," 1970, www .historyisaweapon.com/defcon1/radicalesbianswoman.html.

63 Adler, *Gay Priori*, 86–89; Case, "Missing Sex Talk in the Supreme Court's Same-Sex Marriage Cases," 67–84; Franke, "The Domesticated Liberty of *Lawrence v. Texas*," 1416; Franke, "The Politics of Same-Sex Marriage Politics," 239–40; Godsoe, "Perfect Plaintiffs," 153–54; Robinson and Frost, "The Afterlife of Homophobia," 221–22; Willse and Spade, "Marriage Will Never Set Us Free."

64 Weinrib, *The Taming of Free Speech*; Goluboff, *The Lost Promise of Civil Rights*.

65 Bill Vlasic, "In Michigan, Gay Couples Marry in Mass Ceremony," *NYT*, June 26, 2014.

66 "1st Gay Couple in Mass. to Wed Rejoice in Ruling," *Boston Herald*, June 27, 2015; Kera Bolonik, "I'd Never Thought I'd See the Day," *Salon*, June 27, 2015, www .salon.com/2015/06/27/i_never_thought_id_see_this_day_partner/; Claire Galofaro, "Some Officials Not Ready to Issue Same-Sex Licenses," *Detroit News*, June 26, 2015.

67 Chauncey, *Why Marriage?*, 66–70.

68 Cott, *Public Vows*, 202; Lefkovitz, *Strange Bedfellows*, 3.

69 Peck, *Not Just Roommates*, 10.

70 Cott, *Public Vows*, 205–06; Self, *All in the Family*, 328–29.

71 Dinner, "The Divorce Bargain," 112, 124–25; Lefkovitz, *Strange Bedfellows*, 11; Mayeri, "Foundling Fathers," 2297–300.

72 Self, *All in the Family*, 5–6.

73 Bérubé, *Coming Out under Fire*; Canaday, *The Straight State*; Johnson, *The Lavender Scare*; Stein, *Sexual Injustice*.

74 Carpenter, *The Forging of Bureaucratic Autonomy*; Goluboff, *The Lost Promise of Civil Rights*; Klarman, *From Jim Crow to Civil Rights*; Lee, *The Workplace Constitution*; Mayeri, *Reasoning from Race*; Tani, *States of Dependency*; Weinrib, *The Taming of Free Speech*.

75 Brown-Nagin, *Courage to Dissent*; Hanhardt, *Safe Space*; Stewart-Winter, *Queer Clout*.

76 Edwards, *Gendered Strife and Confusion*; Hartog, *Man and Wife in America*; Jones, *Birthright Citizens*; Kornbluh, *The Battle for Welfare Rights*; Lvovsky, *Vice Patrol*; Rivers, *Radical Relations*.

77 Eskridge, *Dishonorable Passions*; Klarman, *From the Closet to the Altar*; Leachman, "From Protest to *Perry*"; NeJaime, "Marriage Equality and the New Parenthood"; NeJaime, "The Legal Mobilization Dilemma."

78 Kornbluh and Tani, "Siting the Legal History of Poverty," 329–30; Tani, *States of Dependency*, 20–21.

79 Polletta, *It Was Like a Fever*, 19.

80 Guinier and Torres, "Changing the Wind," 2752; McCann, "Law and Social Movements," 29–30; Siegel, "Constitutional Culture, Social Movement Conflict and Constitutional Change," 1360–61; Zemans, "Legal Mobilization," 697–98.

81 Cummings, "The Social Movement Turn in Law," 373, 395; Klarman, *From Jim Crow to Civil Rights*, 467–68; Rosenberg, *The Hollow Hope*, 427; Scheingold, *The Politics of Rights*, 130.

82 Stein, "Crossing the Border to Memory," 95–96.

83 Record from the Immigration and Naturalization Service, Boutilier v. Immigration and Naturalization Service, No. 440 (U.S. Nov. 28, 1966), at 13, https://outhistory .org/files/original/82de81d7d40bb8e9feee9e80a733454a.pdf.

84 Stein, "Crossing the Border to Memory," 96.

85 Record from the Immigration and Naturalization Service, 3. Boutilier's immigration case file does not indicate how the men came to the attention of the police.

86 Stein, "Crossing the Border to Memory," 94.

87 Record from the Immigration and Naturalization Service, 14–15.

88 Ibid., 15; Stein, "Crossing the Border to Memory," 101.

89 Yoshino, "The Epistemic Contract of Bisexual Erasure," 364–68, 397–99. Historical documents overwhelmingly refer to gays and lesbians, leaving out bisexuals. This book's account is consequently limited to gay and lesbian rights advocacy, although many of the battles likely involved bisexuals and necessarily implicated their rights.

90 George, "Expanding LGBT," 245–47; George, "The LGBT Disconnect," 538–48.

91 Johnson, *This Is Our Message*, 63; Bob Mercer, "Give Pies a Chance," *Georgia's Straight* (Vancouver), Dec. 14, 1977, Box 4, Folder labeled "Pie File," Tom Higgins Papers.

92 Margalit Fox, "Barbara Gittings, 74, Prominent Gay Rights Activist since '50s, Dies," *NYT*, Mar. 15, 2007.

93 The surviving historical documents are clear that police arrested Chapman because he was engaged in some kind of sexual activity with another adult man, but they do not provide more specifics as to the nature of that activity or how the men came to the police's attention.

94 Kelly Ochodnicky, Office of the Livingston County Clerk, email to Sally Irvin, June 10, 2018, on file with author.

95 People v. Chapman, 301 Mich. 584, 584, 589, 591–94 (1942); "The High Price of Being 'Queer': 31 Years," *Advocate*, Dec. 22, 1971.

Part I

1 White, "Dale Jennings," 84; White, *Pre-Gay L.A.*, 21–22.

2 D'Emilio, *Sexual Politics, Sexual Communities*, 71; Goluboff, *Vagrant Nation*, 49; White, *Pre-Gay L.A.*, 24–25.

3 *Hope Along the Wind*, dir. Eric Slade (San Francisco, Calif.: Frameline, 2001), DVD.

4 White, *Pre-Gay L.A.*, 18.

5 D'Emilio, *Sexual Politics, Sexual Communities*, 71–74; White, *Pre-Gay L.A.*, 27.

6 "William Dale Jennings; Pioneering Gay Activist," *LAT*, May 19, 2000.

Chapter 1

1 People v. Earl, 216 Cal. App. 2d 607, 608–09 (1963).
2 Chauncey, *Gay New York*, 4, 9.
3 Leslie, "Creating Criminals," 136.
4 LMNDF, *Mom's Apple Pie*, Apr. 1975, Box 3000, Folder labeled "Visitation Rights," ACLU Records.
5 Bernstein, "Nothing Ventured, Nothing Gained?," 364; Kane, "Timing Matters," 214.
6 Chauncey, *Gay New York*, 13–14; Canaday, *The Straight State*, 11.
7 Canaday, *The Straight State*, 81.
8 Ibid., 3.
9 Stein, *Rethinking the Gay and Lesbian Movement*, 17.
10 Ibid., 17.
11 Canaday, *The Straight State*, 29; Terry, *An American Obsession*, 43, 46–47.
12 Canaday, *The Straight State*, 21, 27, 34.
13 Robertson, *Crimes against Children*, 207, 209–11, 213; Schmeiser, "The Ungovernable Citizen," 220–21, 223–24.
14 Denno, "Life before the Modern Sex Offender Statutes," 1339, 1341–42; Freedman, "Uncontrolled Desires," 88–89.
15 Robertson, *Crimes against Children*, 209–10; Schmeiser, "The Ungovernable Citizen," 223–24.
16 Robertson, *Crimes against Children*, 209–10; Schmeiser, "The Ungovernable Citizen," 223–24.
17 Irma Hewlett, "What Shall We Do about Sex Offenders?," *Parents' Magazine*, Aug. 1950, 38.
18 Denno, "Life Before the Modern Sex Offender Statutes," 1363–66; Eskridge, *Gaylaw*, 354–55; Galliher and Tyree, "Edwin Sutherland's Research on the Origins of Sexual Psychopath Laws," 103; Lave, "Only Yesterday," 561–64; Massachusetts Special Commission Investigating the Prevalence of Sex Crimes, House Doc. 2, 169, *Final Report of the Special Commission Investigating the Prevalence of Sex Crimes* (Boston: Wright & Porter Printing Co., 1948) (hereafter "Massachusetts Report"), 4; New York City Mayor's Committee for the Study of Sex Offenses, *Report of Mayor's Committee for the Study of Sex Offenses* (New York: 1940) (hereafter "NYC Committee Report"), 10–11; Virginia Commission to Study Sex Offenses, Senate Document No. 18, *The Sex Offender and the Criminal Law: Report of the Commission to Study Sex Offenses to the Governor and the General Assembly of Virginia* (Richmond: Commonwealth of Virginia, 1951) (hereafter "Virginia Report"), 2.
19 Chauncey, "The Postwar Sex Crime Panic," 167.
20 Hewlett, "What Shall We Do about Sex Offenders?," 38.
21 Freedman, "Uncontrolled Desires," 91 n.18.
22 Lvovsky, *Vice Patrol*, 120.
23 Corbin Page, "Challenging the Sexual Carceral State: The Fight against Sexual Psychopath Laws" (presentation, American Society for Legal History, Chicago, Ill., Nov. 11, 2022).
24 Lvovsky, *Vice Patrol*, 120.
25 Order that Defendant is a Sexual Psychopath, Oct. 29, 1962, People v. Earl, 4 Crim. 1867, California State Archives.
26 Act of Apr. 14, 1950, chap. 6, 1950 CA Laws 438; Brakel and Cavanaugh, "Of Psychopaths and Pendulums," 72; McNaughton, "Atascadero, Dachau for Queers," 60–61.

27 Bérubé, *Coming Out under Fire*, 8–12, 15, 164–69, 201–03, 230; Canaday, *The Straight State*, 138.
28 D'Emilio, *Sexual Politics, Sexual Communities*, 42.
29 Kunzel, *Criminal Intimacy*, 87.
30 Ibid.
31 Ibid.
32 D'Emilio, *Sexual Politics, Sexual Communities*, 23–24, 31–32.
33 Bérubé, *Coming Out under Fire*, 271; D'Emilio, *Sexual Politics, Sexual Communities*, 32.
34 D'Emilio, *Sexual Politics, Sexual Communities*, 58, 103; Meeker, "Behind the Mask of Respectability," 79, 91.
35 D'Emilio, *Sexual Politics, Sexual Communities*, 59.
36 Paul V. Coates, "Well, Medium and Rare," *Los Angeles Mirror*, Mar. 12, 1953.
37 Johnson, *The Lavender Scare*, 34–35.
38 Ibid., 166.
39 Boyd, *Wide-Open Town*, 114–15; Nickola v. Munro, 328 P.2d 271 (Cal. App. Ct. 1958).
40 Goluboff, *Vagrant Nation*, 2–3, 46–47.
41 Eskridge, *Gaylaw*, 79.
42 Dal McIntire, "Tangents," *One*, Dec. 1955, 10, 11 (Baltimore, 162 people; Pittsburgh, 150 people); Dal McIntire, "Tangents," *One*, Apr.–May 1956, 14 (Redwood City, 200 people); Dal McIntire et al., "Tangents," *One*, Dec. 1961, 8 (Tampa, 200 people).
43 McIntire, "Tangents," Dec. 1955, 10, 11; McIntire, "Tangents," Apr.–May 1956, 14; McIntire, "Tangents," Dec. 1961, 8.
44 Goluboff, *Vagrant Nation*. 47.
45 Lyn Pedersen, "Miami Hurricane," *One*, Nov. 1954, 8. Miami was unique in taking extensive efforts to curtail homosexual bars. In 1954, Miami prohibited establishments with liquor licenses to knowingly employ a homosexual person, sell alcohol to homosexuals, or allow two or more homosexuals to congregate within the business. Inman v. City of Miami, 197 So.2d 50, 51 (Fla. Dist. Ct. App. 1967).
46 Mosk, "The Consenting Adult Homosexual and the Law," 719.
47 Pedersen, "Miami Hurricane," 7.
48 D'Emilio, *Sexual Politics, Sexual Communities*, 51; Stewart-Winter, *Queer Clout*, 20.
49 Mosk, "The Consenting Adult Homosexual and the Law," 688 n.17, 694, 707 n.137; Lvovsky, *Vice Patrol*, 104.
50 Lvovsky, *Vice Patrol*, 104.
51 Philip Dawson, "Controversy Flares over Morals Cases," *WP*, Apr. 5, 1954; Kelly v. United States, 194 F.2d 150, 152 (D.C. Cir. 1952); Mosk, "The Consenting Adult Homosexual and the Law," 691 n.30.
52 Lvovsky, *Vice Patrol*, 52–53; D'Emilio, *Sexual Politics, Sexual Communities*, 98–99.
53 Dal McIntire, "Tangents," *One*, Oct.–Nov. 1957, 19.
54 Goluboff, *Vagrant Nation*, 47.
55 People v. Bentley, 102 Cal. App. 2d 97, 98 (1951); People v. Hensel, 233 Cal. App. 2d 834, 836 (1965); People v. Maldonado, 240 Cal. App. 2d 812, 813 (1966); People v. Metcalf, 22 Cal. App. 3d 20, 22 (1971); People v. Strahan, 153 Cal. App. 2d 100, 101–02 (1957); People v. Young, 214 Cal. App. 2d 131, 133 (1963); State v. Bryant, 287 Minn. 205, 206 (1970); State v. Coyle, 181 So. 2d 671, 672 (Fla. Dist. Ct. App. 1966).
56 Kroehler v. Scott, 391 F. Supp. 1114, 1116 (E.D. Pa. 1975).

57 These campaigns targeted gay men in particular, with sodomy arrests for consensual homosexual activity rising dramatically after World War II. Robertson, "Shifting the Scene of the Crime," 240–42.

58 Kroehler v. Scott, 391 F. Supp. 1114, 1116 (E.D. Pa. 1975); People v. Roberts, 256 Cal. App. 2d 488, 490 (1967); People v. Sellers, 103 Cal. App. 2d 830, 831 (1951); Shaw v. Pitchess, 324 F. Supp. 781, 782 (C.D. Cal. 1969); Smayda v. United States, 352 F.2d 251, 252 (9th Cir. 1965); People v. Norton, 209 Cal. App. 2d 173, 174 (1962).

59 Clerk's Transcript on Appeal at 106, People v. Mason, Crim. 5230, California State Archives.

60 Ibid., 106–07.

61 McIntire, "Tangents," Apr.–May 1956, 14; Mosk, "The Consenting Adult Homosexual and the Law," 176 and n.192, 717 n.197; Robertson, "Shifting the Scene of the Crime," 240–42.

62 Lvovsky, *Vice Patrol*, 196.

63 Ibid., 195.

64 Ibid., 195–97.

65 Ibid., 195.

66 "Alexandrian Loses Appeal of Conviction," *WP*, February 17, 1951; "Senator's Son Convicted on Morals Charge," *WP*, Oct. 7, 1953; "Rule of Thumb is Given with Morals Conviction," *WP*, Apr. 2, 1954; "U.S. Employe [sic] Cleared in Morals Case," *WP*, May 19, 1954; "Usefulness of Sex Squad Questioned by Kronheim," *WP*, June 5, 1954.

67 D'Emilio, *Sexual Politics, Sexual Communities*, 49; Stewart-Winter, *Queer Clout*, 20.

68 Gutterman, *Her Neighbor's Wife*, 106–07; Stewart-Winter, "The Fall of Walter Jenkins and the Hidden History of the Lavender Scare," 213, 225–26.

69 Eskridge, *Gaylaw*, 72–73; Frank C. Wood, Jr., "The Homosexual and the Police," *One*, May 1963, 21–22.

70 Florida Bar v. Kimball, 96 So.2d 825 (Fla. 1957); E.R. Shipp, "The Law: Homosexual Lawyers Keep Fighting Barriers," *NYT*, February 3, 1989.

71 E. Carrington Boggan et al., *The Rights of Gay People: The Basic ACLU Guide to a Gay Person's Rights* (New York: Avon Books, 1975), 211–35; In re Boyd, 307 P.2d 625 (Cal. 1957); McLauglin v. Board of Medical Examiners, 111 Cal. Rptr. 353 (App. 1973); Wood, "The Homosexual and the Police," 21–22; Marcus, *Making History*, 57, 149–51.

72 Duberman, *Stonewall*, 117.

73 D'Emilio, *Sexual Politics, Sexual Communities*, 49.

74 Michael Rumaker, *Robert Duncan in San Francisco* (San Francisco: Grey Fox Press, 1996), 16.

75 Stewart-Winter, *Queer Clout*, 16–17.

76 William McGowan, "The Chickens and the Bulls," *Slate*, Jul. 11, 2012, www.slate.com/articles/life/history/2012/07/the_chickens_and_the_bulls_the_rise_and_incredible_fall_of_a_vicious_extortion_ring_that_preyed_on_prominent_gay_men_in_the_1960s_.single.html.

77 Ibid.

78 McIntire, "Tangents," Oct.–Nov. 1957, 18.

79 D'Emilio, *Sexual Politics, Sexual Communities*, 87, 103, 115–16, 235–36; Meeker, "Behind the Mask of Respectability," 83–88.

80 Jones, *Alfred C. Kinsey*, 13, 41.

81 Ibid., 14.

82 Ibid., 146–48.
83 Ibid., 293.
84 Ibid., 349.
85 Ibid.
86 D'Emilio, *Sexual Politics, Sexual Communities*, 34; Igo, *The Averaged American*, 237.
87 Igo, *The Averaged American*, 237.
88 Ibid.
89 D'Emilio, *Sexual Politics, Sexual Communities*, 34; Igo, *The Averaged American*, 237.
90 Alfred C. Kinsey, Wardell B. Pomeroy, and Clyde E. Martin, *Sexual Behavior in the Human Male* (Bloomington: Indiana University Press, 1948), 623, 625, 627, 650, 665.
91 Jones, *Alfred C. Kinsey*, 372–73, 378–80, 521–22, 645–46.
92 Kinsey, Pomeroy, and Martin, *Sexual Behavior in the Human Male*, 623, 627, 660, 665.
93 Jones, *Alfred C. Kinsey*, 619.
94 Ibid., 618–19.
95 Ibid.
96 Ibid.
97 Ibid., 674–75.
98 Ibid., 675.
99 Alfred C. Kinsey et al., *Sexual Behavior in the Human Female* (Philadelphia: W. B. Saunders Co., 1953), 20.
100 Ibid.
101 Ibid.
102 Morris Ploscowe, "Comments of Morris Ploscowe," *Journal of Legal Education* 20, no. 4 (1968): 446.
103 Morris Ploscowe to Charles D. Breitel, Counsel to the Governor, Mar. 31, 1947, in "Veto Jacket" for Senate Bill no. 2790, 38 (hereafter "Veto Jacket"); Prison Association of New York, *The One Hundred and Third Annual Report of the Prison Association of New York* (New York: Publishers Printing Co., 1947), 39.
104 "Thomas E. Dewey Is Dead at 68," *NYT*, Mar. 17, 1971.
105 Thomas Dewey, memorandum filed with Senate Bill no. 2790, Apr. 9, 1947, in Veto Jacket, 3.
106 NYC Committee Report, 66.
107 Walker, "The Engineer as Progressive," 1176–79.
108 Assembly Interim Committee on Judicial System and Judicial Process, *Preliminary Report of the Subcommittee on Sex Crimes of the Assembly Interim Committee on Judicial System and Judicial Process* (Sacramento, 1950) (hereafter "California Preliminary Report"), 9, 27, 114.
109 Michigan Governor's Study Commission on the Deviated Criminal Sex Offender, *Report of the Governor's Study Commission on the Deviated Criminal Sex Offender* (Lansing, 1951) (hereafter "Michigan Report"), v.
110 New Jersey Commission on the Habitual Sex Offender, *The Habitual Sex Offender: Report and Recommendations of the Commission on the Habitual Sex Offender as formulated by Paul W. Tappan, Technical Consultant* (Trenton, 1950) (hereafter "New Jersey Report"), 12.
111 Most legislatures appropriated funds to cover expenses, with the exception of the New York City Mayor's Committee for the Study of Sex Offenses. NYC Committee Report, 6.

112 George, "The Harmless Psychopath," 237–50.

113 California Preliminary Report 9, 27.

114 Eskridge, *Dishonorable Passions*, 119.

115 Lloyd E. Ohlin to Alfred C. Kinsey, May 14, 1952, Folder labeled "Illinois Academy of Criminology," Alfred C. Kinsey Correspondence Collection; Lloyd E. Ohlin to Alfred C. Kinsey, February 27, 1952, Folder labeled "Illinois Academy of Criminology," Alfred C. Kinsey Correspondence Collection, 1; Michigan Report, iv.

116 Alfred C. Kinsey to Marshall Korshak, Jul. 18, 1952, Folder labeled "Illinois Sex Offenders Commission," Alfred C. Kinsey Correspondence Collection; "Kinsey Praises Group Study on Sex Offenders: 4 Sectional Meetings Set for Today," *Chicago Daily Tribune*, Sept. 26, 1952; Illinois Commission on Sex Offenders, *Report of the Illinois Commission on Sex Offenders to the 68th General Assembly of the State of Illinois* (Springfield, 1953) (hereafter "Illinois Report"), iv–v, 52.

117 Pennsylvania Joint State Government Commission, *Sex Offenders: A Report of the Joint State Government Commission to the General Assembly of the Commonwealth of Pennsylvania* (Pa., 1951) (hereafter "Pennsylvania Report"), 11–12, 15–24.

118 Ibid., 13, 18.

119 California Preliminary Report, 27.

120 New Jersey Report, 14–16, 28–29.

121 Lvovsky, *Vice Patrol*, 120.

122 David Abrahamsen, "Study of 102 Sex Offenders at Sing Sing," *Federal Probation* 14, no. 3 (1950): 26–32; Assembly Interim Committee on Judicial System and Judicial Process, *Progress Report to the Legislature 1951 Regular Session: Final Report of the Subcommittee on Sex Crimes* (Sacramento, 1951) (hereafter "California Final Report"), 141–42; Illinois Report, 8; Massachusetts Report, 8, 38; Minnesota Legislative Interim Commission on Public Welfare Laws, *Report of the Minnesota Legislative Interim Commission on Public Welfare Laws: Sex Psychopath Laws: Submitted to the Legislature of the State of Minnesota* (Minn., 1959), 9; Pennsylvania Report, 11–12, 15–24; New Jersey Report, 11; Virginia Report, 11.

123 California Final Report, 120–24; California Preliminary Report, 25, 45, 48, 267; Illinois Report, 27, 30, 52; New Jersey Report, xx, 22; Michigan Report, 24 n.12, 135, 156; Pennsylvania Report, 15–24.

124 Pennsylvania Report, 15–24.

125 Michigan Report, 24 n.12, 32, 37, 135, 150, 156–57, 190, 193; California Final Report, 141–42. The 1950 New York report did not recommend reducing consensual sodomy to a misdemeanor, but the committee overseeing the report made this change in the proposed bill it submitted to the legislature. Eskridge, *Dishonorable Passions*, 119.

126 Illinois Report, 2.

127 Freedman, "Uncontrolled Desires," 84.

128 Act of Apr. 11, 1949, chap. 20, 1949 NJ Laws 65; Act of June 8, 1950, chap. 207, 1950 NJ Laws 454.

129 Act of Apr. 14, 1950, chap. 6, 1950 CA Laws 438; Act of Jul. 28, 1949, chap. 1325, 1949 CA Laws 2311.

130 California Preliminary Report, 47.

131 Lindman and McIntyre, *The Mentally Disabled and the Law*, 303.

132 Brakel and Cavanaugh, "Of Psychopaths and Pendulums," 72.

133 Act of Apr. 11, 1950, chap. 525, 1950 NY Laws 1271, sec. 15.

134 "M.S. Guttmacher, Psychiatrist, Dies," *NYT*, Nov. 8, 1966; "Medical Services Division," Circuit Court for Baltimore City, 2023, www.baltimorecitycourt.org/court-administration/medical-services-office/.

135 Manfred S. Guttmacher to Alfred Kinsey, June 14, 1951, Folder labeled "Guttmacher, Manfred," Alfred C. Kinsey Correspondence Collection.

136 Alfred Kinsey to Manfred S. Guttmacher, June 18, 1951, Folder labeled "Guttmacher, Manfred," Alfred C. Kinsey Correspondence Collection.

137 Alfred Kinsey to Manfred Guttmacher, Aug. 26, 1950, Folder labeled "Guttmacher, Manfred," Alfred C. Kinsey Correspondence Collection.

138 Manfred S. Guttmacher to Alfred C. Kinsey, February 20, 1948, Folder labeled "Guttmacher, Manfred," Alfred C. Kinsey Correspondence Collection; Manfred S. Guttmacher, "The Kinsey Report and Society," *Scientific Monthly* 70, no. 5 (1950): 293–94.

139 Manfred Guttmacher to Alfred Kinsey, Apr. 24, 1948, Folder labeled "Guttmacher, Manfred," Alfred C. Kinsey Correspondence Collection.

140 Guttmacher, "The Kinsey Report," 293.

141 Manfred Guttmacher and Henry Weihofen, "Sex Offenses," *Journal of Criminal Law, Criminology, and Political Science* 43, no. 2 (1952): 156.

142 Goodrich and Wolkin, *The Story of the American Law Institute*, 5–7; Hazard, *The American Law Institute: What It Is and What It Does*, 3.

143 "Past and Present ALI Projects," American Law Institute, www.ali.org/media/filer_public/d5/00/d500d44f-c3f9-4871-9e10-a9cd0b3b9768/ali-projects-past-and-present-09202022.pdf.

144 Robinson and Dubber, "The American Model Penal Code," 321; Herbert Wechsler, "The Challenge of a Model Penal Code," *Harvard Law Review* 65, no. 7 (1952): 1100–01.

145 Allyn, "Private Acts/Public Policy," 421–22.

146 Advisory Committee Meeting Minutes, June 15, 1951, Box 3, Folder 17, MPC Records, 45–46, 102–8; Morris Ploscowe, *Sex and the Law* (New York: Prentice-Hall, 1951).

147 Ploscowe, *Sex and the Law*, 209, 213, 229.

148 Draft of Article 207 – Sexual Offenses, Jan. 7, 1955, Box 8, Folder 8, MPC Records, 134–36.

149 Ibid., 137.

150 MPC Tentative Draft no. 4, Apr. 25, 1955, Box 7, Folder 3, MPC Records, 276.

151 Ibid., 93; Council Draft no. 8 of Article 207 – Sexual Offenses, Mar. 1, 1955, Box 5, Folder 6, MPC Records.

152 Advisory Committee Meeting Minutes, May 19, 1995, Box 4, Folder 19, MPC Records, 83–84, 127–29.

153 Eskridge, *Dishonorable Passions*, 124; Gunther, *Learned Hand*, xv.

154 Eskridge, *Dishonorable Passions*, 124.

155 "The Law: Sin & Criminality," *Time*, May 30, 1955.

156 Louis B. Schwartz to Alfred C. Kinsey, Jul. 8, 1955, Folder labeled "Schwartz, Louis B.," Alfred C. Kinsey Correspondence Collection.

157 1961 Illinois Penal Code § 35-1.

158 Bernstein, "Nothing Ventured," 363–64; John D'Emilio, "Back To Basics: Sodomy Law Repeal," *National Gay and Lesbian Task Force*, February 25, 1997, www.qrd.org/qrd/orgs/NGLTF/1997/sodomy.law.repeal-02.25.97; Eskridge, *Gaylaw*, 106; Kane, "Timing Matters," 214; Robinson and Dubber, "The American Model Penal Code," 326.

159 Robinson and Dubber, "The American Model Penal Code," 326.

160 Kane, "Timing Matters," 234.

161 Eskridge, *Gaylaw*, 106.

162 Ibid. Six other states decriminalized consensual heterosexual sodomy but kept its homosexual counterpart a crime. Ibid.; Eskridge, *Dishonorable Passions*, 176–84.

163 Bernstein, "Nothing Ventured," 361–62.

164 Chicago Gay Liberation, "Working Paper for the Revolutionary People's Constitution Convention Plenary Session, Philadelphia, Sept. 1970," in *Out of the Closets: Voices of Gay Liberation*, ed. Karla Jay and Allen Young (New York: Douglas Book, 1972), 348.

165 Laura Dominguez, "The Black Cat: Harbinger of LGBTQ Civil Rights," *KCET*, February 11, 2017, www.kcet.org/shows/lost-la/the-black-cat-harbinger-of-lgbtq-civil-rights; Murdoch and Price, *Courting Justice*, 143.

166 Lvovsky, *Vice Patrol*, 258–59.

167 Ibid., 124–32; Stuntz, "The Uneasy Relationship between Criminal Procedure and Criminal Justice," 5.

168 Lvovsky, *Vice Patrol*, 118.

169 Ibid., 129.

170 Robert C. Doty, "Growth of Overt Homosexuality in City Provokes Wide Concern," *NYT*, Dec. 17, 1963, 1, 33; Gaeton J. Fonzi, "The Furtive Fraternity," *Mattachine Interim*, Jan. 1963, 11, reprinted from *Greater Philadelphia Magazine*, Dec. 1962; William J. Helmer, "New York's 'Middle-Class' Homosexuals," *Harper's Magazine*, Mar. 1, 1963, 85–92; Dick Herbert, "They Meet without Fear in 'Gay' Bars around City," *Atlanta Constitution*, Jan. 3, 1966, 1; Paul Welch, "Homosexuality in America," *Life*, June 26, 1964, 66; Louis Wille, "Chicago's Twilight World: The Homosexuals – A Growing Problem," *Chicago Daily News*, June 20, 1966.

171 Welch, "Homosexuality in America," 66.

172 Helmer, "New York's 'Middle-Class' Homosexuals"; Herbert, "They Meet without Fear in 'Gay' Bars around City"; Wille, "Chicago's Twilight World."

173 Lvovsky, *Vice Patrol*, 229.

174 Ibid., 237.

175 Patricia A. Spence, "Letters to the Editors," *Life*, Jul. 17, 1964, 28.

176 Tom Tendal, "Letters to the Editors," *Life*, Jul. 17, 1964, 28.

177 "The Law and the Homosexual Problem," *Life*, June 11, 1965, 4.

178 Igo, *The Known Citizen*, 224–27; Seo, "Democratic Policing before the Due Process Revolution"; James A. Wechsler, "Entrapment Inc.," *New York Post*, Mar. 7, 1966, 2.

179 Klarman, *From Jim Crow to Civil Rights*, 423–41.

180 "Support for Police Seen at Low Point," *NYT*, Feb. 4, 1966.

181 Hanhardt, *Safe Space*, 70; Lvovsky, *Vice Patrol*, 258.

182 Bill Kruse, "Police Beaten!," *BAR*, Jul. 11, 1974.

183 Cain, *Rainbow Rights*, 54; Goluboff, *Vagrant Nation*, 50.

184 Goluboff, *Vagrant Nation*, 3, 13, 16, 44, 52.

185 Ibid., 123.

186 Ibid., 112.

187 Ibid., 113.

188 Ibid., 138–39; Shuttlesworth v. City of Birmingham, 382 U.S. 87, 91 (1965).

189 Goluboff, *Vagrant Nation*, 123.

190 Ibid., 127.

191 Alegata v. Commonwealth, 231 N.E.2d 201 (Mass. 1967); Cal. Penal Code 647 (Supp. 1961); *In re* Hoffman, 434 P.2d 353 (Cal. 1967); City of Seattle v. Drew,

423 P.2d 522 (Wash. 1967); Fenster v. Leary, 229 N.E.2d 426 (N.Y. 1967); City of
    Reno v. Second Judicial Dist. Court, 427 P.2d 4 (Nev. 1967); Parker v. Municipal
    Judge of Las Vegas, 427 P.2d 642 (Nev. 1967).
192 Goluboff, *Vagrant Nation*, 148.
193 Palmer v. City of Euclid, 402 U.S. 544 (1971); Coates v. City of Cincinnati, 402
    U.S. 611 (1971); Papachristou v. City of Jacksonville, 405 U.S. 156 (1972).
194 *Papachristou*, 405 U.S. at 162–63, 168.
195 Murdoch and Price, *Courting Justice*, 143.
196 Lvovsky, *Vice Patrol*, 259; Stewart-Winter, "Queer Law and Order," 69–70.

Chapter 2

1 "Lesbian in a Texas Trial, Loses Son to Ex-Husband," *NYT*, Dec. 23, 1975.
2 Kitty Cotter, "Mary Jo: What Next?," *The Lesbian Feminist*, n.d., ca. 1976, Box
    125, Folder 2, Phyllis Lyon and Del Martin Papers.
3 "Lesbian Fighting to Keep Her Son," *NYT*, Dec. 21, 1974.
4 Untitled Article, *Time*, Jan. 12, 1976, Box 88, Folder 19, NGLTF Records.
5 Friends of Mary Jo Risher, Mailing, n.d., ca. 1975, Box 125, Folder 2, Phyllis Lyon
    and Del Martin Papers.
6 Larry D. Gerbrandt, "Lesbian Mother Loses Custody," *National Courier*,
    Jan. 23, 1976.
7 Cervini, *The Deviant's War*, 24–25.
8 Johnson, *The Lavender Scare*, 179–80; D'Emilio, *Sexual Politics, Sexual
    Communities*, 151.
9 Cervini, *The Deviant's War*, 16, 28.
10 Canaday, *Queer Career*, 107–08.
11 D'Emilio, *Sexual Politics, Sexual Communities*, 151; Cervini, *The Deviant's War*, 49.
12 Cervini, *The Deviant's War*, 208.
13 Ibid., 208–09.
14 Ibid.
15 Although women participated in gay liberation activities, many lesbians created their
    own organizations that blended the ideologies of gay liberation, second-wave femi-
    nism, and other radical movements. Enszer, "How to Stop Choking to Death,"
    182–85; Stein, *Rethinking the Gay and Lesbian Movement*, 91.
16 D'Emilio, *Sexual Politics, Sexual Communities*, 24–25, 152–53.
17 Stein, *Rethinking the Gay and Lesbian Movement*, 103.
18 Stewart-Winter, *Queer Clout*, 95.
19 Stein, *Rethinking the Gay and Lesbian Movement*, 85.
20 D'Emilio, *Sexual Politics, Sexual Communities*, 234–35.
21 Ibid.
22 Bayer, *Homosexuality and American Psychiatry*, 83, 91; Minton, *Departing from
    Deviance*, 252–53.
23 In 1985, the National Gay Task Force changed its name to the National Gay and
    Lesbian Task Force (NGLTF). In 2014, it became the National LGBTQ
    Task Force.
24 "Lambda Legal History," Lambda Legal, www.lambdalegal.org/about-us/history.
25 Evelyn Hooker, "The Changing Status of Gays and Lesbians: 1954–1985," Aug. 24,
    1985, Box 2, Folder 5, Evelyn C. Hooker Papers; Frank Kameny to Ralph Temple
    et al., Dec. 16, 1973, Box 122, Folder 9, Kameny Papers; Minton, *Departing from
    Deviance*, 242.

26 Johnson, *The Lavender Scare*, 35–36.
27 D'Emilio, *Sexual Politics, Sexual Communities*, 154, 162.
28 Gay Organizations in New York City, Memorandum to Committee on Nomenclature of the American Psychiatric Association, 1973, Box 164, Folder 36, NGLTF Records, 10.
29 Ibid.
30 Transcript of Rehearing in Motion for Custody at 67, Nadler v. Nadler, No. 177331 (Cal. Super. Ct. Nov. 15, 1967), Box 124, Folder 8, Phyllis Lyon and Del Martin Papers.
31 Ibid.
32 Ibid., 68.
33 Ibid., 49–50.
34 Ibid., 50; Del Martin and Phyllis Lyon, *Lesbian/Woman*, 20th anniversary ed. (Volcano, Calif.: Volcano Press, 1991), 135.
35 Rivers, *Radical Relations*, 49–51.
36 Ibid., 57–59.
37 Ibid., 48.
38 Johnson, "A Narrative Life Story," 88–89.
39 Barbara Gittings, "Show and Tell," in *American Psychiatry and Homosexuality*, ed. Drescher and Merlino, xvi.
40 Bayer, *Homosexuality and American Psychiatry*, 105; Clendinen and Nagourney, *Out for Good*, 204.
41 Bayer, *Homosexuality and American Psychiatry*, 109; Minton, *Departing from Deviance*, 258.
42 Bayer, *Homosexuality and American Psychiatry*, 110.
43 David L. Scasta, "John E. Fryer, MD, and the Dr. H. Anonymous Episode," in *American Psychiatry and Homosexuality*, ed. Drescher and Merlino, 22, 25.
44 Evelyn Hooker, "The Adjustment of the Male Overt Homosexual," *Journal of Projective Techniques* 21 (1957): 18, 30; Minton, *Departing from Deviance*, 234.
45 Minton, *Departing from Deviance*, 228.
46 Ibid., 231.
47 Ibid., 3, 260–61.
48 Franklin E. Kameny, typewritten note, Box 122, Folder 10, Frank Kameny Papers.
49 Bayer, *Homosexuality and American Psychiatry*, 129.
50 National Gay Task Force, "Psychiatric Turnaround: The Greatest Gay Victory – A Major Socio-Historic Change," Dec. 8, 1973, Box 164, Folder 40, NGLTF Records.
51 Donald N. Mager, interview by Tim Retzloff, Oct. 18, 2009, https://bentley.mivideo.it.umich.edu/media/1_8fep255u; Rivers, *Radical Relations*, 117.
52 Don Mager, "Faggot Fathers," *Gay Liberator* (Detroit, Mich.), June 1973, 8–9.
53 Ibid.
54 Rivers, *Radical Relations*, 80–82, 114–18.
55 Kruse, *One Nation under God*, 96, 170; Lienesch, *In the Beginning*, 52; Martin, *With God on Our Side*, 16–22.
56 Dochuk, *From Bible Belt to Sun Belt*, 229–30, 332–33; McGirr, *Suburban Warriors*, 132–36, 143–46, 211–15; Stone, *Gay Rights at the Ballot Box*, 4–5.
57 Dochuk, *From Bible Belt to Sun Belt*, 357–58.
58 Ibid., 365; Kenneth L. Woodward et al., "Born Again!," *Newsweek*, Oct. 25, 1976, 69.
59 Self, *All in the Family*, 349.
60 410 U.S. 113 (1973).

61 Frank, "The Civil Rights of Parents"; Self, *All in the Family*, 277–78; Stone, *Gay Rights at the Ballot Box*, 4–5; Ziegler, *After* Roe, ch. 6.

62 Self, *All in the Family*, 328.

63 Dowland, *Family Values*, 8–12; May, *Homeward Bound*, 7–8, 13–14, 91–94; Sandbrook, *Mad as Hell*, 383–84; Self, *All in the Family*, 6, 10, 309–11, 349, 362, 369.

64 Greg Goldin, "The 15 Per Cent Solution: How the Religious Right Is Building from Below to Take Over from Above," *Village Voice*, Apr. 6, 1993, 19; Irvine, *Talk About Sex*, 65, 69–72.

65 Eskridge, "No Promo Homo," 1329; Murray, "Marriage Rights and Parental Rights," 359; Rosky, "Fear of the Queer Child," 641; Rosky, "No Promo Hetero," 428.

66 Irvine, *Talk About Sex*, 173.

67 Tim LaHaye and Beverly LaHaye, *The Act of Marriage: The Beauty of Sexual Love* (Grand Rapids: Zondervan Publishing, 1976), 261.

68 Denno, "Life before the Modern Sex Offender Statutes," 1339, 1341–42; Freedman, "Uncontrolled Desires," 103; Schmeiser, "The Ungovernable Citizen," 215.

69 Eskridge, "No Promo Homo," 1328, 1366; Rosky, "Fear of the Queer Child," 608.

70 Eskridge, "No Promo Homo," 1328, 1366; Rosky, "Fear of the Queer Child," 608.

71 Frank, "The Civil Rights of Parents," 142.

72 Anita Bryant, *The Anita Bryant Story: The Survival of Our Nation's Families and the Threat of Militant Homosexuality* (Old Tappan, NJ: Revell, 1977), 62; Morton Kondracke, "Anita Bryant Is Mad about Gays," *New Republic*, May 7, 1977, 14.

73 Clendinen and Nagourney, *Out for Good*, 299, 303–04, 308; Fejes, *Gay Rights and Moral Panic*, ch. 5.

74 Fejes, *Gay Rights and Moral Panic*, 172–74, 176–77; Stone, *Gay Rights at the Ballot Box*, 14.

75 Klarman, *From the Closet to the Altar*, 17–18, 22–26; Self, *All in the Family*, 222–23, 230–31; Stein, *Rethinking the Gay and Lesbian Movement*, chs. 3–4; Rivers, *Radical Relations*, 53–54.

76 Rhonda Rivera, "Where We Stand: Gay Parent," *Metro Gay News*, Feb. 1977, Box 88, Folder 17, NGLTF Records.

77 Rivers, *Radical Relations*, 72–73.

78 Despite the large number of cases, only a small fraction left any record, as family court decisions are typically unreported and sealed for the protection of the parties involved. Determining what happened in these closed courtrooms requires piecing together descriptions of cases from lawyers' and advocates' files, organizational newsletters, and newspaper reports. The vast majority of the surviving case records involve white mothers, in part because the most publicized cases were those of white middle-class lesbian mothers battling their ex-husbands, resulting in a dearth of material on queer parents of color. The remaining records also obscure the number of gay and lesbian parents who never sought custody or visitation, afraid of having their sexual orientation revealed or convinced that it was futile to attempt a court battle.

79 *Mom's Apple Pie: The Heart of the Lesbian Mothers' Custody Movement*, dirs. Jody Laine, Shan Ottey, and Shad Reinstein (San Francisco: Frameline, 2006), DVD.

80 Rivers, *Radical Relations*, 86–87.

81 Gilmore, *Groundswell*, 54; Lefkovitz, *Strange Bedfellows*, 3.

82 Rivers, *Radical Relations*, 80, 82–86; Meeker, *Contacts Desired*, 227.

83 Rivers, *Radical Relations*, 103–04; *Not All Parents Are Straight*, dir. Kevin White (San Francisco: Filmmakers Collaborative, 1988), DVD.

84 Rivers, *Radical Relations*, 103.

85 Ibid., 85–86.

86 Ibid., 106.

87 Ibid., 83–84, 111.

88 Ibid., 84.

89 Gay fathers also generally did not appeal their losses. Many consequently became estranged from their children. Ibid., 133.

90 *Not All Parents Are Straight.*

91 Rivers, *Radical Relations*, 112.

92 In the 1980s, the imbalance became even more pronounced as a result of the AIDS crisis, which decimated queer communities. By the middle of the decade, there were simply fewer gay fathers alive to fight for custody. Ibid., 133–35.

93 Barbara Price, Draft of Lesbian Mother Case Summary, Box 3000, Folder labeled "Custody Articles," ACLU Records, 28–29.

94 Appellant's Opening Brief, *In re* Deanna P. and Constance P., 1 Civil 34007-8 (Cal. App. Ct. Dec. 29, 1973), Box 124, Folder 20, Phyllis Lyon and Del Martin Papers, 7–8.

95 Price, Draft of Lesbian Mother Case Summary, 26.

96 Ibid.; Carol Parrott, interview by Andrew Hill, KPIX, Oct. 3, 1973, https://diva.sfsu .edu/collections/sfbatv/bundles/239315.

97 Price, Draft of Lesbian Mother Case Summary, 26.

98 Ball, *Same Sex Marriage and Children*, 59–60; DiFonzo and Stern, "The Winding Road from Form to Function," 24; Fineman, "Dominant Discourse, Professional Language, and Legal Change in Child Custody Decisionmaking," 739–40; Self, *All in the Family*, 328.

99 Dinner, "The Divorce Bargain," 113–15.

100 Ibid.; Shapiro, "Custody and Conduct," 633.

101 People v. Brown, 212 N.W.2d 55, 57 (Mich. Ct. App. 1973).

102 Ibid., 57–58; Nancy Woodhull, "Lesbian Mothers Work to Rebuild Family," *Free Press*, n.d., ca. 1973, Box 196, Folder 3, Phyllis Lyon and Del Martin Papers.

103 *Brown*, 212 N.W.2d at 57; Hunter and Polikoff, "Custody Rights of Lesbian Mothers," 711–12; Price, Draft of Lesbian Mother Case Summary, 25.

104 Fineman, *The Illusion of Equality*, 85.

105 "California Victory," *Lesbian Tide*, 1978, Box 125, Folder 1, Phyllis Lyon and Del Martin Papers.

106 Ibid.; Lynn Scott Ransom Defense Committee Flier, Box 125, Folder 1, Phyllis Lyon and Del Martin Papers.

107 "California Victory"; "Lesbian Mother Wins," n.d., ca. 1978, Box 88, Folder 14, NGLTF Records.

108 "Lesbian Mother Wins"; LMNDF, LMNDF Materials List and Order Form, 4, Box 71, Folder 51, NGLTF Records; Eric Nagourney, "Wardell B. Pomeroy, 87: Aided Kinsey's Studies on Sex," *NYT*, Sept. 12, 2001.

109 Rivers, *Radical Relations*, 76–77, 92.

110 Brief of Amici Curiae Lambda Legal Defense and Education Fund and National Center for Lesbian Rights at 36, Walsh v. Walsh, no. 88-713 (Iowa), Box 88, Folder 9, NGLTF Records; Brief of Amici Curiae National Center for Lesbian Rights and Lambda Legal Defense and Education Fund at 9, Lamberson v. Lamberson, no. 1202321 (Mich. Ct. App.), Box 88, Folder 15, NGLTF Records; Palmore v. Sidoti, 466 U.S. 429, 433 (1984).

111 Chauncey, *Why Marriage?*, 107–08; Stone, "The Moral Dilemma," 741–42.

112 Johnson v. Schlotman, 502 N.W.2d 831, 834 (N.D. 1993).

113 Pamela J. Laws, "Court Hears Final Arguments: Child Custody Case Pits Lesbian against Husband, Former Lover," *Metro Gay News* (Mich.), June 1977, Box 139,

Folder 37, NGLTF Records; Karlis Streips, "Sexuality Is Crux of Visitation Dispute," *Gay Life* (Chicago), Dec. 9, 1982, Box 88, Folder 17, NGLTF Records.

114 Rosky, "Like Father, Like Son," 291.

115 Richman, *Courting Change*, 29–30.

116 Ibid., 67–72; Ball, *The Right to be Parents*, 27; Mezey, *Gay Families and the Courts*, 17; Richman, *Courting Change*, 28, 48, 53; Polikoff, "Raising Children," 312; Briggs, *Somebody's Children*, 248–49.

117 LMNDF, "$$$," *Mom's Apple Pie*, Jan. 1976, Gale Archives of Sexuality and Gender, 1.

118 Jil Clark, "Activist Lesbian Mother Wins N.J. Custody Battle," *GCN*, Aug. 16, 1980; "Colorado Judge Rules Mother's Lesbianism Is Bar to Good Parenting," *Advocate*, June 12, 1980; "Washington State Lesbian Mother Wins Custody," Box 88, Folder 14, NGLTF Records.

119 "Court Uses Live-in Lover to Deny Custody," *GCN*, Jan. 19–25, 1992; J.L.P. v. D.J.P., 643 S.W.2d 865, 872 (Mo. Ct. App. 1982).

120 Price, Draft of Lesbian Mother Case Summary, 9, 33.

121 Gitlin, "Sexual Morality and the Children of Divorce," 468–69.

122 *In re* J.S. & C., 324 A.2d 90, 97 (N.J. Super. Ct. Ch. Div. 1974); "State Court Rules Gay Activism Harmful to Children," *Psychiatric News*, Sept. 4, 1974, Box 88, Folder 17, NGLTF Records.

123 In re *J.S. & C.*, 324 A.2d at 97.

124 Shapiro, "Custody and Conduct," 642.

125 "Out of the Closet into the Courts: Eleanor Stevens Reports on Discrimination against Lesbian Mothers in Custody Battles," *Spare Rib*, Sept. 1976, 6–8.

126 Brief of Appellant, Teegarden v. Teegarden, No. 38A04–0406-CV-212, 1994 WL 16461688, at *16 n.4 (Ind. App. Ct. Jul. 5, 1994); Brief of Appellee, Bottoms v. Bottoms, No. 94-1166, 1994 WL 16199380, at *16 n.6 (Va. Dec. 28, 1994); *In re* Adoption of Evan, 583 N.Y.S.2d 997, 1001 n.1 (Surrogate's Ct. 1992).

127 Susan Golombok, interview by author, Aug. 28, 2014.

128 Susan Golombok, Ann Spencer, and Michael Rutter, "Children in Lesbian and Single-Parent Households: Psychosexual and Psychiatric Appraisal," *Journal of Child Psychology and Psychiatry* 24, no. 4 (1983): 568.

129 These studies did not address the cause of sexual orientation, although they implied sexual orientation was immutable, an issue that would become relevant in later equal protection arguments for gay and lesbian rights. Knauer, "Science, Identity, and the Construction of the Gay Political Narrative," 74–78.

130 Meyerowitz, *How Sex Changed*, ch. 2.

131 Kessler, *Lessons from the Intersexed*, 14.

132 Richard Green and John Money, "Incongruous Gender Role: Nongenital Manifestations in Prepubertal Boys," *Journal of Nervous and Mental Disease* 131 (1960): 166–67.

133 Bayer, *Homosexuality and American Psychiatry*, 112; Richard Green, "Homosexuality as a Mental Illness," *International Journal of Psychiatry* 10 (Mar. 1972): 77–98; Richard Green, interview by author, May 31, 2014.

134 Rivers, *Radical Relations*, 69.

135 Richard Green, "Sexual Identity of 37 Children Raised by Homosexual or Transsexual Parents," *American Journal of Psychiatry* 135, no. 6 (1978): 696; Richard Green et al., "Lesbian Mothers and Their Children: A Comparison with Solo Parent Heterosexual Mothers and Their Children," *Archives of Sexual Behavior* 15, no. 2 (1986): 180; Mary E. Hotvedt and Jane Barclay Mandel,

"Children of Lesbian Mothers," in *Homosexuality: Social, Psychological, and Biological Issues*, ed. William Paul et al. (Beverly Hills: SAGE Publications, 1982), 276, 281, 285.

136 Richardson, "Theoretical Perspectives on Homosexuality," 24.

137 The pro-gay and lesbian parenting research pointed to early childhood as the time when sexual orientation became fixed, although adolescence continued to be an important, albeit less critical phase. M.J.P v. J.G.P., 640 P.2d 966, 968–69 (Okla. 1982).

138 Transcript of Examination of Richard Green, Hall v. Hall, No. 55900 (Ohio C.P. Licking County, Apr. 26, 1974), Box 124, Folder 10, Phyllis Lyon and Del Martin Papers, 27.

139 Ibid., 25–26.

140 Ibid., 26.

141 Price, Draft of Lesbian Mother Case Summary, 14.

142 "Children of Homosexuals Seen Headed Straight," *Psychology Today*, Nov. 1978; Green, "Sexual Identity of 37 Children Raised by Homosexual or Transsexual Parents," 695–96.

143 Green, "Sexual Identity of 37 Children Raised by Homosexual or Transsexual Parents," 695–96.

144 Gottman, "Children of Gay and Lesbian Parents," 180.

145 Martha Kirkpatrick, Catherine Smith, and Ron Roy, "Lesbian Mothers and their Children: A Comparative Survey," *American Journal of Orthopsychiatry* 51, no. 3 (1981): 545–51.

146 Ibid., 549.

147 Although Kirkpatrick was married when the study began, by the time the team published its research, she had divorced her husband and met Nadia Doubins, who would become her life-long partner. Kirkpatrick feared that her sexual history would impact how others would perceive the study, in that "it would be considered to be something I was doing for my own benefit, to get the right result to comfort me." Martha Kirkpatrick, interview by author, June 16, 2014; Vernon Rosario, "An Interview with Martha J. Kirkpatrick, MD," in *American Psychiatry and Homosexuality*, ed. Drescher and Merlino, 209–10. Her concerns ultimately proved unfounded, as the few critiques her study engendered focused on the team's research methodology and the study's small sample size. Paul Cameron, "Oddities in Kirkpatrick, et al.'s Study of Children of Lesbian Mothers," *Psychological Reports* 96 (2005): 397–407; Walter R. Schumm, "A Review and Critique of Research on Same-Sex Parenting and Adoption," *Psychological Reports* 119, no. 3 (2016): 693.

148 Beverly Hoeffer, "Children's Acquisition of Sex-Role Behavior in Lesbian-Mother Families," *American Journal of Orthopsychiatry* 51, no. 3 (1981): 536–37; "Study Finds Advantages to Custody Awards to Lesbians," *Los Angeles Daily Journal*, Mar. 21, 1981, Box 88, Folder 19, NGLTF Records.

149 Ellen Lewin, "Lesbianism and Motherhood: Implications for Child Custody," *Human Organization* 40, no. 1 (1981): 6–14.

150 Ellen Lewin, email message to Joanne Meyerowitz, Aug. 19, 2014, author's possession; Ellen Lewin, interview by author, Sept. 19, 2014.

151 Lewin, "Confessions of a Reformed Grant Hustler," 111.

152 Ibid., 116; Ellen Lewin, Curriculum Vitae, Jan. 2013, author's possession, 3.

153 Lewin, "Confessions of a Reformed Grant Hustler," 116, 122.

154 Ibid., 117; William Proxmire, Golden Fleece Awards, 1975–987, Box 158, Folders 1–5, William Proxmire Papers.

155 J.L.P. (H.) v. D.J.P., 643 S.W.2d 865, 869 (Mo. Ct. App. 1982).

156 Ibid.

157 Marilyn Elias, "Are Gays Fit Parents?," *SFC*, Sept. 3, 1979, Box 141, Folder 38, NGLTF Records.

158 Brian Miller, "Gay Fathers and Their Children," *The Family Coordinator* 28, no. 4 (1979): 546–47.

159 Ibid., 551.

160 Jerry J. Bigner and Frederick W. Bozett, "Parenting by Gay Fathers," in *Homosexuality and Family Relations*, ed. Frederick W. Bozett and Marvin B. Sussman (New York: Harrington Park Press, 1990), 163; Frederick W. Bozett, "Children of Gay Fathers," in *Gay and Lesbian Parents*, ed. F.W. Bozett (New York: Praeger, 1987), 39.

161 Paul Cameron, interview by author, June 4, 2014.

162 Ibid.

163 Paul Cameron et al., "Child Molestation and Homosexuality," *Psychological Reports* 58 (1986): 328; Institute for the Scientific Investigation of Sexuality (ISIS), Survey, 1984, Box 13, Folder 49, Equality Colorado Records.

164 ISIS, Survey.

165 Cameron et al., "Child Molestation and Homosexuality," 331; Paul Cameron and Kirk Cameron, "Does Incest Cause Homosexuality?." *Psychological Reports* 76, no. 1 (1995): 611–21, 614.

166 American Sociological Association, Resolution adopted Aug. 1985, http://psychology .ucdavis.edu/faculty_sites/rainbow/html/ASA_resolution_1985.PDF; Barton, *Pray the Gay Away*, 142–43; Gregory M. Herek, "Bad Science in the Service of Stigma: A Critique of the Cameron Group's Survey Studies," in *Stigma and Sexual Orientation: Understanding Prejudice against Lesbians, Gay Men, and Bisexuals*, ed. Gregory M. Herek (Thousand Oaks: SAGE Publications, 1998), 245–47; Todd G. Morrison, "Children of Homosexuals and Transsexuals More Apt to Be Homosexual: A Reply to Cameron," *Journal of Biosocial Science* 39 (2007): 153–54; Max Seigel to Paul Cameron, Dec. 2, 1983, http://psychology.ucdavis.edu/faculty_sites/ rainbow/html/Cameron_apaletter.html; Chuck Stewart, *Homosexuality and the Law: A Dictionary* (Santa Barbara: ABC-CLIO, 2001), 222; David Reyes and Marlene Cimons, "Gays Assail Dannemeyer for Hiring Researcher," *LAT*, Aug. 20, 1985.

167 Herek, "Bad Science in the Service of Stigma," 245.

168 Family Research Institute, "About FRI: FRI Scientists," www.familyresearchinst .org/about/; Herek, "Bad Science in the Service of Stigma," 223–24; Judith Stacey and Timothy J. Biblarz, "(How) Does the Sexual Orientation of Parents Matter?," *American Sociological Review* 66 (2001): 161.

169 Wuest, *Born This Way*, 56–58.

170 Richardson, "Lesbian Mothers," 156.

171 Stein, *Sexual Injustice*, 97.

172 Researchers like Lewin and Bozett, whose studies focused on family structures rather than future sexual orientation, did not adopt this position. However, because their work did not address the concerns of judges, it had less impact on custody and visitation cases.

173 Richardson, "Lesbian Mothers," 156.

174 Cathy Cade, "Jeanne Jullion: Fighting for Custody," n.d., Box 9, Folder 12, Cathy Cade Photograph Archive.

175 Ibid.

176 Ibid.

177 "Lesbian Mother Fights Back," n.d., ca. 1978, Box 124, Folder 14, Phyllis Lyon and Del Martin Papers.

178 The appellate court returned the younger son to his mother's custody and granted Jullion more extended visitation with her older son, who remained in his father's care. "Lesbian Mother Wins Custody on Appeal," 1978, Box 88, Folder 14, NGLTF Records.

179 Ibid.

180 Ibid.; "Lesbian Mother Fights Back."

181 "Lesbian Mother Fights Back."

182 Friends of Mary Jo Risher, Mailing.

183 G. Guy Gibson, "Homosexuality on Trial," n.d., ca. 1975, Box 125, Folder 2, Phyllis Lyon and Del Martin Papers.

184 Friends of Mary Jo Risher, Mailing; "Lesbian Mother Fights Back"; LMNDF, "Custody Decision a Disaster," *Mom's Apple Pie*, 1993, Box 105, Folder 14, Phyllis Lyon and Del Martin Papers.

185 Meeker, *Contacts Desired*, 227; Rivers, *Radical Relations*, 82–86.

186 LMNDF, "A Dollar a Day Keeps the Husbands Away," *Mom's Apple Pie*, Jul./Aug. 1977, Box 125, Folder 11, Phyllis Lyon and Del Martin Papers.

187 LMNDF, "Case Updates," *Mom's Apple Pie*, Jan. 1976, Gale Archives of Sexuality and Gender, 2.

188 Philip S. Gutis, "Homosexual Parents Winning Some Custody Cases," *NYT*, Jan. 21, 1987.

189 "Gay Wins Custody of Twin Sons," *Advocate*, Nov. 1982.

190 Blew v. Varta, 617 A.2d 31, 36 n.2 (Pa. Super. Ct. 1992).

191 Conkel v. Conkel, 509 N.E.2d 983, 986–87 (Ohio Ct. App. 1987).

192 National Gay Task Force, "Gay Parent Support Packet," 1973, Box 105, Folder 7, NGLTF Records.

193 Ibid.

194 Ibid.

195 "Lesbians Win Custody in AZ Court," *Sunday's Childe* (Phoenix, Ariz.), Apr. 1980, Box 88, Folder 19, NGLTF Records; Brent Whiting, "Phoenix Lesbian Wins Custody of Young Daughters from Court," *Arizona Republic* (Phoenix), Apr. 14, 1980.

196 Dean B. Mitchell to National Gay Task Force, Apr. 23, 1980, Box 88, Folder 19, NGLTF Records.

197 Nan Hunter, interview by author, Mar. 18, 2014.

198 Findings of Fact at 2, Hulett v. Hulett, 79 D 653 (Kans. D. Ct. Feb. 28, 1980), Box 124, Folder 13, Phyllis Lyon and Del Martin Papers.

199 Gutis, "Homosexual Parents Winning Some Custody Cases."

200 George, "The Custody Crucible," 498–99; LMNDF, *Mom's Apple Pie*, Apr. 1975; Molly Moore and Tom Sherwood, "Homosexual Father Must Give Up Custody," *WP*, Jan. 19, 1985.

201 Transcript of Court's Oral Decision at 5–6, Schuster v. Schuster, No. 36868 (Wash. Super. Ct. King County, Sept. 3, 1974), Box 196, Folder 10, Phyllis Lyon and Del Martin Papers.

202 Ibid.

203 Nancy Faber, "Lesbians Madeleine Isaacson and Sandy Shuster Find 'Marriage' Happy but Hardly Untroubled," *People*, Jul. 9, 1979; Roger L. Winters, "Sandy & Madeleine: 'We Won It All,'" *Seattle Gay News*, Oct. 13, 1978, Box 125, Folder 5, Phyllis Lyon and Del Martin Papers.

204 Faber, "Lesbians Madeleine Isaacson and Sandy Shuster Find 'Marriage' Happy but Hardly Untroubled."

205 George, "The Custody Crucible," 497.

206 "Gay Wins Custody of Twin Sons"; Gutis, "Homosexual Parents Winning Some Custody Cases"; Donna J. Hitchens and Ann G. Thomas, *Lesbian Mothers and Their Children: An Annotated Bibliography of Legal and Psychological Materials* (San Francisco: Lesbian Rights Project, 1980), 2; Linda Kohl, "Lesbian Granted Custody," *St. Paul Pioneer Press*, June 2, 1978; LMNDF, "A Dollar a Day Keeps the Husbands Away"; National Gay Task Force, "NGTF Action Report," May 1979, Box 125, Folder 13, Phyllis Lyon and Del Martin Papers; "Oklahoma Lesbian Mother Wins Custody (June 1979)," 1979, Box 88, Folder 19, NGLTF Records; Whiting, "Phoenix Lesbian Wins Custody"; "Washington State Lesbian Mother Wins Custody."

207 "Lover Gets Custody of Gay Man's Son," *SFC*, Nov. 6, 1987, Box 1, Folder 7, Wendell Ricketts Papers.

Chapter 3

1 "Will Fiercely Disputed," *The Front Page* (Raleigh, NC), Jul. 10, 1990.

2 Ibid.

3 Ibid.

4 Chauncey, *Why Marriage?*, 96. Lesbians also contracted HIV, but at a far lower rate than gay men.

5 Ibid., 98–99.

6 Ibid.; Rivers, *Radical Relations*, 193.

7 "Will Fiercely Disputed."

8 NeJaime, "Before Marriage," 160–63.

9 Jeffrey Weinstein, interview by author, Feb. 28, 2022.

10 Miriam Frank and Desma Holcomb, "Pride at Work: Organizing for Lesbian and Gay Rights in Unions," 1990, 46, https://labornotes.org/sites/default/files/Pride-at-Work-1990.pdf; Richard Green, "Domestic Partner Benefits: A Status Report to the ACLU," June 1987, Box 1, Folder 59, Charles W. Gossett Papers, 4; Weinstein, interview by author.

11 Bertrand B. Pogrebin to Celine Keating, Jul. 28, 1982, author's possession; "Village Voice Bargains 'Spousal Equivalents' into Contract," District 65 UAW, n.d., ca. Jul. 8, 1982, author's possession; Weinstein, interview by author.

12 Green, "Domestic Partner Benefits," 4; Kirk Honeycutt, "Same-Sex Health Plan Coming to Warner Bros.," *Hollywood Reporter*, Jul. 1, 1993; Joanne Wojcik, "Newspaper First to Offer Domestic Partner Plan," *Business Insurance*, Mar. 11, 1991.

13 Canaday, *Queer Career*, 39; D'Emilio, *Sexual Politics, Sexual Communities*, 44, 46, 208–09; Johnson, *The Lavender Scare*, ch. 6; Teimeyer, *Plane Queer*, 62, 68–69.

14 Johnson, *The Lavender Scare*, ch. 6.

15 Graves, *And They Were Wonderful Teachers*.

16 Canaday, *Queer Career*, 230.

17 Ibid., 84–85, 162.

18 Ibid., 155, 229; Theresa M. Melbourne, Skylar Rolf, and Steven Schlachter, "The Case for Employee Resource Groups: A Review and Social Identity Theory-Based Research Agenda," *Personnel Review* 46, no. 8 (2017): 1816–17.

19 Canaday, *Queer Career*, 236.

20 Tom Brougham, interview by author, Oct. 27, 2022.

21 City of Berkeley, Cal., Ordinance 5106-NS (Oct. 10, 1978), *codified at* Berkeley Mun. Code. 13.28.010; Pierceson, *Same-Sex Marriage in the United States*, 43.

22 Brougham, interview by author.

23 Ibid.; David Lester, "Public Employees Seek Benefits for Spouses," *SFS*, Apr. 15, 1982.

24 Matthew Coles, interview by author, Oct. 27, 2022.

25 Ibid.

26 Ibid.

27 Evelyn Hsu and Larry Leibert, "Feinstein 'Live-in Lover' Veto Gets Strong, Mixed Reaction," *SFC*, Dec. 11, 1982; Jackson Rannells and H.G. Reza, "Live-in Lover Plan Vetoed," *SFC*, Dec. 10, 1982.

28 Coles, interview by author.

29 Brougham, interview by author; Hsu and Leibert, "Feinstein 'Live-in Lover' Veto Gets Strong, Mixed Reaction"; Jack Sullivan, "HRCF Snubs Feinstein," *Voice* (San Francisco), Dec. 17, 1982.

30 Hsu and Leibert, "Feinstein 'Live-in Lover' Veto Gets Strong, Mixed Reaction"; Rannells and Reza, "Live-In Lover Plan Vetoed."

31 Brougham, interview by author; City of Berkeley, Domestic Partnership Information Sheet, n.d., ca. 1985, Box 8, Folder 13, Thomas F. Coleman and Jay M. Kohorn Papers; Katharine J. Kleine, Memorandum to City of Berkeley Mayor and Members of the City Council, Jan. 17, 1984, Box 8, Folder 13, Thomas F. Coleman and Jay M. Kohorn Papers.

32 Tom Brougham, "Domestic Partnership Policy Turns 40," *BAR*, Aug. 14, 2019; Brougham, interview by author; Rob Hotakainen, "California Cities First to Extend Insurance to Domestic Partners," *Star-Tribune* (Minn.), Apr. 1, 1990.

33 Hotakainen, "California Cities First to Extend Insurance to Domestic Partners"; John Laird, interview by author, Mar. 17, 2022.

34 Gamble, "Putting Civil Rights to Popular Vote," 258; Laird, interview by author.

35 Laird, interview by author.

36 City of Santa Cruz, Cal., Resolution NS-17,185 (Sept. 23, 1986).

37 West Hollywood, Cal., Ordinance 22 (Feb. 21, 1985), *codified at* West Hollywood Mun. Code §§ 4220–28.

38 "Court Denies Gay Man's Right to Bereavement Leave," *NYN*, Sept. 30, 1985; Peter Schrag, "The ACLU's Gay Funeral Case," *Sacramento Bee*, Jul. 7, 1982.

39 Dawn Garcia, "S.F. Effort to Develop Policy on Unmarried Couples' Rights," *SFC*, Mar. 8, 1989.

40 "Secretary Sues for Funeral Leave," *WB*, Aug. 16, 1985.

41 Schrag, "The ACLU's Gay Funeral Case."

42 "Court Denies Gay Man's Right to Bereavement Leave."

43 Ibid.

44 "Domestic Partner Benefits: Employer Considerations," *Employee Benefit Practices*, Fourth Quarter 1994, Box 9, Folder 9, HRC Records, 4–5; Catherine Iannuzzo and Alexandra Pinck, "Benefits for the Domestic Partners of Gay and Lesbian Employees at Lotus Development Corporation," Nov. 1991, Box 1, Folder 55, Charles W. Gossett Papers; Elizabeth Murphy, "Understanding the Domestic Partner Dilemma: Perspectives of Employer and Insurer," 1992, Box 21, Folder 4, ACLU of Southern California Gay and Lesbian Rights Chapter Records, 33; Joanne Wojcik, "Few Offer Benefits to Unwed Couples," *Business Insurance*, Mar. 11, 1991; Richard Worsnop, "Domestic Partners: The Issues," *C.Q. Researcher*, Sept. 4, 1992, 765–67.

45 Jane Galvin to Charles W. Gossett, Jan. 12, 1990, Box 1, Folder 61, Charles W. Gossett Papers; Paul Liberatore, "Debate over Health Benefits for City Workers' Lovers," *SFC*, Nov. 11, 1982; Alex Linn, "Domestic Partners: Fodder for Debate," *SFE*, Nov. 18, 1982.

46 David Lester, "Passage Likely, But Will Industry Offer Partner Benefits?," *SFS*, Jul. 22, 1982.

47 Bruce Shutan, "Benefits Battle: Should Live-Ins Join the Company Health Plan?," *Employee Benefit News*, Sept. 1989.

48 Wojcik, "Few Offer Benefits to Unwed Couples."

49 Association of Maryland Health Maintenance Organizations to Charles W. Gossett, Mar. 2, 1990, Box 1, Folder 62, Charles W. Gossett Papers.

50 Jane Bryant Quinn, "Pressure to Insure Domestic Partners Grows," *Boston Herald*, Apr. 30, 1991.

51 Shutan, "Benefits Battle"; Quinn, "Pressure to Insure Domestic Partners Grows."

52 Green, "Domestic Partner Benefits," 4.

53 Ibid., 3–4.

54 City of Berkeley, Domestic Partnership Information Sheet; City of West Hollywood, Employee/Domestic Partner Health Insurance Information Sheet, Box 1, Folder 53, Charles W. Gossett Papers; Steve Taravella, "Michigan City May Cover Domestic Partners," *Business Insurance*, Apr. 7, 1986, 34; Weinstein, interview by author.

55 NeJaime, "Before Marriage," 161–63.

56 Coles, interview by author.

57 City of Berkeley, Domestic Partnership Information Sheet; City of West Hollywood, Employee/Domestic Partner Health Insurance Information Sheet; Taravella, "Michigan City May Cover Domestic Partners"; Weinstein, interview by author.

58 Vider, *Queerness of Home*, 83–84, 95–102.

59 Jan Gillingham to Dick Cushing, Dec. 22, 1993, Box 1, Folder 37, Charles W. Gossett Papers; Hedy R. Griffiths, "Domestic Partners as Related to Employee Benefits," Apr. 14, 1993, Box 1, Folder 33, Charles W. Gossett Papers.

60 Cliff Edwards, "Few Employees Take Advantage of Domestic Partner Benefits Study Finds," *SV*, Aug. 24, 1995; Quinn, "Pressure to Insure Domestic Partners Grows."

61 Canaday, *Queer Career*, 233–34, 239–40.

62 Griffiths, "Domestic Partners as Related to Employee Benefits"; Murphy, "Understanding the Domestic Partner Dilemma," 21; Shutan, "Benefits Battle."

63 Epstein, *Impure Science*, 188–89; Mark H. Furstenberg, "AZT The First AIDS Drug," *WP*, Sept. 15, 1987.

64 Shutan, "Benefits Battle."

65 Griffiths, "Domestic Partners as Related to Employee Benefits."

66 Ball, *From the Closet to the Courtroom*, 22–24, 29.

67 Ibid., 26–27.

68 Epstein, *Impure Science*, 199.

69 Ball, *From the Closet to the Courtroom*, 29.

70 Ibid., 21, 30.

71 Ibid., 30.

72 United States Department of Health and Human Services, A Timeline of HIV and AIDS, www.hiv.gov/hiv-basics/overview/history/hiv-and-aids-timeline.

73 CDC, "Current Trends Mortality Attributable to HIV Infection/AIDS – United States, 1981–1990," *Morbidity and Mortality Weekly Report*, Jan. 25, 1991.

74 Murray, "Free for All Lesbians," 251–53; Rivers, *Radical Relations*, 147–48.

75 Schulman, *Let the Record Show*, 32–33, 55–56; Stein, *Rethinking the Gay and Lesbian Movement*, 148–50.

76 Schulman, *Let the Record Show*, 10; Petro, *After the Wrath of God*, 140–41.

77 Chambers, "Tales of Two Cities," 184; Klarman, *From the Closet to the Altar*, 41–42, 71.

78 Bowers v. Hardwick, 478 U.S. 186 (1986).

79 Cain, "Litigating for Lesbian and Gay Rights," 1587; Eskridge, *Dishonorable Passions*, 235.

80 Eskridge, *Dishonorable Passions*, 238–39, 242.

81 Lewis J. Powell, Memorandum to Michael Mosman, Mar. 31, 1986, File 85-140, *Bowers v. Hardwick*, Lewis F. Powell, Jr. Archives.

82 Justice Lewis F. Powell, Bowers – Possible Footnote, June 24, 1986, File 85-140, *Bowers v. Hardwick*, Lewis F. Powell, Jr. Archives.

83 *Bowers*, 478 U.S. at 194.

84 Ibid., 197 (Burger, C.J., concurring).

85 Boutcher, "Mobilizing in the Shadow of the Law," 186–87; Eskridge, *Dishonorable Passions*, 242, 249.

86 Boutcher, "Mobilizing in the Shadow of the Law," 187.

87 Ibid., 192.

88 Chauncey, *Why Marriage?*, 44.

89 Boutcher, "Mobilizing in the Shadow of the Law," 192.

90 ACLU, "ACLU Seeks to Encourage Domestic Partnership Laws," Jan. 9, 1991, Box 21, Folder 4, ACLU of Southern California Gay and Lesbian Rights Chapter Records; Paul Horowitz, "Winning Passage of the Domestic Partnership Bill: A 12 Month Strategy," Feb. 18, 1992, Box 49, Folder 2, Empire State Pride Agenda Papers; NCLR, "Recognizing Lesbian and Gay Families: Strategies for Obtaining Domestic Partners Benefits," 1992, Box 8, Folder 18, Thomas F. Coleman and Jay M. Kohorn Papers; Christina Smith, "Do We Really Need Domestic Partnership Laws?," *Windy City Times*, Feb. 22, 1990.

91 CDC, "Average Age at Death from HIV Disease, by Sex – United States, 1987–2013," *Morbidity and Mortality Weekly Report*, Nov. 6, 2015.

92 Ibid.

93 Chauncey, *Why Marriage?*, 111.

94 Bill Sweigart, "Karen Thompson: 'I Wasn't "Family,"'" *Partners*, Sept. 1988, Newsletter Collection; "Sharon & Karen: First Legal Break in 4½ Years," *Partners*, Apr. 1988, Newsletter Collection; Karen D. Thompson to Friend of Lambda, n.d., ca. 1989, Lambda Legal Subject File; Thompson and Andrzejewski, *Why Can't Sharon Kowalski Come Home?*, 1, 3–5.

95 Thompson and Andrzejewski, *Why Can't Sharon Kowalski Come Home?*, 29.

96 Ibid., 79.

97 "Bring Sharon Home: Lesbian Fights to Be United with Her Lover," *Partners*, Apr. 1987, Newsletter Collection; "Sharon & Karen: First Legal Break in 4½ Years"; Sweigart, "Karen Thompson: 'I Wasn't "Family"'"; Thompson and Andrzejewski, *Why Can't Sharon Kowalski Come Home?*, 20–22, 26, 30, 67, 119, 155–56.

98 *In re* Guardianship of Kowalski, 382 N.W.2d 861 (Minn. Ct. App. 1986); *In re* Guardianship of Kowalski, 392 N.W.2d 310 (Minn. Ct. App. 1986).

99 *In re* Guardianship of Kowalski, 478 N.W.2d 790, 791 (Minn. Ct. App. 1991).

100 "Sharon & Karen: First Legal Break in 4½ Years"; Sweigart, "Karen Thompson: 'I Wasn't "Family."'"

101 Charles, *The Sharon Kowalski Case*, 60–61, 100, 114, 152–53.

102 Thompson and Andrzejewski, *Why Can't Sharon Kowalski Come Home?*, 20–22.
103 In re *Guardianship of Kowalski*, 382 N.W.2d at 863; In re *Guardianship of Kowalski*, 392 N.W.2d at 312.
104 Charles, *The Sharon Kowalski Case*, 140–41, 147–48, 169, 172–74, 183, 186–87, 234, 247–50, 252.
105 Ann Hardie, "Elderly Gays Face Special Problems," *AJC*, Mar. 21, 1993.
106 Mayor's Lesbian/Gay Task Force, "Domestic Partnership Survey Results," *A Family Affair* (Seattle), Oct. 1988, Gay and Lesbian Task Force Records.
107 Rivera, "Lawyers, Clients, and AIDS," 892–95.
108 Chambers, "Tales of Two Cities," 197.
109 Braschi v. Stahl Assocs., 543 N.E.2d 49, 50–51, 53, 55 (N.Y. 1989); Chambers, "Tales of Two Cities," 195.
110 In re Guardianship of Kowalski, 478 N.W.2d 790, 797 (Minn. Ct. App. 1991).
111 "Kowalski May Come Home," *Partners*, Winter 1992, Newsletter Collection.
112 Coles, interview by author.
113 Coles, *Try This at Home!*, 233–36.
114 Karen D. Thompson to Friend of Lambda.
115 Jill Rackmill, "City Council Approves Domestic Partnerships," *Cornell Daily Sun*, Sept. 10, 1990.
116 Domestic partnership programs were not the only way that gays and lesbians pressed for relationship recognition. In 1990, a Los Angeles attorney named Thomas Coleman registered his family as a non-profit association with the California Secretary of State. The certificate he obtained, which featured the state's gold seal, read "Family of Thomas F. Coleman and Michael A. Vasquez." He publicized the option to other gays and lesbians around the country, creating a manual that included six states' application forms. Coleman devised the creative maneuver as a step toward broader acceptance of queer life, recognizing that state recognition would help the American public understand that gays and lesbians formed families just like theirs. For that same reason, Christian conservatives denounced the action. In a mailing from 1991, the Traditional Values Coalition warned its members that California had certified "unholy matrimony," describing Coleman as having launched "the first assault on historic, constitutional biblical standards." Thomas F. Coleman, "California Families Can Register with the Secretary of State," Dec. 11, 1990, Box 8, Folder 14, Thomas F. Coleman and Jay M. Kohorn Papers; Senator Newton Russell, Memorandum to Bion Gregory, Jan. 17, 1991, Box 8, Folder 12, Thomas F. Coleman and Jay M. Kohorn Papers; "Non-Traditional Households Use Old Law to Register as Families," *NYN*, Dec. 31, 1990; Traditional Values Coalition, "California Certifies Unholy Matrimony," *Traditional Values Report*, Feb./Mar. 1991, Box 8, Folder 13, Thomas F. Coleman and Jay M. Kohorn Papers.
117 Paula L. Ettelbrick to "Friend," Nov. 28, 1989, Lambda Legal Subject File.
118 Christina Smith, "Do We Really Need Domestic Partnership Laws?," *Windy City Times*, Feb. 22, 1990.
119 Ibid.; "Lesbian Survey Ranks Partnership Rights as #1 Issue," *Human Rights Campaign Fund Newsletter*, Spring 1990, Box 98, Folder 5, Phyllis Lyon and Del Martin Papers.
120 Christopher Elliott, "Gay, Lesbian Couples Get 'Partnered' in San Francisco," *LAT*, Feb. 15, 1991.
121 K. Connie Kang and Larry D. Hatfield, "Renne Won't Join an Override Attempt," *SFE*, Dec. 9, 1982.
122 Ibid.; Coles, interview by author.

123 Al Lewis, "SF Religious Members against Domestic Partnership Ordinance," *San Francisco Post*, Aug. 16, 1989; Office of the Registrar of Voters, San Francisco Voter Information Pamphlet, 1989, San Francisco Voter Information Pamphlets and Ballots, 138–39, 146–48.

124 Office of the Registrar of Voters, San Francisco Voter Information Pamphlet & Sample Ballot, 1990, San Francisco Voter Information Pamphlets and Ballots, 153.

125 Elliott, "Gay, Lesbian Couples Get 'Partnered' in San Francisco."

126 Dowland, *Family Values*, 8.

127 Self, *All in the Family*, 348.

128 Dowland, *Family Values*, 3–4; Self, *All in the Family*, 5–6.

129 Dowland, *Family Values*, 9; Self, *All in the Family*, 3–11.

130 Karen Diegmueller, "Extended Definition of Family Fuels Partnership Controversy," *Insight*, Aug. 7, 1989; Mary Goodavage, "S.F. Takes Step toward Same-Sex Matrimony," *USA Today*, Feb. 14, 1991; Philip S. Gutis, "Family Redefines Itself, and Now the Law Follows," *NYT*, May 28, 1989; David Shaffer, "Proposed Ordinance Redefines Family," *St. Paul Pioneer Press*, Aug. 6, 1990.

131 Janet Naylor, "Partners Law Safe, Council Hopes," *Washington Times*, May 7, 1992.

132 Ibid.

133 Dowland, *Family Values*, 158; Self, *All in the Family*, 221.

134 Petro, *After the Wrath of God*, 24.

135 Ibid.; Alwood, *Straight News*, 219, 223, 235; Mendicino, "Characterization and Disease," 241–42; Stein, *Rethinking the Gay and Lesbian Movement*, 23–24.

136 Alwood, *Straight News*, 228–29, 241–45; Chauncey, *Why Marriage?*, 44.

137 Chauncey, *Why Marriage?*, 105; Deborah Hastings, "'L.A. Law' Lesbian Kiss Hailed by Gay Rights Group," *Associated Press*, Feb. 8, 1991; John J. O'Connor, "Gay Images: TV's Mixed Signals," *NYT*, May 19, 1991; Polikoff, *Beyond (Straight and Gay) Marriage*, 85–86.

138 Jeffrey Schmalz "Gay Politics Goes Mainstream," *NYT Magazine*, Oct. 11, 1992.

139 Chauncey, *Why Marriage?*, 48.

140 Ellen Hume, "Gay Community Is Holding on to Political Gains Despite AIDS, Pressure from Some Conservatives," *WSJ*, Apr. 22, 1986.

141 Karlyn Bowman and Adam Foster, "Attitudes about Homosexuality and Gay Marriage," *AEI Studies in Public Opinion*, June 3, 2008, 4–6, 21; "Theoretically Gay," *Partners*, Jul. 1989, Newsletter Collection.

142 Charly L. Coward, "Activists Say: 'This Is Not a Gay Marriage Bill,'" *WB*, Nov. 1, 1991; Lisa Keen, "Domestic Partnership Laws Are under Attack," *WB*, Nov. 18, 1994; Rene Sanchez, "D.C. Council Rethinks Live-In Partners Bill," *WP*, Apr. 5, 1992.

143 NeJaime, "Before Marriage," 160–63.

144 Paula Ettelbrick, "Since When Is Marriage a Path to Liberation?," *Out/Look*, Fall 1989, 9.

145 Jerome J. Davis and Cynthia Goldstein, S.F. Human Rights Commission, "Domestic Partnerships," n.d., ca. 1990, Box 2, Folder 10, Jerry (Jerome Joel) Davis Papers; Gary Schweikhart, "Britt: Benefits an 'Alternative to Marriage,'" *SFS*, Nov. 23, 1982.

146 Thomas B. Stoddard, "Why Gay People Should Seek the Right to Marry," *Out/Look*, Fall 1989, 12.

147 "Marry Us, Insist Lesbian and Gay Couples," *Partners*, May/June 1991, Newsletter Collection.

148 Fischer and Hout, *Century of Difference*, ch. 4.
149 Lefkovitz, *Strange Bedfellows*, 11, 31.
150 Peck, *Not Just Roommates*, 10.
151 Katrine Ames et al., "Domesticated Bliss," *Newsweek*, Mar. 23, 1992; Diegmueller, "Extended Definition of Family Fuels Partnership Controversy"; Gutis, "Family Redefines Itself"; Mimi Hall, "Percentage of Marrieds Is Smallest in 200 Years," *USA Today*, June 11, 1991; "Nuclear Family Still in Decline, Census Reports," *SFE*, Jan. 30, 1991.
152 Michelle Buehler, Dianne Goodman, and Katherine J. Hamilton, "Los Angeles City Task Force on Family Diversity Research Team on Governmental Employee Benefits," 1987, Box 1, Folder 60, Charles W. Gossett Papers, 3; Shelly F. Cohen, "Domestic Partner Benefits under the Seattle Fair Employment Practices Ordinance," Nov. 8, 1988, Published Documents Collection, 2–3; Coward, "Activists Say: 'This Is Not a Gay Marriage Bill'"; Domestic Partners Organizing Committee, "Domestic Partners," Box 1, Folder 1, Brian J. Coyle Papers.
153 George L. Blum, "Property Rights Arising from Relationship of Couple Cohabitating without Marriage," *ALR 5th* 69 (2019): 219; William H. Danne, Jr., "'Palimony' Actions for Support Following Termination of Nonmarital Relationships," *ALR 6th* 21 (2007): 351; Marvin v. Marvin, 557 P.2d 106 (Cal. 1976) (en banc).
154 Los Angeles City Task Force on Family Diversity, *Strengthening Families: A Model for Community Action* (Los Angeles: Los Angeles City Council, 1988), 24.
155 Coward, "Activists Say: 'This Is Not a Gay Marriage Bill'"; Domestic Partners Organizing Committee, "Domestic Partners."
156 Joint Select Task Force on the Changing Family, "Planning a Family Policy for California," 1989, Box 8, Folder 17, Thomas F. Coleman and Jay M. Kohorn Papers, 100; Los Angeles City Task Force on Family Diversity, *Strengthening Families*.
157 Griffiths, "Domestic Partners as Related to Employee Benefits"; Murphy, "Understanding the Domestic Partner Dilemma," 20; James Bryant Quinn, "Pressure to Insure Domestic Partners Grows," *Boston Herald*, Apr. 30, 1991.
158 Ames et al., "Domesticated Bliss."
159 Austin, Tex., Resolution 930902-41 (Sept. 2, 1993); Gary S. Chafetz, "Cambridge Ordinance Extends Benefits to City Workers' Partners," *BG*, Sept. 15, 1992; Ithaca, N.Y., Ordinance No. 90-7 (Aug. 1, 1990); Madison, Wis., Substitute Ordinance No. 10,039 (May 17, 1990); Marin County, Cal., Ordinance No. 3140 (Apr. 27, 1993); "Mayor Signs Benefits and Registry Bills," *WB*, Apr. 22, 1994 (Rochester, N.Y.); Minneapolis, Minn., Ordinance 91-08-015 (Jan. 25, 1991); New York City, Exec. Order No. 48 (Jan. 7, 1993); Northampton, Mass., Ordinance to amend sections 14-22 through 14-27 (May 18, 1995); "Partners Get Benefits," *WB*, Sept. 4, 1993 (Ann Arbor, Mich.); Press Release, "Remarks by Mayor Dinkins to Announce New Citywide Registration Program for Domestic Partnerships," Jan. 7, 1993, Box 49, Folder 3, Empire State Pride Agenda Papers; Sacramento, Cal., Ordinance No. 92-062 (Nov. 5, 1992); San Francisco, Cal., Proposition K (Nov. 6, 1990); Tacoma Park, Md., Administrative Procedure No. 93-01 (Nov. 8, 1993); Washington, D.C., Law 9-188 (Apr. 15, 1992).
160 Minneapolis, Ordinance 91-08-015.
161 Photograph and accompanying note, Box 1, Folder 12, Brian J. Coyle Papers.
162 Findings of Fact, Conclusions of Law, and Order for Judgment, Anglin v. City of Minneapolis, 88180-EM-12 (Minn. Comm'n on Civ. Rts. Nov. 17, 1992), Box 4,

Folder 7, Charles W. Gossett Papers; "Librarians Throw the Book at Library Board," *Partners*, May 1989, Newsletter Collection.

163 David Anger, "Domestic Partnership Battle Begins," *Equal Time* (St. Paul, Minn.), Aug. 17–31, 1990.

164 Ibid.

165 Jon Jeter, "Watered-Down Domestic Partners Plan Passes," *Star Tribune* (Minneapolis), Jan. 26, 1991.

166 Minneapolis, Minn., Resolution 93R-342 (Sept. 2, 1993).

167 Stevie Bryant, "L.A. O.K.s 'No-Cost' Benefits for Domestic Partners," *Partners*, Nov. 1988, Newsletter Collection; City of Seattle, Fact Sheet: Domestic Partner Benefits, Jan. 1991, Box 1, Folder 47, Charles W. Gossett Papers; "D.C. Adopts Leave Benefits," *Partners*, Nov./Dec. 1990, Newsletter Collection; Peter Freiberg, "City Workers Get Partners Benefits," *WB*, Nov. 5, 1993; Wade Lambert, "Domestic Partners of Seattle Workers Get Health Benefits," *WSJ*, May 7, 1990; New York City, Exec. Order No. 48; NYC Mayor's Office for the Lesbian and Gay Community, "Mayor Edward I. Koch Issues Executive Order Granting Bereavement Leave to Domestic Partners," Aug. 7, 1989, Domestic Partner Benefits – U.S. – New York Subject File; Press Release, "Remarks by Mayor Dinkins to Announce New Citywide Registration Program for Domestic Partnerships"; Washington, D.C., Law 9-188.

168 Maynard Jackson to the Honorable President and Members of Atlanta City Council, June 29, 1993, Box 15, Folder labeled Domestic Partnership, GLAAD Records.

169 Maynard Jackson to Marvin S. Arrington and Members of Atlanta City Council, Jul. 2, 1993, Box 15, Folder labeled Domestic Partnership, GLAAD Records; David Pendered and Holly Morris, "Mayor Broke Promise, Gays, Lesbians Assert," *AJC*, Jul. 1, 1993; K.C. Wildmoon, "Mayor Jackson Says Financial Questions Led to Partnership Veto," *SV*, Jul. 8, 1993.

170 Richard Shumate, "Days of Rage," *SV*, Jul. 8, 1993.

171 Ibid.

172 Ibid.; Holly Morris and Mary Louise Kelly, "Holiday Events to Fuel Gays' Mayoral Protests," *AJC*, Jul. 2, 1993.

173 Shumate, "Days of Rage"; Holly Morris, "Tensions Mount Between City, Gays in Domestic Partnership Battle," *AJC*, Jul. 12, 1993.

174 Jackson to Arrington and Members of Atlanta City Council, Jul. 2, 1993.

175 Atlanta, Ga., Ordinance 93-0-1057 (Aug. 9, 1993); City of Atlanta v. McKinney, 454 S.E.2d 517, 520–21 (Ga. 1995).

176 Ga. Const., art. 3 § 6, ¶ IV.

177 *McKinney*, 454 S.E.2d at 520–21.

178 Ibid., 520.

179 Austin, Resolution 930902-41; Kristina Cambpell, "Vt. City Gives Benefits," *WB*, Jan. 29, 1993 (Burlington, Vt.); "City Passes Partners Law," *WB*, Nov. 13, 1992 (East Lansing, Mich.); Domestic Partner Benefit Program, n.d., ca. 1993, Box 1, Folder 16, Charles W. Gossett Papers (King County, Wash.); Charles W. Gossett, "Domestic Partnership Benefits: Public Sector Patterns," paper presented at the 54th National Training Conference of the American Society for Public Administration, San Francisco, Calif., Jul. 19, 1993, Box 2, Folder 4, Charles W. Gossett Papers, 24; Philip J. LaVelle, "City OKs Benefits for Unwed Partners," *San Diego Union-Tribune*, June 3, 1994; Los Angeles, Calif., Ordinance No. 168238 (Sept. 16, 1992); "OR County Gives Go-Ahead to Domestic Partner Coverage," *SV*, Dec. 17, 1992 (Multnomah County, Or.); Portland, Or., Resolution No. 35281 (June 8, 1994); Sheila Walsh, "Baltimore Extends Benefits to Gay Couples," *WB*, Dec. 24, 1993.

180 "Boston Partners Bill Defeated," *Partners*, Sept./Oct. 1991, Newsletter Collection; Rick Holguin, "City Kills Plan to Offer Benefits to Non-Traditional Families," *LAT*, June 3, 1993.

181 "Benefits for Partners Out in Atlanta," *WB*, May 13, 1994; Lisa Keen, "Loss in Austin: City Repeals Its Partnership Law," *WB*, May 13, 1994; Mary Rowland, "Hurdles for Unmarried Partners," *NYT*, May 22, 1994.

182 Keen, "Loss in Austin."

183 "Domestic Partner Bill Vetoed in California," *NYT*, Sept. 13, 1994; "Health Laws for Ill.," *Partners*, Nov./Dec. 1991, Newsletter Collection; Mass., Exec. Order 340 (Sept. 23, 1992); Mass., Exec. Order 341 (Sept. 23, 1992); Sheila Walsh, "Vermont OKs Partner Benefits for Its Workers," *WB*, June 17, 1994.

184 Brantley, *Brewing a Boycott*, 2.

185 Ibid., 90.

186 Baker, Straub, and Henning, *Cracking the Corporate Closet*, 100–01.

187 Ibid., 100.

188 Brantley, *Brewing a Boycott*, 178–79.

189 David J. Jefferson, "Gay Employees Win Benefits for Partners at More Corporations," *WSJ*, Mar. 18, 1994.

190 Ibid.

191 Weinstein, interview by author.

192 Ibid.; Canaday, *Queer Career*, 246; Iannuzzo and Pinck, "Benefits for the Domestic Partners of Gay and Lesbian Employees at Lotus Development Corporation."

193 E. Scott Reckard, "Gay Workers Gaining Benefits for Partners," *SFE*, Jul. 2, 1993.

194 "Gay Benefits at Genentch," *SFE*, May 26, 1994; Honeycutt, "Same-Sex Health Plan Coming to Warner Bros."; Jefferson, "Gay Employees Win Benefits for Partners at More Corporations"; Julia Lawlor, "Gay Make Gains in Health Care," *USA Today*, Apr. 23, 1993; "Levi Strauss OKs Benefits for Unmarried Partners," *LAT*, Feb. 24, 1992; Barbara Presley Noble, "HBO Grants Benefits to Staff's Same-Sex Partners," *NYT*, Jul. 2, 1993; Jennifer Pendleton, "Viacom Adds Benefits for Gay Partners," *Daily Variety*, Oct. 28, 1992; E. Scott Reckard, "Hollywood Moving Forward on Recognizing Needs of Gay Employees," *Bay Windows*, Jul. 8, 1993; Chris Woodyard and Don Lee, "Disney to Extend Health Benefits to Gay Partners," *LAT*, Oct. 7, 1995.

195 Canaday, *Queer Career*, 245.

196 Reckard, "Gay Workers Gaining Benefits for Partners."

197 Ibid.

198 Judi C. Casey, "Employee Resource Groups: A Strategic Business Resource for Today's Workplace," Boston College Center for Work and Family, Nov. 2021, www.bc.edu/content/dam/files/centers/cwf/research/publications3/executivebriefing series-2/ExecutiveBriefing_EmployeeResourceGroups.pdf; "Exploring the History and Evolution of Employee Resource Groups," DiversityInc, Aug. 4, 2020, www .diversityinc.com/history-and-evolution-of-employee-resource-groups-ergs/.

199 Baker, Straub, and Henning, *Cracking the Corporate Closet*, 15–16.

200 "One in Four Corporations Protect Gays," *WB*, Jul. 29, 1994.

201 Woods and Lucas, *The Corporate Closet*, 249.

202 Ibid., 251.

203 "One in Four Corporations Protect Gays."

204 Joseph E. Slater, "The 'American Rule' that Swallows the Exceptions," *Employment Rights and Employment Policy Journal* 11, no. 1 (2007): 98.

205 Matthew Corey, "Gays Faring Better in Workplace," *WB*, Dec. 3, 1993; Meryl Davids, "Good for Business: Why Companies Are Bringing Gay Rights Out of the

Closet," *Working Woman*, Oct. 1991; Iannuzzo and Pinck, "Benefits for the Domestic Partners of Gay and Lesbian Employees at Lotus Development Corporation"; Jefferson, "Gay Employees Win Benefits for Partners at More Corporations."

206 Woods and Lucas, *The Corporate Closet*, 250.

207 Jefferson, "Gay Employees Win Benefits for Partners at More Corporations."

208 Ibid.; Corey, "Gays Faring Better in Workplace"; Davids, "Good for Business."

209 Jefferson, "Gay Employees Win Benefits for Partners at More Corporations."

210 Ibid., 251.

211 Woods and Lucas, *The Corporate Closet*, 249.

212 Ibid.

213 Ibid.

214 Canaday, *Queer Career*, 236–42.

215 Ibid., 239.

216 Claudia H. Deutsch, "Gay Rights, Issue of the 90s," *NYT*, Apr. 28, 1991.

217 Canaday, *Queer Career*, 240.

218 Ibid., 239–40; Lawlor, "Gays Make Gains in Health Care."

219 Lisa M. Keen, "Domestic Partners Suit Filed against AT&T," *WB*, Aug. 31, 1990; Tamar Lewin, "Suit over Death Benefits Asks, What Is a Family?," *NYT*, Sept. 21, 1990.

220 Keen, "Domestic Partners Suit Filed against AT&T"; Lewin, "Suit over Death Benefits Asks, What Is a Family?"

221 Canaday, *Queer Career*, 239–40; Lawlor, "Gays Make Gains in Health Care."

222 "Benefits for Gay Partners," *WSJ*, Mar. 30, 1993; "Our Commitment to the LGBTQ+ & Ally Community," AT&T, 2019, https://watch.att.com/lgbtq/share-your-truth/.

223 Edward Iwata, "Making Strides: Gays Finding Acceptance, Recognition in Corporate America," *SFE*, Apr. 22, 1996.

224 M.V. Lee Badgett, "Influence of Family-Related Institutions on Lesbian and Gay Couples' Decision-Making" (presentation, American Political Science Association Annual Meeting, New York, NY, Sept. 1–4, 1994), Box 2, Folder 6, Charles W. Gossett Papers, 4.

225 "Benefits at U. of Iowa," *WB*, Nov. 27, 1992; "Chicago, Swarthmore Extend Benefits to Gays," *Frontiers*, Jan. 29, 1993; Michele N.-K. Collison, "Benefits for Gay Couples," *Chronicle of Higher Education*, Nov. 3, 1993; Anthony DePalma, "2 Universities Give Gay Partners Same Benefits as Married Couples," *NYT*, Dec. 24, 1992; "Duke to Offer Same-Sex Benefits," *SV*, Jan. 19, 1995; John Gallagher, "Benefits for the Fringe," *Advocate*, Jan. 25, 1994; "Harvard Offers Benefits for Same-Sex Partners," *Voice*, June 3, 1993, Box 2, Folder 7, Charles W. Gossett Papers; "Homosexuals Gain Benefits," *NYT*, June 13, 1993; "New Mexico," *USA Today*, Apr. 15, 1994; Lesbian and Gay Families Project, NGLTF Policy Institute, "Domestic Partners/Non-Traditional Family Recognition in Campus Benefit Policies," 1990, Box 2, Folder 6, Charles W. Gossett Papers.

226 Aslan Brooke, "Gay Couple Sues Nation's 5th Largest Bank," *Frontiers*, Feb. 10, 1995; "A Car for Two," *Partners*, Nov./Dec. 1991, Newsletter Collection; "Insurance Discrimination in Texas," *Partners*, Apr. 1987, Newsletter Collection; National Gay Rights Advocates, "Couples Rights Litigation a Major Priority for NGRA," Monthly Litigation Update, May 1987, Box 1, Folder 17, Betty Berzon Papers.

227 David Tuller, "Trying to Avoid an Insurance Debacle," *NYT*, Feb. 22, 1987.

228 Ibid.

229 "Clerk Demands Spousal Rights," *Partners*, Mar. 1990, Newsletter Collection; "Frequent Flyer Bonus," *WB*, June 18, 1993; "If at First You Don't Succeed," *Partners*, Nov. 1989, Newsletter Collection; Village of Shorewood Hills, Wis., Resolution No. 90-03 (Aug. 20, 1990).

230 "Credit Where Credit Is Due," *Partners*, Feb. 1989, Newsletter Collection; John Hammond, "TWA Settles Lambda Suit," *NYN*, Jul. 31, 1989.

231 Jefferson, "Gay Employees Win Benefits for Partners at More Corporations"; Cliff O'Neill, "Right Wingers to Boycott Levi Strauss, Wells Fargo," *Frontiers*, Sept. 11, 1992; Rachel Timoner, "Levi Strauss Stands Up for Gays, Lesbians," *Update*, June 3, 1992.

232 Jefferson, "Gay Employees Win Benefits for Partners at More Corporations."

233 Kathleen Sullivan, "Companies Committed to Gay Benefits," *SFE*, Dec. 2, 1993.

234 "Lawmakers Condemn Disney for Offering Benefits for Gay Partners," *Contax Guide: Your National Gay Entertainment & Contact Magazine* (Tampa), Nov. 1, 1995.

235 "Disney's Gay Partner Benefits Criticized," *SFE*, Oct. 20, 1995.

236 Sullivan, "Companies Committed to Gay Benefits."

237 Ibid.

238 Ibid.

239 Iwata, "Making Strides."

Chapter 4

1 "Antiretroviral Drug Discovery and Development," National Institute of Allergy and Infectious Disease, last modified Nov. 26, 2018, www.Niaid.Nih.Gov/Diseases-Conditions/Antiretroviral-Drug-Development; Report of the Alameda County Social Services Agency at 1, *In re* Adoption Petition of Jessen, No. 18380 (Cal. Super. Ct. Jul. 3, 1989), Box 2, Folder 9, Wendell Ricketts Papers.

2 "Policy against Adoptions by Unmarrieds Is Assailed," *Sunday Star-Bulletin & Advertiser* (Honolulu), Nov. 19, 1989; Dexter Waugh, "Lesbian Pair Adopt Child with AIDS," *SFE*, Nov. 16, 1989.

3 "California's Adoption Policy Is Criticized," *NYT*, Nov. 16, 1989.

4 NCLR, Current Case Docket, 1989, Box 88, Folder 63, NGLTF Records; Report of the Alameda County Social Services Agency, 3.

5 CDSS, All-County Letter No. 87-80, June 15, 1987, author's possession; Donna Hitchens, interview by Wendell Ricketts, Jul. 14, 1988, Box 2, Folder 12, Wendell Ricketts Papers, 4.

6 Report of the Alameda County Social Services Agency, 3.

7 Carole S. Cullum, "Co-Parent Adoptions; Lesbian and Gay Parenting," *Trial*, June 1993, 28, Box 105, Folder 15, Phyllis Lyon and Del Martin Papers; Gina Kolata, "Lesbian Partners Find the Means to be Parents," *NYT*, Jan. 30, 1989; Sue Zemel, "Legal Frontier: Donor Insemination of Lesbians," *SFS*, Mar. 18, 1982.

8 Sharon Kahn, interview by Wendell Ricketts, Dec. 13, 1986, Box 2, Folder 12, Wendell Ricketts Papers, 1; "Experience and Education," on Sharon Kahn's website, accessed Jan. 12, 2022.

9 Given the sensitive nature of the case, I have used pseudonyms for the parents. The children's first names are a matter of public record. *In re* Nathaniel P., No. A038967 (Cal. Ct. App. Mar. 29, 1989), https://caselaw.findlaw.com/ca-court-of-appeal/1772327.html.

10 Ibid.

11 Kathy Barbell and Madelyn Freundlich, *Foster Care Today* (Washington, D.C.: Casey Family Programs, 2001) v, www.hunter.cuny.edu/socwork/nrcfcpp/down loads/policy-issues/foster_care_today.pdf.

12 Adoption Assistance and Child Welfare Act of 1980, Pub. L. No. 96-272, 94 Stat. 500, *amended by* Adoption and Safe Families Act of 1997; Adoption and Safe Families Act of 1997, Pub. L. No. 105-89, 111 Stat. 2115, *codified as amended at* 42 U.S.C. §§ 670 et seq. (2012).

13 Barbell and Freundlich, *Foster Care Today*, 13.

14 Ibid.

15 "Families by Adoption: A Gay Reality," *Advocate*, Aug. 28, 1974, 1.

16 "Agency Reveals Kids Placed with Gay Couples," *Advocate*, Aug. 15, 1973, 2; "Gay Ban Claimed in Chicago Child Placement," *Advocate*, Aug. 29, 1973, 22; "Illinois Agency Boiling: New Row over Gay Foster Homes," *Advocate*, Jul. 3, 1974, A-6.

17 Randy Shilts, "Foster Homes for Gay Children: Justice or Prejudice?," *Advocate*, Dec. 17, 1975, Box 1, Folder 4, Wendell Ricketts Papers, 11–12.

18 Ibid., 13.

19 "Foster Care/Adoption," n.d., Box 32, Folder 17, Phyllis Lyon and Del Martin Papers.

20 Koren, interview by Ricketts, 1.

21 Massachusetts Executive Office of Human Services, "Review of States' Policies Regarding Foster Placements," 1985, Box 1, Folder 11, Wendell Ricketts Papers, 7.

22 David Perry, "Homes of Last Resort: Is America Dumping Its Unwanted Children on Gays Hoping to Adopt?," *Advocate*, Dec. 5, 1985.

23 Ibid., 46–47.

24 "Board Discusses Treatment Book, Prospective Payment," *Psychiatric News*, Aug. 1, 1986, 8; NASW, "Lesbian and Gay Issues," 1987, Box 2, Folder 19, Wendell Ricketts Papers; "National Committee on Lesbian, Gay, Bisexual, Transgender, & Queer+ Issues (NCLGBTQ+)," NASW, www.socialworkers.org/ About/Governance/National-Appointments/National-Committees/Committee-on-LGBT-Issues.

25 NASW, "Lesbian and Gay Issues."

26 Richard A. Barnett, letter, Apr. 16, 1981, Adoption by Gays or Lesbians Subject File; Kevin McKinney, "How to Become a Gay Father," *Advocate*, Dec. 8, 1987; Brian Quinn, interview by Wendell Ricketts, Nov. 18, 1986, Box 2, Folder 12, Wendell Ricketts Papers.

27 New York Department of Social Services, "Standards of Practice for Adoption Services," 1981, Box 139, Folder 2, NGLTF Records, 18.

28 Massachusetts Executive Office of Human Services, "Review of States' Policies Regarding Foster Placements," 5–6.

29 Lofton v. Sec'y of the Dep't of Children & Family Servs., 377 F.3d 1275, 1302–03 (11th Cir. 2004).

30 Kay Longcope, "States' Policies Differ on Issue of Gay Foster Parents," *BG*, May 12, 1985.

31 George, "Bureaucratic Agency," 94–102; Lee, *The Workplace Constitution*, 105; Tani, *States of Dependency*, 20–21.

32 Frank Galvan, "Gays as Adoptive Parents: A Study Contrasting Policies in Public Adoption Agencies in Los Angeles County," 1980, Adoption by Gays or Lesbians Subject File, 3.

33 Steven Fritsch Rudser, interview by Wendell Ricketts, Jul. 31, 1988, Box 2, Folder 12, Wendell Ricketts Papers, 3.

34 Ibid.

35 Ellen Goodman, "Children's Needs," *SFE*, May 31, 1985.
36 Ibid.
37 Kenneth J. Cooper, "Placement of Foster Children with Gay Couple Is Revoked," *BG*, May 9, 1985.
38 Kay Longcope, "Gay Couple Express Anger, Grief and Hope: Media, Politics Blamed in Loss of Boys," *BG*, May 16, 1985.
39 Kenneth J. Cooper, "Some Oppose Foster Placement with Gay Couple," *BG*, May 8, 1985, 21, 24; Wendell Ricketts, *Lesbians and Gay Men as Foster Parents* (Portland: National Child Welfare Resource Center, 1991), 68.
40 Scot Lehigh and Neil Miller, "The Damage Done: The Breaking of a Foster Family," *Boston Phoenix*, May 21, 1985.
41 Ibid.; Cooper, "Some Oppose Foster Placement with Gay Couple."
42 "Youths Terrorize Gay Couple," *Boston Herald*, Sept. 21, 1985.
43 Koren, interview by Ricketts, 1.
44 Clara Germani, "Foster Care by Homosexuals: A Survey of States and Their Policies," *Christian Science Monitor*, June 21, 1985; Lofton v. Sec'y of the Dep't of Children & Family Servs., 377 F.3d 1275, 1302–03 (11th Cir. 2004); Massachusetts Executive Office of Human Services, "Review of States' Policies Regarding Foster Placements," 5–6.
45 MDSS, 110 CMR § 7-101 (1986), Box 1, Folder labeled New DSS Regulations, 1986, GLDC Collection.
46 Kevin Cathcart, interview by Wendell Ricketts, Oct. 1986, Box 2, Folder 12, Wendell Ricketts Papers, 4–5.
47 Anita Diamant, "In the Best Interest of the Children: A Recent Controversy Raises Questions about the State's Foster Care System – and What Constitutes an American Family," *BG Magazine*, Sept. 8, 1985, 14, 92, 96.
48 Cathcart, interview by Ricketts, 4–5; Kenneth J. Cooper, "New Policy on Foster Care," *BG*, May 25, 1985; Christine Guilfoy, "Outrage Grows against Gay Foster Policy," *GCN*, June 8, 1985; Teresa M. Hanafin, "State Social Services Chief to Be Sworn In," *BG*, Jul. 19, 1991.
49 Paul R. Lessard, "Sexuality Issue Raised in Foster Child Care Case," *UL* (Manchester, NH), June 19, 1985.
50 David A. Bundy, Memorandum, June 28, 1985, Box 23, Folder 7, GLAD Records; David Bundy, interview by author, Sept. 24, 2014; John Distaso, "House Okays Smoking Ban but Rejects Homosexual Bill," *UL*, Feb. 13, 1986; "Foster Parent Rules Rewritten, Set for Hearings," *UL*, Jul. 15, 1986, 3; "House Kills Bill Barring Gays as Foster Parents," *Nashua Telegraph*, Feb. 13, 1986; Jack Lightfoot, interview by author, Nov. 12, 2014; "'Practicing' Gays Can't Have Kids," *BAR*, Sept. 12, 1985; Donna Sytek, New Hampshire Republican Party Chair 1981–1984, interview by author, Oct. 4, 2014; Donn Tibbetts, "House Opposes Homosexual Bill," *UL*, Jan. 22, 1986.
51 John DiStaso, "Bill on Homosexuals Gets Strong Reaction," *UL*, Feb. 4, 1987.
52 Clay Wirestone, "In 1987, the New Hampshire Legislature Targeted Gay People as Unfit for Parenting," *CM*, June 29, 2013.
53 Distaso, "Bill on Homosexuals Gets Strong Reaction"; H.R. 70, 1987 Gen. Court, Reg. Sess. (N.H. 1987).
54 David Olinger, "Who Will Take a Foster Child?," *CM*, June 5, 1985; Ed Roberts, "Foster Care: NH Needs Money, Homes," *UL*, Sept. 28, 1986; "Sununu Will Continue to Make Child Welfare a Major Concern," *UL*, Dec. 30, 1986; Barbara Tetreault, "North Country Needs More Foster Families," *UL*, Sept. 27, 1986.

55 N.H. House of Representatives, Definition and Majority Response; N.H. House of Representatives, Judiciary Committee, Committee Report, Feb. 2, 1987, House of Representatives File for H.B. 70 (1987), Senate and House of Representatives Legislative Files.

56 Christine Guilfoy, "Foster Policy Activists Keep Pressure on Dukakis," *GCN*, Jul. 6, 1985; GLDC, "Facts of Interest," Box 1, Folder labeled Facts of Interest Concerning Proposed D.S.S. Foster Care Policy, GLDC Collection.

57 Guilfoy, "Outrage Grows against Gay Foster Policy."

58 Ibid.

59 Babets v. Dukakis, C.A. No. 81083, slip op. 1, 13–15 (Mass. Super. Ct. Sept. 18, 1986), Box 1, Folder labeled Babets vs. Gov. of Commonwealth – Memorandum, GLDC Collection.

60 GLAD, "Massachusetts Changes Foster Care Regulations," Apr. 4, 1990, Box 88, Folder 44, NGLTF Records; Kay Longcope, "Foster-Care Ban on Gays Is Reversed," *BG*, Apr. 5, 1990; "Massachusetts Acts to Permit Homosexual Foster Parents," *NYT*, Apr. 6, 1990.

61 GLAD, "Massachusetts Changes Foster Care Regulations"; Longcope, "Foster-Care Ban on Gays is Reversed"; "Massachusetts Acts to Permit Homosexual Foster Parents."

62 Ellen Musinsky, interview by Ricketts, Aug. 9, 1988, Box 2, Folder 12, Wendell Ricketts Papers, 2.

63 Bundy, interview by author; National Defense Authorization Act of 1994, P.L. 103–160 (1993), *codified at* 10 U.S.C. §654, *repealed by* Don't Ask, Don't Tell Repeal Act of 2010, P.L. 111–321 (2010).

64 Pat Hammond, "Foster Parents Crisis Feared," *UL*, Sept. 27, 1987; Ben Stocking, "Lawmakers Split over Enforcement of Gay Ban," *CM*, Nov. 25, 1987.

65 Ellen Musinsky, interview by author, Oct. 1, 2014.

66 Massachusetts Executive Office of Human Services, "Review of States' Policies Regarding Foster Placements," 5–6; Ben Stocking, "Official's Task: Defining Homosexuality," *CM*, Jul. 18, 1987.

67 "NH Will Be First State to Enforce Law Banning Homosexual Foster Parents," *UL*, Jul. 24, 1987.

68 Ibid.

69 Ibid.

70 Act of May 3, 1999, 1999 N.H. Laws 18.

71 Lofton v. Sec'y of the Dep't of Children & Family Servs., 377 F.3d 1275 (11th Cir. 2004).

72 Contemporary reproductive justice advocates no longer use the term "artificial insemination," as it makes a harmful distinction between "natural" and assisted reproduction. At the time of the lesbian baby boom, however, "artificial insemination" was how individuals referred to the practice.

73 Bonnie Pfister, "'Always Wanted to Be Mom': Lesbians Use Artificial Insemination," *Arizona Republic*, Aug. 6, 1989.

74 Chauncey, *Why Marriage?*, 105.

75 Higdon, "Constitutional Parenthood," 1486.

76 Cahn and Carbone, "Custody and Visitation in Families with Three (Or More) Parents," 56; Douglas NeJaime, "Who Is a Parent?," *ABA Family Advocate*, May 10, 2021.

77 Ball, *The Right to Be Parents*, 83–84; Rivers, *Radical Relations*, 175.

78 Martin Curie-Cohen, Lesleigh Luttrell, and Sander Shapiro, "Current Practice of Artificial Insemination by Donor in the United States," *New England Journal of Medicine* 300, no. 11 (1979): 585.

79 Rivers, *Radical Relations*, 176–78.
80 Robert Cooke, "Some Single Women Inseminating Selves Artificially," *BG*, Apr. 5, 1984.
81 Susan Stern, "A Different Type of Baby Boom in S.F.," *Synapse* (University of California, San Francisco), Dec. 6, 1979, Box 125, Folder 14, Phyllis Lyon and Del Martin Papers.
82 Sarah and Mary Anonymous (pseud.), *Woman Controlled Conception* (San Francisco: Womanshare Books, 1979); Jack and Jill (pseud.), *Artificial Insemination: An Alternative Conception* (San Francisco: Lesbian Health Information Project, 1979); Mary O'Donnell et al., *Lesbian Health Matters!* (Santa Cruz, Calif.: Santa Cruz Women's Health Center, 1979).
83 Jil Clark, "Sperm Bank Welcomes Unmarried Recipients," *GCN*, Oct. 20, 1982, 3.
84 Ibid.
85 Kolata, "Lesbian Partners Find the Means to Be Parents."
86 Ball, *The Right to Be Parents*, 85.
87 Laurene Mascola and Mary Guinan, "Semen Donors as the Source of Sexually Transmitted Diseases in Artificially Inseminated Women: The Saga Unfolds," *Journal of the American Medical Association* 257, n. 8 (1987): 1093–94.
88 Ball, *The Right to Be Parents*, 87; Kate Kendell and Robert Haaland, *Lesbians Choosing Motherhood: Legal Implications of Alternative Insemination and Reproductive Technologies* (3d ed.) (San Francisco: NCLR 1996), 4–9; LMNDF, "Sperm Donor Declared Father," *Mom's Apple Pie*, Fall 1993, 5, Box 105, Folder 14, Phyllis Lyon and Del Martin Papers.
89 Suzanne Lynn, "Artificial Insemination: Unmarried Women Are Eligible," *Civil Liberties* (ACLU), Nov. 1980, Artificial Insemination Subject File; "Sperm Bank Holdup," *Partners*, Winter 1992, Newsletter Collection.
90 Rivers, *Radical Relations*, 175.
91 Ibid., 189–90.
92 Lesbian Mothers' Defence Fund, "Custody News: USA," *Grapevine* (Canada), Spring 1985, https://riseupfeministarchive.ca/wp-content/uploads/2016/02/Grapevine-Spring-1985.pdf.
93 Marsha Ginsburg, "Lesbian 'Father' Wins Visitation Rights," *SFE*, Nov. 21, 1984; "Lesbians Fight over Child," *USA Today*, Apr. 29, 1983.
94 Ginsburg, "Lesbian 'Father' Wins Visitation Rights."
95 Rivers, *Radical Relations*, 174–75.
96 Ibid., 175.
97 Ibid.
98 Ibid.
99 Donna J. Hitchens, *Lesbians Choosing Motherhood: Legal Issues in Donor Insemination* (San Francisco: NCLR, 1984), 10–11.
100 Ibid., 10.
101 Lost: Alison D. v. Virginia M., 572 N.E.2d 27 (N.Y. 1991); Curiale v. Reagan, 222 Cal. App. 3d 1597 (1990); In re Z.J.H., 471 N.W.2d 202 (Wis. 1991); LMNDF, "Lesbian Co-Parents Update," *Mom's Apple Pie*, n.d., ca. 1991 (Kulla v. McNulty); "Lesbian Loses Suit over Child," *Outlook*, Dec. 16, 1989, Lesbian Mother Subject File (Sabol v. Bowling); NCLR Annual Report, 1990, Box 1, Folder 35, Wendell Ricketts Papers (Angela C. v. Robin R.); Statement of Decision, Fitzsimmons v. Becker, No. 897 036 (Cal. Super. Ct. Mar. 31, 1989), Box 11, Folder 11, Wendell Ricketts Papers. Won: *A State by State Guide to Child Custody* (San Francisco: NCLR, 1996), 10–11 (Jhordan C. v. Mary K.); Order, ACC v. CID,

89191039 (Md. Cir. Ct. 1990). The coparents were more successful when their former partners died and the issue before the court was whether the intended mother or another relative would have custody. Final Judgment, *In re* Pearlman, No. 87-24926 DA (Fla. Cir. Ct. Mar. 31, 1989), Box 88, Folder 12, NGLTF Records; "Relatives Lose in Custody Ruling," *New Orleans Times-Picayune*, Jul. 1, 1989 (*In re* Estate of Hamilton).

102 Lambda Legal Defense and Education Fund, "Cooperating Attorney Update," Jan/Feb 1990, Box 97, Folder 1, Phyllis Lyon and Del Martin Papers; Nancy S. v. Michele G., 228 Cal. App. 3d 831, 834 (1991).

103 *Nancy S.*, 228 Cal. App. 3d at 839; Polikoff, "This Child Does Have Two Mothers," 495–99.

104 NeJaime, "Differentiating Assimilation," 14.

105 Ibid., 14–15.

106 One notable exception was Tubwon v. Weisberg, 394 N.W.2d 601 (Minn. Ct. App. 1986), where the Minnesota Court of Appeals granted legal custody to a nonmarital, nonbiological father.

107 Kathleen Hendrix, "A Case of 2 'Moms' Tests Definition of Parenthood," *LAT*, Aug 15, 1990.

108 Ibid.

109 *Nancy S.*, 228 Cal. App. 3d at 841.

110 Ibid., 834.

111 NeJaime, "The Nature of Parenthood," 2272.

112 Chauncey, *Why Marriage?*, 105; Polikoff, *Beyond (Straight and Gay) Marriage*, 85.

113 In the 1980s, gay and lesbian parents increasingly adopted children from Latin America. Briggs, *Somebody's Children*, 257.

114 LMNDF, "First Adoption Exemplifies Benefits," *Mom's Apple Pie*, Winter 1996, 8, Box 105, Folder 14, Phyllis Lyon and Del Martin Papers; *In re* Adoption of Minor (M. & T.), 17 Fam. L. Rep. 1523 (D.C. Super. Ct. 1991); Deb Price, "Blessed with Two Mommies," *Detroit News*, Dec. 31, 1993, Box 1, Folder 193, Same-Sex Marriage Collection; Report and Recommendation, *In re* L.S. and V.L., Nos. A269–90 & A270–90 (D.C. Super. Ct. Mar. 8, 1991), Box 1, Folder 21, Ettelbrick Papers.

115 Polikoff, *Beyond (Straight and Gay) Marriage*, 53.

116 Additional Submission, *In re* Petition of LS and VL, No. 269-90 (D.C. Super. Ct. n. d., ca. 1991), Box 1, Folder 21, Ettelbrick Papers; Polikoff, *Beyond (Straight and Gay) Marriage*, 53.

117 Polikoff, *Beyond (Straight and Gay) Marriage*, 53.

118 Rivers, *Radical Relations*, 191–92, 195–96.

119 Klarman, *From the Closet to the Altar*, 51; Lambda Legal Defense and Education Fund, Inc., Flier for Securing Our Relationships/Creating Our Families, Apr. 13, 1985, Lambda Legal Subject File.

120 "Gay Family Project," *Partners*, Sept. 1988, Newsletter Collection; Paula L. Ettelbrick to "Friend," Nov. 28, 1989, Lambda Legal Subject File.

121 Rivers, *Radical Relations*, 192–93.

122 Brief for Petitioner, *In re* Adoption Petition of Nancy L. Davis, No. 18086 (Super. Ct. S.F. Cty. Sept. 21, 1987), Box 1, Folder 31, Ettelbrick Papers.

123 Ibid., Exhibit E.

124 Hitchens, interview by Ricketts, 4.

125 George, "Agency Nullification," 409–10.

126 "Strategy for Second-Parent Adoptions," *Partners*, Fall 1992, Newsletter Collection, 21.

127 "Lesbian and Gay Parenting," *Etc.*, Nov. 24, 1995, Box 5, Folder 12, Charles W. Gossett Papers.

128 George, "Agency Nullification," 409–10.

129 *In re* Adoption of Dana, 1993 WL 764519 (N.Y. Fam. Ct. Sept. 9, 1993), *rev'd*, *In re* Jacob, 660 N.E.2d 397 (N.Y. 1995); *In re* Adoption of Jane Doe, 719 N.E.2d 1071 (Ohio Ct. App. 1998); *In re* Adoption of T.K.J., 931 P.2d 488 (Colo. Ct. App. 1997); *In re* Angel Lace M., 516 N.W.2d 678 (Wis. 1994); *In re* Christine Carole G.M., 1884 NYLJ LEXIS 9125 (N.Y. Surrog. Ct. June 16, 1994).

130 *A State By State Guide to Child Custody*, 28.

131 *In re* Adoption of Caitlin, 622 N.Y.S.2d 835, 838 (N.Y. Fam. Ct. 1994).

132 Alison D. v. Virginia M., 572 N.E.2d 27 (N.Y. 1991).

133 *In re* Adoption of B.L.V.D., 628 A.2d 1271, 1272 (Vt. 1993); *In re* Adoption of Evan, 583 N.Y.S.2d 997, 999 (Sur. Ct. 1992); *In re* Adoption by J.M.G., 632 A.2d 550, 552 (N.J. Super. Ct. 1993).

134 In re *Evan*, 583 N.Y.S.2d at 999.

135 Ibid.

136 In re *Adoption of B.L.V.D.*, 628 A.2d at 1275; *In re* Adoption of Caitlin, 622 N.Y.S.2d at 839; *In re* Adoption by H.N.R., 666 A.2d 535, 539–40 (N.J. Super. Ct. 1995); *In re* Adoption by J.M.G., 632 A.2d at 553; *In re* Camilla, 620 N.Y.S.2d 897, 902 (Fam. Ct. 1994); *In re* Jacob, 660 N.E.2d 397, 404–05 (N.Y. 1995); *In re* Petition of E.S. and R.L., No. 90 Coa 1201, 1994 WL 157949, at *2 (Ill. Cir. Ct. 1994). Some courts disagreed, reading the stepparent provision strictly. *In re* Angel Lace M., 516 N.W.2d 678, 684 (Wis. 1994).

137 In re *Evan*, 583 N.Y.S.2d at 1001 n.1; In re *J.M.G.*, 632 A.2d at 554; In re *Caitlin*, 622 N.Y.S.2d at 841.

138 *In re* Adoption of E.O.G., 28 Pa. D. & C. 4th 262, 267–68 (Com. Pl. 1993); *In re* Adoption of Tammy, 619 N.E.2d 315, 317 (Mass. 1993); Findings of Fact and Conclusions of Law at 2, *In re* Adoption of R.C., No. 9088, (Vt. Prob. Ct. Dec. 9, 1991), Box 1, Folder 7, Ettelbrick Papers.

139 In re *BLVD*, 628 A.2d at 1276; In re *Evan*, 583 N.Y.S.2d at 998–99.

140 In re *J.M.G.*, 632 A.2d at 554–55.

141 Susan Chira, "Gay Parents Become Increasingly Visible," *NYT*, Sept. 30, 1993.

142 Chauncey, *Why Marriage?*, 111; April Martin, *Lesbian and Gay Parenting Handbook: Creating and Raising Our Families* (New York: HarperPerennial, 1993), 1.

143 Chauncey, *Why Marriage?*, 111.

144 Ibid.; D'Vera Cohn, "For Gay Parents, A Cloud of Conflicts," *WP*, May 9, 1995; David W. Dunlap, "Gay Parents Ease into Suburbia," *NYT*, May 16, 1996; Mary Jane Fine, "Gay Moms," *CT*, Jun 7, 1987; Jean Latz Griffin, "The Gay Baby Boom," *CT*, Sept. 3, 1992; Jane Gross, "New Challenge of Youth: Growing Up in Gay Home," *NYT*, Feb. 11, 1991; Polikoff, *Beyond (Straight and Gay) Marriage*, 85.

145 Chira, "Gay Parents Become Increasingly Visible."

146 Ibid.; Rivers, *Radical Relations*, 202–03.

147 Rivers, *Radical Relations*, 202–03.

148 Cohn, "For Gay Parents, A Cloud of Conflicts."

149 Ibid.

150 Telephone Notes from Sharon Kahn, Dec. 13, 1986, Box 2, Folder 14, Wendell Ricketts Papers, 4.

151 Lesléa Newman, *Heather Has Two Mommies* (Los Angeles: Alyson Publications, 1989).

152 Michael Willhoite, *Daddy's Roommate* (Los Angeles: Alyson Publications, 1990).
153 Lance Morrow, "Family Values," *Time*, Aug. 31, 1992; Donna Seese, "Kids' Book about Gay Father Sets Town Abuzz," *Raleigh News and Observer*, Jul. 24, 1992.
154 Morrow, "Family Values"; Willhoite, *Daddy's Roommate*.
155 Morrow, "Family Values"; Seese, "Kids' Book about Gay Father Sets Town Abuzz."
156 "100 Most Frequently Challenged Books: 1990–1999," American Library Association, www.ala.org/advocacy/bbooks/frequentlychallengedbooks/decade1999.
157 Rivers, *Radical Relations*, 205.
158 Amy Graves, "Suffer the Children?," *Bay Windows*, Sept. 17, 1992.
159 Ann Heron and Meredith Maran, *How Would you Feel if Your Dad Was Gay?* (Los Angeles: Alyson Publications, 1991); Lesléa Newman, *Gloria Goes to Gay Pride* (Los Angeles: Alyson Publications, 1991).
160 Harriet Henderson to PFLAG, Jan. 4, 1995, Box 2, Folder 9, Starr (Adele) Collection on PFLAG.
161 Cullum, "Co-Parent Adoptions; Lesbian and Gay Parenting," 28.
162 Chira, "Gay Parents Become Increasingly Visible."

Part II

1 Dirk Johnson, "Coming Home, with AIDS, to a Small Town," *NYT*, November 2, 1987.
2 Ibid.
3 Chauncey, *Gay New York*, 4; Eskridge, *Gaylaw*, 7–8; Lvovsky, *Vice Patrol*, 56, 112.
4 Johnson, "Coming Home, with AIDS, to a Small Town."
5 Murray, *Not In This Family*, 139–43.
6 Lester Omstead-Rose to Robert Schroder et al., February 14, 1989, Box 34, Folder 8, CUAV Records, 1; Cliff O'Neill, "Task Force Stats Show Anti-Gay Crimes Up Yet Again in '91," *Frontiers*, April 10, 1992.

Chapter 5

1 Boyd, *Wide-Open Town*, 107.
2 Randy Schell, "CUAV: Recent Incidents," *BAR*, June 9, 1983.
3 NGTF, "Anti-Gay/Lesbian Victimization," June 1984, Box 2, Folder 33, Starr (Adele) Collection on PFLAG.
4 CUAV, "Reports of Anti-Gay/Lesbian Incidents Reach Record High in 1987," June 7, 1988, Box 67, Folder 5, CUAV Records.
5 "'Justified' Gay Killings," *SFC*, Mar. 14, 1983; "Kalamazoo Lesbians, Gays Slam Acquittal of Murdering Bigot," *Workers World Newspaper*, Mar. 13, 1986; Miriam Friedlander, NYC Council Member, Memorandum, Dec. 18, 1980, Violence against Gays and Lesbians Subject File; "Murderer of Gay Man Sentenced to Life," *NYN*, Dec. 17, 1984; Steve Quester et al. to David N. Dinkins, NYC Mayor, Aug. 29, 1990, Violence against Gays and Lesbians Subject File; Michael Reese, "The Growing Terror of 'Gay Bashing,'" *Newsweek*, Mar. 23, 1981; "Two Convicted in Brutal Murder," *WB*, Dec. 18, 1981.
6 David M. Lowe, "Fighting Back!," *SFS*, May 15, 1987.
7 Campaign to Count and Counter Hate Crimes, "Anti-Gay and Lesbian Violence and Victimization Increases in Key U.S. Cities," Mar. 6, 1991, Box 2, Minnesota GLBT Movement Papers, 3; "Gay Bar Bombed; 2nd Site Threatened," *USA Today*,

Dec. 28, 1983; NGLTF, "Anti-Gay Violence, Victimization & Defamation in 1989," Box 61, Folder 8, CUAV Records.

8 Kevin Berrill, "Anti-Gay Violence: Causes, Consequences, Responses," 1986, Box 10, Folder 59, NGLTF Records, 1.

9 Gregory M. Herek, "The Community Response to Violence in San Francisco: An Interview with Wendy Kusuma, Lester Olmstead-Rose, and Jill Tregor," in *Hate Crimes*, 250.

10 Education Exploration Center, "A Sampler for Social Change," Spring 1981, Education Subject File, 42.

11 Ibid.; Dennis McMillan, "Community Forum on Gay Violence," *NYN*, Sept. 18, 1989.

12 Davis and Sandoval, *Suicidal Youth*, 116; "Educators Doubt Gay High Schools Will Catch On," Education Subject File; NCLR, "Project to Stop Mental Health Care Abuse of Lesbian, Gay, Bisexual and Transgender Youth," May 1994, Folder labeled Studies & Surveys, Jessea Greenman P.E.R.S.O.N. Project Records.

13 Paul Gibson, "Gay Male and Lesbian Youth Suicide," in United States Department of Health and Human Services, *Report of the Secretary's Task Force on Youth Suicide*, ed. Marcia R. Feinleib (Washington, D.C.: Government Printing Office, 1989), vol. 3, 110; United States Department of Health and Human Services, *Report of the Secretary's Task Force on Youth Suicide*, vol. 1, iii. Rates of suicide were almost twice as high for gay youth as for lesbians. Joyce Murdoch, "Gay Youths' Deadly Despair: High Rate of Suicide Attempts Tracked," *WP*, Oct. 24, 1988.

14 George, "Bureaucratic Agency," 89.

15 Antiviolence organizations also drew attention to the hate crimes against gender nonconformists, but they primarily focused on the plight of gay men and lesbians. George, "The LGBT Disconnect," 546.

16 Hugo Martin, "Gays Form Patrols to Battle Hate Crimes," *LAT*, Dec. 3, 1991.

17 Pat Riese, "Street Patrol Bolsters Safety," *SFS*, Sept. 15, 1993; Street Patrol, press release, n.d., ca. 1991, Box 98, Folder 17, San Francisco Street Patrol Records Collection; Hank Wilson to Terry Person, Aug. 11, 1997, Box 37, Folder 2, CUAV Records.

18 Dodge, "Bashing Back," 319–20; Hanhardt, *Safe Space*, 81–82.

19 Eric Barnes, "Streetcats Prowl West Hollywood," *Vanguard*, Sept. 4, 1992; Elizabeth Fernandez, "Assault on Man Increases Gay-Bashing Statistics," *SFE*, May 19, 1990; Susan Hightower, "Murder Leads to Protection for Gays," *LAT*, Mar. 22, 1992; Martin, "Gays Form Patrols to Battle Hate Crimes"; Don Terry, "'Pink Angels' Battle Anti-Gay Crime," *NYT*, Apr. 7, 1992.

20 "Gay Group Can't Call Itself Pink Panthers," *NYT*, Oct. 5, 1991; Constance L. Hays, "Gay Patrol and MGM in a Battle over Name," *NYT*, May 27, 1991; Jim Merrett, "Gay and Lesbian Anticrime Patrol Prowls the Streets of New York," *Advocate*, Oct. 9, 1990.

21 Dodge, "Bashing Back," 319.

22 Fernandez, "Assault on Man Increases Gay-Bashing Statistics"; Peter Freiberg, "Antigay Violence: Is It on the Rise?," *Advocate*, Dec. 22, 1983; "Murders of Gays Are More Brutal, Study Says," *Star Tribune* (Minneapolis), Dec. 21, 1994; NGLTF, "Anti-Gay/Lesbian Violence, Victimization & Defamation in 1991," 1992, Box 61, Folder 10, CUAV Records (hereafter "1991 Report"); NGLTF, "Some Facts about Anti-Gay Violence," n.d., ca. 1988, Box 61, Folder 10, CUAV Records; Ruth Snyder, "'Gay Bashing' – AIDS Fear Cited as Attacks on Male Homosexuals Grow," *LAT*, Apr. 10, 1986.

23 Perry, *In the Name of Hate*, 55–56, 110–18; Todres, "Law, Otherness, and Human Trafficking," 607–08.

24 Ruth and Reitz, *The Challenge of Crime*, 15–17.
25 D'Emilio, *Sexual Politics, Sexual Communities*, 5–36; Stein, *Rethinking the Gay and Lesbian Movement*, 84.
26 NGTF Violence Project, "The NGTF Violence Project," n.d., ca. 1983, Box 68, Folder 38, NGLTF Records.
27 Snyder, "Gay Bashing."
28 Dirk Johnson, "Fear of AIDS Stirs New Attacks on Homosexuals," *NYT*, Apr. 24, 1987.
29 CUAV, "Anti-Gay/Lesbian Violence in 1994," 1995, Box 57, Folder 6, CUAV Records (hereafter "1994 Report"), 16.
30 Michael Thompson to Arlo Smith, May 18, 1993, Box 40, Folder 1, CUAV Records.
31 Wertheimer, "The Emergence of a Gay and Lesbian Antiviolence Movement," 269.
32 NGLTF, 1991 Report, 15.
33 CUAV, 1994 Report, 16.
34 Lowe, "Fighting Back!"
35 Ibid.
36 Laurence Zuckerman, "Open Season on Gays," *Time*, Mar. 7, 1988.
37 CUAV, 1994 Report; New York City Gay and Lesbian Anti-Violence Project, "1990 Annual Report," 1991, Box 64, Folder 2, CUAV Records; New York City Gay and Lesbian Anti-Violence Project, "Gay/Lesbian-Related Homicides in the United States, 1992–1994," 1994, Box 58, Folder 9, CUAV Records; NGLTF, "Anti-Gay/Lesbian Violence, Victimization & Defamation in 1987," 1988, Box 61, Folder 8, CUAV Records; NGLTF, "Anti-Gay/Lesbian Violence, Victimization & Defamation in 1988," 1989, Box 61, Folder 8, CUAV Records; NGLTF, "Anti-Gay/Lesbian Violence, Victimization & Defamation in 1989," 1990, Box 61, Folder 8, CUAV Records; NGLTF, "Anti-Gay/Lesbian Violence, Victimization & Defamation in 1990," 1991, Box 61, Folder 8, CUAV Records (hereafter "1990 Report"); NGLTF, 1991 Report; NGLTF, "Anti-Gay/Lesbian Violence, Victimization & Defamation in 1992," 1993, Box 61, Folder 10, CUAV Records (hereafter "1992 Report"); NGLTF, "Anti-Gay/Lesbian Violence, Victimization & Defamation in 1993," 1994, Box 7, Folder 44, HRC Records (hereafter "1993 Report").
38 Freiberg, "Antigay Violence"; NGLTF, "Reports of Anti-Gay/Lesbian Incidents Reach Record High in 1987," June 7, 1988, Box 56, Folder 19, NGLTF Records.
39 Snyder, "Gay Bashing."
40 William Greer, "Violence against Homosexuals Rising, Groups Seeking Wider Protection Say," *NYT*, Nov. 23, 1986, 36.
41 Wertheimer, "The Emergence of a Gay and Lesbian Antiviolence Movement," 271.
42 Bayley, *Police for the Future*, 50.
43 Snyder, "Gay Bashing"; Wertheimer, "The Emergence of a Gay and Lesbian Antiviolence Movement," 268.
44 Greer, "Violence against Homosexuals Rising."
45 Tommi Avicolli, "Violence: Task Force to Meet with Police Commissioner," *Philadelphia Gay News*, Nov. 1987.
46 Greer, "Violence against Homosexuals Rising"; Snyder, "Gay Bashing."
47 CUAV, "Halt Assault," n.d., ca. 1979, CUAV Subject File; "Gay Safety Patrols Begin," *SFS*, Jul. 13, 1979; NGTF Violence Project, "The NGTF Violence Project"; Reese, "The Growing Terror of 'Gay Bashing'"; Snyder, "'Gay Bashing.'"
48 Avicolli, "Violence"; David France, "Queerbashing and the Social Contract," *NYN*, Jul. 2–15, 1984; Larry Gordon, "Gays Call LAPD Prejudiced," *LAT*, Apr. 8, 1987; Snyder, "Gay Bashing."

49 France, "Queerbashing and the Social Contract"; Peter Freiberg, "Gays and Police: Old Problems, New Hope," *Advocate*, June 11, 1985; Snyder, "Gay Bashing."

50 Zuckerman, "Open Season on Gays."

51 Ibid.

52 Lvovsky, *Vice Patrol*, 258–59.

53 Hanhardt, *Safe Space*, 104.

54 "Anti-Gay Violence on Increase," *Philadelphia Inquirer*, June 16, 1987; Kevin Berrill, Testimony, Police Misconduct, Hearings before the Subcommittee on Criminal Justice, 98th Congress, 1396 (Washington, D.C.: Government Printing Office, 1983) (Kevin Berrill, Director, NGTF Violence Project); Comstock, *Violence against Lesbians and Gay Men*, 160–61; France, "Queerbashing and the Social Contract"; Ray O'Loughlin, "Call the Police," *BAR*, Feb. 12, 1989; Kim Remesch, "Opening the Closets: Several Cities Begin Recruiting Gay Cops," *Police*, Dec. 1990; Snyder, "Gay Bashing"; Stewart-Winter, "The Law and Order Origins of Urban Gay Politics," 829.

55 Gordon, "Gays Call LAPD Prejudiced."

56 Freiberg, "Gays and Police"; Stewart-Winter, "The Law and Order Origins of Urban Gay Politics," 829; Stewart-Winter, *Queer Clout*, 211.

57 Berrill, Testimony, 1396; Freiberg, "Gays and Police."

58 Berrill, Testimony, 1396.

59 NGLTF, "Anti-Violence Project Update," Jul. 1987, Box 65, Folder 7, CUAV Records, 4.

60 "Anti-Gay Violence on Increase."

61 Ibid.; Avicolli, "Violence."

62 Police Department, City of New York, "Background Information on Bias Incident Investigating Unit," n.d., ca. 1989, Box 61, Folder 9, CUAV Records.

63 Freiberg, "Gays and Police."

64 Leo Treadway, interview by author, Jul. 25, 2022.

65 CUAV, 1994 Report, 24; National Coalition of Anti-Violence Projects and CUAV, "Anti-Lesbian, Gay, Bisexual and Transgendered Violence in 1996," n.d., ca. 1997, Box 60, Folder 7, CUAV Records, 19–20 (hereafter "1996 Report"); National Coalition of Anti-Violence Projects, "Anti-Lesbian, Gay, Bisexual and Transgendered Violence in 1997," 1997, Box 61, Folder 6, CUAV Records, 39 (hereafter "1997 Report"); National Coalition of Anti-Violence Projects, "Anti-Lesbian, Gay, Bisexual and Transgender Violence in 1998," 1999, Box 61, Folder 1, CUAV Records, 27, 62; NGLTF, 1990 Report, 24; NGLTF, 1991 Report, 32; NGLTF, 1992 Report, 43; NGLTF, 1993 Report, 39.

66 Freiberg, "Gays and Police."

67 Leo Treadway, interview by Obie Holmen, Nov. 10, 2017, 29–30, https://lgbtqreligiousarchives.org/media/oral-history/leo-treadway/LTreadway.pdf; Treadway, interview by author.

68 Treadway, interview by Holmen, 27.

69 Ibid., 16–17.

70 Elaine F. Valadez to Leo Treadway, Oct. 30, 1987, Box 6, Minnesota GLBT Movement Papers; Treadway, interview by author.

71 Mark Kasel, "Task Force Begins Writing Report on Prejudice and Violence," *Twin Cities Gaze*, Feb. 11, 1988.

72 Governor's Task Force on Prejudice and Violence, Minutes, Nov. 7, 1987, Box 6, Minnesota GLBT Movement Papers, 2.

73 Kasel, "Task Force Begins Writing Report on Prejudice and Violence."

74 Governor's Task Force on Prejudice and Violence, "Summary of Incident Reports," n.d., ca. 1988, Box 29, Senate Judiciary Committee Papers; Treadway, interview by author.

75 Governor's Task Force on Prejudice and Violence, "Summary of Incident Reports"; Kasel, "Task Force Begins Writing Report on Prejudice and Violence"; Virginia Lane, *Bias-Motivated Crimes: A Summary Report of Minnesota's Response* (St. Paul: Minnesota POST, 1990), 20–22.

76 Laws of Minnesota, ch. 643, H.F. No. 2340 (1988), *codified at* Minn. Stat. 626.5531.

77 Jenness and Grattet, *Making Hate a Crime*, 1–2.

78 Ibid., 80–86, 92–98.

79 Hanhardt, *Safe Space*, 163–64.

80 Lawrence, *Punishing Hate*, 9.

81 Ibid., 163–64; Jenness and Grattet, *Making Hate a Crime*, 1; Perry, *In the Name of Hate*, 112–14.

82 Hanhardt, *Safe Space*, 165–66, 170.

83 California Initiative Measure 7, approved Nov. 7, 1978, eff. Nov. 8, 1978; Law of Aug. 21, 1981, ch. 785, 1981 Or. Laws 1103; Law of May 18, 1981, ch. 267, 1981 Wash. Laws 1106.

84 Law of Sept. 25, 1984, ch. 1482, 1984 Cal. Laws 5178.

85 Law of Apr. 21, 1988, ch. 348, 1987 Wis. Laws 1232.

86 Atlanta, Ga., Ordinance 89-0-1123 (Jul. 24, 1989) (statistics); Columbus, Ohio, Ordinance 3790-88 (Dec. 1, 1988) (criminal penalties); Herek and Berrill, *Hate Crimes*, 291; Seattle, Wash., Ordinance 11,1714 (June 11, 1984); St. Louis, Mo., Ordinance 61277 (Feb. 22, 1989) (statistics, criminal penalties, civil penalties).

87 Herek and Berrill, *Hate Crimes*, 291. California, Minnesota, Nevada, Oregon, Wisconsin, and the District of Columbia all had some type of hate crimes statute that included protections for sexual orientation. Law of Apr. 21, 1988, ch. 348, 1987 Wis. Laws 1232 (penalty enhancement and civil remedy); Law of Aug. 7, 1989, ch. 1029, 1989 Or. Laws 2079 (standalone criminal statute); Law of June 21, 1989, ch. 416, 1989 Nevada Laws 897 (penalty enhancement); Law of May 25, 1989, ch. 261, 1989 Minn. Laws 892 (penalty enhancement); Law of Sept. 25, 1984, ch. 1482, 1984 Cal. Laws 5178 (data collection); Washington, D.C., Bias-Related Crime Act of 1989 (Dec. 21, 1989) (data collection, penalty enhancement, and civil remedy). New Jersey's attorney general issued a directive in 1987, which required the state's law enforcement agencies to report bias incidents to capture data on the problem. Although the directive did not initially require it, these reports soon included hate crimes involving sexual orientation. New Jersey Attorney General, Executive Directive No. 1987-3 (1987), *reprinted in* Federal Bureau of Investigation, *Hate Crimes Statistics: A Resource Book* (Washington, D.C.: Department of Justice, 1990), Appendix C; New Jersey State Police, 1991 Bias Incident Report, 1992, 5–6, www.ojp.gov/pdffiles1/Digitization/136967NCJRS.pdf.

88 Anne McGraw, "Homosexuals Press for Anti-Intimidation Law," *Morning Call* (Pa.), Apr. 10, 1990; "Minnesota Bias Crimes Legislation," n.d, ca. 1988, Box 67, Folder 17, NGLTF Records; "N.Y. Sen. Nixes Hate Bill," *Philadelphia Gay News*, June 16, 1989; Alan K. Ota, "Legislature Revives Bill, Bans Intimidation of Homosexuals," *Oregonian*, Jul. 3, 1989.

89 McGraw, "Homosexuals Press for Anti-Intimidation Law."

90 Hate Crimes Statistics Act, Pub. L. No. 101-275, 104 Stat. 140, *codified as amended at* 28 U.S.C. § 534.

91 Jacobs and Potter, *Hate Crimes*, 89.

92 Ibid.

93 Ibid., 90.

94 Cameron Erney, "Hate Crimes Statistics Act: Analysis and Recommendation," Dec. 21, 1988, Box 56, Folder 48, NGLTF Records, 4.

95 NGLTF, "House of Representatives Passes Hate Crimes Act," June 27, 1989, Box 56, Folder 19, NGLTF Records; NGLTF, "Hate Crimes Bill Not Brought to Senate Floor," Nov. 1, 1988, Box 56, Folder 19, NGLTF Records.

96 Harding, *The Book of Jerry Falwell*, 261; Johnson, *This Is Our Message*, 93; Williams, *God's Own Party*, 222.

97 Williams, *God's Own Party*, 222–23.

98 Harding, *The Book of Jerry Falwell*, 261; Johnson, *This Is Our Message*, 93.

99 "Falwell: Bakker Set to Meet Accusers," *CT*, May 19, 1987.

100 Hertzke, *Echoes of Discontent*, 159; Williams, *God's Own Party*, 213, 216–19.

101 Jonathan Alter, "Pat Robertson: The TelePolitician," *Newsweek*, Feb. 22, 1988; R.W. Apple, Jr., "Bush Takes Resounding Victory in First of the Southern Primaries," *NYT*, Mar. 6, 1988; Fred Barnes, "Rarin' to Go: Pat Robertson Hears the Call," *New Republic*, Sept. 19, 1986; E.J. Dionne, Jr., "Dole Wins in Iowa, with Robertson Next," *NYT*, Feb. 9, 1988; Doug Hill, "Preacher for President?," *TV Guide*, Mar. 15, 1986; Wayne King, "The Record of Pat Robertson on Religion and Government," *NYT*, Dec. 27, 1987.

102 Williams, *God's Own Party*, 220–21.

103 Ibid., 221.

104 Ibid., 222, 231; Hertzke, *Echoes of Discontent*, 184.

105 Hanhardt, *Safe Space*, 163; Rex Wockner, "Bush Invites Gays to White House Ceremony," *Outlines*, May 1990.

106 Jacobs and Potter, *Hate Crimes*, 91–92.

107 Hate Crimes Statistics Act, Pub. L. No. 101–275; Leung, "Points of Departure," 40; Nolan, Akyama, and Berhanu, "The Hate Crime Statistics Act of 1990," 143–47.

108 Hate Crimes Statistics Act, Pub. L. No. 101-275, 104 Stat. 140, *codified as amended at* 28 U.S.C. § 534.

109 Cameron Erney, "Hate Crimes Statistics Act: Analysis and Recommendation," Dec. 21, 1988, Box 56, Folder 48, NGLTF Records.

110 Wuest, *Born This Way*, 55–60.

111 Stein, *Rethinking the Gay and Lesbian Movement*, 120.

112 Clarke, "Against Immutability," 14–16; Klarman, *From Jim Crow to Civil Rights*, 195–96; Konnoth, "Created in Its Image," 340–52; Mayeri, *Reasoning from Race*, 4, 66–62.

113 George, "Regulating Same-Sex Sexuality in Twentieth Century America," 13–14.

114 Herek and Berrill, *Hate Crimes*, 291.

115 Ibid.

116 Jamie Nabozny, Written testimony to the Subcommittee on Oversight and Investigations, Dec. 5, 1995, Folder labeled Hoekstra-Sheldon Hearings, Jessea Greenman P.E.R.S.O.N. Project Records; Jamie Nabozny to Friends, May 1996, Lambda Legal Subject File.

117 Nabozny, Written testimony.

118 Gibson, "Gay Male and Lesbian Youth Suicide," 110; Murdoch, "Gay Youths' Deadly Despair."

119 United States Department of Health and Human Services, *Report of the Secretary's Task Force on Youth Suicide*, vol. 1, iii.

120 David W. Dunlap, "Jeanne Manford, 92, Who Stood Up for Her Gay Son, Inspiring Others, Dies," *NYT*, Jan. 10, 2013; Murray, *Not In This Family*, 110.

121 Murray, *Not In This Family*, 110.
122 "Our Story," PFLAG, https://pflag.org/our-story.
123 Dunlap, "Jeanne Manford."
124 Broad, "Social Movement Selves," 329–30.
125 Ibid., 330.
126 Charles Faber, "Parents and Friends and an Organization to Support Them," *Advocate*, Jan. 6, 1983.
127 Schulman, *Let the Record Show*, chs. 3, 4, 12, 16, 21, 29.
128 Murray, *Not In This Family*, 113.
129 Ibid.
130 Broad, "Social Movement Selves," 328.
131 Broad, "Coming Out for Parents, Families and Friends of Lesbians and Gays," 406.
132 Fields, "Normal Queers," 172–74.
133 George, "Expressive Ends," 805–06.
134 Drescher, "I'm Your Handyman," 26–30; Erzen, *Straight to Jesus*, 146; George, "Expressive Ends," 817–18.
135 Fields, "Normal Queers," 171.
136 PFLAG, "Why Ask Why?: Addressing the Research on Homosexuality and Biology," 1995, Box 43, Folder 50, PFLAG Records, 4.
137 Field, "Normal Queers," 172.
138 George, "Regulating Same-Sex Sexuality in Twentieth Century America," 13–14.
139 PFLAG, Summary Sheet, June 26, 1986, Box 7, Folder 18, Starr (Adele) Collection on PFLAG.
140 "Adele Starr: Founder," PFLAG Los Angeles, 2022, www.pflagla.org/founder/.
141 Parents FLAG, "About Our Children," 1979, Box 7, Folder 21, Starr (Adele) Collection on PFLAG, 4.
142 Ibid., 5.
143 Ibid.
144 Adele Starr to Bill Honig, Dec. 19, 1986, Box 3, Folder 7, Starr (Adele) Collection on PFLAG; "Our Story."
145 Davis and Sandoval, *Suicidal Youth*, 116; "Educators Doubt Gay High Schools Will Catch On"; NCLR, "Project to Stop Mental Health Care Abuse of Lesbian, Gay, Bisexual and Transgender Youth."
146 Governor's Task Force on Bias-Related Violence, *Final Report* (Albany, NY: Governor's Task Force on Bias-Related Violence, 1988); Seattle Commission on Children and Youth, *Report on Gay and Lesbian Youth in Seattle* (Seattle Commission on Children and Youth, 1988), 7.
147 Davis and Sandoval, *Suicidal Youth*, 113, 116; Anthony R. D'Augelli and Scott L. Hershberger, "Lesbian, Gay, and Bisexual Youth in Community Settings: Personal Challenges and Mental Health Problems," *American Journal of Community Psychology* 21, no. 4 (Aug. 1993): 437; John C. Gonsiorek, "Mental Health Issues of Gay and Lesbian Adolescents," *Journal of Adolescent Health Care* 9, no. 2 (Mar. 1988): 120–21; Curtis D. Proctor and Victor K. Groze, "Risk Factors for Suicide and Gay, Lesbian, and Bisexual Youths," *Social Work* 39, no. 5 (Sept. 1994): 510.
148 Dowland, *Family Values*; Petrzela, *Classroom Wars*.
149 Nickerson, *Mothers of Conservatism*, 91–92.
150 Ibid., 94–95; Dowland, *Family Values*, 32, 44, 51, 158.
151 Robert L. Simonds, *A Guide to the Public Schools* (Costa Mesa, Calif.: NACE/CEE, 1993), 111; Robert L. Simonds, *How to Elect Christians to Public Office* (Costa Mesa, Calif.: NACE/CEE, 1985), 65.

152 National Center for Education Statistics, "Digest of Education Statistics," 2012, Table 98, https://nces.ed.gov/programs/digest/d12/tables/dt12_098.asp; Thomas Toch and Kukula Glastris, "Who's Minding the Schools?," *U.S. News & World Report*, Apr. 18, 1994, 78.

153 Simonds, *A Guide to the Public Schools*, 93; Chris Bull, "Why Johnny Can't Learn about Condoms: How the Religious Right Censors Sex Education across the U.S.," *Advocate*, Dec. 15, 1992, 39, 78; Greg Goldin, "The 15 Per Cent Solution: How the Religious Right Is Building from Below to Take Over from Above," *Village Voice*, Apr. 6, 1993, 20.

154 Simonds, *A Guide to the Public Schools*, 111; Simonds, *How to Elect Christians to Public Office*, 65.

155 Robert Simonds, "President's Report," Dec. 1993, Box 2, Folder labeled CEE, Jessea Greenman P.E.R.S.O.N. Project Records, 2.

156 Kevin Fagan, "Banner of 'Decency' Leads Parade to Ban Books in Schools," *Oakland Tribune*, Sept. 6, 1992; Gay and Lesbian Educators of Southern California, Recent Attempts to Ban Schoolbooks, *The Chalkboard*, Oct. 1987, Newsletter Collection, 7; "Parents Demand Curbs on School Topics," *San Diego Union*, Feb. 6, 1985; People for the American Way, "Attacks on the Freedom to Learn, 1990–1991," Box 1, Ronald H. Schmidt Papers; People for the American Way, "Fight from the Right," *SFS*, June 16, 1994; Toch and Glastris, "Who's Minding the Schools?," 79; Kenneth L. Woodward, "The Sound of Empty Barrels," *Newsweek*, May 16, 1993, 62.

157 Dowland, *Family Values*, 158–59.

158 Ibid.

159 Ibid.

160 Adele Starr to Nancy Keene, Sept. 13, 1985, Box 7, Folder 18, Starr (Adele) Collection on PFLAG; Adele Starr to Principal, Oct. 25, 1984, Box 7, Folder 18, Starr (Adele) Collection on PFLAG.

161 Starr to Keene.

162 Starr to Honig.

163 Marian Wirth to Chicago Resource Center, May 5, 1986, Box 7, Folder 18, Starr (Adele) Collection on PFLAG.

164 Colorado for Family Values, "Stop Special Class Status for Homosexuality," in ACLU, Briefing Book: Anti-Gay Ballot Initiatives, Aug. 1993, Box 19, Folder 2, ACLU of Southern California Lesbian and Gay Rights Chapter Records.

165 Wirth to Chicago Resource Center.

166 Armstrong, "The Silent Minority within a Minority," 86 n.129.

167 Friends of Project 10, "Project 10 Handbook," 1989, Project 10 Collection, 1; Zsa Zsa Gershick, "Virginia Is for Students," *Advocate*, Sept. 7, 1993, 56–57; Martin Schoenhals, "Lesbian and Gay Affirmative Educational Initiatives in Selected U.S. Cities and Counties," 1992, Box 6, Folder labeled Organizing, Jessea Greenman P.E.R.S.O.N. Project Records, 16; Mary Yarber, "Project 10 Gives Gay Students Help When They Need It Most," *LAT*, Mar. 28, 1991.

168 Dell Richards, "Helping Gay High School Students," *Frontiers*, Nov. 2–16, 1988.

169 Virginia Uribe, "A Call to Conscience" (speech delivered at the Lambda Democratic Club 10th Anniversary Dinner, Long Beach, Calif., Oct. 14, 1989), Box 2, Folder labeled Project 10 LA, Jessea Greenman P.E.R.S.O.N. Project Records.

170 Friends of Project 10, "Project 10 Handbook," vii; Virginia Uribe and Karen M. Harbeck, "Addressing the Needs of Lesbian, Gay, and Bisexual Youth: The Origins of PROJECT 10 and School-Based Intervention," in Harbeck, *Coming Out of the Classroom Closet: Gay and Lesbian Students, Teachers, and Curricula*, 19;

Schoenhals, "Lesbian and Gay Affirmative Educational Initiatives in Selected U.S. Cities and Counties," 16.

171 Friends of Project 10, "Project 10 Handbook," vi–vii.

172 Uribe and Harbeck, "Addressing the Needs of Lesbian, Gay, and Bisexual Youth," 19.

173 "Virginia Uribe, 1933–2019," *LAT*, Apr. 4–7, 2019; Susan Wood, "Who's Afraid of Virginia Uribe?," *Advocate California*, Feb. 14, 1989, 5–6.

174 Connell, *School's Out*, 42.

175 Janet Barker, "Project 10 Tells Students It's 'OK to Be Gay,'" *Daily Breeze*, May 4, 1986, Box 1, Folder 6, Project 10 Collection; Gershick, "Virginia Is for Students"; Dell Richards, "Never Will Gay Student Be Forced Out Again," *Bay Windows*, Nov. 10, 1988; Wood, "Who's Afraid of Virginia Uribe?," 5.

176 "Questions and Answers about Project 10," n.d., Box 2, Folder 21, Starr (Adele) Collection on PFLAG.

177 Stephen Braun, "Fairfax Pilot Project Quietly Seeks to Cut Gay Student Dropout Rate," *LAT*, Nov. 14, 1985.

178 Bell, "*Brown v. Board of Education* and the Interest-Convergence Dilemma," 523.

179 Marla Jo Fisher, "Project for Gays Gets a '10,'" *Pasadena Star News*, ca. 1992, Project 10 Subject File.

180 Gail Rolf, interview by author, May 2, 2022.

181 Bruce Mirken, "Gay Teens," *Genre*, n.d., ca. 1990, Youth Subject File, 32; Beverly LaHaye to Concerned Friend, n.d., ca. 1988, Project 10 Subject File.

182 Neil Genzlinger, "Louis Sheldon, Anti-Gay Minister with Political Clout, Dies at 85," *NYT*, June 5, 2020; John Needham, "Foe of Gay Rights, Abortion Takes Fight Beyond Pulpit," *LAT*, Oct. 14, 1985.

183 Matt Schudel, "Louis P. Sheldon, Inflammatory Anti-Gay Crusader of 'Traditional Values,' Dies at 85," *LAT*, June 6, 2020.

184 Peter Erbland, "Founder of High School Program for Gays Tells of Trial and Tribulations of First Years," *Bay Windows*, Mar. 8–14, 1990; Murdoch, "Gay Youths' Deadly Despair."

185 Deborah Anderluh, "Long, Angry Debate on Counseling for Gay Teens," *Los Angeles Herald-Examiner*, n.d., ca. 1988, Project 10 Subject File; Phillip D. Wyman et al. to Bill Honig, Mar. 27, 1989, Project 10 Subject File.

186 Murdoch, "Gay Youths' Deadly Despair"; Manley Witten, "Project 10: What Schools Teach Children about Gay Sex," *Valley Magazine*, Aug. 1988, 28.

187 Steven Lee Myers, "School Board Out in New York Fight," *NYT*, Dec. 2, 1992.

188 Aslan Brooke, "LaFollette Amendment Foiled," publication unknown, June 8, 1988, Box 1, Folder 7, Project 10 Collection.

189 Mark Gabrish Conlan, "Lesbian Educator Speaks to S.D. Democratic Club," *Bravo! News*, June 1, 1989, Box 1, Folder 6, Project 10 Collection; "Legislative Update," Project 10 Update, Spring 1989, Box 2, Folder labeled Project 10 LA, Jessea Greenman P.E.R.S.O.N. Project Records.

190 Brooke, "LaFollette Amendment Foiled"; Myers, "School Board Out in New York Fight"; Diane E. Watson to Lu Belle Boice, May 27, 1988, Box 1, Folder 3, Project 10 Collection.

191 Act of June 1, 1989, ch. 1195, § 1.03, 1989 Tex. Gen. Laws 4854; David Muralt, Testimony, Texas House Committee on Public Health on H.B. 1901, Apr. 17, 1989, 51:53–52:34, http://columbialawreview.org/wp-content/uploads/2017/10/TX_House_Committee_on_Public_Health_3_of_5.mp3.

192 Biggers, *Morality at the Ballot Box*, 172.

193 Paul Cameron and Mark Olson, interview by Chuck Baker, KVOR Radio Talk Show, Jan. 30, 1992, Box 13, Folder 48, Equality Colorado Records.

194 No Special Rights, "Vote YES on Measure 9!," n.d., ca. 1992, Box 21, Folder 10, Equality Colorado Records, 1.

195 Aslan Brooke, "Religious Right Escalates Project 10 Attack," *Dispatch*, Mar. 30, 1988, Box 1, Folder 6, Project 10 Collection; Jerry Gillam and Patricia Ward Biederman, "School Funds, Gay Counselor Linked," *LAT*, Mar. 11, 1988.

196 Erbland, "Founder of High School Program for Gays Tells of Trial and Tribulations of First Years."

197 Friends of Project 10, "Project 10 Handbook," i; Craig Wilson, "Teacher Takes Homophobia to Task," *USA Today*, Feb. 12, 1991.

198 Marv. Shaw, "Uribe Goes to War in San Jose," *BAR*, Dec. 9, 1993. In 1993, the Massachusetts Board of Education unanimously recommended that school districts offer support groups for gay and lesbian students. Patricia Manghan, "School Pledge for Gays Sparks Storm," *Boston Herald*, May 19, 1993.

199 Fisher, "Project for Gays Gets a '10'"; Jessica Lloyd-Rogers, "Project 10 Founder Honored at San Jose Reception," *OutNOW!*, Dec. 14, 1993, Box 2, Folder labeled Project 10 LA, Jessea Greenman P.E.R.S.O.N. Project Records.

200 Erica Gordon Sorohan, "School Districts Reach Out to Gay and Lesbian Youth," *School Board News*, June 19, 1990, 12.

201 Zane Meckler, "Fairfax Teacher Testifies before U.S. Senate," Nov. 1989, Box 1, Folder 8, Project 10 Collection.

202 Adele Starr to Leonard M. Brittan, Jul. 10, 1987, Box 3, Folder 22, Starr (Adele) Collection on PFLAG.

203 Lisa Atkinson, "Mass. Begins Teacher Training on Helping Support Gay Students," *BG*, Jul. 4, 1993; "Gov. Weld Asks Schools to Aid Gay Students," *NYT*, Jul. 4, 1993.

204 Rolf, interview by author.

Chapter 6

1 Federation of Parents and Friends of Lesbians and Gays, Inc., "Parents Decry Society's Cruelty to Gay and Lesbian Adolescents," n.d., ca. 1989, Box 154, Folder 46, NGLTF Records; "Project 10 Aired on Capitol Hill," *PFLAGpole*, Fall 1989, Project 10 Subject File; William Trombley, "Religious Right Wins Textbook Battle on Sex," *LAT*, Aug. 2, 1992.

2 Trombley, "Religious Right Wins Textbook Battle on Sex."

3 Ibid.

4 Ibid.

5 Ibid.; "Fundamentalists Lose Battle on Sex Education," *LAT*, May 31, 1992.

6 Louis P. Sheldon to Friend of Traditional Values, Aug. 1995, Folder labeled Hoekstra-Sheldon Hearings, Jessea Greenman P.E.R.S.O.N. Project Records.

7 Shilts, *And the Band Played On*, 55, 273, 293–98, 328–29, 397–99, 452–53, 473–74, 525–27, 572–73, 585–89. Gay men disproportionately contracted HIV.

8 Frances A. Schaeffer, C. Everett Koop, and Jeremy C. Jackson, *Whatever Happened to the Human Race?* (Gospel Films Video, 1979), VHS.

9 Martin, *With God on Our Side*, 239–39.

10 Ibid., 239.

11 Ibid.

12 John B. Judis, "The Unlikely Celebrity of C. Everett Koop," *New Republic*, Feb. 26, 2013.

13 Michael Specter, "Postscript: C. Everett Koop, 1916–2013," *New Yorker*, Feb. 26, 2013.

14 Martin, *With God on Our Side*, 249.

15 C. Everett Koop, *Surgeon General's Report on Acquired Immune Deficiency Syndrome* (Washington, D.C.: Department of Health and Human Services, 1986), 31; John Leo, "Sex and Schools: AIDS and the Surgeon General Add a New Urgency to an Old Debate," *Time*, Nov. 24, 1986, 54; Shilts, *And the Band Played On*, 587.

16 Leo, "Sex and Schools," 54.

17 Peter Freiberg, "Sex Education and the Gay Issue: What Are They Teaching about Us in the Schools?," *Advocate*, Sept. 1, 1987, 43; "Schools, Groups Work to Help Gay Youth," *Empty Closet*, Jul. 1990, Gay Youth Subject File.

18 Bill Stokes, "Researcher Says Gay Teens Need to Develop Self-Esteem," *Las Vegas Review-Journal*, Apr. 16, 1987.

19 U.S. House of Representatives Select Committee on Children Youth, and Families, *A Decade of Denial: Teens and AIDS in America* (Washington, D.C.: Government Printing Office, 1992), 1.

20 Petro, *After the Wrath of God*, 55; Alessandra Stanley, "AIDS Becomes a Political Issue," *Time*, Mar. 23, 1987, 24.

21 Martin, *With God on Our Side*, 242–43.

22 Ibid., 243.

23 Brier, *Infectious Ideas*, 80; "HIV/AIDS: Snapshots of an Epidemic," amfAR, www.amfar.org/thirty-years-of-hiv/aids-snapshots-of-an-epidemic/.

24 Ellen Flax, "Study Finds Fast Growth in Sex Education, But Sentiment for Classes in Lower Grades," *Education Week*, May 10, 1989, 1.

25 Leo, "Sex and Schools," 55; "School Districts Beginning to Offer Comprehensive Sex Ed," *Edline*, June 15, 1990. Those states were Kansas, Maryland, and New Jersey. Ibid.

26 "School Districts Beginning to Offer Comprehensive Sex Ed." Twenty-three states recommended, but did not require, sex education. Ibid.

27 Ali Kielwasser, "GLAAD/Project 21 Fact Sheet," June 1992, Box 1, Folder 47, GLAAD Papers.

28 Josh Barbanel, "Chancellor Has Plans to Distribute Condoms to Students in New York," *NYT*, Sept. 26, 1990; Leo, "Sex and Schools," 55.

29 People for the American Way, "Religious Right's Candidates Win Big," *SFS*, Nov. 23, 1994.

30 Rosky, "Anti-Gay Curriculum Laws."

31 Act of June 1, 1989, ch. 1195, § 1.03, 1989 Tex. Gen. Laws 4854; Act of Sept. 1, 1991, ch. 14, §§ 36, 51, 1991 Tex. Gen. Laws 42, 63, 83, *codified at* Tex Health & Safety Code Ann. 85.007(b)(2) (1991); Act of May 21, 1992, No. 92-590, § 2, 1992 Ala. Laws 1216, 1218–19, *codified at* Ala. Code 16-40A-2(c)(8) (1992).

32 Chris Bull, "Back to the Future," *Advocate*, Nov. 15, 1994, 28–29; Chris Bull, "Why Johnny Can't Learn about Condoms: How the Religious Right Censors Sex Education Across the U.S.," *Advocate*, Dec. 15, 1992, 36; Gallagher and Bull, *Perfect Enemies*, 220–21.

33 Bull, "Why Johnny Can't Learn about Condoms," 37; Gallagher and Bull, *Perfect Enemies*, 220–21; Michael Granberry, "Backlash to Teaching Chastity," *LAT*, Feb. 15, 1994.

34 Klarman, *From the Closet to the Altar*, 71; Jeffrey Schmalz, "Gay Politics Goes Mainstream," *NYT Magazine*, Oct. 11, 1992.

35 Eskridge, *Dishonorable Passions*, Appendix; Jerome Hunt, "A State-by-State Examination of Nondiscrimination Laws and Policies," June 2012, www .americanprogress.org/wp-content/uploads/issues/2012/06/pdf/state_ nondiscrimination.pdf; Klarman, *From the Closet to the Altar*, 41–42, 71.

36 Jeffrey Schmalz, "Poll Finds an Even Split on Homosexuality's Cause," *NYT*, Mar. 5, 1992.

37 Ibid.

38 Jeffrey Schmalz, "Survey Finds U.S. Divided over Gays," *Oregonian* (Portland, Or.), Mar. 5, 1993.

39 Lesléa Newman, *Heather Has Two Mommies* (Los Angeles: Alyson Publications, 1989).

40 Shannon Maughan, "A Second Life for 'Heather Has Two Mommies,'" *Publishers Weekly*, Mar. 16, 2015; Rachel Rosenberg, "Heather Has How Many Mommies?," *Book Riot*, June 24, 2022, https://bookriot.com/the-creation-of-heather-has-two-mommies/.

41 Felicia R. Lee, "Intolerance Will Be Topic for Students," *NYT*, Sept. 18, 1989.

42 Ralph Blumenthal, "Black Youth Is Killed by Whites," *NYT*, Aug. 25, 1989; Montgomery Brower, "The Racial Murder of Yusuf Hawkins Inflamed New York City, Forcing His Parents to Relive Their Anguish," *People*, June 4, 1990.

43 New York City Board of Education, "Statement of Policy on Multicultural Education and Promotion of Positive Intergroup Relations," Nov. 9, 1989, Box 4, Folder 215, LGTANY Collection.

44 "The Coalition for Lesbian and Gay Rights Speaks Out vs. 'Woeful' AIDS Education in New York City Schools," *Gay Teachers Association Newsletter*, Apr. 1987, Box 1, Folder 38, LGTANY Collection, 1; "Dear Paul," *Gay Teachers Association Newsletter*, Sept. 1989, Box 1, Folder 41, LGTANY Collection, 1; Governor's Task Force on Bias-Related Violence, *Final Report* (Albany, 1988), 97.

45 New York City Public Schools, Memorandum to Reporters et al., Sept. 8, 1992, Box 4, Folder 217, LGTANY Collection, 4.

46 NYC Public Schools, *Children of the Rainbow: First Grade* (1991), Box 10, Folder 342, Jan Carl Park Files, 372.

47 Ibid., 145.

48 Vic Ostrowidzki, "Families of Yore Fading Away," *SFE*, Aug. 25, 1992.

49 NYC Public Schools, *Children of the Rainbow*, 371.

50 Joseph Fernandez to Mary A. Cummins, Nov. 6, 1992, Box 2, Folder 21, LGTANY Collection.

51 Donna Minkowitz, "Wrong Side of the Rainbow," *Nation*, June 28, 1993, 901.

52 Ibid.

53 Ibid.; Steven Lee Myers, "Schools Find that Diversity Can Place Values in Conflict," *NYT*, Oct. 6, 1992.

54 Mary A. Cummins to Parents, Community School District 24, Aug. 28, 1992, Box 4, Folder 217, LGTANY Collection; Myers, "Schools Find that Diversity Can Place Values in Conflict."

55 Cummins to Parents, Aug. 28, 1992; Myers, "Schools Find that Diversity Can Place Values in Conflict."

56 Adam Entous, "Christian Right Targets 20 City School Boards," *New York Observer*, Mar. 8, 1993; Mary Jordan, "Opposition to New York Curriculum Guide Continues To Explode," *Daily Californian*, Dec. 8, 1992, 8; Irvine, *Talk About Sex*, 156; Dana Kennedy, "N.Y. School Chief in Flap with Parents over Gay Curriculum," *Phoenix Gazette*, Dec. 11, 1992; Minkowitz, "Wrong Side of the Rainbow," 902.

57 Irvine, *Talk About Sex*, 155; Minkowitz, "Wrong Side of the Rainbow," 901–02.

58 Josh Barbanel, "Under 'Rainbow,' a War: When Politics, Morals and Learning Mix," *NYT*, Dec. 27, 1992; Sam Dillon, "New York School Fight Shifts to Local Boards," *NYT*, Feb. 17, 1993; Gallagher and Bull, *Perfect Enemies*, 220; Sam Roberts, "New York School Fight Highlights Role of Catholic Church," *NYT*, Dec. 15, 1992.

59 "In N.Y., Educrats vs. Parents," *Boston Herald*, Dec. 12, 1992, 16; Minkowitz, "Wrong Side of the Rainbow," 902.

60 Peg Byron, "NYC Parents Protest 'Children of the Rainbow,'" *BAR*, Sept. 10, 1992.

61 Steven Lee Myers, "How a 'Rainbow Curriculum' Turned into Fighting Words," *NYT*, Dec. 13, 1992.

62 Chris Bull, "N.Y. Curriculum Fight Gets Physical," *Advocate*, Jan. 26, 1993, 21; Roberts, "New York School Fight Highlights Role of Catholic Church."

63 Fernandez to Cummins, Nov. 6, 1992.

64 Myers, "How a 'Rainbow Curriculum' Turned into Fighting Words."

65 "Rainbow Curriculum Abandoned by Board of Ed," *San Francisco Bay Times*, Feb. 23, 1995.

66 Tom Wilson, "Elizabethtown 'Pro-Family' Resolution," *Pennsylvania Expose*, Oct. 22, 1996, Box 6, Folder labeled PA Action Alerts, Jessea Greenman P.E.R.S.O.N. Project Records.

67 "School Officials in Pennsylvania Ban the Village People," *Church & State*, Dec. 1996, 17.

68 Wilson, "Elizabethtown 'Pro-Family' Resolution."

69 PERSON Project, "The P.E.R.S.O.N. Organizing Manual," Box 10, Jessea Greenman P.E.R.S.O.N. Project Records.

70 Al Kielwasser, "Muppet Love," *BAR*, Jan. 6, 1994.

71 "Virginia District Will Address Homosexuality in Curricula," *The Daily Digest*, June 18, 1990, Box 4, Folder labeled Hate Violence P21, Jessea Greenman P.E.R.S.O.N. Project Records.

72 Erica Gordon Sorohan, "School Districts Reach Out to Gay and Lesbian Youth," *School Board News*, June 19, 1990, Box 4, Folder labeled Hate Violence P21, Jessea Greenman P.E.R.S.O.N. Project Records, 12.

73 Ibid., Tammerlin Drummond and Bettina Boxall, "Gay Rights Fight Moves on Campus," *LAT*, Jan. 10, 1994; Steven Lee Myers, "School Board Out in New York Fight," *NYT*, Dec. 2, 1992.

74 GLAAD San Francisco Bay Area Chapter, "New State Health Education Policy Mandates Lesbian, Gay, Bisexual Inclusion," Dec. 11, 1992, Box 1, Folder 47, GLAAD/San Francisco Bay Area Clippings; GLAAD San Francisco Bay Area, "Project 21 Achieves Historic Victory," GLAAD Update, Jan. 1993, Box Labeled Extra/Old GLAAD Files, Folder labeled Update Jul. 91–Feb 94, Jessea Greenman P.E.R.S.O.N. Project Records, 1–2.

75 "New State Health Education Policy Mandates Lesbian, Gay, and Bisexual Inclusion," *Your Paper* (Santa Clara Valley), Dec. 16, 1992, 1, Box 1, Folder 47, GLAAD/San Francisco Bay Area Clippings; Mary Ann Swissler, "Cal Board of Ed OKs G-Word in Health Class Curriculum," *BAR*, Oct. 19, 1995. California school districts were not required to use the state-approved curricula. Claire D. Brindis, Sara P. Geierstanger, and Adrienne Faxio, "The Role of Policy Advocacy in Assuring Comprehensive Family Life Education in California," *Health Education and Behavior* 36, no. 6 (2009): 1096.

76 Phyllida Burlingame, *Sex Education in California Public Schools: Are Students Learning What They Need to Know?* (San Francisco: ACLU of Southern California, 2003), 10, 13; Swissler, "Cal Board of Ed OKs G-Word in Health Class Curriculum."

77 Patricia Manghan, "School Pledge for Gays Sparks Storm," *Boston Herald*, May 19, 1993.

78 Act of Dec. 10, 1993, ch. 282, 1993 Mass. Session Laws 1160, *codified at* Mass. Gen. Laws 76 § 5.

79 Gary Putka, "Uncharted Course: Effort to Teach Teens about Homosexuality Advances in Schools," *WSJ*, June 12, 1990.

80 Rod Paul, "Sex and God Split Small Town in New England," *SFE*, May 9, 1996.

81 Chris Ager, "Letter to the Editor," *Merrimack Village Crier*, Aug. 1, 1995.

82 Nancy Roberts Trott, "School District Anti-Gay Policy Splits N.H. Town," *LAT*, Mar. 17, 1996.

83 Peter Freiberg, "Gay Issues in Schools Now a 'Front-Burner Issue,'" *WB*, Jan. 19, 1996; Irvine, *Talk About Sex*, 163; PERSON Project, "The P.E.R.S.O.N. Organizing Manual."

84 A handful of teachers did invite PFLAG parents to present to their classes, but no district implemented a school-wide policy.

85 "Gays Reunite with Estranged Parents," *The Oprah Winfrey Show*, episode 07136, OWN, 1992.

86 Ibid.

87 Murray, *Not In This Family*, 138, 166–78.

88 PFLAG, "Homosexuality Is Largely Determined at Birth, Can Not Be Reversed, Scientists Say," Dec. 7, 1988, Box 36, Folder 8, PFLAG Records; PFLAG, "Why Is My Child Gay?," n.d., ca. 1988, Box 17, Folder 28, PFLAG Records.

89 PFLAG, "Homosexuality Is Largely Determined at Birth."

90 PFLAG, "Why Is My Child Gay?," 1.

91 J. Michael Bailey & Richard C. Pillard, "A Genetic Study of Male Sexual Orientation," *Archives of General Psychiatry* 48, no. 12 (1991): 1094.

92 Dean H. Hamer et al., "A Linkage between DNA Markers on the X Chromosomes and Male Sexual Orientation," *Science* 261, no. 5119 (1993): 321–27.

93 Lancaster, *The Trouble with Nature*, 240; Stein, "Immutability and Innateness Arguments about Lesbian, Gay, and Bisexual Rights," 629–33.

94 Mbugua, "Sexual Orientation and Brain Structures," 175.

95 Lancaster, *The Trouble with Nature*, 240; Stein, "Immutability and Innateness Arguments about Lesbian, Gay, and Bisexual Rights," 605, 629–33.

96 Ruth Abramson, "Genetics: How Our Jewels Are Set into the Crown" (PFLAG National Convention, Charlotte, NC, Oct. 12–14, 1991), Box 11, Folder 91-24, PFLAG Records.

97 PFLAG, "Celebrating Real Family Values," 1993, Box 49, Folder 59, PFLAG Records, 12.

98 Ibid.

99 PFLAG, "Why Ask Why?: Addressing the Research on Homosexuality and Biology," 1995, Box 43, Folder 50, PFLAG Records.

100 Ibid., 26.

101 Wuest, *Born This Way*, 127.

102 John D'Emilio, "Born Gay?," in *The World Turned: Essays on Gay History, Politics, and Culture* (Durham, NC: Duke University Press, 2002), 162.

103 Ibid., 160–63.

104 Ibid., 164.

105 Halley, "'Like Race' Arguments," 52; Halley, "Sexual Orientation and the Politics of Biology," 564; Hequembourg and Arditi, "Fractured Resistances," 664, 668–71; Sedgwick, *Epistemology of the Closet*, 13; Wuest, *Born This Way*, 128.

106 PFLAG, "Why Ask Why?," 8–9.

107 Sarah B. Ames, "Petition Drive Aimed at Homosexuals," *Oregonian*, Feb. 23, 1988; Betsy Brown, "Anti-Gay Measure Passes in Oregon," *GCN*, Nov. 13–19, 1988; "Constructing Homophobia: Colorado's Right-Wing Attack on Homosexuals," *The Public Eye*, Mar. 1993, 3–4, in ACLU, "Briefing Book: Anti-Gay Ballot Initiatives," Aug. 1993, Box 19, Folder 2, ACLU of Southern California Lesbian and Gay Rights Chapter Records; "Hostile Climate: A State-By-State Report on Anti-Gay Activity," Nov. 1993, Box 5, Folder 11, Ettelbrick Papers, 8–9; "An Overview of Anti-Gay Organizing in the US," Box 311, Folder 1, NGLTF Records, 96.

108 Biggers, *Morality at the Ballot Box*, 172; Keen and Goldberg, *Strangers to the Law*, 3–4, 45.

109 ACLU, "Briefing Book: Anti-Gay Ballot Initiatives," Appendix of Polling Results; William E. Dannemeyer to Colleague, June 26, 1989, Box 56, Folder 42, NGLTF Records; Minnesota Bias Crime Legislation, n.d., ca. 1988, Box 67, Folder 17, NGLTF Records.

110 Garretson and Suhay, "Scientific Communications about Biological Influences on Homosexuality," 25.

111 Ibid.

112 Ibid., 22.

113 "Gays vs. Dukakis," *Guide to Gay New England*, Jul. 1985, Box 1, Folder labeled Information Packet: "Gays vs. Dukakis," GLDC Collection, 7.

114 Ibid., 6.

115 Klarman, *From the Closet to the Altar*, 43.

116 Broad, "Social Movement Selves," 321; Chauncey, *Why Marriage?*, 48.

117 Pam Walton, "To Save Our Children," *BAR*, June 29, 1992.

118 Broad, "Coming Out for Parents, Families and Friends of Lesbians and Gays," 409–10.

119 Ibid., 410.

120 Ibid., 407.

121 Ibid.

122 Ibid., 408; Broad, "Social Movement Selves," 324; Murray, *Not In This Family*, 189–91.

123 Karlyn Bowman and Adam Foster, "Attitudes about Homosexuality & Gay Marriage," *AEI Studies in Public Opinion*, June 3, 2008 (on file with author), 2–8, 11–15.

124 PFLAG, "Why Ask Why?," 26.

125 Broad, "Social Movement Selves," 325.

126 PLFAG, "Interim Project Open Mind National Report," Feb. 19, 1997, Box 19, Folder 18, PFLAG Records, 1.

127 EDK Associates, Inc., "Fact vs. Belief: Shaping the Conflict Over Gay & Lesbian Equality," Nov. 1995, Box 19, Folder 17, PFLAG Records, 2–4.

128 Ibid., 8.

129 Ibid., 7.

130 PFLAG, "Celebrating Real Family Values," 12; PLFAG, "Interim Project Open Mind National Report," 2; PFLAG, "Parents Decry Society's Cruelty to Gay and Lesbian Adolescents."

131 Paul Gibson, "Gay Male and Lesbian Youth Suicide," in United States Department of Health and Human Services, *Report of the Secretary's Task Force on Youth Suicide*, ed. Marcia R. Feinleib (Washington, D.C.: Government Printing Office, 1989), vol. 3, 110. These statistics matched the experiences of gay and lesbian youth services providers in New York. Joyce Murdoch, "Gay Youths' Deadly Despair: High Rate of Suicide Attempts Tracked," *WP*, Oct. 24, 1988.

132 PLFAG, "Interim Project Open Mind National Report," 2–7.

133 PFLAG, Gun, Zimmerman & Markman, 1995, www.adrespect.org/common/adli
brary/ad-details.cfm?clientID=11064&QID=180.

134 PLFAG, "Interim Project Open Mind National Report," 9.

135 Ibid., 7.

136 Ibid., 8.

137 Ibid., 6.

138 Ibid.

139 Ibid., 9.

140 Ibid.

141 Howard Chua-Edan, "That's Not a Scarecrow," *Time*, Oct. 19, 1998; "Nebraska
Man Found Shepard's Body," *Casper Star-Tribune* (Wyo.), Oct. 15, 1998.

142 Janes Brooke, "Gay Murder Trial Yields Guilty Plea by Wyoming Man," *NYT*,
Apr. 6, 1999; Kerry Drake, "4 Charged as Laramie Man Clings to Life," *Casper
Star-Tribune*, Oct. 10, 1998; "Gay Student Dies after Robbery, Severe Beating,"
Minnesota Daily, Oct. 13, 1998; Todd Lewan and Steven K. Paulson, "Laramie
Wrestles with Killing in Rich-Poor Midst," *Casper Start-Tribune*, Oct. 18, 1998;
"Victim Was Cautious about Revealing Gay Lifestyle," *Billings Gazette* (Wyo.),
Oct. 13, 1998.

143 Rebecca Isaacs, Memorandum to NGLTF Board Members, Oct. 22, 1998, Box
293, NGLTF Records; Robert Roten, "Media Storm Following Killing of Matthew
Shepard Year's Top Story," *Laramie Boomerang* (Wyo.), Dec. 31, 1998; Melanie
Thernstrom, "The Crucifixion of Matthew Shepard," *Vanity Fair*, Mar. 1989, 272.

144 Thernstrom, "The Crucifixion of Matthew Shepard," 272.

145 Justin Gillis and Patrice Gaines, "America's Hidden Climate of Hate," *SFE*,
Oct. 18, 1998.

146 Ott and Aoki, "The Media Framing of the Matthew Shepard Murder," 489–90.

147 Shepard, *The Meaning of Matthew*, 42, 53–54; "Shepard's Life Recalled," *Billings
Gazette* (Mont.), Oct. 13, 1998.

148 Robert O. Blanchard, "The 'Hate State' Myth," *Reason*, May 1999; Elise Harris,
"Writing the Book of Matthew," *Out*, Mar. 1999.

149 Hillel Gray, "They're Still Here: The Curious Evolution of the Westboro Baptist
Church," *Religion News*, Jul. 17, 2018, https://religionnews.com/2018/07/17/
theyre-still-here-the-curious-evolution-of-westboro-baptist-church/.

150 Jude Sheerin, "Matthew Shepard: The Murder that Changed America," *BBC*,
Oct. 26, 2018, www.bbc.com/news/world-us-canada-45968606; Jason Marsden,
"The Murder of Matthew Shepard," *Wyoming State Historical Society*, Nov. 8,
2014, www.wyohistory.org/encyclopedia/murder-matthew-shepard.

151 Merrit Kennedy, "'Angels' from Orlando's Theater Community Guard Mourners
from Protestors," *NPR*, June 19, 2016, www.npr.org/sections/thetwo-way/2016/
06/19/482698337/angels-from-orlandos-theater-community-guard-mourners-
from-protesters.

152 Jonathan Alter, "Trickle-Down Hate," *Newsweek*, Oct. 26, 1998; Blanchard, "The
'Hate State' Myth"; Chua-Egan, "That's Not a Scarecrow"; Howard Fineman,
"Echoes of a Murder in Wyoming," *Newsweek*, Oct. 26, 1998.

153 Bettina Boxall, "Long Arm of Hatred," *LAT*, Nov. 6, 1998; Gillis and Gaines,
"America's Hidden Climate of Hate."

154 Gillis and Gaines, "America's Hidden Climate of Hate."

155 Judy Shepard, interview by author, Apr. 27, 2022.

156 Murray, *Not In This Family*, 183–85, 187–89; Shepard, interview by author.

157 Shepard, *The Meaning of Matthew*, 134.

158 Shepard, interview by author.

159 Ibid.; Shepard, *The Meaning of Matthew*, 260.

160 "Judy Shepard," GLSEN, 1999, www.adrespect.org/common/adlibrary/ad-details
.cfm?clientID=11064&QID=133.

161 "Judy Shepard Launches Anti-Gay Harassment Campaign," *Laramie Boomerang*
(Wyo.), Oct. 5, 1999.

162 "Judy Shepard/Parenthood," Human Rights Campaign, 1999, www.adrespect.org/
common/adlibrary/adlibrarydetails.cfm?QID=403&ClientID=11064.

163 Elizabeth Birch and David M. Smith, Memorandum, Nov. 5, 1999, Box 2, Folder
25, HRC Records.

164 Shepard, *The Meaning of Matthew*, 194.

165 Moisés Kaufman and the Members of the Tectonic Theater Project, *The Laramie
Project* (New York: Vintage Books, 2001).

166 John Moore, "How 'The Laramie Project' Changed Theater – And the World,"
DCPA News Center, Feb. 25, 2020, www.denvercenter.org/news-center/how-the-
laramie-project-changed-theatre-and-the-world/.

167 Matthew Shepard and James Byrd, Jr., Hate Crimes Prevention Act, 18 U.S.C. §
249 (2009).

168 Sam Fulwood, III, "Dissent Blocks Tougher Hate Crimes Laws," *LAT*, Oct. 14,
1998; NGLTF, "Legislative Update," Mar. 19, 1999, Box 293, NGLTF Records, 2.

169 Hanhardt, *Safe Space*, 163; Scott Holleran, "Thoughts of Hate Are Not a Crime,"
Casper Star Tribune (Wyo.), Nov. 7, 1998; William Raspberry, "Hate Crimes,
Thought Police," *WP*, Sept. 11, 2000.

170 Lisa Neff, "The Best Defense: Activists Plan Demonstrations in 50 States to Fight
for Basic Human Rights," *Advocate*, Mar. 16, 1999; George, "The LGBT
Disconnect," 514.

171 Gillis and Gaines, "America's Hidden Climate of Hate."

172 George, "The LGBT Disconnect," 514.

173 Fulwood, "Dissent Blocks Tougher Hate Crimes Laws"; NGLTF, "Legislative
Update," 2.

174 AB 537, ch. 587, 1999 Cal. Laws 5155; "Judy Shepard Launches Anti-Gay
Harassment Campaign."

175 Thernstrom, "The Crucifixion of Matthew Shepard," 275.

176 National Coalition of Anti-Violence Programs, "Anti-Lesbian, Gay, Transgender
and Bisexual Violence in 1999," 2000, Box 61, Folder 5, CUAV Records; National
Coalition of Anti-Violence Programs, "Anti-Lesbian, Gay, Transgender and
Bisexual Violence in 2000," 2001, Box 61, Folder 7, CUAV Records; National
Coalition of Anti-Violence Programs, "Anti-Lesbian, Gay, Transgender and
Bisexual Violence in 2001," 2002, Box 61, Folder 5, CUAV Records.

Part III

1 Brief of PFLAG, Inc. as *Amicus Curiae* in Support of Petitioners at 5, Obergefell
v. Hodges, No. 14-556, 2015 WL 1004714 (U.S. Mar. 6, 2015).

2 Ibid., 5–6.

3 Ibid., 6.

4 Ibid., 8.

5 Ibid.

6 Ibid., 9.

7 Ibid., 5, 9.

8 Ibid., 8.

Chapter 7

1 Jackie Young, "Protect Our Constitution Is a Coalition of Groups," *Honolulu Star-Bulletin*, Aug. 17, 1998.
2 Kevin Dayton, "Former Hawaii Lawmaker Jackie Young Dies at 84," *Honolulu Star Advertiser*, Feb. 13, 2019.
3 Baehr v. Lewin, 852 P.2d 44 (Haw. 1993).
4 Coolidge, "The Hawai'i Marriage Amendment," 101.
5 HRC, "Aoki," 1998, Starr Siegel Communications, www.adrespect.org/common/adlibrary/adlibrarydetails.cfm?QID=405&ClientID=11064; HRC, "Miyasoto," 1998, Starr Siegel Communications, www.adrespect.org/common/adlibrary/adlibrarydetails.cfm?QID=408&ClientID=11064; HRC, "Truth," 1998, Starr Siegel Communications, www.adrespect.org/common/adlibrary/adlibrarydetails.cfm?QID=407&ClientID=11064; Protect Our Constitution, "Dr. Rodney Powell," 1998, video no. 79898, Julian P. Kanter Political Commercial Archive; Protect Our Constitution, "Endorsements," 1998, video no. 79900, Julian P. Kanter Political Commercial Archive; Protect Our Constitution, "Honolulu Advertiser," 1998, video no. 79904, Julian P. Kanter Political Commercial Archive; Protect Our Constitution, "Japanese," 1998, video no. 79901, Julian P. Kanter Political Commercial Archive; Protect Our Constitution, "Jennifer E. Frank, MD," 1998, video no. 79896, Julian P. Kanter Political Commercial Archive; Protect Our Constitution, "The Kern Family," 1998, video no. 79899, Julian P. Kanter Political Commercial Archive; Protect Our Constitution, "League of Women Voters," 1998, video no. 79903, Julian P. Kanter Political Commercial Archive; Protect Our Constitution, "Walter Tagawa," 1998, video no. 79895, Julian P. Kanter Political Commercial Archive.
6 Protect Our Constitution, "Dr. Rodney Powell."
7 HRC, "Aoki."
8 Protect Our Constitution, "Endorsements"; Protect Our Constitution, "Japanese."
9 Klarman, *From the Closet to the Altar*, 66.
10 Ibid., 68.
11 Camp, "Mobilizing the Base and Embarrassing the Opposition," 719; Hunter, "Varieties of Constitutional Experiences," 1680; Klarman, *From the Closet to the Altar*, 83–84, 95–96, 105–06.
12 Cases: Goodridge v. Dep't of Pub. Health, 798 N.E.2d 941, 961 (Mass. 2003); Kerrigan v. Comm'n of Pub. Health, 957 A.2d 407 (Conn. 2008); Lewis v. Harris, 908 A.2d 196 (N.J. 2006). Statutes: An Act Relating to Civil Marriage, ch. 3, 2009 Vt. Acts & Resolves 33, *codified at* 15 Vt. Stat. Ann. § 8; D.C. Act No. 18–248, 57 D.C. Reg. 27 (2010); H.B. 436, 2009 Reg. Sess. (N.H. 2009); Marriage Equality Act, 2011 N.Y. Laws 749, *codified at* N.Y. Dom. Rel. Law Ann. §§ 10-a, 10-b, 13.
13 Frank Newport, "For the First Time, Majority of Americans Favor Legal Gay Marriage," *Gallup News*, May 20, 2011.
14 Sunnivie Brydum, "Win Claimed in Washington: Voters Affirm Marriage Equality," *Advocate*, Nov. 7, 2012.
15 Eskridge and Riano, *Marriage Equality*, Appendix 1.
16 Godsoe, "Perfect Plaintiffs," 139.
17 Gash, *Below the Radar*, 34; Gary J. Gates, LGBT Parenting in the United States, Feb. 2013, https://williamsinstitute.law.ucla.edu/wp-content/uploads/LGBT-Parenting-Feb-2013.pdf, 1; United States Census Bureau, Same-Sex Couple Households: American Community Survey Briefs, Sept. 2011, 2.
18 Issenberg, *The Engagement*, 60–62; Keck, "Beyond Backlash," 178.

19 Dominic Holden, "Meet the Women Who Won the First Same-Sex Marriage Court Case 19 Years Ago," *BuzzFeed News*, Apr. 27, 2105, www.buzzfeednews.com/article/dominicholden/these-brave-women-won-the-first-same-sex-marriage-court-case; Sasha Issenberg, "The Surprising Honolulu Origins of the National Fight Over Same-Sex Marriage," *Politico*, May 31, 2021.

20 Issenberg, *The Engagement*, 25–26.

21 Ibid., 26.

22 Baehr v. Lewin, 852 P.2d 44 (Haw. 1993).

23 Although queer couples had applied for marriage licenses in 1970s, each event was an act of protest against the state's discriminatory policies, rather than a sincere effort to secure marriage rights. Boucai, *Glorious Precedents*, 2, 4–5.

24 Issenberg, *The Engagement*, 26–31, 65, 69.

25 Ibid., 31.

26 Issenberg, *The Engagement*, 60–62; Keck, "Beyond Backlash," 178.

27 Thomas B. Stoddard, "Why Gay People Should Seek the Right to Marry," *Out/Look*, Fall 1989, 12.

28 Klarman, *From the Closet to the Altar*, 55; Pinello, *America's Struggle for Same-Sex Marriage*, 24–25.

29 Paula Ettelbrick, "Since When Is Marriage a Path to Liberation?," *Out/Look*, Fall 1989, 9.

30 Ibid., 14.

31 Ettelbrick, "Since When Was Marriage the Path to Liberation?," 9, 14, 17; Pinello, *America's Struggle for Same-Sex Marriage*, 24–25; Stone, *Gay Rights at the Ballot Box*, 129.

32 Klarman, *From the Closet to the Altar*, 48.

33 Baehr v. Lewin, 852 P.2d 44 (Haw. 1993).

34 Ibid.

35 Eskridge and Riano, *Marriage Equality*, 89.

36 Hull and Ortyl, "Same-Sex Marriage and Constituent Perceptions of the LGBT Rights Movement," 81–82.

37 States follow the principle of comity unless doing so violates their public policy. Cox, "Same-Sex Marriage and Choice of Law," 1041; Evan Wolfson, "Winning and Keeping Equal Marriage Rights: What Will Follow Victory in *Baehr v. Lewin*?," Mar. 20, 1996, cited in Defense of Marriage Act: Hearing Before the Subcomm. on the Constitution, 104th Cong. 14 (Washington, D.C.: U.S. Government Printing Office, 1996).

38 Sant'Ambrogio and Law, "*Baehr v. Lewin* and the Long Road to Marriage Equality," 708 n.22.

39 Eskridge and Riano, *Marriage Equality*, 117–18.

40 Ibid., 117–19.

41 Ibid., 120.

42 Defense of Marriage Act, 1 U.S.C.A. § 7 and 28 U.S.C.A. § 1738C (1996), *held unconstitutional by* United States v. Windsor, 133 S. Ct. 2675 (2013).

43 Defense of Marriage Act: Hearing before the Subcomm. on the Constitution, 8, 32 (statement of Rep. Sensebrenner, Member. H. Comm. on the Judiciary).

44 Actions Overview, H.R. 3396 – Defense of Marriage Act, 1995–1996, www.congress.gov/bill/104th-congress/house-bill/3396/actions.

45 Richard Socarides, "Why Bill Clinton Signed the Defense of Marriage Act," *New Yorker*, Mar. 8, 2013.

46 Peter Baker, "Now in Defense of Gay Marriage, Bill Clinton," *NYT*, Mar. 25, 2013.

47 Klarman, *From the Closet to the Altar*, 59.

48 Eskridge and Riano, *Marriage Equality*, 143–44; Haider-Markel, "Lesbian and Gay Politics in the States," 307.
49 Eskridge and Riano, *Marriage Equality*, 121; *The Ultimate Target of the Gay Agenda: Same-Sex Marriage* (Lancaster, CA: The Report, 1996), VHS.
50 Klarman, *From the Closet to the Altar*, 59.
51 Connie Cain Ramsey, "1989 Custody Case Put Attention on Equal Rights," *Burlington Free Press* (Vt.), Aug. 7, 2014.
52 Ibid.; Eskridge and Riano, *Marriage Equality*, 171; Moats, *Civil Wars*, 84–89.
53 Eskridge and Riano, *Marriage Equality*, 171.
54 Bonauto, "The Litigation," 69.
55 Ibid., 69–70; Eskridge and Riano, *Marriage Equality*, 172–73, 177–78.
56 An Act Relating to Adoptions, 1996 Vt. Laws P.A. 161, S. 136, *codified at* 15A V.S.A. § 1-102; Eskridge and Riano, *Marriage Equality*, 171–72; *In re B.L.V.B.*, 628A.2d 1271 (1993).
57 An Act Related to Intimidation and Vandalism, 1990 Vt. Laws P.A. 172, H. 504, *codified at* Vt. Stat. Ann. § 13-31-1455; An Act Relating to Discrimination on the Basis of Sexual Orientation, 1992 Vt. Laws P.A. 135, S. 131, *codified at* 21 V.S.A. § 495.
58 Baker v. State, 744 A.2d 864 (Vt. 1999).
59 Ibid., 878–79. This analysis differs substantially from the multitiered standard that federal courts use when adjudicating challenges under the U.S. Equal Protection Clause.
60 Bonauto, "Equality and the Impossible," 1507 n.146.
61 Ibid.; Bonauto, Murray, and Robinson, "The Freedom to Marry for Same-Sex Couples," 413.
62 Bonauto, "The Litigation," 70.
63 *Baker*, 744 A.2d at 881, 884.
64 Ibid., 882.
65 Ibid., 884–85.
66 Ibid., 996. The Vermont Supreme Court adopted the same approach two years earlier, when it ruled that the state's educational funding system was unconstitutional. Brigham v. State, 692 A.2d 384 (Vt. 1997).
67 *Baker*, 744 A.2d 884–85, 887.
68 An Act Relating to Civil Unions, 2000 Vt. Laws P.A. 91, H. 847, *codified at* 15 V.S.A. § 1201.
69 Chris Graff, "Legislators Draw on Family in Civil-Union Debate," *Burlington Free Press* (Vt.), Apr. 23, 2000.
70 Klarman, *From the Closet to the Altar*, 79; Adam Lisberg, "Dean Signs Civil Unions into Law," *Burlington Free Press* (Vt.), Apr. 27, 2000.
71 Klarman, *From the Closet to the Altar*, 79.
72 Bonauto, "The Litigation," 73.
73 Eskridge and Riano, *Marriage Equality*, 212.
74 Bonauto, "The Litigation," 71.
75 Complaint, Goodridge v. Dep't of Pub. Health, No. 01-1647A, 2001 WL 35920963 (Mass. Super. Ct. Apr. 11, 2001).
76 Bonauto, "*Goodridge* in Context," 28; Godsoe, "Perfect Plaintiffs," 136–37.
77 Goodridge v. Dep't of Pub. Health, 798 N.E.2d 941, 959 (Mass. 2003).
78 Ibid.
79 Ibid., 961.
80 Ibid., 964.
81 Ibid., 962 n.24.

82 Ibid., 964.
83 *In re* Opinions of the Justices to the Senate, 802 N.E.2d 565, 569 (Mass. 2004).
84 Klarman, *From the Closet to the Altar*, 94.
85 Eskridge and Riano, *Marriage Equality*, 236.
86 Tovia Smith, "Lawyer Reflects on Nation's First Gay Marriages: 'The Cage Had Been Lifted,'" *NPR*, May 15, 2014.
87 Ibid.
88 Klarman, *From the Closet to the Altar*, 103.
89 Ibid., 96.
90 Pinello, *America's Struggle for Same-Sex Marriage*, 71; "Quotes of Note," *BG*, Sept. 17, 2005.
91 Klarman, *From the Closet to the Altar*, 92.
92 Ibid., 96.
93 Ibid.; Bonauto, "*Goodridge* in Context," 21.
94 One of the important changes during this period was the increased visibility of same-sex sexuality on television screens. Indeed, the same year that the Massachusetts high court issued its *Goodridge* opinion, Ellen DeGeneres, who had suffered professional backlash years earlier by coming out as a lesbian, began hosting her popular daytime talk show. Polls would later show that DeGeneres did more to influence Americans' attitudes concerning same-sex sexuality than any other public figure or celebrity. Brent Lang, "Ellen DeGeneres Influenced Gay Rights Views More Than Any Other Celebrity," *Variety*, June 30, 2015.
95 "San Franciscans Pick Newsom as Mayor," *WP*, Dec. 10, 2003.
96 Josh Harkinson, "Sweet Vindication for Gavin Newsom, Who Staked His Career on Same-Sex Marriage," *Mother Jones*, June 27, 2015; Melanie Mason, "When Gavin Newsom Issued Marriage Licenses in San Francisco, His Party Was Furious; Now It's a Campaign Ad," *LAT*, May 15, 2018.
97 Pinello, *America's Struggle for Same-Sex Marriage*, 73–74.
98 Ibid., 74.
99 Stone, *Gay Rights at the Ballot Box*, 34.
100 Pinello, *America's Struggle for Same-Sex Marriage*, 79.
101 Anne Hull, "Just Married, after 51 Years Together," *WP*, Feb. 29, 2004.
102 Ibid.
103 Ibid.
104 Ibid.
105 Pinello, *America's Struggle for Same-Sex Marriage*, 79.
106 Ibid.
107 Heather Knight, "The Flowering of Love," *San Francisco Gate*, Feb. 21, 2004.
108 Keck, "Beyond Backlash," 163–64.
109 Mezey, *Queers in Court*, 94–96; Lockyer v. City and County of San Francisco, 95 P.3d 459, 462 (Cal. 2004).
110 Camp, "Mobilizing the Base and Embarrassing the Opposition," 719.
111 Stone, *Gay Rights at the Ballot Box*, 133.
112 Ibid., 135.
113 Ibid., 65, 68–73.
114 ACLU, "Briefing Book: Anti-Gay Ballot Initiatives," Aug. 1993, Box 19, Folder 2, ACLU of Southern California Lesbian and Gay Rights Chapter Records, 6, 46, 56, 64–65, Appendix of EPOColorado Campaign Literature.
115 No on 9, advertisements, *Oregonian*, Nov. 1, 1992; No on 9, advertisements, *Oregonian*, Nov. 2, 1992.

116 Basic Rights Oregon, "Simple," 2004, www.adrespect.org/common/11064/view-page
.cfm?clientID=11064&CompanyID=31102; Basic Rights Oregon, "Surgery," 2004,
www.adrespect.org/common/adlibrary/ad-details.cfm?clientID=11064&QID=2797;
Basic Rights Oregon, "Worry," 2004, www.adrespect.org/common/11064/view-page
.cfm?clientID=11064&CompanyID=31102; No on Constitutional Amendment 36,
"Judge Tanzer," 2004, video no. 103256, Julian P. Kanter Political Commercial
Archive; Stone, *Gay Rights at the Ballot Box*, 133–34. As a legal matter, same-sex
couples could contract into many, but not all, of the benefits associated with marriage.
117 No on Constitutional Amendment 36, "Judge Tanzer."
118 No on Constitutional Amendment 36, "Goes Too Far," 2004, video no. 103255,
Julian P. Kanter Political Commercial Archive; No on Knight/No on Prop 22,
"Intend," video no. 81962, Julian P. Kanter Political Commercial Archive.
119 Equality Florida, "Vote NO on Amendment #2," 2008, www.youtube.com/user/
EqualityFlorida; Fair Wisconsin Committee, "Arlyn," 2006, video no. 107441,
Julian P. Kanter Political Commercial Archive.
120 Camp, "Mobilizing the Base and Embarrassing the Opposition," 719.
121 Ibid. Pundits also attributed George W. Bush's reelection to Ohio's marriage ballot
measure, claiming it drove conservative voters to the polls. Although political
scientists later disputed this claim, it further augmented LGBT rights advocates'
sense of loss. Fiorina, Abrams, and Pope, *Culture War*, 145–57; Smith, DeSantis,
and Kassel, "Same-Sex Marriage Ballot Measures and the 2004 Presidential
Election" 78–79, 87–88.
122 Klarman, *From the Closet to the Altar*, 113.
123 Michael Adams et al., "Winning Marriage: What We Need to Do," June 21, 2005,
3, author's possession.
124 Ibid., 2, 15.
125 GLAAD and Movement Advancement Project, "Talking to the Moveable Middle
about Marriage: Guidelines for Talking to the Moveable Middle about LGBT
Issues," 2008, author's possession.
126 Ibid., 7.
127 Ibid.
128 Ibid., 14.
129 Cal. Fam. Code § 297.1 (2001); Conn. Gen. Stat. § 46b-38rr (2009); Haw. Rev.
Stat. § 572-1.7 (1998); Lewis v. Harris, 908 A.2d 196 (N.J. 2006); 22 Me. Rev.
Stat. § 2710 (2003); N.J. Stat. § 37:1–30 (2006); Wash. Stat. § 26.60.100 (2012).
130 *In re* Marriage Cases, 183 P.3d 384 (Cal. 2008); Kerrigan v. Comm'r of Pub.
Health, 957 A.2d 407 (Conn. 2008).
131 Keck, "Beyond Backlash," 165–67, 169–70.
132 George, "Framing Trans Rights," 562.
133 In re *Marriage Cases*, 183 P.3d at 422.
134 Ibid., 451.
135 Ibid. (quoting Hernandez v. Robles, 855 N.E.2d 1, 30 (N.Y. 2006) (Kaye,
C.J., dissenting)).
136 Ibid., 452.
137 "Secretary of State Debra Bowen Certifies Eight Measure for Nov. 4, 2008, General
Election," California Secretary of State, June 2, 2008, https://admin.cdn.sos.ca.gov/
press-releases/2008/DB08–068.pdf.
138 Gary J. Gates and Christopher Ramos, "Census Snapshot: California Lesbian, Gay,
and Bisexual Population," Williams Institute, 2008; Stone, *Gay Rights at the Ballot
Box*, 138. Proposition 8 was not the first time California citizens had been asked to
vote on same-sex marriage. In 2000, 61 percent of California voters had approved a

statutory ballot measure reserving marriage to different-sex couples. However, the California Supreme Court struck down the statute in the spring of 2008. In re *Marriage Cases*, 183 P.3d at 453; Perry v. Schwarzenegger, 704 F. Supp. 2d 921, 928 (N.D. Cal. 2010).

139 Klarman, *From the Closet to the Altar*, 122.
140 "More Than $83 Million Spent on Prop 8," *NBC News*, Feb. 2, 2009, www .nbcnews.com/id/wbna28985504.
141 Initiative and Referendum Institute, "Same-Sex Marriage: Will Voters Break the Firewall?," *Ballotwatch*, Sept. 2012.
142 California, Proposition 22 (Nov. 8, 2000).
143 Lewis and Gossett, "Why Did Californians Pass Proposition 8?," 4.
144 Frank Schubert and Jeff Flint, "Passing Prop 8," *Politics*, Feb. 2009, 45.
145 Yes on 8, "It's Already Happened," 2008, www.youtube.com/watch?v= oPgjcgqFYP4.
146 Ibid.; Home page, Pepperdine Caruso School of Law, accessed Aug. 16, 2023, https://law.pepperdine.edu/.
147 Yes on 8, "It's Already Happened."
148 Ibid.
149 Yes on 8, "Everything to Do with Schools," 2008, www.youtube.com/watch?v= 7352ZVMKBQM.
150 Perry v. Schwarzenegger, 704 F. Supp. 2d 921, 988 (N.D. Cal. 2010).
151 Ibid.
152 Ball, *Same-Sex Marriage and Children*, 112; David Fleischer, *The Prop 8 Report: What Defeat in California Can Teach Us about Winning Future Ballot Measures on Same-Sex Marriage* (Los Angeles: LGBT Mentoring Project, 2010), 32–35.
153 Ben Ehrenreich, "Anatomy of a Failed Campaign," *Advocate*, Nov. 19, 2008.
154 Eskridge and Riano, *Marriage Equality*, 278–79.
155 Klarman, *From the Closet to the Altar*, 122.
156 No on Prop 8, "History," 2008, video no. 130109, Julian P. Kanter Political Commercial Archive.
157 No on Prop 8, "Why Society Is Dumb," 2008, video no. 108930, Julian P. Kanter Political Commercial Archive.
158 Initiative and Referendum Institute, "Same-Sex Marriage: Will Voters Break the Firewall?"
159 Klarman, *From the Closet to the Altar*, 124.
160 Molly Ball, "The Marriage Plot: Inside This Year's Epic Campaign for Gay Equality," *Atlantic*, Dec. 11, 2012.
161 Let California Ring, "Garden Wedding," 2007, www.youtube.com/watch?v= GG7ddWLF_Fk.
162 Ball, "The Marriage Plot."
163 California Secretary of State, "Statement of Vote," 2008, 60–62, https:// elections.cdn.sos.ca.gov/sov/2008-general/sov_complete.pdf; "Gay Marriage Ban: A Tale of Two Votes," *LAT*, Sept. 16, 2014; "Proposition 8," Howard University Law Library, 2018, https://library.law.howard.edu/civilrightshis tory/lgbtq/prop8.
164 McGirr, *Suburban Warriors*, 4–5.
165 "Freedom to Marry – The Early Years," Freedom to Marry, www.freedomtomarry .org/pages/Freedom-to-Marry-The-Early-Years.
166 Thalia Zepatos, "The Marriage Movement's Secret Weapon: Radical Cooperation," *Huffington Post*, June 26, 2015, www.huffpost.com/entry/the-mar riage-movements-se_b_7665696.

167 Freedom to Marry, "Alabama: All Families Deserve Respect," 2015, www .freedomtomarry.org/video/category/tv-ads#category.
168 Freedom to Marry, "Utah Family Supports Marriage for Gay Couples," 2014, www.freedomtomarry.org/video/category/tv-ads#category.
169 Freedom to Marry, "Messaging, Messengers, and Public Support," www .freedomtomarry.org/pages/Messaging-Messengers-and-Public-Support.
170 Freedom to Marry, "Chris Morningstar for Washington United for Marriage," 2012, www.freedomtomarry.org/video/category/tv-ads#category.
171 Barth and Parry, "2>1+1?," 45–46; Herek and Capitanio, "'Some of My Best Friends," 420–22; Lewis, "The Friends and Family Plan," 228, 231–35.
172 Klarman, *From the Closet to the Altar*, 73.
173 Newport, "For the First Time, Majority of Americans Favor Legal Gay Marriage."
174 Jessica Yellin, "Biden Says He Is 'Absolutely Comfortable' with Same-Sex Marriage," CNN.com, May 6, 2012, http://politicalticker.blogs.cnn.com/2012/ 05/06/biden-says-he-is-absolutely-comfortable-with-same-sex-marriage/.
175 Ball, "The Marriage Plot."
176 Judy Harrison, "Mainers Approve Gay Marriage Referendum," *Bangor Daily News* (Me.), Nov. 6, 2012.
177 Equality Maine, "Clear," 2009, www.youtube.com/watch?v=vPS-fMXogsg; Equality Maine, "Stand," 2009, www.youtube.com/watch?v=ID8qo2opSiU; Equality Maine, "Together," 2009, www.youtube.com/watch?v=74kiByvu8R4.
178 Mainers United for Marriage, "Cathy and Phil Curtis," 2012, www.youtube.com/ watch?v=TL48VDCsG-4; Mainers United for Marriage, "Gardner Family of Machias," 2012, www.youtube.com/watch?v=2dTdP-XLZzk; Mainers United for Marriage, "Pat and Dan Lawson of Monroe," 2012, www.youtube.com/watch?v= FdUCLgjxanQ; Mainers United for Marriage, "Will and Arlene Brewster," 2012, www.youtube.com/watch?v=rizfhtN6UVc.
179 Mainers United for Marriage, "Cathy and Phil Curtis."
180 Mainers United for Marriage, "Will and Arlene Brewster."
181 Sunnivie Brydum, "Win Claimed in Washington: Voters Affirm Marriage Equality," *Advocate*, Nov. 7, 2012; Hunter, "Varieties of Constitutional Experience," 1697.
182 United States v. Windsor, 570 U.S. 744, 764 (2013).
183 Affidavit of Edith Schlain Windsor, Windsor v. United States., 10 Civ. 8435 (S.D.N.Y. June 23, 2011), author's possession; Robert D. McFadden, "Edith Windsor, Whose Same-Sex Marriage Fight Led to Landmark Ruling, Dies at 88," *NYT*, Sept. 12, 2009.
184 Ariel Levy, "The Perfect Wife: How Edith Windsor Fell in Love, Got Married, and Won a Landmark Case for Gay Marriage," *New Yorker*, Sept. 30, 2012.
185 *Windsor*, 570 U.S. at 750–52.
186 Ibid., 774, 77.
187 Ibid., 771–72.
188 Windsor had "desperately" wanted to be a parent, but she had met Spyer, a psychologist, at the time when mental health professionals believed that homosexuality was an illness. In light of the potential impact of their sexual orientation on a child – which at the time was unknown – the women agreed to forgo parenthood. Levy, "The Perfect Wife."
189 Andersen v. King County, 138 P.3d 963, 982–83 (Wash. 2006); Baskin v. Bogan, 766 F.3d 648 (7th Cir. 2014); Bishop v. Smith, 760 F.3d 1070, 1080–81 (10th Cir. 2014); Bostic v. Schaefer, 760 F.3d 352, 381, 383 (4th Cir. 2014); Citizens for Equal Protection v. Bruning, 455 F.3d 859, 867 (8th Cir. 2006); Conaway

v. Deane, 932 A.2d 571, 630 (Md. 2007); DeBoer v. Snyder, 772 F.3d 388, 404–05 (6th Cir. 2014); Griego v. Oliver, 316 P.3d 865, 877 (N.M. 2013); Hernandez v. Robles, 855 N.E.2d 1, 7 (N.Y. 2006); *In re* Alabama Policy Institute, 200 So.3d 495, 546 (Ala. 2015); *In re* Marriage Cases, 183 P.3d 384, 431–33 (Cal. 2008); Kitchen v. Herbert, 755 F.3d 1193, 1219 (10th Cir. 2014); Latta v. Otter, 771 F.3d 456, 468–69 (9th Cir. 2014); Perry v. Brown, 671 F.3d 1052, 1086 (9th Cir. 2012); Varnum v. Brien, 763 N.W.2d 862, 873 (Iowa 2009).

190 *Baskin*, 766 F.3d at 654.

191 *Bostic*, 760 F.3d at 383; "APA Amicus Briefs by Issue," American Psychological Association, www.apa.org/about/offices/ogc/amicus/index-issues.

192 Baehr v. Miike, CIV No. 91-1394, 1996 WL 694235, at *10–16 (Haw. Cir. Ct. Dec. 3, 1996); DeBoer v. Snyder, 973 F. Supp. 2d 757, 761–63 (E.D. Mich. 2014); Perry v. Schwarzenegger, 704 F. Supp. 2d 921, 935 (N.D. Cal. 2010); Varnum v. Brien, No. CV5965, 2007 WL 2468667 (Iowa Dist. Ct. Aug. 30, 2007).

193 *DeBoer*, 973 F.Supp.2d at 761.

194 *Griego*, 316 P.3d 865; In re *Marriage Cases*, 183 P.3d 384; Kerrigan v. Comm'n of Pub. Health, 957 A.2d 407 (Conn. 2008); Lewis v. Harris, 908 A.2d 196 (N.J. 2006); *Perry*, 671 F.3d 1052; *Varnum*, 763 N.W.2d 862. They had also lost several cases. Andersen v. King Co., 138 P.3d 963 (Wash. 2006) (en banc); *Bruning*, 455 F.3d 859; *Conaway*, 932 A.2d 571; *Hernandez*, 855 N.Ed. 2d 1.

195 Eskridge and Riano, *Marriage Equality*, 555.

196 Ibid., 555–56; Sofia Resnick, "New Family Structures Study Intended to Sway Supreme Court on Gay Marriage, Documents Show," *Huffington Post*, Mar. 10, 2013, www.huffpost.com/entry/supreme-court-gay-marriage_n_2850302.6.

197 Mark Regnerus, "How Different Are the Adult Children of Parents Who Have Same-Sex Relationships? Findings from the New Family Structures Study," *Social Science Research* 41, no. 6 (2012): 752–70.

198 Gary J. Gates et al., "Letter to the Editors and Advisory Editors of *Social Science Research*," *Social Science Research* 41, no. 6 (2012): 1350.

199 DeBoer v. Snyder, 973 F. Supp. 2d 757, 766 (E.D. Mich. 2014).

200 The one exception was Bostic v. Schaefer, 760 F.3d 352, 383 (4th Cir. 2014).

201 Baskin v. Bogan, 766 F.3d 648, 659–60, 671–72 (7th Cir. 2014); *Bostic*, 760 F.3d at 374, 378–79, 383; Kitchen v. Herbert, 755 F.3d 1193, 1207–08, 1213–14 (10th Cir. 2014); Latta v. Otter, 771 F.3d 456, 465–66, 472–73 (9th Cir. 2014). For the states recognizing same-sex marriage between *Windsor* and *Obergefell*, see Eskridge and Riano, *Marriage Equality*, Appendix 1.

202 *DeBoer*, 973 F.Supp.2d 388; *In re* Alabama Policy Institute, 200 So.3d 495 (Ala. 2015).

203 Eskridge and Riano, *Marriage Equality*, Appendix 1.

204 Obergefell v. Hodges, 576 U.S. 644, 667–69 (2015).

205 Ibid., 658.

206 Godsoe, "Perfect Plaintiffs," 137–38.

207 Ibid., 678.

208 Brief for Gary J. Gates as Amicus Curiae in Support of Petitioners, *Obergefell v. Hodges*, 2015 WL 1021451, at *4 (U.S. Mar. 6, 2015).

209 *Obergefell*, 576 U.S. at 668.

210 Ibid., 681.

211 Avianne Tan, "Celebrations Break Out after Same-Sex Marriage Legalized Nationwide," *ABC News*, June 26, 2015.

212 Alex Dickinson, "Here's How America Celebrated the Supreme Court Gay Marriage Decision," *Bloomberg News*, June 26, 2015.

213 Jordan Fabian, "White House Lights Up Rainbow Colors to Celebrate SCOTUS Ruling," *The Hill*, June 26, 2015.

214 Juliet Eilperin, "For Obama, Rainbow White House was 'A Moment Worth Savoring,'" *WP*, June 30, 2015.

215 "US Landmarks Light Up in Rainbows over Gay Marriage Ruling," *Guardian*, June 26, 2015; "A Surprising Number of National Buildings Turned Rainbow Last Night," *ATTN:*, June 27, 2015, www.attn.com/stories/2176/cities-and-monu ments-lit-marriage-equality.

216 Godsoe, "Perfect Plaintiffs," 138.

217 Levy, "The Perfect Wife."

218 Godsoe, "Perfect Plaintiffs," 139.

219 Issenberg, *The Engagement*, 745.

220 Mary Kaye Ritz, "Canadian Wedding Bells Ring for Island Gay Couples," *Honolulu Advertiser*, Aug. 3, 2003.

221 Chad Graham, "Life after Gay Marriage," *Advocate*, Mar. 2, 2004.

222 "Obituaries: William Everett Woods," *Honolulu Advertiser*, Sept. 30, 2008.

223 "William Woods Obituary," *Decatur Herald & Review* (Ill.), Nov. 9, 2008.

Epilogue

1 Frank, *Awakening*, 357.

2 Ibid., 93–94, 357–58.

3 Ibid., 358.

4 U.S. Census Bureau, "U.S. Census Bureau Releases CPS Estimates of Same-Sex Households," Nov. 19, 2019, www.census.gov/newsroom/press-releases/2019/ same-sex-households.html.

5 Some critics of the marriage equality movement persisted in their criticisms. Adler, *Gay Priori*, 86–89; Franke, *Wedlocked*, 9–10.

6 George, "Expanding LGBT," 262–63; George, "Framing Trans Rights," 559–60.

7 George, "Expanding LGBT," 273–79, 286–95, 301–09.

8 David A. Fahrenthold, Kevin Sullivan, and Niraj Chokshi, "Opponents Divided on How – or Whether – to Resist Justices' Ruling," *WP*, June 26, 2015; Heyman, "A Struggle for Recognition," 6–10.

9 Heyman, "A Struggle for Recognition," 9–10.

10 Masterpiece Cakeshop, Ltd. v. Colo. Civil Rts. Comm'n, 138 S. Ct. 1719, 1721 (2018).

11 Dobbs v. Jackson Women's Health Organization, 142 S. Ct. 2228, 2301 (2022) (Thomas, J., concurring); Girgis, "Nervous Victors, Illiberal Measures," 407; NeJaime and Siegel, "Religious Accommodation, and Its Limits, in a Pluralist Society," 73.

12 Ibid., 2309.

13 Solcyre Burga, "The Implications of Supreme Court's 303 Creative Decision Are Already Being Felt," *Time*, Jul. 16, 2023; Jodi Miesen and Jacob Johnson, "Traverse City Hair Salon No Longer Servicing Certain LGBTQ Members," *9&10 News* (Northern Mich.), Jul. 10, 2023, www.9and10news .com/2023/07/11/traverse-city-hair-salon-no-longer-servicing-lgbtq-members/ #google_vignette.

14 George, "Framing Trans Rights," 584–91; George, "The LGBT Disconnect," 514–15.

15 George, "Framing Trans Rights," 556–58.

16 Annette Choi, "Record Number of Anti-LGBTQ Bills Have Been Introduced this Year," *CNN*, Apr. 6, 2023, www.cnn.com/2023/04/06/politics/anti-lgbtq-plus-state-bill-rights-dg/index.html; Marie-Amélie George, "'Don't Say Gay' Laws Harm Students Already at Risk," *AJC*, Feb. 13, 2023.

17 Maggie Astor, "G.O.P. State Lawmakers Push a Growing Wave of Anti-Transgender Bills," *NYT*, Jan. 25, 2023.

18 "For the First Time Ever, Human Rights Campaign Official Declares 'State of Emergency' for LGBTQ+ Americans," HRC, June 6, 2023, www.hrc.org/press-releases/for-the-first-time-ever-human-rights-campaign-officially-declares-state-of-emergency-for-lgbtq-americans-issues-national-warning-and-guidebook-to-ensure-safety-for-lgbtq-residents-and-travelers.

19 Hunter, "Varieties of Constitutional Experience," 1683.

20 Transcript of Oral Argument at 109, United States v. Windsor, No. 12-307 (U.S. Mar. 26, 2013).

21 Case, "Missing Sex Talk in the Supreme Court's Same-Sex Marriage Cases," 678–84; Franke, "The Politics of Same-Sex Marriage Politics," 239–40; Franke, "The Domesticated Liberty of *Lawrence v. Texas*," 1416.

22 Tom Brougham, interview by author, Oct. 27, 2022.

23 Act of May 12, 1975, ch. 71, 1975 Cal. Laws 131 (effective Jan. 1, 1976).

24 Brougham, interview by author.

Bibliography

Archival Collections

Bancroft Library, University of California, Berkeley, Berkeley, Calif.
    Cathy Cade Photograph Archive
Biddle Law Library, University of Pennsylvania, Philadelphia, Pa.
    American Law Institute MPC Records
Carl A. Kroch Library, Cornell University, Ithaca, NY
    Empire State Pride Agenda Papers
    Paula L. Ettelbrick Papers
    GLAAD Records
    HRC Records
    NGLTF Records
    PFLAG Records
    Wendell Ricketts Papers
Charles E. Young Research Library, University of California at Los
  Angeles, Los Angeles, Calif.
    Evelyn C. Hooker Papers
Denver Public Library, Denver, Colo.
    Equality Colorado Records
GLBT Historical Society, San Francisco, Calif.
    CUAV Records
    Phyllis Lyon and Del Martin Papers
    San Francisco Street Patrol Records Collection
    Ronald H. Schmidt Papers
The History Project, Boston, Mass.
    GLDC Collection

Julian P. Kanter Political Commercial Archive, University of
Oklahoma, Norman, Okla.
Kinsey Institute Library, Indiana University Bloomington, Bloomington, Ind.
    Alfred C. Kinsey Correspondence Collection
LGBT Community Center, New York, NY
    LGTANY Collection
Library of Congress, Washington, D.C.
    Frank Kameny Papers
Manuscripts and Archives, Yale University, New Haven, Conn.
    GLAD Records
Minnesota Historical Society, St. Paul, Minn.
    Brian J. Coyle Papers
    Tom Higgins Papers
    Minnesota GLBT Movement Papers
    Senate Judiciary Committee Papers
New Hampshire State Archives, Concord, NH
    Senate and House of Representatives Legislative Files
New York City Municipal Archives, New York, NY
    Jan Carl Park Files
ONE National Gay and Lesbian Archives, Los Angeles, Calif.
    ACLU of Southern California Gay and Lesbian Rights
        Chapter Records
    Betty Berzon Papers
    Thomas F. Coleman and Jay M. Kohorn Papers
    Charles W. Gossett Papers
    Newsletter Collection
    Project 10 Collection
    Same-Sex Marriage Collection
    Starr (Adele) Collection on PFLAG
    Subject Files
Seattle City Archives, Seattle, Wash.
    Gay and Lesbian Task Force Records
    Published Documents Collection
San Francisco Public Library, San Francisco, Calif.
    Jerry (Jerome Joel) Davis Papers
    GLAAD/San Francisco Bay Area Clippings
    Jessea Greenman P.E.R.S.O.N. Project Records
    San Francisco Voter Information Pamphlets and Ballots
Seeley G. Mudd Manuscript Library, Princeton University, Princeton, NJ
    ACLU Records
Sydney Lewis Hall, Washington and Lee School of Law, Lexington, Va.
    Lewis F. Powell, Jr. Archives
Wisconsin Historical Society Archives, Madison, Wis.
    William Proxmire Papers

Selected Secondary Sources

Alsott, Anne L. "Neoliberalism in U.S. Family Law." *Law and Contemporary Problems* 77, no. 4 (2014): 25–42.

Adler, Libby. *Gay Priori: A Queer Critical Legal Studies Approach to Law Reform*. Durham, NC: Duke University Press, 2018.

Allyn, David. "Private Acts/Public Policy: Alfred Kinsey, the American Law Institute and the Privatization of American Sexual Morality." *Journal of American Studies* 30, no. 3 (1996): 405–28.

Alwood, Edward. *Straight News: Gays, Lesbians, and the News Media*. New York: Columbia University Press, 1996.

Armstrong, Kelli K. "The Silent Minority within a Minority: Focusing on the Needs of Gay Youth in Our Public Schools." *Golden Gate University Law Review* no. 24 (1994): 67–97.

Baker, Daniel B., Sean O'Brien Straub, and Bill Henning. *Cracking the Corporate Closet*. New York: HarperBusiness, 1995.

Ball, Carlos A. *From the Closet to the Courtroom: Five LGBT Rights Lawsuits That Have Changed Our Nation*. Boston: Beacon Press, 2010.

  The Right to Be Parents: LGBT Families and the Transformation of Parenthood. New York University Press, 2012.

  Same Sex Marriage and Children: A Tale of History, Social Science, and Law. New York: Oxford University Press, 2014.

Barth, Jay and Janine Parry. "2 > 1 + 1?: The Impact of Contact with Gay and Lesbian *Couples* on Attitudes about Gays/Lesbians and Gay-Related Policies." *Politics and Policy* 37, no. 1 (2009): 31–50.

Barton, Bernadette. *Pray the Gay Away: The Extraordinary Lives of Bible Belt Gays*. New York University Press, 2012.

Bayer, Ronald. *Homosexuality and American Psychiatry: The Politics of Diagnosis*. 2nd ed. Princeton University Press, 1987.

Bayley, David. *Police for the Future*. Oxford University Press, 1996.

Bell, Derrick A. Jr., "*Brown v. Board of Education* and the Interest-Convergence Dilemma," *Harvard Law Review* 93, no. 3 (1980): 518–33.

Bernstein, Mary. "Nothing Ventured, Nothing Gained? Conceptualizing Social Movement 'Success' in the Lesbian and Gay Movement." *Sociological Perspectives* 46, no. 3 (2003): 353–79.

Bernstein, Mary and Verta Taylor eds. *The Marrying Kind?: Debating Same-Sex Marriage within the Lesbian and Gay Movement*. Minneapolis: University of Minnesota Press, 2013.

Bérubé, Allan. *Coming Out under Fire: The History of Gay Men and Women in World War II*, 20th anniversary ed. Chapel Hill: University of North Carolina Press, 2010.

Biggers, Daniel R. *Morality at the Ballot Box: Direct Democracy and Political Engagement in the United States*. New York: Cambridge University Press, 2014.

Bonauto, Mary L. "Equality and the Impossible: State Constitutions and Marriage." *Rutgers University Law Review* no. 68 (2017): 1481–533.

"*Goodridge* in Context." *Harvard Civil Rights-Civil Liberties Law Review* 40 (2005): 1–69.

"The Litigation: First Judicial Victories in Vermont, Massachusetts, and Connecticut." In *Love Unites Us: Winning the Freedom to Marry in America*, ed. Kevin M. Cathcart and Leslie J. Gabel-Brett, 50–72. New York: The New Press, 2016.

Bonauto, Mary L., Susan M. Murray, and Beth Robinson. "The Freedom to Marry for Same-Sex Couples: The Opening Appellate Brief of Plaintiffs Stan Baker et al. in *Baker et al. v. State of Vermont*." *Michigan Journal of Gender and Law*, no. 5 (1999): 409–75.

Boucai, Michael. "Glorious Precedents: When Gay Marriage Was Radical." *Yale Journal of Law & Humanities* 27 (2015): 1–82.

Boutcher, Steven A., "Mobilizing in the Shadow of the Law: Lesbian and Gay Rights in the Aftermath of *Bowers v. Hardwick*." *Research in Social Movements, Conflict, and Change* 31 (2011): 175–205.

Boyd, Nan Alamilla. *Wide-Open Town: A History of Queer San Francisco to 1965*. Berkeley: University of California Press, 2003.

Brakel, Samuel Jan and James L. Cavanaugh, Jr. "Of Psychopaths and Pendulums: Legal and Psychiatric Treatment of Sex Offenders in the United States." *New Mexico Law Review* 30, no. 1 (January 2000): 69–94.

Brantley, Allyson P. *Brewing a Boycott: How a Grassroots Coalition Fought Coors and Remade American Consumer Activism*. Chapel Hill: University of North Carolina Press, 2021.

Brier, Jennifer. *Infectious Ideas: U.S. Political Responses to the AIDS Crisis*. Chapel Hill: University of North Carolina Press, 2009.

Briggs, Laura. *Somebody's Children: The Politics of Transracial and Transnational Adoption*. Durham, NC: Duke University Press, 2012.

Broad, K.L. "Coming Out for Parents, Families and Friends of Lesbians and Gays: From Support Group Grieving to Love Advocacy." *Sexualities* 14, no. 4 (2011): 399–415.

"Social Movement Selves." *Sociological Perspectives* 45, no. 3 (2002): 317–36.

Brown-Nagin, Tomiko. *Courage to Dissent Atlanta and the Long History of the Civil Rights Movement*. New York: Oxford University Press, 2011.

Bullough, Vern L. et al., ed. *Before Stonewall: Activists for Gay and Lesbian Rights in Historical Context*. Hoboken: Taylor and Francis, 2014.

Cahn, Naomi and June Carbone, "Custody and Visitation in Families with Three (Or More) Parents." *Family Court Review* 56, no. 3 (2018): 399–409.

Cain, Patricia A. "Litigating for Lesbian and Gay Rights: A Legal History." *Virginia Law Review* 79, no. 7 (1993): 1551–641.

Rainbow Rights: The Role of Lawyers and Courts in the Lesbian and Gay Civil Rights Movement. Boulder: Westview Press, 2000.

Camp, Bayliss J. "Mobilizing the Base and Embarrassing the Opposition: Defense of Marriage Referenda and Cross-Cutting Electoral Cleavages." *Sociological Perspectives* 51, no. 4 (2008): 713–33.

Canaday, Margot. *Queer Career: Sexuality and Work in Modern America*. Princeton University Press, 2023.

The Straight State: Sexuality and Citizenship in Twentieth-Century America. Princeton University Press, 2009.

Carbone, June and Naomi R. Cahn. *Marriage Markets: How Inequality Is Remaking the American Family*. New York: Oxford University Press, 2014.

Carpenter, Daniel P. *The Forging of Bureaucratic Autonomy: Reputations, Networks, and Policy Innovation in Executive Agencies, 1862–1928*. Princeton University Press, 2001.

Case, Mary Anne. "Missing Sex Talk in the Supreme Court's Same-Sex Marriage Cases." *University of Kansas City Law Review* 84, no. 3 (2016): 675–92.

Cervini, Eric. *The Deviant's War: The Homosexual vs. The United States of America*. New York: Farrar, Straus and Giroux, 2020.

Chambers, David L. "Tales of Two Cities: AIDS and the Legal Recognition of Domestic Partnerships in San Francisco and New York." *Law and Sexuality* 2 (1992): 181–208.

Charles, Casey. *The Sharon Kowalski Case: Lesbian and Gay Rights on Trial*. Lawrence: University Press of Kansas, 2003.

Chauncey, George. *Gay New York: Gender, Urban Culture, and the Making of the Gay Male World, 1890–1940*. New York: Basic Books, 1993.

"The Postwar Sex Crime Panic." In *True Stories from the American Past*, ed. William Graebner, 160–78. New York: McGraw-Hill, 1993.

Why Marriage?: The History Shaping Today's Debate over Gay Equality, New York: Basic Books, 2009.

Clarke, Jessica A. "Against Immutability." *Yale Law Journal* 125 (2015): 2–102.

Clendinen, Dudley and Adam Nagourney. *Out for Good: The Struggle to Build a Gay Rights Movement in America*. New York: Touchstone, 1999.

Coles, Matthew. *Try This at Home! A Do-It-Yourself Guide to Winning Lesbian and Gay Civil Rights Policy*. New York: The New Press, 1996.

Comstock, Gary David. *Violence against Lesbians and Gay Men*. New York: Columbia University Press, 1991.

Connell, Catherine. *School's Out: Gay and Lesbian Teachers in the Classroom*. Oakland: University of California Press, 2015.

Coolidge, David Orgon. "The Hawai'i Marriage Amendment: Its Origins, Meaning and Fate." *University of Hawaii Law Review* 22, no. 1 (2000): 20–118.

Cott, Nancy F. *Public Vows: A History of Marriage and the Nation.*
Cambridge, Mass.: Harvard University Press, 2002.

Cox, Barbara. "Same-Sex Marriage and Choice of Law: If We Marry in
Hawaii, Are We Still Married When We Get Home?" *Wisconsin Law
Review* (1994): 1033–118.

Cummings, Scott L. "The Social Movement Turn in Law." *Law and Social
Inquiry* 43, no. 2 (2018): 360–416.

Davis, John M. and Johnathan Sandoval. *Suicidal Youth: School-Based
Intervention and Prevention.* San Francisco: Jossey-Bass, 1991.

D'Emilio, John. *Sexual Politics, Sexual Communities: The Making of a
Homosexual Minority in the United States, 1940–1970.* 2nd ed.
University of Chicago Press, 1998.

D'Emilio, John, William B. Turner, and Urvashi Vaid, eds. *Creating Change:
Sexuality, Public Policy, and Civil Rights.* New York: St. Martin's Press,
2000.

Denno, Deborah W. "Life before the Modern Sex Offender Statutes."
Northwestern University Law Review 92, no. 4 (1997–1998): 1317–413.

DiFonzo, Herbie J. and Ruth C. Stern. "The Winding Road from Form to
Function: A Brief History of Contemporary Marriage." *Journal of the
American Academy of Matrimonial Lawyers* 21 (2008): 1–41.

Dinner, Deborah. "The Divorce Bargain: The Fathers' Rights Movement and
Family Inequalities." *Virginia Law Review* 102, no. 1 (March 2016):
79–152.

Dochuk, Darren. *From Bible Belt to Sun Belt: Plain-Folk Religion, Grassroots
Politics, and the Rise of Evangelical Conservatism.* New York: W.W.
Norton & Co., 2011.

Dodge, Kirstin S. "Bashing Back: Gay and Lesbian Street Patrols and the
Criminal Justice System." *Law and Inequality: A Journal of Theory and
Practice* 11, no. 2 (June 1993): 295–368.

Dowland, Seth. *Family Values and the Rise of the Christian Right.*
Philadelphia: University of Pennsylvania Press, 2015.

Drescher, Jack. "I'm Your Handyman: A History of Reparative Therapies."
Journal of Homosexuality 36, no. 1 (1998): 19–42.

Drescher, Jack and Joseph P. Merlino, eds. *American Psychiatry and
Homosexuality: An Oral History* (New York: Harrington Park Press,
2007).

Duberman, Martin. *Stonewall.* New York: Penguin Books, 1993.

Edwards, Laura F. *Gendered Strife and Confusion: The Political Culture of
Reconstruction.* Urbana: University of Illinois Press, 1997.

Enszer, Julie R. "'How to Stop Choking to Death': Rethinking Lesbian
Separatism as a Vibrant Political Theory and Feminist Practice." *Journal
of Lesbian Studies* 20, no. 2 (2016): 180–96.

Epstein, Steven. *Impure Science: AIDS, Activism, and the Politics of
Knowledge.* Los Angeles: University of California Press, 1996.

Erzen, Tanya. *Straight to Jesus: Sexual and Christian Conversions in the Ex-Gay Movement*. Berkeley: University of California Press, 2006.

Eskridge, William N., Jr. *Dishonorable Passions: Sodomy Laws in America, 1861–2003*. New York: Viking, 2008.

    Gaylaw: Challenging the Apartheid of the Closet. Cambridge, Mass.: Harvard University Press, 1999.

    "No Promo Homo: The Sedimentation of Antigay Discourse and the Channeling Effect of Judicial Review." *New York University Law Review* 75, no. 5 (2000): 1328–411.

Eskridge, William N., Jr., and Christopher R. Riano. *Marriage Equality: From Outlaws to In-Laws*. New Haven: Yale University Press, 2020.

Fejes, Fred. *Gay Rights and Moral Panic: The Origins of America's Debate on Homosexuality*. New York: Palgrave Macmillan, 2008.

Fields, Jessica. "Normal Queers: Straight Parents Respond to Their Children's 'Coming Out.'" *Symbolic Interaction* 24, no. 2 (2001): 165–67.

Fiorina, Morris P., Samuel J. Abrams, and Jeremy C. Pope. *Culture War?: The Myth of a Polarized America*. 3d ed. New York: Longman, 2010.

Fineman, Martha. "Dominant Discourse, Professional Language, and Legal Change in Child Custody Decisionmaking." *Harvard Law Review* 101, no. 4 (1988): 727–74.

    The Illusion of Equality: The Rhetoric and Reality of Divorce Reform. University of Chicago Press, 1991.

Fischer, Claude S. and Michael Hout. *Century of Difference: How America Changed in the Last One Hundred Years*. New York: Russell Sage Foundation, 2006.

Frank, Gillian. "'The Civil Rights of Parents': Race and Conservative Politics in Anita Bryant's Campaign against Gay Rights in 1970s Florida." *Journal of the History of Sexuality* 22, no. 1 (January 2013): 126–60.

Frank, Nathaniel. *Awakening: How Gays and Lesbians Brought Marriage Equality to America*. Cambridge, Mass.: Belknap Press, 2017.

Franke, Katherine M. "The Domesticated Liberty of *Lawrence* v. *Texas*." *Columbia Law Review* 104 (2004): 1399–426.

    "The Politics of Same-Sex Marriage Politics." *Columbia Journal of Gender and Law* 15, no. 1 (2006): 236–48.

    Wedlocked: The Perils of Marriage Equality. New York University Press, 2015.

Freedman, Estelle B. "Uncontrolled Desires: The Response to the Sexual Psychopath, 1920–1960." *Journal of American History* 74, no. 1 (1987): 83–106.

Gallagher, John and Chris Bull. *Perfect Enemies: The Religious Right, the Gay Movement, and the Politics of the 1990s*. New York: Crown, 1996.

Galliher, John F. and Cheryl Tyree. "Edwin Sutherland's Research on the Origins of Sexual Psychopath Laws: An Early Case Study of the Medicalization of Deviance." *Social Problems* 33, no. 2 (1985): 100–13.

Gamble, Barbara S. "Putting Civil Rights to Popular Vote." *American Journal of Political Science* 41, no. 1 (1997): 245–69.

Garretson, Jeremiah and Elizabeth Suhay. "Scientific Communication about Biological Influences on Homosexuality and the Politics of Gay Rights." *Political Research Quarterly* 69, no. 1 (2016): 17–29.

Gash, Alison L. *Below the Radar: How Silence Can Save Civil Rights*. New York: Oxford University Press, 2015.

George, Marie-Amélie. "Agency Nullification: Defying Bans on Gay and Lesbian Foster and Adoptive Parents." *Harvard Civil Rights-Civil Liberties Law Review* 51 (2016): 363–422.

"Bureaucratic Agency: Administering the Transformation of LGBT Rights." *Yale Law and Policy Review* 36, no. 1 (2017): 83–154.

"The Custody Crucible: The Development of Scientific Authority about Gay and Lesbian Parents." *Law and History Review* 34, no. 2 (2016): 487–529.

"Expanding LGBT." *Florida Law Review* 73, no. 2 (2021): 243–319.

"Expressive Ends: Understanding Conversion Therapy Bans." *Alabama Law Review* 68, no. 3 (2017): 793–853.

"Framing Trans Rights." *Northwestern University Law Review* 114, no. 3 (2019): 555–632.

"The Harmless Psychopath: Legal Debates Promoting the Decriminalization of Sodomy in the United States." *Journal of the History of Sexuality* 24, no. 2 (2015): 225–61.

"The LGBT Disconnect: Politics and Perils of Legal Movement Formation." *Wisconsin Law Review* 2018 (2018): 504–91.

"Regulating Same-Sex Sexuality in Twentieth Century America." In *The Cambridge History of Sexuality in the United States*, ed. Jen Manion and Nick Syrett. New York: Cambridge University Press, forthcoming.

Gilmore, Stephanie. *Groundswell: Grassroots Feminist Activism in Postwar America*. New York: Routledge, 2013.

Gilmore, Stephanie and Elizabeth Kaminski. "A Part and Apart: Lesbian and Straight Feminist Activists Negotiate Identity in a Second-Wave Organization." *Journal of the History of Sexuality* 16, no. 1 (2007): 95–113.

Girgis, Sherif. "Nervous Victors, Illiberal Measures: A Response to Douglas NeJaime and Reva Siegel." *Yale Law Journal Forum* 125 (2015–2016): 399–415.

Gitlin, H. Joseph. "Sexual Morality and the Children of Divorce." *Illinois Bar Journal* 92 (2004): 468–73.

Godsoe, Cynthia. "Perfect Plaintiffs." *The Yale Law Journal Forum* 125 (2015): 136–55.

Goluboff, Risa. *The Lost Promise of Civil Rights*. Cambridge, Mass: Harvard University Press, 2007.

Vagrant Nation: Police Power, Constitutional Change, and the Making of the 1960s. New York: Oxford University Press, 2016.

Goodrich, Herbert F. and Paul A. Wolkin, *The Story of the American Law Institute, 1923–1961*. St. Paul, Minn.: American Law Institute Publishers, 1961.

Gottman, Julie Schwartz. "Children of Gay and Lesbian Parents." In *Homosexuality and Family Relations*, ed. Frederick W. Bozett and Marvin B. Sussman, 176–85. New York: Harrington Park Press, 1990.

Graves, Karen. *And They Were Wonderful Teachers: Florida's Purge of Gay and Lesbian Teachers*. Urbana: University of Illinois Press, 2009.

Guinier, Lani and Gerald Torres, "Changing the Wind: Notes toward a Demosprudence of Law and Social Movements." *Yale Law Journal* 123, no. 8 (2014): 2740–804.

Gunther, Gerald. *Learned Hand: The Man and the Judge*. New York: Oxford University Press, 2011.

Gutterman, Lauren Jae. *Her Neighbor's Wife: A History of Lesbian Desire within Marriage*. Philadelphia: University of Pennsylvania Press, 2020.

Haider-Markel, Donald P. "Lesbian and Gay Politics in the States: Interest Groups, Electoral Politics, and Policy." In *The Politics of Gay Rights*, ed. Craig A. Rimmerman, Kenneth D. Wald, and Clyde Wilcox, 301–17. University of Chicago Press, 2000.

Halley, Janet E. "'Like Race' Arguments." In *What's Left of Theory?: New Work on the Politics of Literary Theory*, ed. Judith Butler, John Guillory, and Kendall Thomas, 40–74. New York: Routledge, 2000.

"Sexual Orientation and the Politics of Biology: A Critique of the Argument from Immutability." *Stanford Law Review* 46, no. 3 (1994): 503–68.

Hanhardt, Christina B. *Safe Space: Gay Neighborhood History and the Politics of Violence*. Durham, NC: Duke University Press, 2013.

Harbeck, Karen. *Coming Out of the Classroom Closet: Gay and Lesbian Students, Teachers, and Curricula*. New York: Haworth Press, 1992.

Harding, Susan. *The Book of Jerry Falwell: Fundamental Language and Politics*. Princeton University Press, 2001.

Hartog, Hendrik. *Man and Wife in America: A History*. Cambridge, Mass.: Harvard University Press, 2002.

Harvey, David. *A Brief History of Neoliberalism*. New York: Oxford University Press, 2005.

Hazard, Jr., Geoffrey C. *The American Law Institute: What It Is and What It Does*. Rome: Centro Di Studi e Richerche di Diritto Comparato e Straniero, 1994.

Hequembourg, Amy and Jorge Arditi. "Fractured Resistances: The Debate over Assimilationism among Gays and Lesbians in the United States." *Sociological Quarterly* 40, no. 4 (1999): 663.

Herek, Gregory M. and John P. Capitanio. "'Some of My Best Friends': Intergroup Contact, Concealable Stigma, and Heterosexuals' Attitudes toward Gay Men and Lesbians." *Personality and Social Psychology Bulletin* 22, no. 4 (1996): 412–24.

Herek, Gregory M. and Kevin Berrill. *Hate Crimes: Confronting Violence against Lesbians and Gay Men*. California: Sage Publications, 1992.

Hertzke, Allen D. *Echoes of Discontent: Jesse Jackson, Pat Robertson, and the Resurgence of Populism*. Washington, D.C.: CQ Press, 1993.

Heyman, Steven J. "A Struggle for Recognition: The Controversy over Religious Liberty, Civil Rights, and Same-Sex Marriage." *First Amendment Law Review* 14 (2015): 1–126.

Higdon, Michael J. "Constitutional Parenthood." *Iowa Law Review* 103, no. 4 (2018): 1483–541.

Hirschman, Linda. *Victory: The Triumphant Gay Revolution*. New York: HarperCollins, 2012.

Hull, Kathleen E. and Timothy A. Ortyl. "Same-Sex Marriage and Constituent Perceptions of the LGBT Rights Movement." In *The Marrying Kind?: Debating Same-Sex Marriage within the Lesbian and Gay Movement*, ed. Mary Bernstein and Verta Taylor, 67–102. Minneapolis: University of Minnesota Press, 2013.

Hunter, Nan D. "Varieties of Constitutional Experience: Democracy and the Marriage Equality Campaign." *UCLA Law Review* 64 (2017): 1662–726.

Hunter, Nan D. and Nancy D. Polikoff. "Custody Rights of Lesbian Mothers: Legal Theory and Litigation Strategy." *Buffalo Law Review* 2 (1975–1976): 691–733.

Igo, Sarah E. *The Averaged American: Surveys, Citizens, and the Making of a Mass Public*. Cambridge, Mass.: Harvard University Press, 2007.

  The Known Citizen: A History of Privacy in Modern America. Cambridge, Mass.: Harvard University Press, 2018.

Infanti, Anthony C. "Victims of Our Own Success: The Perils of *Obergefell* and *Windsor*." *Ohio State Law Journal* 79 (2015): 79–85.

Irvine, Janice M. *Talk About Sex: The Battles over Sex Education in the United States*. Berkeley: University of California Press, 2004.

Issenberg, Sasha. *The Engagement: America's Quarter-Century Struggle over Same-Sex Marriage*. New York: Pantheon Publishing, 2021.

Jacobs, James B. and Kimberly Potter. *Hate Crimes: Criminal Law and Identity Politics*. New York: Oxford University Press, 1998.

Jenness, Valerie and Rykin Grattet. *Making Hate a Crime: From Social Movement to Law Enforcement*. New York: Russell Sage Foundation, 2001.

Johnson, David K. *The Lavender Scare: The Cold War Persecution of Gays and Lesbians in the Federal Government*. University of Chicago Press, 2004.

Johnson, Diane Lee. "A Narrative Life Story of Activist Phyllis Lyon and Her Reflections on a Life with Del Martin." Master's thesis. Grand Valley State University, 2012.

Johnson, Emily Suzanne. *This Is Our Message: Women's Leadership in the New Christian Right*. New York: Oxford University Press, 2019.

Jones, James H. *Alfred C. Kinsey: A Public/Private Life*. New York: W. W. Norton, 1997.

Jones, Martha S. *Birthright Citizens: A History of Race and Rights in Antebellum America*. New York: Cambridge University Press, 2018.

Joslin, Courtney G. "The Gay Rights Canon and the Right to Nonmarriage." *Boston University Law Review* 97, no. 2 (2017): 425–88.

Kane, Melinda D. "Timing Matters: Shifts in the Causal Determinants of Sodomy Law Decriminalization, 1961–1998." *Social Problems* 52, no. 2 (2007): 211–39.

Keck, Thomas M. "Beyond Backlash: Assessing the Impact of Judicial Decisions on LGBT Rights." *Law & Society Review* 43, no. 1 (2009): 151–86.

Keen, Lisa and Suzanne B. Goldberg. *Strangers to the Law: Gay People on Trial*. Ann Arbor: University of Michigan Press, 2000.

Kessler, Suzanne J. *Lessons from the Intersexed*. New Brunswick: Rutgers University Press, 1998.

Klarman, Michael J. *From the Closet to the Altar: Courts, Backlash, and the Struggle for Same-Sex Marriage*. New York: Oxford University Press, 2013.

    From Jim Crow to Civil Rights: The Supreme Court and the Struggle for Racial Equality. New York: Oxford University Press, 2004.

Klein, Jennifer. *For All These Rights: Business, Labor, and the Shaping of America's Public–Private Welfare State*. Princeton University Press, 2003.

Knauer, Nancy J. "Science, Identity, and the Construction of the Gay Political Narrative." *Law and Sexuality* 12 (2003): 1–86.

Konnoth, Craig J. "Created in Its Image: The Race Analogy, Gay Identity, and Gay Litigation in the 1950s–1970s." *Yale Law Journal* 119 (2009): 316–72.

Kornbluh, Felicia. *The Battle for Welfare Rights: Politics and Poverty in Modern America*. Philadelphia: University of Pennsylvania Press, 2007.

Kornbluh, Felicia and Karen Tani. "Siting the Legal History of Poverty: Below, Above, and Amidst." In *A Companion to American Legal History*, ed. Sally E. Hadden and Alfred L. Brophy, 329–48. Malden, Mass.: Wiley-Blackwell, 2013.

Kosbie, Jeffrey. "Beyond Queer v. LGBT: Discursive Community and Marriage Mobilization in Massachusetts." In *The Marrying Kind?: Debating Same-Sex Marriage within the Lesbian and Gay Movement*, ed. Mary Bernstein and Verta Taylor, 103–31. Minneapolis: University of Minnesota Press, 2013.

Kruse, Kevin M. *One Nation under God: How Corporate America Invented Christian America*. New York: Basic Books, 2015.

Kunzel, Regina. *Criminal Intimacy: Prison and the Uneven History of Modern American Sexuality*. University of Chicago Press, 2008.

Lancaster, Roger N. *The Trouble with Nature: Sex in Science and Popular Culture*. Berkeley: University of California Press, 2003.

Lave, Tamara Rice. "Only Yesterday: The Rise and Fall of Twentieth Century Sexual Psychopath Laws." *Louisiana Law Review* 69, no. 3 (2009): 549–91.

Lawrence, Frederick M. *Punishing Hate: Bias Crimes under American Law*. Cambridge, Mass.: Harvard University Press, 2002.

Leachman, Gwendolyn M. "From Protest to *Perry*: How Litigation Shaped the LGBT Movement's Agenda." *U.C. Davis Law Review* 47, no. 5 (2014): 1667–752.

Lee, Sophia Z. *The Workplace Constitution from the New Deal to the New Right*. New York: Cambridge University Press, 2014.

Lefkovitz, Alison. *Strange Bedfellows: Marriage in the Age of Women's Liberation*. Philadelphia: University of Pennsylvania Press, 2018.

Leslie, Christopher R. "Creating Criminals: The Injuries Inflicted by 'Unenforced' Sodomy Laws." *Harvard Civil Rights-Civil Liberties Law Review* 35, no. 1 (2000): 103–81.

Leung, Maxwell. "Points of Departure: Re-Examining the Discursive Formation of the Hate Crime Statistics Act of 1990." *Patterns of Prejudice* 52, no. 1 (2018): 39–57.

Levitsky, Sandra R. "To Lead with Law: Reassessing the Influence of Legal Advocacy Organizations in Social Movements." In *Cause Lawyers and Social Movements*, ed. Austin Sarat and Stuart A. Scheingold, 145–63. Stanford University Press, 2006.

Lewin, Ellen. "Confessions of a Reformed Grant Hustler." In *Out in the Field: Reflections of Lesbian and Gay Anthropologists*, ed. Ellen Lewin and William Leap, 11–27. Urbana: University of Illinois Press, 1996.

Lewis, Gregory B. "The Friends and Family Plan: Contact with Gays and Support for Gay Rights." *Policy Studies Journal* 39, no. 2 (2011): 217–38.

Lewis, Gregory B. and Charles W. Gossett. "Why Did Californians Pass Proposition 8?: Stability and Change in Public Support for Same-Sex Marriage." *California Journal of Politics and Policy* 3, no. 1 (2011): 1–20.

Lienesch, Michael. *In the Beginning: Fundamentalism, The Scopes Trial, and the Making of the Antievolution Movement*. Chapel Hill: University of North Carolina Press, 2007.

Lindman, Frank T. and Donald M. McIntyre, Jr. *The Mentally Disabled and the Law*. University of Chicago Press, 1961.

Love, Jean C. and Patricia A. Cain. "Six Cases in Search of a Decision: The Story of *In re* Marriage Cases." In *Women and Law Stories*, ed. Elizabeth M. Schneider and Stephanie M. Wildman, 337–78. New York: Foundation Press, 2011.

Lvovsky, Anna. *Vice Patrol: Cops, Courts, and the Struggle over Urban Gay Life before Stonewall*. University of Chicago Press, 2021.

Marcus, Eric. *Making History: The Struggle for Gay and Lesbian Equal Rights, 1945–1990*. New York: HarperCollins, 1992.

Martin, William. *With God on Our Side: The Rise of the Religious Right in America*. New York: Broadway Books, 1996.

May, Elaine Tyler. *Homeward Bound: American Families in the Cold War Era*. New York: Basic Books, 2008.

Mayeri, Serena. "Foundling Fathers: (Non)-Marriage and Parental Rights in the Age of Equality." *Yale Law Journal* 125, no. 8 (2016): 2292–392.

Reasoning from Race: Feminism, Law, and the Civil Rights Revolution. Cambridge, Mass.: Harvard University Press, 2014.

Mbugua, Karori. "Sexual Orientation and Brain Structures: A Critical Review of Recent Research." *Current Science* 84, no. 2 (2003): 173–78.

McCann, Michael. "Law and Social Movements: Contemporary Perspectives." *Annual Review of Law and Social Science* 2 (2006): 17–38.

McGirr, Lisa. *Suburban Warriors: The Origins of the New American Right*. Princeton University Press, 2001.

McNaughton, Paul Mark. "Atascadero, Dachau for Queers: Examining the Transformation of the Gay Rights Movement from Accommodationism to Militancy, 1954–1973." PhD diss. University of California San Diego, 2020.

Mecca, Tommi Avicolli "Introduction." In *Smash the Church, Smash the State!* San Francisco: City Lights Books, 2009.

Meeker, Martin. "Behind the Mask of Respectability: Reconsidering the Mattachine Society and Male Homophile Practice, 1950s and 1960s." *Journal of the History of Sexuality* 10, no. 1 (2001): 78–116.

Contacts Desired: Gay and Lesbian Communications and Community, 1940s–1970s. University of Chicago Press, 2006.

Mendicino, Thomas R. "Characterization and Disease: Homosexuals and the Threat of AIDS." *North Carolina Law Review* 66, no. 1 (1987): 226–50.

Meyerowitz, Joanne. *How Sex Changed: A History of Transsexuality in the United States*. Cambridge, Mass.: Harvard University Press, 2002.

Mezey, Susan Gluck. *Gay Families and the Courts: The Quest for Equal Rights*. Lanham: Rowman & Littlefield, 2009.

Queers in Court: Gay Rights Law and Public Policy. Lanham: Rowman & Littlefield, 2007.

Minton, Henry L. *Departing from Deviance: A History of Homosexual Rights and Emancipatory Science in America*. University of Chicago Press, 2002.

Mixner, David B. and Dennis Bailey. *Brave Journeys: Profiles in Gay and Lesbian Courage*. New York: Bantam Books, 2000.

Moats, David. *Civil Wars: The Battle for Gay Marriage*. Orlando: Harcourt, 2004.

Mosk, Stanley. "The Consenting Adult Homosexual and the Law: An Empirical Study of Enforcement and Administration in Los Angeles County." *UCLA Law Review* 13, no. 3 (1966): 644–832.

Murdoch, Joyce and Deb Price. *Courting Justice: Gay Men and Lesbians v. the Supreme Court*. New York: Basic Books, 2001.

Murray, Heather. "Free for All Lesbians: Lesbian Cultural Production and Consumption in the United States during the 1970s." *Journal of the History of Sexuality* 16, no. 2 (2007): 251–75.

Not In This Family: Gays and the Meaning of Kinship in Postwar North America. Philadelphia: University of Pennsylvania Press, 2010.

Murray, Melissa. "Marriage as Punishment." *Columbia Law Review* 112, no. 1 (2012): 1–65.

"Marriage Rights and Parental Rights: Parents, the State, and Proposition 8." *Stanford Journal of Civil Rights and Civil Liberties* 5, no. 2 (2009): 357–408.

"*Obergefell v. Hodges* and Nonmarriage Inequality." *California Law Review* 104, no. 5 (2016): 1207–58.

NeJaime, Douglas. "Before Marriage: The Unexplored History of Nonmarital Recognition and Its Relationship to Marriage." *California Law Review* 102, no. 1 (2014): 87–172.

"Differentiating Assimilation." *Studies in Law, Politics, and Society* 75 (2018): 1–42.

"The Legal Mobilization Dilemma." *Emory Law Journal* 61 (2012): 663–736.

"Marriage Equality and the New Parenthood." *Harvard Law Review* 129, no. 5 (2016): 1185–266.

"The Nature of Parenthood," *Yale Law Journal* 126, no. 8 (2017): 2260–381.

NeJaime, Douglas and Reva B. Siegel. "Religious Accommodation, and Its Limits, in a Pluralist Society." In *Religious Freedom, LGBT Rights, and the Prospects for Common Ground*, ed. William N. Eskridge, Jr. and Robin Fretwell Wilson, 69–81. New York: Cambridge University Press, 2018).

Nickerson, Michelle M. *Mothers of Conservatism: Women and the Postwar Right*. Princeton University Press, 2012.

Nolan, James J., III, Yoshio Akiyama, and Samuel Berhanu, "The Hate Crime Statistics Act of 1990: Developing a Method for Measuring the Occurrence of Hate Violence," *American Behavioral Scientist* 46, no. 1 (2002): 136–53.

Ott, Brian L. and Eric Aoki. "The Politics of Negotiating Public Tragedy: Media Framing of the Matthew Shepard Murder." *Rhetoric and Public Affairs* 5, no. 3 (2002): 483–505.

Peck, Elizabeth H. *Not Just Roommates: Cohabitation after the Sexual Revolution*. University of Chicago Press, 2012.

Perry, Barbara. *In the Name of Hate: Understanding Hate Crimes*. New York: Routledge, 2001.

Petro, Anthony M. *After the Wrath of God: AIDS, Sexuality, and American Religion*. New York: Oxford University Press, 2015.

Petrzela, Natalia Mehlman. *Classroom Wars: Language, Sex, and the Making of Modern Political Culture*. New York: Oxford University Press, 2015.

Pierceson, Jason. *Same-Sex Marriage in the United States: The Road to the Supreme Court and Beyond.* Lanham: Rowman & Littlefield, 2014.

Pinello, Daniel R. *America's Struggle for Same-Sex Marriage.* New York: Cambridge University Press, 2006.

Polikoff, Nancy D. *Beyond (Straight and Gay) Marriage: Valuing All Families under the Law.* Boston: Beacon Press, 2008.

"The New 'Illegitimacy': Winning Backward in the Protection of the Children of Lesbian Couples." *American University Journal of Gender, Social Policy and the Law* 20, no. 3 (2012): 721–40.

"Raising Children: Lesbian and Gay Parents Face the Public and the Courts." In *Creating Change: Sexuality, Public Policy, and Civil Rights,* ed. John D'Emilio, William B. Turner, and Urvashi Vaid, 305–35. New York: St. Martin's Press, 2000.

"This Child Does Have Two Mothers: Redefining Parenthood to Meet the Needs of Children in Lesbian-Mother and Other Nontraditional Families." *Georgetown Law Journal* 78, no. 3 (1990): 459–575.

Polletta, Francesca. *It Was Like a Fever: Storytelling in Protest and Politics.* University of Chicago Press, 2006.

Richardson, Diane. "Lesbian Mothers." In *The Theory and Practice of Homosexuality,* ed. John Hart and Diane Richardson, 52–70. Boston: Routledge & Kagan Paul, 1981.

"Theoretical Perspectives on Homosexuality." In *The Theory and Practice of Homosexuality,* ed. John Hart and Diane Richardson, 5–37. Boston: Routledge & Kagan Paul, 1981.

Richman, Kimberly D. *Courting Change: Queer Parents, Judges, and the Transformation of American Family Law.* New York University Press, 2009.

Rivera, Rhonda R. "Lawyers, Clients, and AIDS: Some Notes from the Trenches." *Ohio State Law Journal* 49 (1989): 883–928.

Rivers, Daniel Winunwe. *Radical Relations: Lesbian Mothers, Gay Fathers, and Their Children in the United States since World War II.* Chapel Hill: University of North Carolina Press, 2013.

Robertson, Stephen. *Crimes against Children: Sexual Violence and Legal Culture in New York City, 1880–1960.* Chapel Hill: University of North Carolina Press, 2005.

"Shifting the Scene of the Crime: Sodomy and the American History of Sexual Violence." *Journal of the History of Sexuality* 19, no. 2 (2010): 223–42.

Robinson, Paul H. and Markus D. Dubber. "The American Model Penal Code: A Brief Overview." *New Criminal Law Review: An International and Interdisciplinary Journal* 10, no. 3 (2007): 319–41.

Robinson, Russell K. and David M. Frost, "The Afterlife of Homophobia." *Arizona Law Review* 60 (2018): 213–89.

Robson, Ruthann. "Assimilation, Marriage, and Lesbian Liberation." *Temple Law Review* 75, no. 4 (2002): 709–820.

Rohy, Valeria. *Lost Causes: Narrative, Etiology, and Queer Theory.* New York: Oxford University Press, 2015.

Rosenberg, Gerald N. *The Hollow Hope: Can Courts Bring about Social Change?* 2nd ed. University of Chicago Press, 2008.

Rosenbury, Laura A. "Federal Visions of Private Family Support." *Vanderbilt Law Review* 67, no. 6 (2014): 1835–70.

Rosky, Clifford J. "Anti-Gay Curriculum Laws." *Columbia Law Review* 117, no. 6 (2017): 1461–542.

"Fear of the Queer Child." *Buffalo Law Review* 61, no. 3 (2013): 607–98.

"Like Father, Like Son: Homosexuality, Parenthood and the Gender of Homophobia." *Yale Journal of Law & Feminism* 20, no. 2 (2009): 257–355.

"No Promo Hetero: Children's Right to be Queer," *Cardozo Law Review* 35, no. 2 (2013): 425–510.

Ruth, Henry and Kevin R. Reitz. *The Challenge of Crime: Rethinking Our Response.* Cambridge, Mass.: Harvard University Press, 2006.

Sandbrook, Dominic. *Mad as Hell: The Crisis of the 1970s and the Rise of the Populist Right.* New York: Anchor Books, 2011.

Sant'Ambrogio, Michael D. and Sylvia A. Law. "*Baehr v. Lewin* and the Long Road to Marriage Equality." *University of Hawaii Law Review* 33, no. 2 (2011): 705–53.

Scheingold, Stuart A. *The Politics of Rights: Lawyers, Public Policy, and Political Change.* 2nd ed. Ann Arbor: University of Michigan Press, 2015.

Schmeiser, Susan R. "The Ungovernable Citizen: Psychopathy, Sexuality, and the Rise of Medico-Legal Reasoning." *Yale Journal of Law and the Humanities* 20, no. 2 (2008): 163–240.

Schulman, Sarah. *Let the Record Show: A Political History of Act Up New York, 1987–1993.* New York: Farrar, Straus and Giroux, 2021.

Sedgwick, Eve Kosofsky. *Epistemology of the Closet.* Berkeley: University of California Press, 1990.

Self, Robert O. *All in the Family: the Realignment of American Democracy Since the 1960s.* New York: Hill and Wang, 2012.

Seo, Sarah A. "Democratic Policing before the Due Process Revolution." *Yale Law Journal* 128, no. 5 (2019): 1246–302.

Shapiro, Julie. "Custody and Conduct: How the Law Fails Lesbian and Gay Parents." *Indiana Law Journal* 71, no. 3 (1996): 623–71.

Shepard, Judy. *The Meaning of Matthew: My Sons' Murder in Laramie, and a World Transformed.* New York: Plume, 2010.

Shilts, Randy. *And the Band Played On: Politics, People, and the AIDS Epidemic.* New York: St. Martin's Press, 1987.

Siegel, Reva B. "Constitutional Culture, Social Movement Conflict and Constitutional Change: The Case of the *de facto* ERA." *California Law Review* 94, no. 5 (2006): 1323–419.

Smith, Daniel A., Matthew DeSantis, and Jason Kassel. "Same-Sex Marriage Ballot Measures and the 2004 Presidential Election." *State and Local Government Review* 38, no. 2 (2006): 78–91.

Smith-Rosenberg, Carroll. "The Female World of Love and Ritual: Relations between Women in Nineteenth-Century America." *Signs* 1, no. 1 (1975): 1–29.

Spade, Dean. "Under the Cover of Gay Rights." *N.Y.U. Review of Law and Social Change* 37, no. 1 (2013): 79–100.

Stein, Edward. "Immutability and Innateness Arguments about Lesbian, Gay, and Bisexual Rights." *Chicago-Kent Law Review* 89, no. 2 (2014): 597–640.

Stein, Marc. "Crossing the Border to Memory: In Search of Clive Michael Boutilier (1933–2003)." *Torquere* 6 (2004): 91–115.

Rethinking the Gay and Lesbian Movement. New York: Routledge, 2012.

Sexual Injustice: Supreme Court Decisions from Griswold *to* Roe. Chapel Hill: University of North Carolina Press, 2010.

Stewart, Chuck. *Homosexuality and the Law: A Dictionary.* Santa Barbara: ABC-CLIO, 2001.

Stewart-Winter, Timothy. "The Fall of Walter Jenkins and the Hidden History of the Lavender Scare." In *Intimate States: Gender, Sexuality, and Governance in Modern US History*, ed. Margot Canaday, Nancy F. Cott, and Robert O. Self, 211–34. University of Chicago Press, 2021.

"The Law and Order Origins of Urban Gay Politics." *Journal of Urban History* 41, no. 5 (2015): 825–35.

Queer Clout: Chicago and the Rise of Gay Politics. Philadelphia: University of Pennsylvania Press, 2016.

"Queer Law and Order: Sex, Criminality, and Policing in the Late Twentieth-Century United States." *Journal of American History* 102, no. 1 (2015): 61–72.

Stone, Amy L. *Gay Rights at the Ballot Box.* Minneapolis: University of Minnesota Press, 2012.

Stone, Donald H. "The Moral Dilemma: Child Custody When One Parent is Homosexual or Lesbian – An Empirical Study." *Suffolk University Law Review* 23 (1989): 711–54.

Stuntz, William J. "The Uneasy Relationship between Criminal Procedure and Criminal Justice." *Yale Law Journal* 107, no. 1 (1997): 1–76.

Tani, Karen M. *States of Dependency: Welfare, Rights, and American Governance, 1935–1972.* New York: Cambridge University Press, 2016.

Terry, Jennifer. *An American Obsession: Science, Medicine, and Homosexuality in Modern Society.* University of Chicago Press, 1999.

Thompson, Karen and Julie Andrzejewski. *Why Can't Sharon Kowalski Come Home?* San Francisco: Spinsters/Aunt Lute, 1988.

Tiemeyer, Philip James. *Plane Queer: Labor, Sexuality, and AIDS in the History of Male Flight Attendants*. Berkeley: University of California Press, 2013.

Todres, Jonathan. "Law, Otherness, and Human Trafficking." *Santa Clara Law Review* 49, no. 3 (2009): 605–72.

Vider, Stephen. *The Queerness of Home: Gender, Sexuality, and the Politics of Domesticity after World War II*. University of Chicago Press, 2021.

Walker, Samuel. "The Engineer as Progressive: The Wickersham Commission in the Arc of Herbert Hoover's Life and Work." *Marquette Law Review* 96, no. 4, 2013: 1165–97.

Warner, Michael. *The Trouble with Normal: Sex, Politics, and the Ethics of Queer Life*. Cambridge, Mass.: Harvard University Press, 1999.

Weinrib, Laura M. *The Taming of Free Speech*. Cambridge, Mass.: Harvard University Press, 2016.

Wertheimer, David A. "The Emergence of a Gay and Lesbian Antiviolence Movement." In *Creating Change: Sexuality, Public Policy, and Civil Rights*, ed. John D'Emilio, William B. Turner, and Urvashi Vaid, 261–78. New York: St. Martin's Press, 2000.

White, C. Todd. "Dale Jennings (1917–2000): ONE's Outspoken Advocate." In *Before Stonewall: Activists for Gay and Lesbian Rights in Historical Context*, ed. Vern L. Bullough et al., 83–93. Hoboken: Taylor and Francis, 2014.

Pre-Gay L.A.: A Social History of the Movement for Homosexual Rights. Urbana: University of Illinois Press, 2009.

Williams, Daniel K. *God's Own Party: The Making of the Christian Right*. New York: Oxford University Press, 2010.

Woods, James D. and Jay H. Lucas, *The Corporate Closet: The Professional Lives of Gay Men in America*. New York: Free Press, 1994.

Wuest, Joanna. *Born This Way: Science, Citizenship, and Inequality in the American LGBTQ+ Movement*. University of Chicago Press, 2023.

Yoshino, Kenji. "The Epistemic Contract of Bisexual Erasure." *Stanford Law Review* 52, no. 2 (2000): 353–461.

Speak Now: Marriage Equality on Trial: The Story of Hollingsworth v. Perry. New York: Crown Publishers, 2015.

Zemans, Frances Kahn. "Legal Mobilization: The Neglected Role of the Law in the Political System." *American Political Science Review* 77, no. 3 (1983): 690–703.

Ziegler, Mary. *After Roe: The Lost History of the Abortion Debate*. Cambridge, Mass.: Harvard University Press, 2015.

Index

Studies in Legal History
(*continued from page ii*)

Sara M. Butler, *Pain, Penance, and Protest: Peine Forte et Dure in Medieval England*

Michael Lobban, *Imperial Incarceration: Detention without Trial in the Making of British Colonial Africa*

Stefan Jurasinski and Lisi Oliver, *The Laws of Alfred: The Domboc and the Making of Anglo-Saxon Law*

Sascha Auerbach, *Armed with Sword and Scales: Law, Culture, and Local Courtrooms in London, 1860–1913*

Alejandro de La Fuente and Ariela J. Gross, *Becoming Free, Becoming Black: Race, Freedom, and the Law in Cuba, Virginia, and Louisiana*

Elizabeth Papp Kamali, *Felony and the Guilty Mind in Medieval England*

Jessica K. Lowe, *Murder in the Shenandoah: Making Law Sovereign in Revolutionary Virginia*

Michael A. Schoeppner, *Moral Contagion: Black Atlantic Sailors, Citizenship, and Diplomacy in Antebellum America*

Sam Erman, *Almost Citizens: Puerto Rico, the U.S. Constitution, and Empire*

Martha S. Jones, *Birthright Citizens: A History of Race and Rights in Antebellum America*

Julia Moses, *The First Modern Risk: Workplace Accidents and the Origins of European Social States*

Cynthia Nicoletti, *Secession on Trial: The Treason Prosecution of Jefferson Davis*

Edward James Kolla, *Sovereignty, International Law, and the French Revolution*

Assaf Likhovski, *Tax Law and Social Norms in Mandatory Palestine and Israel*

Robert W. Gordon, *Taming the Past: Essays on Law and History and History in Law*

Paul Garfinkel, *Criminal Law in Liberal and Fascist Italy*

Michelle A. McKinley, *Fractional Freedoms: Slavery, Intimacy, and Legal Mobilization in Colonial Lima, 1600–1700*

Karen M. Tani, *States of Dependency: Welfare, Rights, and American Governance, 1935–1972*

Stefan Jurasinski, *The Old English Penitentials and Anglo- Saxon Law*

Felice Batlan, *Women and Justice for the Poor: A History of Legal Aid, 1863–1945*

Sophia Z. Lee, *The Workplace Constitution from the New Deal to the New Right*

Mitra Sharafi, *Law and Identity in Colonial South Asia: Parsi Legal Culture, 1772–1947*

Michael A. Livingston, *The Fascists and the Jews of Italy: Mussolini's Race Laws, 1938–1943*